INTEGRATION AND DIVISION

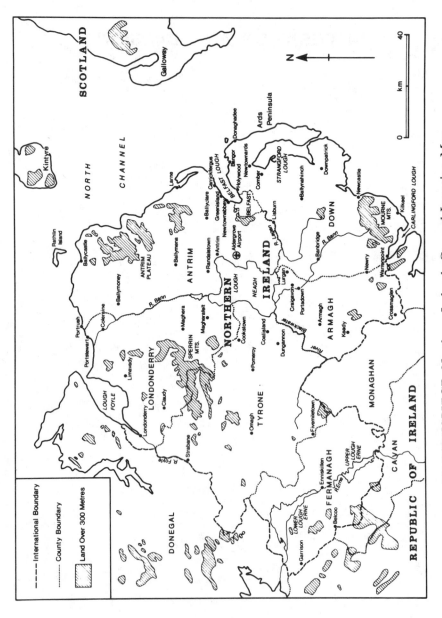

FRONTISPIECE. Northern Ireland: General Location Map.

INTEGRATION AND DIVISION

Geographical Perspectives on the
Northern Ireland Problem

Edited by

Frederick W. Boal and J. Neville H. Douglas

Department of Geography, The Queen's University of Belfast

With the assistance of
Jenitha A. E. Orr

1982

ACADEMIC PRESS

A Subsidiary of Harcourt Brace Jovanovich, Publisher

London   New York
Paris   San Diego   San Francisco   São Paulo
Sydney   Tokyo   Toronto

ACADEMIC PRESS INC. (LONDON) LTD.
24–28 Oval Road
London NW1 7DX

U.S. Edition published by
ACADEMIC PRESS INC.
111 Fifth Avenue
New York, New York 10003

British Library Cataloguing in Publication Data

Integration and division: geographical perspectives on the Northern Ireland problem.

1. Ethnology—Northern Ireland—Addresses, essays, lectures
2. Northern Ireland—Social life and customs—Addresses, essays, lectures
I. Boal, F. W.   II. Douglas, J. N. H.
941.6   GN585.G/

ISBN 0-12-108080-3

LCCCN 81-68978

Typeset by Bath Typesetting Ltd., Bath
and printed in Great Britain by
T. J. Press (Padstow) Ltd., Padstow, Cornwall.

CONTRIBUTORS

Frederick W. Boal, Reader in Geography, The Queen's University of Belfast, Belfast BT7 1NN, Northern Ireland.

Ronald H. Buchanan, Reader in Geography, The Queen's University of Belfast, Belfast BT7 1NN, Northern Ireland.

Paul A. Compton, Senior Lecturer in Geography, The Queen's University of Belfast, Belfast BT7 1NN, Northern Ireland.

Paul Doherty, Lecturer in Geography, Ulster Polytechnic, Jordanstown, Newtownabbey, County Antrim, BT37 0QB, Northern Ireland.

J. Neville H. Douglas, Senior Lecturer in Geography, The Queen's University of Belfast, Belfast BT7 1NN, Northern Ireland.

Anthony G. Hoare, Lecturer in Geography, University of Bristol, Bristol BS8 1TH, England.

Russell Murray, Lecturer in Sociology, University of Edinburgh, 18 Buccleuch Place, Edinburgh EH8 9LN, Scotland.

Robert D. Osborne, Lecturer in Social Policy, Ulster Polytechnic, Jordanstown, Newtownabbey, County Antrim, BT37 0QB, Northern Ireland.

Michael A. Poole, Lecturer in Geography, New University of Ulster, Coleraine, County Londonderry, BT52 1SA, Northern Ireland.

Philip Robinson, Assistant Keeper, Department of Buildings, Ulster Folk and Transport Museum, Cultra, Holywood, County Down, BT18 0EU, Northern Ireland.

Dale Singleton, Lecturer in Town and Country Planning, The Queen's University of Belfast, Belfast BT7 1NN, Northern Ireland.

ACKNOWLEDGEMENTS

Our thanks to Dr Robert Common for providing an initial stimulus to produce this book; to Gillian Alexander, Maura Pringle and Ian Alexander for cartography; to Velma Atcheson and Elizabeth Purdy for typing; to Michael Collins for photographic work related to the cartography; and to Jenitha Orr for an enormous amount of pains-taking editorial assistance. Deepest thanks also to our contributors who enthusiastically accepted the invitation to write for us.

PREFACE

"In Northern Ireland two communities—one Protestant and one Roman Catholic—fight a holy war." Such a perspective on the problems of Northern Ireland remains widespread despite (or perhaps because of) continued analysis in newspapers and journals and on radio and television. The consequence of this perspective is that events in Northern Ireland are easily dismissed as outmoded by those not directly involved —of antique and curiosity value only, in a world where religious pluralism in modern countries is accepted without recourse to violence.

This book rejects absolutely such a simplistic view by setting Northern Ireland in proper perspective as a region with a range of complex problems which commonly beset countries containing culturally and politically diverse communities. Thus the experience and the lessons to be learnt from Northern Ireland are not unique; those who study the region's problems can learn from and add to the general body of knowledge concerning cultural diversity and conflict.

Accepting that Northern Ireland contains a plural society (Chapter 1), the early chapters (Chapters 2 and 3) focus upon the origins of cultural pluralism and demonstrate the existence of an evolving framework of diversity and conflict. More than most regions, Northern Ireland considered apart from its history makes little sense in the contemporary world. How then does cultural diversity show itself? It shows most clearly through the varied range of cultural attributes— demographic, economic, political and social—which characterise each community and which are considered in Chapters 4 to 11 of this volume. These attributes expose starkly the superficiality of the religious perspective. Yet cultural attributes, salient though they be as group identifiers, provide but a static portrait of a dynamic problem. What maintains the diversity and forces it towards conflict or constrains the divisions and encourages integration?

To answer these questions, culture must be viewed not simply as a set of attributes but also as a complex of processes. Such cultural processes are seen in the economic, political and social behaviour of the communities within the plural society. Cultural division and cultural integration are not, therefore, separate entities set far apart but are the two ends of a continuum. On this continuum, which can be compared to a finely balanced see-saw, sits the plural society. Like the see-saw, the continuum is seldom static and its angle of slope towards the division end or towards the counterbalance of integration is controlled by the relative strengths, at any particular time, of integrative or divisive behavioural processes. Partisan and conflict behaviour lends weight to the division end and the plural society slides towards greater division. Co-operative behaviour and contact lowers the gradient and may move the plural society back towards a position of greater integration. Chapters in this book concerned with demographic behaviour (Chapter 4), political behaviour (Chapters 5 and 6), public policy behaviour (Chapter 7), economic behaviour (Chapters 8 and 9), urban residential behaviour (Chapters 10 and 11) and violent behaviour (Chapter 12) demonstrate the importance of cultural processes in maintaining or changing the position of the plural society on the integration–division continuum.

In the final overview chapter (Chapter 13) we use the material concerning cultural attributes and processes to suggest an explanation and develop a simple classification of group relations in Northern Ireland. The concepts of dominance–subordination behaviour, territorial separation and exclusionary policy making, all at work in an environment of competition for scarce economic and political resources, provide frameworks for better understanding of group relations. These considerations lead finally to a brief discussion of solutions or, more realistically, of processes of social and political behaviour which would emphasise co-operation and integration and reduce the division in Northern Ireland's plural society.

While culturally and mentally separated, Northern Ireland's two communities live together, frequently intermingling and "rubbing along" in one territory. All chapters pay particular attention to the spatial characteristics of the plural society. It is, perhaps, too easily forgotten that geographical proximity and interwoven distributions act as important causal influences on both the nature and scale of conflict and so are not simple reflectors of pluralism. Thus maps and diagrams are used throughout this volume as aids to understanding but above all to portray the spatial reality of the Northern Ireland problem.

While the book contains a set of original contributions by separate authors, as editors we have attempted from the outset to provide an integrative core for the work. Initially this took the form of strong guidelines for the authors; this was followed by developing these guidelines into the major themes set out in the introductory chapter. The contributions, therefore, follow a logical sequence, each adding detail to the portrait of cultural integration and division in Northern Ireland. Where chapters overlap or complement each other directly, or where maps, diagrams or tables are of use in more than one contribution, we have provided cross-references to aid the reader.

Although the contributions deal with a wide range of topics we do not claim comprehensive coverage: the content derives from our view of the important issues which exist within the Northern Ireland problem and from our knowledge of the research work of geographers who are currently, or who have been in the past, based at the Geography Department of Queen's University, Belfast.

January, 1982   Frederick W. Boal and J. Neville H. Douglas

Note on Terminology. In this book the term "Ulster" refers to the historic northern province of Ireland. This province is composed of nine counties. "Northern Ireland" refers to the area formed in 1921, being composed of six of the original nine counties of Ulster. We have ensured that the terms "Ulster" and "Northern Ireland" are used in their strict sense except where a "looser" usage occurs in quotations from the work of other authors.

CONTENTS

To Sallie and Rita

CHAPTER 1

THE NORTHERN IRELAND PROBLEM

J. Neville H. Douglas and Frederick W. Boal

INTRODUCTION

Since Northern Ireland came into existence as a separate political unit in 1921 the Northern Ireland problem has forced its way into the world's headlines at intervals—most recently and most persistently in the period of unsurpassed strife which has lasted since 1969. This strife is labelled as conflict between Protestants and Roman Catholics and has been treated, in many instances, as a religious or holy war. Two points must be made at the outset—first, that the Northern Ireland problem pre-dates the existence of Northern Ireland as a political unit, and, secondly, that the holy war interpretation is, at best, a vast over-simplification which enables its adherents to avoid any attempt at real understanding.

Many people, if asked to state the essence of the Northern Ireland problem, would say that the two communities, Roman Catholic and Protestant, cannot live together. A. T. Q. Stewart, on the other hand, claims that the very essence of the problem is that the two communities do live together, and have done so for centuries. As Stewart puts it: "they share the same homeland, and like it or not, the two diametrically opposed political wills must co-exist on the same narrow ground" (1977, p. 180). He goes on to note, however, that the two communities are not intermingled "but they are interlocked, and in ways which it is probably impossible for anyone except a native . . . to understand" (1977, p. 181). The profoundly complex geography implicit in these statements will be an ever-present thread in this book.

The existence and severity of the Northern Ireland conflict indicates great depth of division. The fact that the two communities are at least interlocked suggests, however, that division must be by no means

1

the only theme in Northern Ireland. There are processes at work that divide but there are also others that integrate, or that at least permit the interlocking to survive. Our book will attempt to explore aspects of the interweave of integration and division that comprises the fabric of the Northern Ireland problem as it exists "on the ground".

THE NORTHERN IRELAND PROBLEM: EXPLANATORY MODELS

Clearly focussed description and explanation require sound philosophical foundations. To provide such foundations, two models of the Northern Ireland problem are outlined and the consequences of each briefly considered. The models are not mutually exclusive and therefore they can be brought together to form the first half of the framework which underpins this book.

The Plural Society Model

Northern Ireland as *one* political, territorial unit is populated by *two* distinct communities which form a divided, plural society. Each community is held together by a significant and self-generating level of internal interaction creating distinctive social and political attributes, values and preferences. In contrast to strong intra-community interaction, the amount of inter-community communication is small. The consequent cleavages cut across the whole spectrum of cultural attributes, creating a plural society with communities separated by *social distance* and often also by *physical distance*. Not all scholars accept that the plural society model is applicable to Northern Ireland. Whyte (1978) concludes that the cleavages are neither deep nor wide enough to merit the use of the model. In contrast, Lijphart (1975) emphasises the value of the plural society model in forcing a consideration of a wide number of social, cultural and political cleavages of which religious division is but one. The argument by Smith (1969) that a plural society is a society in which sub-groups differ culturally on matters of public concern strongly supports the use of the model in setting out a general framework for the study of integration and division in Northern Ireland.

The consequences of pluralism within a governmental unit are manifold and form an important consideration in establishing the wide historical, economic and social parameters of this book. However, the consequences react most fundamentally upon the political system. Plurality results in pushing into the public and political arena many economic and social matters which would normally be solved locally and privately. Thus, through publicity, the range of matters causing inter-group conflict is increased, adding to the burdens of government. At the same time, plurality creates difficulties in the actual establishment of government, in its maintenance and in its working efficiency. In plural societies a majority–minority group conflict is usually inherent, and in this situation political choice is governed by the so-called "Law of Contradiction", i.e. the demands of sub-groups are mutually contradictory and both sets of demands cannot be met simultaneously without destroying the existing system (Rabushka and Shepsle, 1972). Frequently this impasse of pluralism is also set within political systems based on the rule of democratic egalitarianism—i.e. one individual, one vote, and the simple majority (that group which gains more than 50% of the vote) establishes the collective choice. Thus the minority group which *de facto* is removed from the decision-making arena can become politically estranged and withhold the sense of legitimacy necessary for consensus government. Political instability thus becomes an important characteristic of the system.

Divisions in political life are paralleled by dichotomous economic and social spheres. Separate living areas and distinct community organisations, different retail service points, schools and places of recreation and worship emphasise the plurality and reinforce the element of instability.

The consequences suggest that the Northern Ireland problem contains strong political elements concerned with the control of power, with decision making and with the nature of the political system. The pluralist model therefore points to an extended range of cultural cleavages beyond the religious dichotomy.

The Double Minority Model

This model, first put forward by Jackson (1971), points to the existence and to the importance of more than one political and territorial scale. In Northern Ireland the Protestant/unionist community forms the majority, while the Roman Catholic/nationalist community is in the minority. However, at the scale of Ireland as a whole—to which Northern Ireland, although politically separate, is territorially bound— the Protestant/unionist group is a numerical minority while the Catholic/ nationalist group is part of a larger majority Catholic population. At the United Kingdom level—to which Northern Ireland, although territorially separated, is politically bound—the Protestant/unionist community is again a minority with ultimate political power beyond its control.

This model reveals the political uncertainty and territorial ambiguity of the Northern Ireland problem. Partition, though a legal reality, has not smothered the Irish Republic's claims of territorial and political interest. Political union with Great Britain, whether with devolved power or with full administrative integration, does not remove the uncertainty of Westminster's final and long-term views concerning Northern Ireland. The double minority model thus suggests several behavioural consequences. The Protestant/unionist community, unable to rest on an unchallenged territorial base and political control, has a heightened sense of insecurity and a very sensitive psychological perception of risk. Thus, although until 1972 it held political power within Northern Ireland, the Protestant/unionist community used that power with many of the trappings of an insecure besieged minority. Too often decision making was seen as risk taking and not as opportunity making. Policy decisions were related back to traditional political values and judged in the light of these. As Stewart (1977) has shown so persuasively, all new decisions bowed to the supremacy of historical precedent and in this way the possibility of unforeseen change was reduced to a minimum. In contrast, the Roman Catholic/nationalist community refused to consider itself as a minority but rather viewed itself as part of the legitimate majority, set within an unredeemed segment of Irish national territory. It could, therefore, make demands for territorial reorganisation from both the Irish Government in Dublin and the United Kingdom Government at Westminster, while refusing to recognise the political legitimacy of Northern Ireland. The varied political scale-levels associated with the Northern Ireland problem thereby create a paradox, imbuing the majority with insecurity and the minority with confidence and resolve.

Together, these models provide a first stage foundation for the study of integration and division in Northern Ireland. In the problem region there exists a plural society comprising two strong communities, separated by an extensive range of social, economic and political cleavages. The plural society is set in an uncertain territorial and political environment which suggests and reflects different possibilities at different scales. Ambiguity and consequent tension provide the behavioural milieu. In this milieu, the one safe and unchanging reference point for decision and action is the individual community store of traditional values and historical precedents.

INTEGRATION AND DIVISION

Given the existence of a plural society in Northern Ireland, the concepts of cultural integration and division emerge as fundamental.

"Culture" is here thought of in its widest sense as the totality of learned behaviour transmitted from one generation to the next. Concern then is simply with integration in the "way of life" in Northern Ireland. Pluralism exists because strong integration at the intra-community level is complemented by equally strong division at the inter-community level. This is not to deny the existence of intra-community division on the basis of factors such as social class and urban–rural and centre–periphery characteristics; nor should inter-group interaction across the middle ground be overlooked. Nonetheless, in terms of depth and intensity and as a basis for social behaviour, intra-community integration and inter-community division dominate in Northern Ireland. Description and explanation of the Northern Ireland problem cannot begin, therefore, without detailed consideration and explicit definitions of cultural integration and division. In providing these, the remainder of this chapter lays down the second half of the framework which underpins this book.

CULTURAL INTEGRATION AND DIVISION AS ATTRIBUTES

Integration and division, in both social and political senses, defy easy recognition. Integration, for example, cannot be seen directly but has to be inferred from empirical study. In one sense lack of integration, i.e. division, is more easily recognised when the level of division is great enough to result in open conflict and disorder. In practice, integration and division must not be thought of as two sides of a coin nor as discrete realities, but rather as connected ends of a continuum. Societies slide along this continuum in either direction as events and information flows create changes in the dynamic social milieu.

Most frequently, however, integration is seen as an attribute of society, i.e. the state of being integrated. Thus integration can be defined as *the sense of community based on common cultural attributes and attitudes, and expressed in an accepted set of social institutions.* These cultural attributes provide the basis for cultural practices that are acceptable and widespread enough to ensure peaceful social activity and change. Political integration can be defined, therefore, as the sense of political community based on common political attributes and views and expressed in an accepted set of political institutions. The attributes create norms regarding political behaviour and commitment to the patterns of political behaviour legitimised by these norms.

Assessing the level of integration can, in theory, be carried out by analysis of the strength of community feeling, the acceptability of institutions and the strength of favourable attitudes towards social structures and objectives. In practice, the assessment of levels of integration through the study of societal attributes faces considerable difficulties. The range of possible indicators is so large and their salience and interrelationships so varied in time and space that no clear and widely accepted set of measures of integration has emerged from the large body of studies on cultural integration (Neuman, 1976). Nevertheless, studies which cover a wide range of cultural attributes provide at least a strong descriptive base and an opportunity for drawing more effective conclusions, even though, in the absence of universally accepted measures, such conclusions will have the ring of subjectivity. While making no attempt to suggest their relative salience, the cultural attributes most commonly considered in studies of integration concern territory and its political organisation, population characteristics, socio-economic aspects of that population and human attitudes and values. The significance of each will be considered briefly.

The Territorial Attribute

All societies, plural or otherwise, are tied to territory; with the urge for security and control, territory becomes bounded politically and political regions or states evolve with a level of independence and power. In essence the political boundary establishes the effective parameters of a society and encloses the space within which all other cultural attributes have meaning. In time the territory enclosed by the political boundary is usually sub-divided into smaller units for the purposes of administration, organised local government and the holding of elections. The nature of the subdivisions and the resulting territorial frameworks are attributes of particular significance in plural societies where political representation of separate cultural groups has increased importance. Further, the political organisation of territory can condition the nature of other attributes. Thus local governments, depending on the degree of delegated power, can influence a wide range of socio-economic characteristics among the population in its area. The electoral framework controls the amount of political representation different communities can achieve, so conditioning their level of power or powerlessness. Ultimately, territorial frameworks affect quite considerably the attitudes held within society and particularly within the communities which form segments of a plural society. Pluralism is also reflected in the jigsaw of less formal territorial patterns that underlie the statutory subdivisions of the political system. Residential areas, segregated by community, with their graffiti-marked boundaries in urban areas testify, not just to the strength of pluralism, but also to the symbolic significance of territory. In rural areas patterns of segregation less tangible to the outsider also exist, recognised by the local population and giving different territories special attributes.

Non-political organisations also operate within specific territorial frameworks: for example the parishes of the Roman Catholic Church provide important community foci which differ in pattern, extent and functional significance from the presbytery areas of the Presbyterian Church. Sports and social organisations also establish diverse territorial unit patterns which reflect both the distribution and the needs of community members. In the final analysis, however, territorial divisions, political and non-political, are more than mere reflectors of pluralism. In many subtle ways they give substance to and help foster the cultural cleavages which influence the relative strengths of integration and division within society.

The Population Attribute

Three aspects of population—size, structure and distribution—have effects upon cultural integration and division. The numerical size of the population in each segment of a plural society reflects, in a general way, the relative strengths and weaknesses and the viability of competing groups. Population numbers invest majority or minority status and thereby bequeath important psychological traits and self-images. These traits, in turn, help condition inter-group attitudes and lay the basis for behaviour. The variations of political groupings within a plural society can range from one extreme in which the society is composed of several groups, all of relatively equal population size and all being minorities, and where association is unavoidable, to the other extreme where the society is made up of only two groups, a majority and a minority, and where association may be desirable but unworkable. It is in this latter case, particularly when the majority is small and the minority large, that Lijphart (1977) finds the limits of applicability for the "democratic" political model.

Population structure, particularly as shown in age characteristics, also influences the nature of plurality. The population pyramid with a wide base, containing large numbers of people in the younger age groups, contrasts strikingly with the narrow-based or top-heavy pyramid which reflects a low-growth or static population. When such structural differences characterise competing communities with strong implications for the balance between majority and minority, the effects on both intra- and inter-community attitudes can be considerable. Population distribution, at both local and regional scales and in the urban and rural patterns, establishes the spatial parameters of plurality. The degree of community intermixing or segregation represents the characteristics of *physical proximity* and *distance* in group relations and reflects the potential for inter-group contact and communication. *Physical distance* between competing communities at regional or at local levels also points to possible differences in access to economic and social opportunities. Thus communities concentrated in regional peripheries and in inner city areas are usually separated economically and socially as well as physically from their suburban and metropolitan centre counterparts.

The Socio-Economic Attribute

Human characteristics are of fundamental significance as reflectors of integration and in studies of pluralism a wide range of social and economic features has been considered. Studies of race, language and religion have been added to, more recently, by the analysis of aspects such as group occupational structure, unemployment and income patterns, and educational attainment levels. Such analyses have given new depth to the study of community attributes and laid a stronger base for the assessment of integration and division. Differences in occupational, income and educational attainment levels between communities are taken as evidence of lack of integration. Also, when such differences coincide with other cleavages between groups, for example in population distribution, the concept of *social distance* can be set alongside that of *physical distance* and used as an aid in describing the balance between integration and division (Jacob and Toscano, 1964, p. 19).

The Attitudes Attribute

In the study of cultural attributes, attitudes sit uneasily alongside territorial frameworks, population and socio-economic characteristics. In the real world, these other attributes create the milieu from which attitudes emerge and towards which, in turn, the attitudes are held. So, for example, patterns of local government, population structures and unemployment rates are all attributes which help mould individual and community attitudes; the attitudes, however, although they will have a spill-over effect on later attitude formation, have meaning only in relation to the attributes which caused their emergence. A change in the attribute may therefore result in a change in attitude. It is thus necessary to recognise the special position of the attitudes attribute before study can proceed (see Fig. 1.1). Once formed, however, attitudes are important in two ways. In the first instance they reflect the views and preferences of the individual and the group and, through these, form a link back to fundamental human values which act as prime motivators. In the second instance they provide a link forward and help explain behaviour and action choices. Surveys of attitudes are therefore a useful means of assessing intra-community solidarity and inter-community relations. Attitudes towards events, situations and personalities can be added to attitudes of communities towards each other to build pictures of community images and stereotypes. In this context, the concept of *cognitive distance* has been used to describe contrasting inter-group perceptions and the differences which exist in mutual knowledge and understanding (Jacob and Toscano, 1964, p. 26). Although *cognitive distance* can be thought of as a factor contributing to the wider concept of *social distance*, it can be usefully kept separate because of its emphasis on images and perceptions, and set alongside *physical distance* and *social distance* as another concept which can be employed in the description of cultural integration and division.

Finally, the place of the historical dimension in the study of attributes must be noted. Cultural attributes are not static features: new elements are constantly being added to the cultural milieu while, through time, existing attributes will change, both in nature and in relative importance as integrators. Both integration and division build upon previous experience and so events long past, in which attempts at co-operation went unrewarded or in which division was necessary for self-defence, can spill over into the present and have all-pervasive effects on contemporary attributes. Consideration of the past, and in particular of those historical periods when new group elements and cultural origins emerged, provides the necessary context for the study of cultural attributes.

The balance between integration and division in plural societies therefore is based upon and reflected in a very extensive range of cultural attributes. Herein are found many opportunities for analysis and also, less fortunately, many problems of assessment. Studies can cover a number of significant attributes and, in so doing, refine and strengthen our understanding of integration and division. Despite such studies, few serious students would claim to have fully described the nature of pluralism. Even with the rise of statistical measures giving quantitative indices of fragmentation and pluralism (Haug, 1967; Rea and Taylor, 1970), the essential nature of the balance remains uncertain. In the real world, cultural integration and division is created, not simply by similarities and differences in cultural attributes, but by the much less tangible salience of each attribute and the intensity of feeling to which it gives rise. It is in the changing relative importance of cultural attributes, through time and from place to place, that the truly elusive essence of integration and division is found.

CULTURAL INTEGRATION AND DIVISION AS PROCESSES

Clearly, the relative levels of integration and division within a plural society are not static: they vary in time and space. Attribute analysis therefore can only describe this dynamic phenomenon at one point or at successive points in time. The dynamism of integration (and division) is recognised in a second definition which states that *integration (i.e. the act of integrating) results from a process whereby members of a culture group develop an escalating sequence of social linkages and contacts which create cohesion and establish behaviour norms which become legitimised through time.* Integration can thus be thought of as the process, i.e. the series of actions and operations, by which co-operation, consensus and community evolve. (The process of division is the converse of this.)

The process of integration is complex, diffuse and multilinear. It is made up of a large number of strands whose effects on levels of integration and division can be varied and contradictory. For example, a government decision to locate a desired facility, such as a new university, in Area A will be generally integrative in this favoured area; it will create process strands resulting in an increased level of support for the political system. At the same time, the decision will have disappointed other areas and Area B, in particular, which had hoped for the facility, will see itself as neglected; this will create process strands resulting in a lowering of support for the political system. Within Area B, however, the perceived neglect may well create links and co-operation between groups which were formerly opposed. Thus the same decision can result in greater integration locally, while creating elements of division at the wider political system level. Further, the shifts in the balance of integration and division resulting from the decision may well continue as the decision is implemented—it may cause perhaps unforeseen environmental change—or as subsequent and related decisions change the meaning of the original decision and alter the acceptability of the information flows to competing groups. Thus all locational decisions, whether concerned with desired or noxious facilities, create gainers and losers and thereby affect the balance and patterns of integration and division within the political system. In a plural society, where such locational decisions are usually perceived to have overtones of community advantage or disadvantage, the many strands in the process of integration and division are particularly significant. In all plural societies, with their increased consciousness of community relations, seemingly unimportant decisions at many different levels can set in motion a range of processes of considerable consequence for cultural integration and division.

Study of integration and division as a process thus encounters problems similar to those met in the analysis of cultural attributes. The process is not separate, distinct and easily recognisable in its own right. All communities are held together or separated by a gross mass of societal processes and all these processes affect the balance of integration and division in any given place. The range of strands and their complexity is such that the mass must be broken down before study can proceed. In most studies this breakdown is carried out by the simple method of including in the study those strands considered to be most significant and omitting the rest. Such a method is not only simple but, inevitably, subjective. Yet, as with attribute studies, the absence of a generally accepted set of salient integrative or disintegrative process strands prevents the development of a more objective approach.

The starting point for process studies is eased by an understanding of the nature of processes. All cultural processes, which comprise a series of actions and operations moving forward in time, are started by the implementation of a decision, whether that decision is made by individual, group, or government. Decision making is thus integrative or divisive and so the study of process can begin with the decision. Yet the question remains as to which decisions should be of greatest concern in the study of integration and division. Government decisions, with the weight of authority to implement them, form one category. In particular, in a plural society, policy decisions concerned with the redistribution of power, i.e. with administrative, local government and electoral reform, are vital. Another category with significance for the balance between integration and division is the whole range of economic and social reform decisions concerned with who gets what, where and when in the competition for scarce resources. In the private sector, a further range of decisions with possibly even greater integrative and divisive significance is encountered. The most important individual decision is certainly the voting decision; it sets in motion a process which results ultimately in the distribution of political power. In aggregate, voting decisions are one of the strongest conditioners of the integration–division balance. The residential decision also has considerable added significance in a plural society. Cumulatively, residential decisions cause the emergence and growth of distinct community settlement patterns and, in a strict sense, create *physical distance* between communities; indirectly they can reinforce *social distance* and establish the environment in which *cognitive distance* increases. Derogatory images and group stereotypes are likely to emerge most strongly in plural societies where competing culture groups are physically separated.

Published work on cultural integration and division has concentrated on attribute description and analysis (Neuman, 1976). However, the importance of cultural interaction as a determinant of the integration and division balance demands, at the very least, that the process element be given more consideration.

THE RELATIONSHIP BETWEEN ATTRIBUTE AND PROCESS

Although integration can be defined as an attribute of society (the state of being integrated) and as a process at work in society (the act of integrating), in reality the attribute and the process are interdependent. The process of integration does not take place in a vacuum but is influenced and moulded by the already existing attributes of society. In turn, society's attributes are the result of processes at work over time and change in attributes reflects the integrative or divisive effects of cultural processes. The relationship is symbiotic and, as with the chicken and the egg, impossible to time-order.

It is important to note, however, that process introduces the element of change and dynamism and it is this which makes the study of integration as a process of such basic importance. While descriptive analysis of attributes can show "what is", only study of process can show how "what is" came about and the direction in which change is leading. Study of integration/division as a process can therefore introduce both the predictive and the prescriptive element into studies. As Merritt (1974, p. 188) notes:

> To the extent that political integration is a process it has policy implications: decision makers may seek to determine which policies are more or less likely to lead to the end state of integration and govern their behaviour accordingly.

The complex relationships between attribute and process are shown in Fig. 1.1. The attributes, together with the historical context, are enclosed in the boxes. The processes are represented by lines and arrows, reflecting flows of activity and information. The processes, influenced

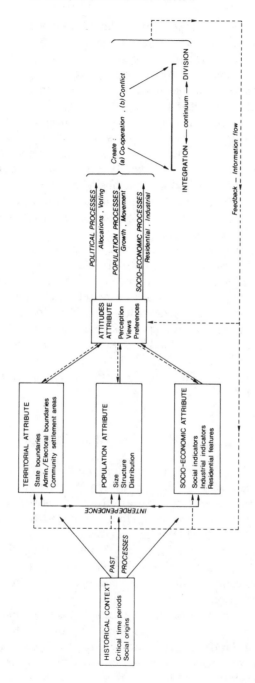

FIGURE 1.1. Integration and Division: Attributes and Processes.

by the attributes, control intra- and inter-group transactions and, to the extent that they are either co-operative or conflicting, they set the position of the plural society on the integration–division continuum. The many aspects of change created by the processes in turn feed back, by means of information flows, to alter or reinforce the nature of the contents in the attribute boxes.

Cultural integration and division is a subject of considerable complexity with its component parts possessing great systemic interdependence. The interweaving of cause and effect makes it difficult to establish with confidence exactly where study should begin. Despite these formidable methodological obstacles, the underlying aim of this book is to contribute to the better understanding of the plural society in Northern Ireland—why it became plural, why it remains so and how plurality grows or declines.

It is our hope that the framework set out here, based upon the plural society model and the concepts of cultural attributes and processes, will ease understanding and aid the reader's progress through the succeeding chapters. The framework sets each chapter in its place; it does more, however—it provides a position for each contribution in the wider scheme of things. Thus the content and findings of each chapter can be related back or carried forward, adding substance to that which has gone before and helping to focus more sharply that which follows. The place and the position of each contribution can now be established.

THE CONTRIBUTIONS

Periods during which population movement and contact create culture change and establish new community patterns are particularly important to students of integration and division. In the new cultural attributes, processes and behaviour are found the origins of historical precedents which spill over into the present and provide the touchstone for contemporary behaviour. In Chapter 2 Philip Robinson considers the Ulster Plantation of the early seventeenth century as such a period. The organisation and legislative background to the Plantation are set out and the processes of population migration and settlement which planted a new cultural element in north-eastern Ireland reviewed. The contemporary consequences of the Plantation in terms of community distributions, land-ownership and competition and origins of settlement segregation are discussed, together with differences in cultural attributes recognisable in the seventeenth century and remaining to the present day. Ronnie Buchanan, in Chapter 3, complements Robinson's work by considering in depth the cultural attributes and folk customs of the Plantation immigrant. Concentrating particularly on the Scottish Planter, he first shows how long-established and frequent movement of population between west and south-west Scotland and north-east Ireland created culture contact and mutual knowledge. Consequent similarities in settlement type, agricultural techniques and folk habits and customs must have greatly eased culture contact and understanding between the Planter and the Gael—the native Irish. Yet, as Buchanan concludes, there were other cultural traits, particularly non-material ones, which signalled difference, rivalry, separation and strong division.

Considerations of the contemporary aspects of the Northern Ireland problem are begun in Chapter 4 with a detailed description and analysis, by Paul Compton, of population attributes and processes. Using religious affiliation as the crucial category, the attributes of population size, structure and distribution are used to provide a clear demographic picture of Northern Ireland's two communities. This is built upon by the analysis of demographic processes, particularly those of population growth and migration, and by the use of the results to consider the future nature of the community population balance. The work also considers the likely social, economic and community relations consequences of differential population growth rates within the Protestant and Roman Catholic communities in the future.

The locus of attention next moves to the territorial attributes of the Northern Ireland political system. In Chapter 5 Neville Douglas outlines the nature and evolution of the spatial frameworks of regional and local government and their associated electoral areas. The work shows how these administrative and electoral frameworks have had persistent and strong effects upon the distribution and use of political power and, through this, upon community perceptions of and attitudes towards the political system and its legitimacy. Equally important, however, is the lesson that the administrative and electoral frameworks which have aroused so much discord can be explained fully and understood properly only in the context of the intra- and inter-community relations which existed at the time of their origin. The work makes clear that territorial frameworks are not simply the cause of cultural division but are equally the result of pre-existing discord and lack of integration.

Bob Osborne, in Chapter 6, concentrates upon the processes involved in, and the integrative and divisive consequences following from, voting behaviour at regional elections between 1921 and 1975. His analysis demonstrates how inflexible community voting led to unchanging patterns of representation and to the predictable political relationship between majority and minority on which was based an uneasy community co-existence which held sway in Northern Ireland until the 1970s. Osborne also shows how attempts to change this relationship—by Terence O'Neill in the 1960s and by the British Government in the 1970s—have met with persistent electoral rejections. The discussion emphasises the importance of elections as a channel of expression for community feeling.

The importance of government decision making as an instigator of integrative and divisive processes is illustrated in Chapter 7. Bob Osborne considers first the several consequences of the decision to locate the New University of Ulster at Coleraine in 1965. Dale Singleton follows with a more recent example of decision making, under Direct Rule from Westminster, examining the effects of the decision to meet housing needs of the Roman Catholic population of west Belfast at Poleglass, close to the suburbs of the predominantly Protestant town of Lisburn.

Economic conditions impinge crucially on any society. In a plural society, such as that in Northern Ireland, questions of economic health in general and unemployment in particular have an increased significance in that they create what is undoubtedly one of the most important material dimensions within which the processes of integration and division operate. By assessing the nature and pattern of a number of indices of economic health, Tony Hoare, at the outset of Chapter 8, demonstrates that Northern Ireland is a problem region with a regional problem. The survey then attempts to explain, with the aid of purpose-built statistical models, the relationships between the established patterns of economic health and wealth and the existing community patterns. Paul Doherty, in Chapter 9, concentrates specifically on the attribute of unemployment and outlines first the dimensions and distribution of the attribute within Northern Ireland and, more particularly, within Belfast. This is followed by an attempt to establish and assess, by means of regression analysis, the major correlates of the persistently high level of unemployment suffered in the region. Finally, the nature of these unfortunate attributes as it relates to the Protestant and Roman Catholic communities and its effects upon community integration and division are considered.

Integration and division can be observed on the ground in the form of the degree of inter-group segregation and mixing. Chapters 10 and 11 focus on the urban aspect of segregation. Fred Boal begins Chapter 10 by outlining the general relationship that exists between the incidence of residential segregation and the levels of integration or assimilation present in ethnically plural societies. After drawing tentative con- clusions, the study traces briefly the evolving character of residential segregation in Belfast before considering areas of residential mixing in the city. The major concern in the analysis of these areas is to find the causes for the variation in mixing observed in different housing en- vironments and to assess the extent to which the mixing that does exist represents either inter-community integration or a transitory phase in the more common process of community segregation.

In Chapter 11 Mike Poole extends the range of study to consider the characteristics and processes of residential segregation in twenty- six towns in Northern Ireland. Having noted the lack of empirical work on the topic, this study uses the dissimilarity index to develop a detailed analysis of painstakingly collected residential data. The analysis shows how significant variations occur in the degree of resi- dential segregation in the study towns. Attempts to explain both the degree of segregation and its variation establish the long-standing nature of both features and consider the significance of town size, group size, and the nature and speed of urban growth as causal factors. In this work the close interweave of attribute and process is clearly shown.

Violence must be the ultimate indicator of community division. At the same time the threat of violence may intensify the degree of integration within individual groups comprising a plural society. In Chapter 12 Russell Murray considers the patterns of violence which have emerged in Northern Ireland during the period 1969–1977. By analysing data on deaths and bombing incidents associated with political violence, he is able to demonstrate the spatial distribution of terrorism and from it develop a map of Northern Ireland's regions of violence. The study concludes by attempting to explain the regional patterns shown on the map in terms of a range of human and physical factors which have operated over a considerable period of time.

Finally, Chapter 13 provides an overview that draws on the contribu- tions to the book but which also introduces further issues that we consider important to a more complete perspective on the Northern Ireland problem. We conclude, briefly, with a comment on possible solutions to the problem.

REFERENCES

Haug, M. R. (1967). Social and Cultural Pluralism as a Concept in Social System Analysis. *American Journal of Sociology* **73,** 298–299.
Jackson, H. (1971). "The Two Irelands: A Dual Study of Inter-Group Tensions." Minority Rights Group, London.

Jacob, P. E. and Toscano, J. V. (1964). "The Integration of Political Communities." Lippincott, Philadelphia.

Lijphart, A. (1975). The Northern Ireland Problem: Cases, Theories and Solutions. *British Journal of Political Science* **5,** 83–106.

Lijphart, A. (1977). "Democracy in Plural Societies." Yale University Press, New Haven, Connecticut.

Merritt, R. L. (1974). Locational Aspects of Political Integration. *In* "Locational Approaches to Power and Conflict" (K. R. Cox, D. R. Reynolds and S. Rokkan, eds.), pp. 187–211. John Wiley, New York.

Neuman, S. G., ed. (1976). "Small States and Segmented Societies." Praeger, New York.

Rabushka, A. and Shepsle, K. A. (1972). "Politics in Plural Societies: A Theory of Democratic Instability." Merrill, Columbus, Ohio.

Rea, D. W. and Taylor, M. (1970). "The Analysis of Political Cleavages." Yale University Press, New Haven, Connecticut.

Smith, M. G. (1969). Some Developments in the Analytic Framework of Pluralism. *In* "Pluralism in Africa" (L. Kuper and M. G. Smith, eds.), pp. 415–458. University of California Press, Berkeley.

Stewart, A. T. Q. (1977). "The Narrow Ground." Faber and Faber, London.

Whyte, J. (1978). Interpretations of the Northern Ireland Problem: An Appraisal. *Economic and Social Review* **9,** 257–282.

CHAPTER 2

PLANTATION AND COLONISATION: THE HISTORICAL BACKGROUND

Philip Robinson

INTRODUCTION

To understand why, and how, sub-regions with differing cultural identities have developed within Northern Ireland, it is essential to gain an historical perspective, both of the cultural landscape and of the often over-simplified relationships between religious denomination, ethnic origin and political affiliation.

The historical focus for any examination of the origins of cultural divisions must undoubtedly be the Ulster Plantation. This event was intended by James I and his government to achieve stability in those parts of west Ulster which had been found by his predecessor, Elizabeth I, to be most ungovernable, and, following the confiscation of vast tracts of land, the plan involved the settlement or "planting" of significant numbers of English and Lowland Scots in Ulster. Although the Plantation period to most historians would include the years up to 1641 (when the native Irish rebelled against the Planters), the actual movement of English and Scots to Ulster followed a rather broader time schedule, extending in fact well into the eighteenth century. In addition, Counties Antrim and Down, although outside the area considered for the official scheme, each received more settlers than any of the other counties in Ulster, being nearest to the British mainland and directly *en route* to many of the Plantation areas to the west. The movement of population in the early seventeenth century was only the start of what was to become a continuous, if somewhat uneven, flow in the following decades. In all probability the peak rates of immigration were reached in the second half of the seventeenth century.

19

The assumption that a single cultural index such as religious denomination can be taken to have ethnic, cultural and political implications
for most individuals may be grossly misleading. While religious denomination was always a crucial factor in determining an individual's
political and cultural allegiances, its current role as the major threshold
in the assimilation process perhaps obscures the former importance of
language and other cultural thresholds. When the twentieth century
Ulster landscape is examined to discover the extent of plantation and
other British settlement survival, the usual index to be mapped is the
proportion of non-Roman Catholics in the total population per unit
area. Figure 2.1 however, although indicating a strikingly similar
pattern, has been mapped on a rather different basis, to suggest different
levels of Irish cultural persistence in the face of settlement by, and

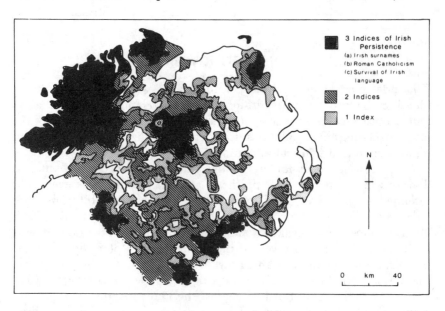

FIGURE 2.1. Irish/British Ethnic and Cultural Survival Areas in Ulster
(Twentieth Century).

The administrative unit employed in the construction of this map is the
district electoral division (D.E.D.). The number of indices of Irish persistence
was ascertained for each rural D.E.D., the indices being: (i) more than 50%
of surnames of Irish origin (*List of Electors for the 1971 Register; Register of
Dail Electors, 1963–1964*); (ii) population more than 50% Roman Catholic
(*Census of Ireland 1911*); (iii) more than 10% survival of the Irish language
(Coimisiún na Gaeltachta, 1927). The numbers of Irish indices at D.E.D.
level were then isoplethed to provide suggestive gradients of acculturation.

assimilation into, the British population. The three basic elements superimposed here are Roman Catholicism, Irish surnames and the survival of the Irish language (this last element is given exaggerated importance as the area represented is only of a 10% survival).

The core areas of Irish persistence are localities where the proportion of Roman Catholics in the total population is generally well in excess of 75% (Compton, 1978, p. 82), and generally correspond to the areas of Irish language survival. Similarly, the area mapped in Fig. 2.1 as showing least Irish cultural persistence can be taken to represent the distributional end-product of several centuries of plantation, colonisation, internal migration and acculturation (Robinson, 1974, pp. 182–196).

In all of these areas there is an obvious correspondence between British settlement and the best of the agricultural land in the principal low-lying areas (Symons and Cruickshank, 1963), with the important qualification that the economic threshold of land desirability for British settlement appears to have been much lower in the east of the province, and also in the coastal areas of the north, than it was in mid and west Ulster. These preferred areas are not only where the physical distance to the points of origin of the settlers in England and Scotland was least, but also where communication and trade with Britain could be maintained.

The direction of colonial spread can be theoretically deduced by lines drawn on a settlement map joining areas of highest to areas of lowest density (Bylund, 1960). Besides suggesting that conventional colonial processes had been operating between Britain and Ulster, the "downslope" gradients in British settlement density suggest a directional movement of colonists mainly from southern Scotland.

In a similar overlay technique to that employed in Fig. 2.1, three present-day criteria have been mapped in Fig. 2.2 to indicate areas where surnames, religious denomination and dialect suggest Scottish rather than English settlement; that is, when these indices are considered only in the context of non-Irish or British surnames, Protestant denominations and variations in dialects of spoken English.

In Ulster, there are three basic linguistic groups which contribute to speech patterns today: Irish Gaelic, Scotch-Irish and Ulster Anglo-Irish. The two primary English dialects of Ulster, called north-eastern or Ulster-Scots dialect and mid-Ulster dialect, are considered to have originated from the seventeenth century dialects of south-west Scotland and the north-west midlands of England respectively (Gregg, 1972; Braidwood, 1964). The extent of the Ulster-Scots dialect in Ulster has been mapped by Gregg, and this distribution forms the core areas representing all three indices of Scottish settlement in Fig. 2.2.

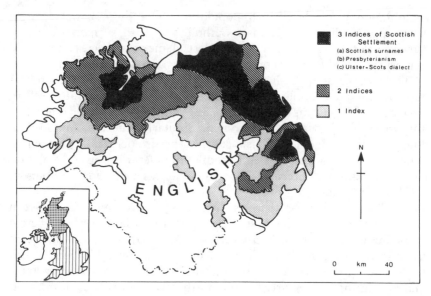

FIGURE 2.2. Scottish/English Settlement and Cultural Areas in Ulster (Twentieth Century).

The administrative units employed in the construction of this map are: (i) rural districts, for Scottish surnames—i.e. Scottish surnames comprising more than 50% of the British surnames in the electoral lists (*List of Electors for the 1971 Register; Register of Dail Electors, 1963–1964*); (ii) baronies, for religious denomination—i.e. more than 50% of Protestant population record- ed as Presbyterian (*Census of Ireland 1911*). The extent of the Ulster-Scots dialect was mapped from fieldwork evidence by Gregg (1972). Some areas in the extreme west and south of the province are not included in the assessment of Scottish traits, i.e. where fewer than 15% of all surnames are of British origin and less than 15% of the total population is Protestant.

Although the two main Protestant denominations in Ulster, Pres- byterianism and Anglicanism, have been broadly associated with Scottish and English settlement respectively, it should be remembered that, while Presbyterianism may have been a dominant philosophy among Scots settlers, it only became established as a distinct religious denomination in Ulster during the later seventeenth century, when it then spread rapidly throughout areas of Scottish settlement (Gailey, 1975).

While dialect and religious denominations have both been subject to processes of assimilation, surnames do provide a more stable and representative index of national origin. The problems associated with the use of surnames in this context are not those of transmission between

English and Scottish settlers, but rather of identifying which surnames are of English, and which of Scottish origin (Robinson, 1974, pp. 217–224). A consensus of this surname, religious and dialect evidence strongly suggests that the present-day British settlement in Ulster comprises two major components: an area to the east, north and west where the non-Irish population is primarily of Scottish origin, and an area in mid and south Ulster predominantly of English origin. The inset to Fig. 2.2 illustrates the relationship of these areas to the source areas of England and Scotland.

However, whether these cultural regions are differentiated on the basis of British–Irish or English–Scottish traits, their foundation was laid during the seventeenth century, by the end of which the present-day cultural patterns of rural settlement had been largely, but not totally, established.

THE BACKGROUND TO COLONIAL VENTURES IN IRELAND

By the end of the sixteenth century, the greater part of south and east Ireland had been subjected to a series of English conquests and colonisations commencing with the Anglo-Norman invasion of 1169, and culminating in the Munster Plantation of 1585 to 1598.

In 1556 Queen Mary indicated her intention of planting Counties Leix and Offaly. However, the failure to attract sufficient numbers of English artisans and tenant-farmers, along with continuing frontier warfare with the displaced Irish, meant that the settlement did not endure (Morton, 1971). Meanwhile, the Earl of Sussex was to drive the Highland Scots out of their settlements in north-east Ulster, and he suggested that a colonising force of 1000 men should be planted in towns there. These plans were postponed until Elizabeth's reign, when in 1567 Sir Henry Sidney proposed a vague scheme to secure Ulster by a network of forts and settlements. However, although Elizabeth wanted to plant Ulster, she desired a scheme which would involve private enterprise and not her own resources. As a result the subsequent proposals to settle Counties Antrim and Down in the 1570s by Sir Thomas Smith and the Earl of Essex involved private armies designed to conquer and settle. Both these ventures perished in the face of Irish opposition and insufficient men (Dunlop, 1925).

Elizabeth's Plantation of Munster (1585–1598) was perhaps most successful of all the sixteenth century plantations in Ireland, although this scheme also failed to establish an enduring English settlement of sufficient numerical strength to provide stability (Quinn, 1966).

Meanwhile in east Ulster the flow of Lowland Scots had already begun before the Ulster Plantation had been formulated. Two Scots, Hugh Montgomery and James Hamilton, had received grants of land in north Down from James I with the requirement ". . . to inhabit the said territory and land with English or Scotchmen" (Perceval-Maxwell, 1973, p. 31). They had no difficulty whatever in attracting large numbers of Scots to their estates and in County Antrim many Scots were also starting to settle on the estate of the Earl of Antrim, Sir Randal Mac-Donnell, who had been re-granted his lands in 1604 to enforce a manorial pattern of land holdings (Perceval-Maxwell, 1973, pp. 48–49).

Nevertheless, the sum total of these English and Lowland Scottish penetrations in Ireland had not substantially affected west Ulster where the Gaelic order remained intact until the early seventeenth century. The Anglo-Norman footholds in Counties Antrim and Down were maintained throughout the Elizabethan period, and so in much of east Ulster English law was enforced. Indeed, although it lacked a substantial English presence, County Monaghan had been divided into freehold estates which were granted mostly to Irish chiefs in 1591 under the policy of "surrender and re-grant".

This meant that in Ulster at the end of the sixteenth century, only the six counties of Armagh, Coleraine (now Londonderry), Cavan, Donegal, Fermanagh and Tyrone retained the Gaelic systems of land tenure (Nicholls, 1972) which were in basic conflict with English law and outside the sphere of influence of the Elizabethan government.

When Hugh O'Neill led the Irish chiefs of these areas in rebellion at the close of Elizabeth's reign, west Ulster was encircled by English military forts and garrisons, and the subjection of Ulster became a vital object for England. After the Ulster-Irish chiefs finally submitted in 1603 they were favourably treated by the new monarch, James I, although his Servitors (i.e. military and civil servants) in Ireland had expected the lands to be parcelled out among them as the Desmonds' lands had been in Munster twenty years earlier. Instead James compelled O'Neill and the other chiefs to accept only their own demesne lands as freehold estates, and to receive a fixed rent from their sub-chiefs.

This frustration of the Servitors' desire for land was short-lived. Sir Arthur Chichester, the most influential Servitor in Ulster (who was also sympathetic to the disappointments of the Irish Servitors generally), was appointed Lord Deputy of Ireland. Almost as soon as the patents of the Irish chiefs' grants had been made out, immense tracts of "termon" and "erenagh" (Church) land were claimed by the Protestant bishops, and the Earls of Tyrone and Tyrconnell (O'Neill and O'Donnell) were continuously harassed by the English officials in Ireland. Eventually through fear of arrest and imprisonment, O'Neill, O'Donnell and a number of other chiefs and followers fled to the Continent from Lough Swilly. This "Flight of the Earls" in 1607 resulted in the eagerly awaited forfeiture of the estates of the earls to the Crown.

While the government was considering the best means of colonising the newly obtained territory, vast additions were made to the lands available for plantation so that by 1608 virtually all the temporal lands in Counties Armagh, Cavan, Coleraine, Donegal, Fermanagh and Tyrone had been either confiscated by or surrendered to the Crown, although many of the Irish chiefs were expecting considerable re-grants of land by James I.

Given the desire for a successful colonisation of Ulster by British Protestants, it had to be remembered that the English Servitors in Ireland were expecting grants of land and that substantial numbers of Irish sub-chiefs were expecting a reallocation of much of their former lands. A further influence on the Plantation scheme was that James wanted to involve Scottish noblemen and to provide grants of land as favours for them and that, following the lessons learnt from earlier plantations, the grants would have to be small with a very strict programme of building and "planting", if the venture was to be successful.

THE SCHEME FOR THE ULSTER PLANTATION

By 1610 a set of Plantation conditions had been endorsed which established that the temporal land of each county involved in the Plantation should be divided into baronies or precincts, and that each barony should be reserved for the use of one particular type of major land grantee (Moody, 1934–1935). The different classes of grantees were to be groups of English Undertakers, Scottish Undertakers, English Servitors and Irish natives. The English Servitors were to receive their grants within the same baronies as the Irish natives, so that they could oversee the Irish, and were not required to plant their estates with British tenants. However, it was the Undertakers, in separate groups of Scots and English, who were to be responsible for the main implementation of the scheme for colonisation.

Each barony allocated either to English or Scottish Undertakers was to be divided into three sorts of proportions or estates: 2000 acres; 1500 acres; and 1000 acres. No Undertaker was to be allowed more than 2000 acres except the chief Undertaker of each barony, who was to be allowed 3000 acres.

In return for these estates, the grantees "undertook" to plant twenty-four able men of eighteen years or more, representing at least ten families of English or inland (Lowland) Scots on every 1000 acres; all tenants were to be planted before November 1611. Of every 1000 acres granted, 300 acres were to be held in demesne with two fee-farmers (freeholders) on 120 acres each, three leaseholders on 100 acres each and four families or more of husbandmen, artificers or cottagers (craftsmen and agricultural labourers) on the remaining 160 acres. No land was to be demised to any Irish or anyone not taking the Oath of Supremacy. The undertenants were to be conformable in religion and take the Oath of Supremacy. Undertakers were to be resident for five years or have an agent resident.

Within three years Undertakers were also to build a stone house and bawn (a defended courtyard) if the estate was of 2000 acres, a stone or brick house and bawn if 1500 acres, and a bawn if the estate was only of 1000 acres.

In addition to these stringent conditions applied to the Undertakers (although the Servitors and natives were also governed by the Plantation building requirements), there was to be a proposed network of corporate towns, one in each barony, along with free schools at selected centres such as Dungannon, Enniskillen and Armagh. The urban network, whose function was largely to facilitate the promotion of a market-based economy, was also to provide administrative centres, although on each estate small nucleations were intended, tenants being required to build their houses in villages near the bawn.

THE ALLOCATION OF LAND

A total of sixty Scottish Undertakers received Plantation estates in nine specially allocated baronies of the Plantation counties, while fifty-three English Undertakers received estates in seven baronies (Fig. 2.3). The nine baronies set aside for Servitors and natives contained fifty-one Servitors' estates, although there were a further four Servitors' estates in other baronies.

Apart from the Irish native grantees, the other two large groups of grantees in the Ulster Plantation were the Protestant bishops and the London companies. Interspersed among the estates in all baronies were vast tracts of land which traditionally had been termon and erenagh lands of the Irish Church. These eventually fell to the Protestant Bishops of Derry, Raphoe, Kilmore and Clogher and the Archbishop of Armagh, who in turn often sub-let to neighbouring Servitors and Undertakers, but included conditions of planting English tenants in their sub-leases.

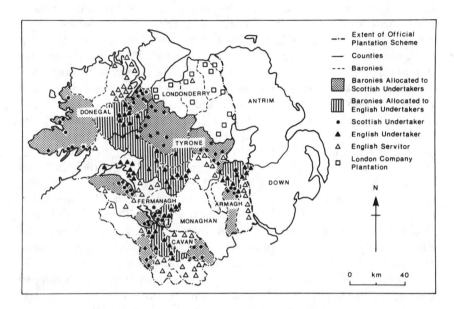

FIGURE 2.3. The Official Allocation of Plantation Lands in Ulster, *circa* 1610. The names of the townlands contained in these individual grants have been collated and printed by Hill (1877, pp. 259–353).

In north Ulster the Barony of Loughinsholin, formerly in County Tyrone, was added to County Coleraine to form the County of Londonderry, which was to be a plantation controlled by twelve different London companies. The Plantation conditions which were applicable to the Undertakers in other counties were applied also to these London companies, but the estates were generally larger, of 3000 acres.

Other exceptions to the general pattern of land allocation were the grant of the entire Barony of Inishowen to Sir Arthur Chichester as a Servitor, the grants of land in Donegal, Fermanagh and Armagh for the maintenance of Trinity College, Dublin, and the smaller fragments granted as glebes to support local Episcopalian clergy, along with certain small grants to support the free schools and corporate towns in each county.

Outside Londonderry, in the other five "escheated" counties, the approximate breakdown of land allocation among the different grantee classes was as follows: English Undertakers 22%; Scottish Undertakers

21%; Church (bishops, abbey land, local glebes, etc.) 24%; English Servitors 13%; Irish natives 15%; Trinity College 3%; corporate towns, forts, schools, etc. 2%. Proportionately, the extent of land which was allocated to the Church was the greatest to any single grantee class, although the English and Scottish Undertakers between them obtained more: about 43%, representing 57% of all the secular (temporal) land. While it is valid to use the Plantation surveyors' estimates of grant sizes for comparative purposes, the absolute sizes of grants (in acres) were always a gross underestimation of the real extent of land involved. This discrepancy was caused by the way in which the land was measured, rather than by any deliberate attempt to discriminate grant sizes in favour of particular grantee classes (Robinson, 1974, pp. 126–139). The escheated lands were estimated in each county simply by enumerating the small Irish land units in each barony, these being slightly different from region to region, but all representing the local prototypes of the present-day townland. These "ballyboes", "polls" and "tates" were estimated by the Plantation surveyors to contain a fixed quantity of profitable land, usually sixty acres (*Analecta Hibernica*, 1931). The real extent of these units, however, was usually well in excess of 300 acres, and they varied greatly in size according to their agricultural potential. Indeed it was the amount of land required to graze a standard number of cattle which probably determined the extent of the ballyboes for the Irish, and certainly not measured area. This meant that, while two estates could bear little resemblance in actual size, their agricultural potential was fairly well equated, with the estate containing the best land being the smaller in actual extent.

In fact, Irish territorial groupings of sixteen ballyboes, polls or tates (of approximately sixty estimated acres each) were known in pre-Plantation Ulster as "ballybetaghs": quasi-political units controlled by sept leaders under the various regional chiefs (Moody, 1939, pp. 451–456; Robinson, 1974, pp. 51–58; Robinson, 1976). These ballybetaghs were estimated therefore to contain 1000 acres of profitable land and were often presented intact as Plantation estates in a way that provided a new social structure with related territorial divisions remarkably similar to the pre-Plantation hierarchical structure.

There is no evidence that the quality of the land received by Irish grantees was poorer than that obtained by any of the other grantee classes, or that their lands were not equally under-estimated in extent by the Plantation surveyors. It was however the *proportion* of the land received which disadvantaged the Irish seriously, along with, of course, the economic sorting of settlement in relation to land values which took place later at tenant-farmer level. British settlers often obtained leases of the best townlands within the Plantation estates, and indeed within Church and Servitors' lands also.

The division of the different counties into baronies to be allocated to Undertakers (Fig. 2.3) resulted in a distribution of English and Scottish Undertakers which, because of the nature of the later colonial processes, bore little, if any, relationship to the eventual pattern of English and Scottish settlement in Ulster (Fig. 2.2).

The Undertakers themselves were grouped in exclusively English or Scottish consorts for each barony under a principal Undertaker. Some of these consorts were of family groups, or of groups from adjacent areas in England or Scotland, while many others were simply mixed groups of English or Scots drawn from quite different parts of their respective countries (Hill, 1877, pp. 117–152; Perceval-Maxwell, 1973, pp. 91–113, 317–358, 368). On balance, relative to the Scots, a slightly higher proportion of the English Undertakers were titled noblemen, and in accord with the fact that the individual wealth of the Scottish Undertakers was not as high, the English generally received a higher proportion of the larger 1500 and 2000 acre estates.

The Scottish Undertakers were drawn, however, from a quite restricted area within Scotland. The vast majority of the Scots Undertakers came from the central lowland belt, especially the Edinburgh-Haddington area in the east and the Renfrew-north Ayrshire area in the west. Apart from a few Undertakers from the east coast of Scotland north of Fife, the only other area from which significant numbers were drawn was the extreme south-west of the country, between Dumfries and Portpatrick.

BRITISH SETTLEMENT IN ULSTER 1610–1670

The earliest quantifiable population statistics of British settlement in Ulster are to be found in the four surviving Plantation surveys of 1611 (*Cal. Carew MSS, 1603–1624*, pp. 68–69, 75–79, 220–251), 1613 (*Hastings MSS*, 1947, pp. 159–182), 1619 (*Cal. Carew MSS, 1603–1624*, pp. 392–423) and 1622 (for printed sources relating to this survey, see note to Fig. 2.4). The intention was to examine the progress of the official Plantation scheme, and therefore they record only the building and settlement programme on the Undertakers' and Servitors' lands within the areas designated for plantation. Additional settlement may be assumed on the Church lands within the Plantation counties, and more especially throughout Counties Antrim and Down, which were outside the official scheme.

In addition to the Plantation surveys, two muster-rolls of adult British males survive for 1618 (*Cal. S.P. Ire.*, *1615–1625*, p. 228) and 1631 (P.R.O.N.I., D. 1759/3C/1–2; T. 808/15164; T. 934). The rather incomplete 1618 muster was compiled by a Captain Alleyne who apparently lacked sufficient authority to summon all the Undertakers to appear (Perceval-Maxwell, 1973, p. 164), although it was probably significant that the majority of those not appearing had, according to the earlier surveys, been the most unsuccessful in terms of "planting" British settlers. On the other hand, the 1631 muster was more thorough and a much more interesting list as it recorded for the first time the numbers of British men on Church lands within the Plantation counties and, more importantly, provides the earliest British settlement statistics for Counties Antrim and Down.

When the surveys and musters of the Plantation period are examined in chronological order, the rate of influx can be assessed. This clearly indicates that there was a slow initial response to the Plantation, with settlement peaks only reached about 1622, ten years after the settlement was originally intended to have been completed. The evidence of the actual population figures of the surveys in respect of a slow take-off is supplemented by the general observations accompanying the various surveys. The first one conducted by Carew in 1611 and the second by Bodley in 1613 noted that, although the building programme had proceeded fairly successfully on almost all estates, the required numbers of settlers had not materialised. James I was intensely displeased at the slow progress of the Plantation, but re-extended to the end of August 1616 the three-year period which had been set for the fulfilment of the Undertakers' obligations (*Cal. S.P. Ire.*, *1615–1625*, p. 26). A further survey by Bodley in 1616 is not extant although it is believed that this again reported unfavourably (Hill, 1877, p. 449). In 1618 a proclamation was issued stipulating that all Irish were to be removed from the estates by May 1619 (Steele, 1910, p. 22). Pynnar's survey of 1619 reported that for the first time a substantial number of Undertakers had fulfilled the Plantation conditions. However, many Irish still remained on the estates, and in 1621 it was decided that one-quarter of each of the Undertakers' estates could be set apart for Irish tenants (*Cal. S.P. Ire.*, *1615–1625*, pp. 322–323). A final official survey was concluded in 1622, and after James I's death in 1625 there was little further interest in enforcing the original Plantation policy.

When British settlement in the official Plantation areas of Ulster is mapped for 1622 (Fig. 2.4), possible explanations of the distribution pattern may best be found in factors relating to the physical environment, such as agricultural land values or distance to the point of entry

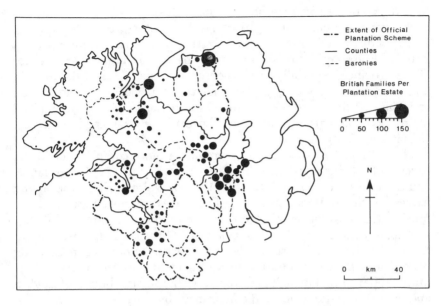

FIGURE 2.4. British Settlement on the Plantation Estates, 1622.
The 1622 survey has been transcribed and printed for each of the counties:
Armagh (Treadwell, 1960); Donegal (Treadwell, 1951–1954; 1954–1957);
Fermanagh (O Gallachair, 1958b); Cavan (O Gallachair, 1958a); Tyrone
(Treadwell, 1964); Londonderry (*Cal. S. P. Ire., 1615–1625*, pp. 364–378).

for the colonists, rather than in any explanation based on the distribution of Undertakers' lands or the "efforts" and "abilities" of individual
Undertakers to effect the Plantation. Indeed, the 1622 British settlement
pattern in west Ulster differs only from the broad pattern of present-
day "British" rural settlement survival in one major respect. This is
that certain areas of central Ulster, especially Cavan, which were
apparently well planted in 1622 despite a degree of isolation from points
of entry, today contain proportionally fewer persons of British origin
in terms of the overall distribution. The underlying inference of this
may be that the 1622 settlement pattern was at least partially influenced
by direct plantations of settlers on estates by Undertakers. Certainly,
the earliest surveys mention Undertakers bringing "followers" and
tenants with them (*Cal. Carew MSS, 1603–1624*, p. 77), but the internal
population movements especially of British labourers or "cottagers"
must have been quite marked. Between the 1619 and 1622 surveys
there were significant settlement changes recorded on many of the
individual estates, some showing an increase and many a decrease

(despite an overall increase in the total British population). Although these differences between the 1619 and the 1622 figures perhaps reflect a certain degree of unreliability in the survey material, a quite distinct pattern of substantial British population loss can be found in the interior of the province, especially in the poorer marginal areas of the Sperrin and Donegal mountains, a loss which was nevertheless more than compensated for by settlement increases in the low-lying valleys and plains of good agricultural land, especially in the north and east (Robinson, 1978).

The 1631 muster-rolls not only provide a more complete territorial coverage for British settlement in Ulster (as they include Church lands, and Counties Antrim and Down), but they also include the actual names of the settlers mustered. These lists of surnames therefore provide the first opportunity to examine the overall nature of British settlement throughout Ulster for evidence of Scottish or English origins. In Fig. 2.5 there can be seen substantial British settlement in Counties Antrim and Down in addition to a settlement pattern in west Ulster quite similar to that of 1622. However, when the distribution of English and Scottish settlement is distinguished by surname analysis and compared to the allocation of land to English and Scottish Under-takers and English Servitors (Figs 2.5 and 2.3), it is apparent that the

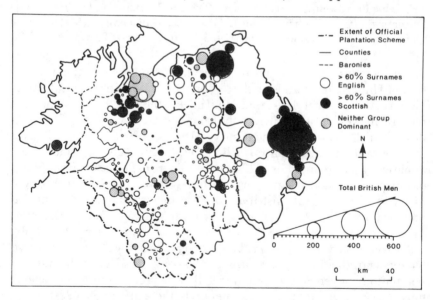

Figure 2.5. English and Scottish Settlement in Ulster, 1631.
Source: P.R.O.N.I., D. 1759/3C/1–2; T. 808/15164; T. 934.

ethnic origin of the settlers does not always coincide with that of the landowner. There is, nevertheless, such a correspondence in areas such as Armagh, most of County Cavan, mid and south Londonderry, and north and west Tyrone. However, in some other areas, concentrations of Scottish settlement appear to have accumulated in areas allocated to English Undertakers, and (less frequently) vice versa with a few areas of predominantly English settlement and Scottish land-ownership. Clearly the areas of Scottish expansion were in south Antrim, north Down, north Antrim and north-east Londonderry, and the "Laggan" area of the Foyle Basin in north-east Donegal and north-west Tyrone. These areas are precisely those of the first four presbyteries of the Presbyterian Church in Ireland, and from which Presbyterianism (as an organisationally separate Church) spread territorially during the seventeenth century (Gailey, 1975). When these areas of English or Scottish settlement in the seventeenth century are compared to the modern survivals of English or Scottish cultural traits (Fig. 2.2), there are two particular localities which have apparently undergone changes in this respect since the mid-seventeenth century and merit closer examination. In the case of County Londonderry the problem is relatively simple: the obvious inference must be that early English settlement was "planted" by the London companies, only to be swamped at a later stage by Scottish settlers arriving from adjacent areas on the British mainland—the colonial process of "spread" rather than "direct plantation". Indeed the first fruits of the colonial spread process can be seen in north Londonderry in Fig. 2.5.

The sequence of British settlement in the other exceptional locality— the Clogher Valley in south Tyrone—is however rather more difficult to interpret. Here the barony was granted to English Undertakers, but was settled largely with Scots by 1631 (and indeed by 1622 for the surnames of the British settlers are available in this area from the 1622 Undertakers' certificates used in the preparation of the 1622 survey) (N.L.I., MS 8014/9). Today this area falls outside the main area of Scottish cultural influence (Fig. 2.2). Scottish Undertakers did buy out some of the estates here from English (Robinson, 1974, pp. 224–225), but generally only *after* these estates were being colonised by Scots. One possible interpretation might be that the Clogher Valley was subjected to two separate influences of a colonial spread type of process, firstly by Scots expanding from their adjacent and convenient points of entry—Londonderry city and Strabane—only to be eclipsed at a later stage by the late seventeenth century flow of English colonists across north Armagh and into south Tyrone from the direction of Belfast. Certainly it was not until after the late 1630s that Belfast superseded

Carrickfergus as the major port in south Antrim (Owen, 1917, p. 11), after which time it became a relatively more important port than Londonderry with a greatly increased sphere of influence (Robinson, 1974, pp. 209–217). During this period the area immediately inland from Belfast—the Lagan Valley, south-west Antrim and north Armagh —recorded substantial increases in the number of persons of pre-dominantly English origin (Braidwood, 1964, pp. 11–17; Morgan, 1976; Crawford, 1975).

The settlement pattern, and the development of English and Scottish settlement concentrations, can only be explained in all localities by reference to three separate colonial processes: direct plantation, colonial spread and internal migration—although internal migration can only be regarded as a distinct and separate process from that of colonial spread if the movement was subsequent to direct plantation, presumably in untenable economic circumstances, and in a direction which cut across any pattern of colonial spread also operating. Direct plantation was probably only a significant settlement influence in the early years of the Plantation, especially in the interior of Ulster and among the larger tenant-farmers. Mobility certainly was most marked among the lower social orders, and subsequent to a period of internal migration and settlement rationalisation in the early seventeenth century, the ever-present process of colonial spread undoubtedly became dominant in the subsequent decades.

The view, therefore, that the pattern of Plantation settlement in Ulster was influenced more by environmental factors than by any aspect of the official governmental scheme is strongly supported, not only by the apparent nature of the colonial processes operating, but also by both the emerging distributional pattern of settlement, and the phases of influx of settlers which indicate late settlement, well after the initial establishment of the estates by the Undertakers.

It is particularly unfortunate that no demographic material survives for British settlement in Ulster between 1631 and *circa* 1660, a period longer than that covered by all the earlier material. This period is important because the 1641 rebellion with its greatly exaggerated stories of massacres of British is sometimes regarded as a cataclysmic event for Plantation settlement. However, the British settlement pattern in 1660 was so similar to that of the pre-1641 period that the rebellion cannot be said to have had any lasting effect in this respect.

Besides the hearth-money rolls and the poll-tax lists of the 1660s, another important demographic source resulted directly from the increased governmental control for taxation purposes which followed the 1641 rebellion and subsequent Cromwellian confiscations. This was the "census" of 1659 which appears to have been compiled from poll-tax material (Pender, 1939), but whose particular value lies in the fact that in it English and Scots are distinguished from Irish, while in the other sources surnames have to be used for this purpose. The accuracy and consistency of the absolute figures provided in this "census" have been challenged (Graham, 1972, pp. 289–292), but when the recorded proportions of British to Irish settlement are examined and mapped (Fig. 2.6), many of the problems of reliability associated with the absolute figures can be discounted (Robinson, 1974, pp. 152–154, 178–181).

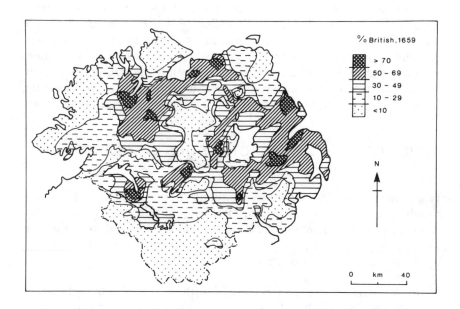

FIGURE 2.6. British Settlement in Ulster, *circa* 1659.

The percentage of British in each parish has been calculated from the 1659 "census" (Pender, 1939) for Counties Armagh, Down, Antrim, Londonderry, Cavan, Fermanagh, Donegal and Monaghan, and the values then isoplethed. Comparable statistics for the County Tyrone parishes were obtained by adjusting the numbers of British and Irish-owned hearths recorded in the hearth-money rolls of 1666 (P.R.O.N.I., T. 307; T. 307c; T. 604; T. 808/15068) by correction factors. These factors were based on a comparison with the fragmentary poll-tax cover which survives for some Tyrone parishes (P.R.O.N.I., T. 1365/3), and this adjustment removes the socially selective imbalance inherent in percentages derived from the hearth-money rolls alone.

The most obvious general inference which may be drawn from a comparison of the British settlement patterns in 1631, 1659 and the early twentieth century (Figs 2.5, 2.6 and 2.1) is one of distributional continuity, and the support this gives to the importance of environmental factors in shaping the pattern of seventeenth century colonisation.

The hearth-money rolls, although socially selective and incomplete in coverage, facilitate further surname analysis to substantiate the broad patterns of British settlement (and indeed the English–Scottish localities) found using the 1631 muster-rolls. Indeed, surnames in many areas are available for 1622, 1631 and 1666, and an examination of these in turn indicates a continuity of English or Scottish predominance in their respective localities during the first half of the seventeenth century (Robinson, 1974, pp. 245–250). Nevertheless, between all three dates the actual individual surnames at any location do change markedly, in some cases almost completely, an aspect which again indicates the high level of internal mobility and population turnover during this period, but a movement which was apparently operating within a state of equilibrium in terms of "ethnic" territoriality.

THE FORM AND CHARACTERISTICS OF PLANTATION SETTLEMENT

When the Plantation scheme was about to be implemented, it was clearly envisaged that the colonisation should consist almost entirely of nucleated settlements, i.e. Plantation towns and villages. Villages were to be the settlement norm on the Plantation estates, as indicated by the articles of the Plantation:

> Every of the said Undertakers shall draw their tenants to build houses for themselves and their families, not scattering, but together, neare the principall house or bawne as well as for their mutuall defence and strength as for the making of villages and townships. (Moody, 1934–1935, p. 181)

However, these small nucleations of farmers and their labourers (cottagers) on each estate were not intended to perform the range of service functions of larger Plantation towns. The towns had market facilities which were to be supplemented by the services offered by churches, tradesmen and artificers. Corporate towns were projected for each of the Plantation baronies ". . . with Markets and Fairs and other reasonable Liberties, and with power to send Burgesses to the Parliament . . ." (Harris, 1770, pp. 108–109).

The land reserved for the support of the towns was normally granted to the principal Undertaker of each barony, who was then charged with the construction of a town on his estate. In practice it was the principal Undertakers who were granted the castles and personal lands of the pre-Plantation Irish chiefs in each barony, so that the towns were often located in positions which had already been established as the lowland centres of power. A good example of this continuity was at Dungannon, where Sir Arthur Chichester received the castle and estate of Hugh O'Neill, Earl of Tyrone (Robinson, 1974, pp. 245–250). An additional 500 acres was granted to Chichester to support the corporate town of Dungannon, and he was required:

> ... to set apart a convenient place of the said 500[a], for the site of the town, to be built streetways; another part for a market place; and another for a church and churchyard; the said borough to consist of 20 burgesses besides cottagers and other inferior inhabitants, for whom he was to build houses and assign proportions of land; and to set apart 60[a] of the said last 500[a] for the common of the said town; with 2[a] more, viz $\frac{1}{2}$ an acre for the site of a public school, and $1\frac{1}{2}$[a] for the exercise of the scholars. (*Cal. Irish Pat. Rolls, James I*, p. 217)

The corporate towns, however, were not by themselves numerically sufficient to provide all the marketing and specialised services that were required by the rural Plantation population. The competitive nature of the market centres is highlighted in a 1612 grant of market rights to Dungannon, which included:

> A prohibition from selling goods by retail within 4 miles of the castle of Dungannon, to all except the inhabitants or those planted there by Sir Arthur. (*Cal. Irish Pat. Rolls, James I*, p. 217)

The effective range of the weekly market centre was recognised in this grant as four miles, a distance which was related to the difficulty of travelling more than eight miles per day to and from the market, rather than to the relative merits of the market centre itself. While the corporate towns were often distances of more than sixteen or twenty miles apart, no area of dense Plantation settlement could function economically with market centres at a separation of more than eight to ten miles. The sizes of the Plantation towns were directly related to the numbers of dispersed rural British residing within a five-mile radius of the market centre, and their distribution was in turn a reflection of the distribution of the dispersed Plantation settlement (Robinson, 1974, pp. 307–314).

By the late seventeenth century a state of equilibrium had been achieved between on the one hand the Plantation towns and the dispersed Plantation population, and on the other between the areas of British and residual Irish settlement. Irish were largely absent from the Plantation towns but the limited Irish rural settlement which did persist within the market influence of these towns must have been much more vulnerable to certain forms of assimilation.

On many of the Plantation estates, villages were not constructed despite substantial Plantation settlement, although on quite a number of others the early surveys do record some initial attempts at village settlement for the agricultural tenants. The interesting aspect of these early villages is that by the 1622 survey they had either been abandoned in favour of dispersed settlement, or had expanded into market centres with artisans and tradesmen forming the majority of the inhabitants (Robinson, 1974, pp. 278–307). There is no evidence of any purely agricultural village surviving as such into the mid-seventeenth century. Indeed, on one estate Pynnar noted in 1619 that:

> All these Tenants do dwell dispersedly upon their own land, and cannot dwell together in a village; because they are bound every one to dwell upon his own Land, which if they do not the Lease is void. (Harris, 1770, p. 198)

Throughout the seventeenth century the ratio of dispersed British settlers (in the form of freeholders, leaseholders and cottagers) to townsmen and artificers remained in the order of four to one. Agriculture was therefore of overwhelming importance to the Plantation economy and even the occupations of the town dwellers were orientated towards providing the essential marketing and processing services necessary to sustain the agricultural economy and to provide an outlet for surplus produce.

SEGREGATION, ASSIMILATION AND POST-PLANTATION SETTLEMENT

According to the articles of the Plantation, British freeholders and leaseholders on the Plantation estates were not permitted to take Irish undertenants, servants, labourers or cottagers, and even some leases of Church lands included requirements that the leasees should plant British undertenants on the land. However, many Irish were in fact retained on the estates. In County Londonderry British lease-holders and freeholders did sub-let lands to Irish (Moody, 1939, p. 333), but in Tyrone it is evident that the Irish were retained mostly on separate townlands.

If undertenants are defined as rural British householders with leases of less than sixty acres of Plantation estimate (a ballyboe), and cottagers as agricultural labourers with no land at all, it is possible to establish an approximate Plantation social structure on the estates. In Tyrone 70% of the British settlers were described in the surveys as under-tenants or cottagers and it was this broad base of English and Scottish labour which was the principal reason for the success of the Plantation, and also what distinguished the Ulster Plantation from the earlier, less successful plantations in Ireland. Although Irish were taken as tenants on the Plantation estates, contrary to the articles of the Plantation, the Undertakers' certificates for Armagh and Tyrone in 1622 clearly show that within the estates there was a segregation of British and Irish (N.L.I., MS8014/9; Robinson, 1974, pp. 326–330); a segregation in the sense of British labourers in British-owned townlands, and Irish labourers in Irish-owned townlands. This pattern of rural segregation along with the broad base of the British social structure found in 1622 were both again present in 1660. Surviving poll-tax lists differentiate between three taxation classes as follows: gentlemen; yeomen and farmers; and servants and labourers. For each townland the names of all heads of households and their designations (i.e. yeoman, labourer, etc.) are given. It may be established from these data that British and Irish surnames of all classes were segregated in most cases at townland level, and when areas of British and Irish settlement are considered in isolation the respective British and Irish social structures for 1660 may be obtained. Of all the British names on the Tyrone poll-tax lists, 32% were recorded as yeomen or farmers, and 68% as labourers and servants. With Irish names a similar social structure can be obtained, although with a marginally stronger labour base of 72% (P.R.O.N.I., T. 1365/3; Robinson, 1974, pp. 326–331).

The segregation of British and Irish settlement in the seventeenth century Plantation areas was enabled by the fact that in many areas the social structure of the Plantation population was sufficiently broad-based to permit it to function almost independently of the Irish. However, it is only at the townland level that it is possible to distinguish areas of complete Irish–British segregation in Plantation Ulster rather than the more general areas of British or Irish settlement predominance.

From his study of the Plantation, Moody (1938) has shown that the processes by which the Irish were driven out of the more fertile land and their places taken by British colonists was a gradual one, and the product of economic forces rather than any deliberate act on the part of the state. Indeed Pynnar noted in his 1619 survey that the presence of Irish on the Undertakers' estates was not totally undesirable, because of the

> ... greater Rents, paid unto them the undertakers by the Irish Tenants who do grease their lands; and if the Irish be put away with their Cattle, the British must either forsake their Dwellings, or endure great Distress in the suddain. Yet the combination of the Irish is dangerous to them, by robbing them, and otherwise. (Harris, 1770, pp. 236–237)

Reflecting a current concern about the continuing presence of Irish, the 1622 survey included an estimate of the numbers of Irish families on each Plantation estate, and this confirmed that their presence was ubiquitous. In Tyrone, for example, the 1622 survey returned a total of 866 British families, and a further 1199 Irish families on the Undertakers' estates alone.

In 1621 it was suggested that the Irish could remain on the Undertakers' estates. By 1628, legislation was finally passed to enable grants to be re-issued with higher Crown rents, but allowing the Undertakers legally to take Irish tenants on a reserved quarter of their estates:

> ... the patentee shall keep three-quarters of his lands occupied by Englishmen, and shall keep two freeholders and two leaseholders at least in every 1,000 acres of his demesne.
> ... If this is broken except in favour of mere Irish who are artificers, it shall be lawful for us to seize unto our hands such parts of the three-quarters as are let to mere Irish ... All the mere Irish, except they are artificers, shall be removed from the three-quarters reserved before 1st May 1629. (*Cal. S.P. Ire.*, *1625–1632*, p. 351)

Inquisitions were then held to determine what land had already been let by the Undertakers to the Irish, and which townlands were most suitable for the proposed Irish settlement of one-quarter of the estates (*Inquisitionum*, 1829). These reserved townlands were invariably those of the poorest quality in the estate and from the surviving inquisitions, in conjunction with 1622 Undertakers' certificates which in some cases name the townlands let to British tenants, it is possible to examine Irish–British segregation within two adjacent Tyrone estates, at townland level (Fig. 2.7). The effect of the 1628 legislation was really to institutionalise the economic segregation of Irish and British settlement which had already taken place on most estates. The two adjacent estates of Ballyconnolly-Ballyneranill and Ballyloughmaguiffe, which between them straddle a section of the Clogher Valley in County

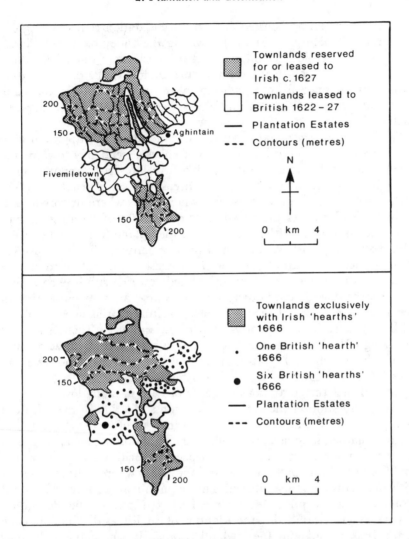

FIGURE 2.7. British and Irish "Segregation" on Two Plantation Estates in the Clogher Valley, County Tyrone: (a) *Circa* 1627; (b) 1666.

Source: 1627: *Inquisitionum* (1829); 1666: P.R.O.N.I., T. 307. The northern estate is Ballyconnolly-Ballyneranill (2000 acres) originally granted to Edward Kingsmill but owned by Sir William Stewart in 1619. The adjacent estate in the south is Ballyloughmaguiffe (1500 acres) originally granted to Captain Edney but owned by Lord Burleigh in 1619.

Tyrone, provide an almost complete picture of Irish and British settlement *circa* 1628. Figure 2.7 clearly shows how British settlement within

these two estates was focussed around the Plantation centres of Aghin-
tain and Ballynelurgan (Fivemiletown) in the valley basin. The lands
which were both let to and reserved for Irish were essentially those
townlands which bordered on the surrounding uplands. The 1666
settlement, mapped from hearth-money roll information for the same
townlands, indicates the continuity of segregation in this area between
1628 and the late seventeenth century.

While complete segregation in the lowland areas was apparent only
at townland level, there was of course a marked tendency towards the
development of broader localities with a British or Irish predominance.
Indeed in poorer marginal upland areas the settlement was often
exclusively Irish, in contrast to the lowland areas where the predominantly British localities did mostly retain a scatter of Irish settlement.
Nevertheless, poorer settlement areas on the upland fringe, which were
often exclusively Irish, retained a distinctive cultural identity. This was
distinguished, for example, by continued seasonal migration to upland
summer pastures, an economy orientated towards subsistence rather
than market-based agriculture, and of course an associated lack of
personal contact with lowland British resulting in the survival of the
Irish language. Even in poorly-drained lowland areas, such as around
the Lough Neagh shore, the orientation of the Irish was towards and
across the lough itself, rather than towards the surrounding more
densely peopled lowland areas of British settlement.

Nevertheless the continuous presence of Irish in many lowland areas
raises the question of the extent to which assimilation of the Irish did
take place. Substantial assimilation in the form of the anglicisation of
personal names, language, religion, or the adoption of new agricultural
practices, house forms, and other aspects of British material culture
could only be anticipated in the lowland areas where cultural contact
with the British was maximised. The requirements of a market-based
economy and the presence of some Irish artificers in the Plantation
towns inevitably resulted in the adoption of English as the first language
of the Irish throughout the lowland regions. In Dungannon, Pynnar
recorded in 1619 that there were thirty-six "Irish Protestants" in the
town (Harris, 1770, p. 209), but this was an exceptional occurrence,
both in terms of a substantial Irish presence in a Plantation town, and
in the implication of religious assimilation. It is interesting to note that
the names of these Irish Protestants in 1622 had not been anglicised.

Table 2.1 contains the county totals of British and Irish for all the
Ulster counties, except Cavan and Tyrone, abstracted from the 1659
census. Clearly the actual proportions of British recorded in the different
counties in 1659, if accurate, represent densities of British settlement

TABLE 2.1. British and Irish Households in Ulster, County Totals, 1659.

	Total	English and Scots		Irish
Antrim	17 001	7567	(45%)	9434
Armagh	6748	2393	(35%)	4355
Donegal	12 001	3412	(28%)	8589
Down	15 183	6540	(43%)	8643
Fermanagh	7102	1800	(25%)	5302
Londonderry	8682	3856	(44%)	4826
Monaghan	4083	434	(11%)	3649
Total	70 800	26 002	(37%)	44 798

Source: Pender (1939).

which have since substantially increased relative to Irish settlement. Most historians familiar with the period agree that the late seventeenth century witnessed a massive increase in British settlement in Ulster (Cullen, 1975; Morgan, 1976; Crawford, 1975), and the levels reached in the eighteenth century (Fig. 2.8) represent the culmination of what had been more than a century of successive waves of incoming settlers.

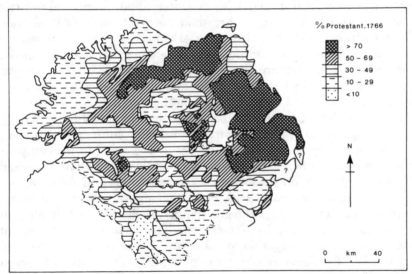

FIGURE 2.8. The Distribution of Protestants (Established Church and Dissenters) in Ulster, 1766.

The originals of the *Parliamentary Religious Returns, 1766* were destroyed by fire in the Public Record Office of Ireland, 1922, but transcripts survive in the Library of the Representative Church Body, Dublin. The author is indebted to Mr. W. H. Crawford of the Public Record Office of Northern Ireland for providing him with these statistics.

In the areas of densest British settlement, for example in south Antrim and north Down, the Irish were greatly outnumbered, and there is some evidence that in these areas especially many Irish became Protestant and were assimilated into the surrounding culture. Lists of early Presbyterian congregations in these "Protestant" areas of east Ulster indeed display a substantial proportion of local, pre-Plantation Irish surnames (Latimer, 1895). When this fact is considered in conjunction with the known historical phases of substantial conversions to the Established Church in Ireland (such as the recorded increase in "recantations of popery" in the eighteenth century, and the "bread and butter reformation" of the early nineteenth century) (Bowen, 1978), it cannot be assumed that the Protestant areas in Ulster represent populations of exclusively "British" ethnic origin. Similarly, in the predominantly "Irish" areas of west Ulster, it is difficult to establish the extent to which the British surnames of a proportion of Roman Catholics represent the hibernicisation of people of Plantation origin, or the anglicisation of Irish surnames.

It should be noted, however, that many of the effects of cultural contact between British and Irish in Ulster could be more accurately described as acculturation rather than assimilation. This is because contact between the distinctive material culture of the two groups, for example in house-types, did not result in the general adoption of the phenomena of one culture (Robinson, 1979). Instead there often was a mutual adoption by both groups of common material culture elements which were developed and adjusted from both sources.

While the broad pattern of British settlement in Ulster remained remarkably consistent from the early seventeenth century to the present, one extremely significant change did occur, this being in the composition of the Ulster towns. Irish settlement was always found in or around the few pre-Plantation towns such as Carrickfergus and Armagh, but the market towns associated with Plantation and subsequent settlement were the economic and strategic centres of British settlement, and almost totally peopled by Protestants. The change to the present patterns of urban segregation in many towns, and the development of towns with Roman Catholic majorities which previously had been British Plantation towns (e.g. Strabane), can be largely explained by the massive rural–urban migrations associated with the industrialisation and agricultural crises within nineteenth century Ulster.

The development of the present pattern of English and Scottish localities in Ulster was probably more significant in political terms in the late eighteenth century than it is today, for at that time the English localities were giving birth to the Orange Order with its loyalist-conservative philosophy, while in many of the Scottish localities Presbyterians were being caught up in the idealist spirit of French republicanism, culminating in the 1798 United Irishmen rising in Counties Antrim and Down. Significant membership of the Orange Order by Presbyterians in the Scottish localities of Ulster was not established until after the Act of Union and well into the nineteenth century.

REFERENCES

Analecta Hibernica (1931). Survey of the Escheated Counties in Ulster, 1608. *Analecta Hibernica* **3,** 151–218.

Bowen, D. (1978). "The Protestant Crusade in Ireland, 1800–1870." Gill and Macmillan, Dublin.

Braidwood, J. (1964). Ulster and Elizabethan English. *In* "Ulster Dialects" (G. B. Adams, ed.), pp. 5–109. Ulster Folk Museum, Cultra.

Bylund, E. (1960). Theoretical Considerations regarding the Distribution of Settlement in Inner North Sweden. *Geografiska Annaler* **42,** 225–231.

Calendar of the Carew Manuscripts, 1603–1624.

Calendar of the Irish Patent Rolls of James I.

Calendar of the State Papers relating to Ireland, 1615–1625.

Calendar of the State Papers relating to Ireland, 1625–1632.

Census of Ireland 1911. His Majesty's Stationery Office, London.

Coimisiún na Gaeltachta (1927). "Maps Showing in respect of the 1925 Special Enumeration." Stationery Office, Dublin.

Compton, P. A. (1978). "Northern Ireland: A Census Atlas." Gill and Macmillan, Dublin.

Crawford, W. H. (1975). Landlord–Tenant Relations in Ulster, 1609–1820. *Irish Economic and Social History* **2,** 5–21.

Cullen, L. M. (1975). Population Trends in Seventeenth-Century Ireland. *Economic and Social Review* **6,** 152–157.

Dunlop, R. (1925). Sixteenth Century Schemes for the Plantation of Ulster. *Scottish Historical Review* **22,** 51–60, 115–126, 199–212.

Gailey, A. (1975). The Scots Element in North Irish Popular Culture. *Ethnologia Europaea* **8,** 2–21.

Graham, B. J. (1972). "The Settlement Pattern of Anglo-Norman East-meath, 1170–1660." Unpublished Ph.D. Thesis, Queen's University, Belfast.

Gregg, R. J. (1972) The Scotch-Irish Dialect Boundaries in Ulster. *In* "Patterns in the Folk Speech of the British Isles" (M. F. Wakelin, ed.), pp. 109–139. Athlone Press, London.

Harris, W., ed. (1770). "Hibernica: Or Some Ancient Pieces relating to Ireland." John Milliken, Dublin.

Hastings Manuscripts, 4 (Royal Commission on Historical Manuscripts, 1947). His Majesty's Stationery Office, London.

Hill, G. (1877). "An Historical Account of the Plantation in Ulster at the Commencement of the Seventeenth Century, 1608–20." McCaw, Stevenson and Orr, Belfast.

Inquisitionum in Officio Notulorium Cancellarie Hiberniae Asservatarum, II (1829). Record Commissioners, Dublin.

Latimer, W. T. (1895). The Old Session-Book of Templepatrick Presbyterian Church. *Journal of the Royal Society of Antiquaries in Ireland* **25**, 130–134.

List of Electors for the 1971 Register (Counties of Antrim, Armagh, Down, Fermanagh, Londonderry and Tyrone). Her Majesty's Stationery Office, Belfast.

Moody, T. W., ed. (1934–1935). The Revised Articles of the Ulster Plantation, 1610. *Bulletin of the Institute of Historical Research* **12**, 178–183.

Moody, T. W. (1938). The Treatment of the Native Population under the Scheme for the Plantation in Ulster. *Irish Historical Studies* **1**, 59–63.

Moody, T. W. (1939). "The Londonderry Plantation, 1609–41." William Mullan and Son, Belfast.

Morgan, V. (1976). A Case Study of Population Change over Two Centuries: Blaris, Lisburn 1661–1848. *Irish Economic and Social History* **3**, 5–16.

Morton, G. (1971). "Elizabethan Ireland." Longman, London.

National Library of Ireland. *Rich Papers*: MS 8014/9 (1622 Undertakers' Certificates).

Nicholls, K. (1972). "Gaelic and Gaelicised Ireland in the Middle Ages." Gill and Macmillan, Dublin.

O Gallachair, P., ed. (1958a). 1622 Survey of Cavan. *Breifne* **1**, 60–75.

O Gallachair, P., ed. (1958b). A Fermanagh Survey. *Clogher Record* **2**, 293–310.

Owen, D. J. (1917). "A Short History of the Port of Belfast." Mayne, Boyd and Son, Belfast.

Parliamentary Religious Returns, 1766 (Transcripts in the Library of the Representative Church Body, Dublin).

Pender, S., ed. (1939). "A Census of Ireland, *circa* 1659." Stationery Office, Dublin.

Perceval-Maxwell, M. (1973). "The Scottish Migration to Ulster in the Reign of James I." Routledge and Kegan Paul, London.

Public Record Office of Northern Ireland. D. 1759/3C/1–2 (1630–1631 Muster-Rolls: Counties Down, Antrim and Londonderry).

Public Record Office of Northern Ireland. T. 307; T. 307c; T. 604; T. 808/15068 (Hearth-Money Rolls).

Public Record Office of Northern Ireland. T. 808/15164 (1631 Muster-Roll: County Tyrone).

Public Record Office of Northern Ireland. T. 934 (1631 Muster-Roll: Counties Armagh, Fermanagh and Tyrone).

Public Record Office of Northern Ireland. T. 1365/3 (Fragment of a Poll Money Book, 1660).

Quinn, D. (1966). The Munster Plantations: Problems and Opportunities. *Journal of the Cork Historical and Archaeological Society* **71,** 19–40.

Register of Dail Electors, 1963–1964 (Counties of Cavan, Donegal and Monaghan). Stationery Office, Dublin.

Robinson, P. (1974). "The Plantation of County Tyrone in the Seventeenth Century." Unpublished Ph.D. Thesis, Queen's University, Belfast.

Robinson, P. (1976). Irish Settlement in Tyrone before the Ulster Plantation. *Ulster Folklife* **22,** 59–69.

Robinson, P. (1978). British Settlement in County Tyrone 1610–1666. *Irish Economic and Social History* **5,** 5–26.

Robinson, P. (1979). Vernacular Housing in Ulster in the Seventeenth Century. *Ulster Folklife* **25,** 1–28.

Steele, R., ed. (1910). "Tudor and Stuart Proclamations, 1485–1714," II. Clarendon Press, Oxford.

Symons, L. and Cruickshank, J. G. (1963). Land Classification. *In* "Land Use in Northern Ireland" (L. Symons, ed.), pp. 109–113. University of London Press, London.

Treadwell, V. W., ed. (1951–1954). The Plantation of Donegal—A Survey. *Donegal Annual* **2,** 511–517.

Treadwell, V. W., ed. (1954–1957). The Plantation of Donegal—A Survey (continued). *Donegal Annual* **3,** 41–47.

Treadwell, V. W., ed. (1960). A Survey of Armagh and Tyrone, 1622. *Ulster Journal of Archaeology* **23,** 126–137.

Treadwell, V. W., ed. (1964). A Survey of Armagh and Tyrone, 1622 (continued). *Ulster Journal of Archaeology* **27,** 140–154.

CHAPTER 3

THE PLANTER AND THE GAEL: CULTURAL DIMENSIONS OF THE NORTHERN IRELAND PROBLEM

Ronald H. Buchanan

INTRODUCTION

Among the many traditions which influence community relations and affect political attitudes in Northern Ireland is the belief that Protestant and Roman Catholic belong to two distinct cultures which have maintained an uneasy co-existence since the Plantation of the early seventeenth century. The Protestant version of this belief is that the Planter was a tough, hard-working and independent pioneer who brought civilisation to a barbarous and superstitious people. Conversely, the Roman Catholic sees his ancestors as proud Celts, dispossessed of their inheritance by the alien Saxon oppressor who some day must be forcibly ejected from the fair land of Ireland, or else made to conform to Irish ways. Simplistic though it may be, this view of Irish history plays a not unimportant role in shaping political attitudes and behaviour in Northern Ireland today. For that reason it seems appropriate to examine the basis of this contemporary folk belief, to see if there was a marked cultural contrast between Planter and Gael in the seventeenth century, and to see what adjustments were made between the cultures in later centuries. First the tradition itself will be considered in a little more detail.

CONTEMPORARY VIEWS OF THE TWO CULTURES

Traditional belief represents the collective memory of an older generation, handed on to the next by word of mouth and interpreted by them

49

according to inherited values. This process continues today, but folk belief in contemporary society is greatly influenced by external opinion, working through formal education and the "media". In the present context, the work of professional historians has tended to reinforce the traditional belief that Planter and Gael belonged to two distinct and contrasting cultures. One recent author (de Paor, 1970, p. 24) states, for example:

> ... the contrast of religions was only one of many contrasts between the planters and the dispossessed natives, since they differed also in language, law, custom, economy, thought and art.

Moreover the differences persisted; in the words of another historian (Beckett, 1972, p. 24):

> ... a large proportion of the settlers resisted complete surrender to the influence of Ireland, and the traditions, ideas and institutions they had imported not only survived, though in modified form, but profoundly affected the earlier population. Sometimes they were freely accepted, more often they were imposed by force; but however they operated, the effect was the same; and among the whole Gaelic population a way of life that had been produced by Irish conditions was challenged, and in some measure submerged, by a way of life that had grown up in Britain.

According to T. W. Moody (1974, p. 9), both cultures have preserved their individual identities intact:

> The overwhelming fact is that to this day neither has assimilated the other, and that the dividing lines remain clear and distinct, not only in the heart but even on the ground.

Students in classes in English as well as those in history are also made aware of the basic differences between Planter and Gael, as in the following extract from John Hewitt's poem, "The Colony" (Hewitt and Montague, 1970):

> ... you may distinguish
> if you were schooled with us, by pigmentation,
> by the cast of features or by turn of phrase,
> or by the clan-names on them which are they,
> among the faces moving in the street.

> They worship Heaven strangely, having rites
> we snigger at, are known as superstitious,
> cunning by nature, never to be trusted,
> given to dancing and a kind of song
> seductive to the ear, a whining sorrow.

The effect of this work by professional writers is to reflect and so reinforce traditional beliefs, a point well illustrated in this excerpt from an essay on the cultural differences between Protestant and Roman Catholic, written by a Roman Catholic student in 1978:

> The Protestants have a spirit of enterprise and are willing to work, probably because of the initial threat they felt at being planted in a foreign land even though it is not far from England. Their strict work and prayer schedule brought many Protestant business men to the fore while the Catholics lacked this drive. The Catholic attitude is "God takes care of me", while the Protestant would say "God helps those who help themselves". In other social spheres their lives tend to differ. Catholics have big families, harking back to the old Gaelic times when the idea of the family clan was strong: the dependence of the Gael on his family is similar to that of the Protestant's reliance on the Crown. Since Irish clans were always fighting they could only trust their own families but while the Protestants stood together they need not have large families. The Gael is also interested in the original sports of Ireland, hurling and gaelic football, while the Planter has brought his own games over with him, like cricket, soccer and tennis. In music also their tastes differ, the Gael preferring Irish traditional music, while the Planters stick to their original music and bands.

This account may bear little resemblance to the history the young man was taught at school, but it represents the homely mixture of learned fact and heard tradition which is the essence of contemporary folk belief. For him there was little doubt that Protestant and Roman Catholic belong to two very different cultural traditions.

In academic writing the "two traditions" view of Roman Catholic–Protestant relations has been accepted until quite recently. Over twenty years ago, T. W. Moody (1957, p. 234) did acknowledge that:

> ... some attributes of a common society have long existed in Ulster speech (though it is English), in Ulster humour, in a certain stern and realistic attitude to life.

But it was geographers who first laid emphasis on the cultural elements shared by people in Northern Ireland regardless of the divisions apparent in religion and politics. The Dutch geographer, Max Heslinga, drew attention to this in a perceptive study published in 1962; and, more recently, Estyn Evans (1973, p. 74), drawing on his unrivalled knowledge of Irish prehistory and folklife, has written:

> ... the two communities in the north, however deeply divided by religion, share an outlook on life which is different from that prevailing in the south and which bears the stamp of a common heritage.

The political analyst Richard Rose (1971, p. 24) notes the same sense of regional identity shared by Northern Ireland people and differentiating them from their neighbours in the Irish Republic and Great Britain. But one of the most telling points is made in a recent study by the historian, A. T. Q. Stewart (1977, p. 41):

> There never was any true confrontation of archetypal Planter and Gael. The essentially mixed character of the pre-plantation population has for so long been denied, or deliberately obscured, in the cause of Gaelic nationalism, that it is almost with a shock of new discovery that we find it was perfectly recognised by contemporaries at the time of the Ulster plantation.

This comment clearly underlines the need to review accepted wisdom on the cultural background of Northern Ireland's two communities.

For the historian the chief problem has been a lack of evidence, for events in this obscure corner of the British Isles were rarely given prominence in official documents, thus denying him the use of the tool with which he is most familiar. Moreover the facts of culture which are most relevant to ordinary people are rarely mentioned in government records: there is little information about the tools and implements people used at work, the houses they lived in, their patterns of speech or the customs which influenced their behaviour. Yet it is in these aspects of folklife that cultural differences are most likely to be apparent, especially when immigrant and native first come in contact. If the elements of culture associated with either group persist virtually unchanged then the cultures may be said to have retained their separate identities, but if changes are recorded then assimilation has occurred to some degree. Archaeologists and ethnologists use concepts such as these in their work, and the findings of the latter discipline are especially relevant to the present study. As yet there is little archaeological research on mediaeval or seventeenth century Ulster, and, while ethnologists work mainly with folk material from the nineteenth century, inferences about earlier periods can be drawn from their studies as well as from other historical sources. It is this literature upon which the following discussion is largely based, with the emphasis on such basic elements of rural life as the house, methods of farming and farm implements, language and the customs associated with seasonal festivals. If Planter and native differed profoundly in their cultural backgrounds it is in such common features of daily life that the contrasts should be most apparent.

FOLKCULTURE IN ULSTER BEFORE THE PLANTATION

Ulster at the time of the seventeenth century Plantation struck contemporary observers—mostly English officials and soldiers—as wild and uncivilised, its extensive woods and bogs relieved only by rough pasture and the occasional patch of cultivated land (Hayes-McCoy, 1964). Farmsteads were mostly scattered in the countryside, although some were grouped in the clusters to which the term "clachan" has been given; but there were no villages, and virtually no towns except for the small settlements associated with religious centres like Armagh, or the tiny seaports of the eastern coasts (Buchanan, 1970). Houses were small and unpretentious, and appear to have been of two main types (Robinson, 1979, pp. 9–10). One was a single-room dwelling, usually circular in plan, built with a light timber frame with walls of wattle and a thatched roof. These structures, known as "creats", were frequently used as temporary dwellings, but they belong to a tradition of post-and-wattle house which in Ireland can be traced back to prehistory. Houses in the second group, often called "coupled houses" in contemporary documents, were more substantial, their distinguishing features being walls built of clay or of earth-and-post construction. In plan they were sub-rectangular, normally without internal partitions and with hipped roofs supported by principal rafter trusses. Like the creats they rarely had chimneys. Little is known of the relative distribution of these two house-types in the early seventeenth century. It is thought that mud walling was introduced within the Norman Pale in mediaeval times, but at the Plantation it was certainly widespread in Ulster and may well have been the dominant type. One other type of house was the stone-built tower, erected by families of high social status such as the Maguires of Enniskillen, and similar in form to those introduced to the Pale in the early fourteenth century. Besides these, archaic homesteads such as the ring-fort and the "crannog" were still occasionally in use.

Fields were unenclosed except for temporary fences; spades were used to prepare the ground for oats, the main crop, but so too were light ploughs, "drawn by the horsetails", a practice strongly deprecated by English officials as was the prevailing custom of burning the straw to separate the grain. The farm economy was dominated by cattle, which represented capital for the wealthy, and provided the staple diet for the ordinary farmer (Buchanan, 1973). The movement of the livestock to seasonal pastures on uplands and lake margins was an essential feature in the pattern of land use, and this accentuated the importance of the two great festivals of Beltaine and Hallowe'en,

occurring at the beginning and end of the growing season in May and
October respectively (Danachair, 1959). Other major festivals were
Lammas in August and St. Brigid's Day in February, the latter cele-
brating the Irish saint whose special concern for cattle was probably
as important to the average countryman as was her undoubted Christian
piety. With this one exception, the religious festivals of the calendar
year appear to have been less significant than might be expected in a
society which was totally Roman Catholic in religion. Finally, Ulster
people were almost all Gaelic-speakers, with the exception of a few
living near ports such as Carrickfergus where some English was spoken
(Gregg, 1964, p. 189).

CULTURAL INNOVATIONS OF THE PLANTATION

The effect of the Plantation on this existing way of life was first made
apparent in the new forms of settlement and land-holding laid down as
official government policy in the document known as the Articles of
Plantation. The new towns were a major innovation, established at
strategic military sites and intended to act also as economic growth
centres. They had a lasting impact, providing the markets which
stimulated a new commercial approach to farming and the means for
conducting external trade. Initially they also provided a social milieu
for the colonists, for although the Irish soon settled in the towns they
formed a minority. One of the major conditions of the Plantation
scheme was that the colonists should live in villages, building their
houses near the bawn or defended courtyard which each Undertaker
was required to build on his property to act as a strong-point. In fact
the colonists rarely did so: two years after the Plantation began, the
then Lord Deputy complained that the tenants "lie not in town rids
together as they were appointed, but lie scattered up and down upon
their proportions" (Edwards, 1938, p. 74). The convenience of living
on the farm rather than in a distant village apparently encouraged
the colonist to adopt the form of settlement already common in the
Ulster countryside.

The settlers also introduced their own styles of vernacular building,
and there are frequent references in surveyors' reports to timber-frame
houses, built "of cage-work after the English manner". Quite clearly
these were very different from the Irish coupled house; for example,
houses shown on the Philips Maps of County Londonderry are of
box-frame construction with central hearth and door, and exposed
timbers, in appearance very similar to styles then current in lowland

England, from south Lancashire to Shropshire, and in the south-east. The settlers also built houses in stone, and brick was used in the lowland corridor stretching from the Lagan Valley to Fermanagh. Thatch was the main roofing material, but shingles, slate and tile were also used (Robinson, 1979).

More pretentious in style were the larger houses of the principal Undertakers, some of which were built to designs then common among the minor English gentry. Castlecaulfield in County Tyrone is a good example (Jope, 1958). But the more prudent preferred homes which could be more easily defended, and certainly the most durable dwellings proved to be stone-built towers such as Monea in County Fermanagh. In appearance these were very similar to the tower-houses of the Irish chiefly families, and they were built mostly by Scottish Undertakers who had themselves long been aware of the need for defensible houses (Simpson, 1968, p. 182).

At the other end of the social scale it seems that lesser tenants and cottagers of British origin were living in what the surveyors called "Irish" houses. In several instances these were built by the Undertakers themselves, sometimes as temporary homes for incoming tenants. In Dungannon, for example, it was noted: "families of English and other civil men who for the present have built houses of coples, but are bound to build of cage-work or stone after the English" (Robinson, 1979).

New systems of land-holding were also introduced, based on the English concept of leasing land from the Crown for a specific period and for a specified rent (Crawford, 1975, pp. 6–8). This contrasted with the native system, in which land was regarded as the property of a particular clan, whose members each had a share which could be reallocated from time to time. Under the leases granted to British tenants there must have been a greater emphasis on individual enterprise as opposed to the communal work in common fields which was a feature of the native system (Buchanan, 1973, pp. 603–605). It must also have resulted in a more permanent pattern of land-holding and of enclosure, although hedged fields were rare in Ulster until the end of the seventeenth century (Robinson, 1977, p. 61). Unfortunately there is very little information about the techniques and methods of farming during the Plantation period. Officially, ploughing by the tail and burning the straw were both prohibited. There are indications that a heavier plough may have been introduced by the colonists (Robinson, 1974, p. 61), but oats and cattle remained the mainstay of the economy, though now commercially organised to the extent of providing an export trade with Britain (Perceval-Maxwell, 1973, pp. 293–295).

In non-material culture the colonists differed from the natives in two major respects. In religion the great majority were Protestants, although as Perceval-Maxwell remarks (1973, p. 273): "initially they do not seem to have possessed strong religious convictions". English colonists were mainly members of the Established Church whereas the Scots were mostly Calvinists (Harrison, 1882, Ch. IV; Woodburn, 1914, Ch. VII), although a few were Roman Catholic, including a group who settled in Strabane (Perceval-Maxwell, 1973, p. 272). English was also pre-eminently the language of the Planters, although in speech it was remarkably varied: the dialect spoken by the Lowland Scots, for example, differed from that of Warwickshire in much the same way as Danish does from Swedish today (Adams, 1976, p. 86). But some of the Galloway Scots did speak Gaelic as their native language (Lorrimer, 1949; MacQueen, 1973), and they would have been easily understood on the Ulster side of the Irish Sea. For them at least, language was not a barrier to cultural exchange.

To summarise, the innovations associated with the Plantation were the introduction of the English language and the Protestant religion, as well as new forms of settlement and land-holding, the last two a direct consequence of government policy. In total they provided a new framework within which dramatic changes could occur in the existing way of life. That this did not happen suggests that the cultural gap between Planter and native Irish was not as great as might be supposed. To explore this point further it is necessary to look at the cultural background of the colonists themselves.

HOMELANDS OF THE PLANTERS

The British colonists in Ulster came from both England and Scotland, the former from three main areas: Devon, the west midland counties of Warwickshire and Staffordshire, and from Lancashire, Cheshire and Flint (Braidwood, 1964). Within the planted counties of Ulster the English settled in County Londonderry and in a broad belt extending westward from north Armagh to Fermanagh, but they were also numerous in areas outside the official Plantation, in the Lagan Valley, and in south Antrim and north Down. Their principal innovations were the English language and the house-types to which reference has already been made. But apart from this there is little direct information about their cultural contribution. However they did form a minority among the colonists both locally and in total, some estimates suggesting that they were outnumbered by the Scots by as much as five to one (Gailey, 1975, p. 4). The culture of the Planters as presented here is biased towards the Scots about whom much more is known, but since they were the dominant group their culture pattern was more likely to prevail. As Stewart (1977, p. 37) says: ". . . the English aspect of the Plantation, which was to have been all-important, was in time to be overshadowed, though never completely overwhelmed".

The Scots who settled in Ulster in the early seventeenth century came from Galloway in the south-west, from Ayrshire, Renfrew and Lanark, from the Borders and the area in the vicinity of Edinburgh (Perceval-Maxwell, 1973, Ch. XI). The Undertakers were mainly landed gentry, but the colonists included an entire "cross-section of lowland society, though the less well-off and less stable elements probably predominated" (Perceval-Maxwell, 1973, p. 289). To these Scotsmen Ireland was no unknown country. The Ulster coast is only about twenty kilometres from the Mull of Kintyre, thirty-five kilometres from the Rhinns of Galloway. Both countries are inter-visible on a clear day and, although the North Channel has strong tidal streams, the sea passages are short and land-falls are numerous on either side. British Rail's Sealink Ferries stress the advantages of the short crossing in their advertising today, but such passages were a common practice in earlier times. For example, in the summer of 1607, the author of the *Montgomery MSS* recalls:

> . . . people came from Stranraer, four miles, left their horses at the port [Portpatrick], hired horses at Donaghadee, came with their wares and provisions to Newtown, and sold them, dined there, stayed two or three hours, and returned to their houses the same day by bedtime, their land journey but twenty miles. (Hill, 1879, p. 60)

Likewise in the north the men of Islay regarded Ballycastle in Antrim as their market town, and some still make an annual journey to the town's Lammas Fair. For men used to its ways, the sea was and is the easiest of natural highways, and like other enclosed sea basins the Irish Sea has long facilitated movement and cultural contact.

The reciprocity between Ireland and Scotland is furthered by marked similarities in the natural environment. The Dalradian rocks of Argyll are much older than the tertiary basalts which face them across the Channel in Antrim, but wild moorlands are dominant in both landscapes, interspersed with narrow and cultivated glens. Further south, both Down and Galloway are underlain by the same palaeozoic rocks, although people from the broad peninsula of the Machairs or the higher hills of Carrick would have found the Ulster land much more productive than their own. Environmental links should not be over-stressed; neither should they be overlooked, for landscapes reminiscent of home and responsive to known skills can ease the colonist's adjustment to his new location, especially when the lines of communication are as easily maintained as those across the Irish Sea. This must have been as true in earlier times as it was for the Planters of the seventeenth century, for the archaeological record gives ample evidence of culture contact from even the most remote prehistoric times. For example the first colonists of Ireland are thought to have been the mesolithic peoples who pioneered the short sea route from Galloway to Antrim early in the seventh millennium B.C. In the present context, the most relevant period is the first millennium A.D., for the Scotsmen who crossed to Ulster in the seventeenth century inherited a culture whose essential features were developed at this time, when connections with Ulster were particularly strong. It may indeed be here that the origins of a culture, common to both native and Planter, are to be found.

THE DALRADIAN SEA AS A CULTURAL PROVINCE

The close ties that linked Ulster and Scotland during the early historic period are best exemplified in the sixth century kingdom of Dál Riada, when for a time western Argyll and north Antrim were ruled by the same Irish dynasty, based first in Ulster and then in Scotland (Chadwick, 1949, pp. 121–122; Alcock, 1973, p. 353). What began as a military adventure ended three centuries later as a major political enterprise, for under Kenneth MacAlpin the Dalradian kings came to rule over all Scotland, north of the Forth and the Clyde. From this same movement Scotland gained its Gaelic language, for the Q-Celtic speech of the Dalradians ultimately displaced the P-Celtic of the indigenous population. Finally the missionary St. Columba, who followed the Dalradians to Scotland, establishing his monastery at Iona in 563, was largely responsible for the conversion of Scotland to Christianity. Even the name Scotland was Irish in origin, for "Scotti" was the name by which the Irish were known in Britain at this time.

For a time contact between the two sectors of Dál Riada was broken by the Norse penetration of the Irish Sea during the early ninth century. But they themselves were soon gaelicised, and from them came the people and the dynasty who were to revive the political and cultural link between Argyll, the Scottish Islands and Antrim during the mediaeval period. The immigrants were known as Gallowglasses, mercenaries from the Islands who first came to Ireland at the invitation of the O'Donnells in the late thirteenth century. They continued to arrive, "sometymes upon one occasion and sometymes upon another" (Perceval-Maxwell, 1973, p. 2), over the next 300 years, although opinions differ on how many may actually have settled in Ireland (Perceval-Maxwell, 1973, p. 2; Stewart, 1977, p. 36). The family which provided the main dynastic link were the MacDonnells, Lords of the Isles, who gained land in Antrim through marriage in the fourteenth century. Under pressure from the Scottish Crown the family removed its main seat to Antrim in the late fifteenth century, accompanied, it is said, by many refugees (Stewart, 1977, p. 45). In fact the MacDonnells were not alone in establishing Irish connections, for both the Gaelic families of Argyll and the feudal magnates of Galloway seem to have made regular alliances through marriage across the Irish Sea (Greeves, 1955–1956, 1957–1958; Sellar, 1971).

Long before the Plantation there was thus a major Scottish colony in Ulster, whose significance is best summarised in the words of Kenneth Jackson (1951, p. 77):

... until at least the end of the sixteenth century, Ireland and the Highlands formed a single culture province. The "sea-divided Gael" as they were called, were closely linked not only by their language but also by their civilisation, their customs and traditions, by intermarriage between their noble kindred, and by their aristocratic social system.

O'Rahilly makes a similar point (1932, p. 123):

To the Gaelic-speaking Scotsman of the past Ireland was the mother country, whose culture and whose traditions belonged no less to himself than to his kinsmen in Ireland.

Undoubtedly their common language was an important bond, for it ensured the survival of a common oral tradition which is still evident in the folktales told in Ulster and the Hebrides today (Gailey, 1968–1969, p. 138).

The Highland Scots were not themselves directly involved in the Plantation, for as Roman Catholics their loyalty was suspect in the eyes of the Crown. Instead it was people from south-west Scotland who provided most of the immigrants, first in the pre-Plantation settlement of north Down, and later throughout Ulster. What is often forgotten is that these Lowlanders shared the same Gaelic heritage as the men from Argyll for in the late fifth century A.D., about the same time as Fergus crossed the North Channel from Antrim to Argyll, Gaelic-speakers from Ireland were settling in the Rhinns and in other parts of Galloway and Carrick. MacQueen (1973, p. 17) believes that this was a "substantial" settlement, influenced perhaps by religious motives, for Galloway was especially venerated through its association with St. Ninian, whose church at Whithorn was a major centre of pilgrimage (Chadwick, 1963, p. 73). But this settlement was only a part of a wider circulation, inspired by Celtic churchmen, which took place across the whole northern sector of the Irish Sea from the sixth century onwards. As Emrys Bowen has shown (1972, p. 87), monasteries from the Hebrides south to Iona and Donegal, from Bangor and Nendrum in County Down, and Whithorn, all were in constant communication. Through these journeys of monks and itinerant craftsmen a cultural province was defined, that of the "Dalradian Sea", which linked northern Ireland with western Scotland, not only in religion but in many aspects of secular culture (Alcock, 1973, p. 52). Archaeologists like Laing (1975, p. 260), for example, note a uniformity in the type of artifacts used in this area over a period of more than 600 years; and in settlement the hill-fort, crannog and souterrain were common on both sides of the Irish Sea. Only the ring-fort, the most Irish of Dark Age settlement forms, was absent from Scotland.

Towards the end of the seventh century, the connection with Galloway and Strathclyde was interrupted by the westward spread of Angles from Northumberland, but, in the tenth century, Norse Irish from the Isles spread south along the Irish Sea coast and into the Solway (Laing, 1975, pp. 38–47). It was these settlers who ensured that Galloway remained Gaelic-speaking into the sixteenth century (MacQueen, 1973, pp. 27–28). In later mediaeval times this culture pattern must have been affected by the economic and social changes taking place in the eastern lowlands. But western Scotland was remote from the centre of political power in Edinburgh, and political events did not disrupt the traffic across the Irish Sea. Much of the common culture linking Antrim, Argyll and Galloway in earlier times must have survived into the seventeenth century. This point will be examined next.

FOLKCULTURE OF THE SCOTTISH PLANTERS

As in Ireland, evidence on Scottish folklife before the nineteenth century is limited, but a review of the available material suggests that the seventeenth century Scottish colonist would have found little that was unfamiliar in the way of life of the Ulster people among whom he had come to live. Rural housing in Scotland for example had the same simplicity of style and construction as in Ireland, the typical dwelling being a rectangular building, its walls most commonly built of clay or turf, with a thatched roof supported on a cruck frame (Whyte, 1975, p. 58). Stone was also used, either by itself or in alternate layers of turf and stone. Unlike Ulster, wattles were rarely used in Lowland houses by the seventeenth century, although the practice continued in the Highlands until well into the eighteenth (Gailey, 1962b, pp. 237–238). Evidence on construction details is rare before the early nineteenth century, but even at this late date there are many similarities between the houses of the two countries, with the implication that the resemblance would have been at least as strong in earlier times. For example, a style of timber roof-truss, described in Ulster by Desmond McCourt (1964–1965), is found in the Highlands and south-west Scotland (Walton, 1957, pp. 118–120; Stell, 1972, p. 39), and houses in the same areas had their thatch secured by a network of ropes as in Donegal (Fenton, 1976a). In Argyll there is also a localised thatching technique which elsewhere is found only along a narrow stretch of the north Antrim coast (Buchanan, 1957, p. 138), a distribution which is similar to that of the aptly-named Dalradian house-type, first recognised by Colin Sinclair in Argyll (1953) but with affinities in north Antrim (Gailey, 1962b, p. 228).

Throughout Scotland, the dominant house-type in the seventeenth century was the long-house, a building in which dwelling, byre and barn were combined under the one roof. An early description of a Highland house, dated 1577, is very reminiscent of travellers' accounts of Irish houses of a later period (Dunbar, 1971, p. 236):

> ... their houses are very simply built with pibble stones, without any chimneys, the fire being in the middest thereof. The good man, wife, children and other of their familie eate and sleepe on the one side of the house, and their catell on the other, very beastlie and rudely in respect of civilitie.

Estate inventories show that Lowland houses conformed to the same basic plan, but the byre and barn were normally separated from the dwelling by partition walls. By the mid-seventeenth century, Lowland farmsteads also varied in length and size according to the wealth and social status of the tenants who lived in them (Whyte, 1975, p. 64).

The form and pattern of settlement in western Scotland was also similar to Ireland. Towns were rare in the western Highlands but, as in Down and Antrim, the Galloway coast had several small mediaeval seaports, at Wigtown, Kirkcudbright and Dumfries. Rural settlement included both scattered farmsteads and house clusters, known as "clachans" in the Highlands and "fermtouns" in the Lowlands. In form and function the Scottish clachan was essentially the same as its Irish counterpart (Fairhurst, 1960; Caird, 1964), and, like it, was associated with a common field system which in the nineteenth century appears to have been similar in its organisation and practice to rundale in Ireland (Whittington, 1973; Dodgshon, 1973). Scottish farmers used tools and implements which closely resembled those of Ireland, including the one-eared spade and the "flachter". A wider range of ploughs was probably used in Scotland, but two practices condemned by the English in Ireland were followed here too: ploughing by the tail, and burning the grain in the straw (Fenton, 1976b, Ch. 2; Gailey and Fenton, 1970). A comparison of two such standard works as Evans' "Irish Folk Ways" (1957) and Fenton's "Scottish Country Life" (1976b) extends the list of parallels in the material folkculture of both countries, and underlines the similarity in many aspects of folk custom, including those associated with the major seasonal festivals. For example, in Scotland as in Ireland, Beltaine and Hallowe'en were the high points of the year. Lammas and St. Brigid's Day were of less significance in Scotland; the only major point of difference was the celebration of Hogmanay, for Scotland's New Year festival was never an important date in Ireland (Buchanan, 1962, 1963).

From this review it is apparent that in his homeland the Scottish Planter had a way of life little different from that of his Irish neighbour. They lived in similar houses, used similar tools and implements, and marked the changing seasons with the same festivals and customs. In no sense can their settlement among the Irish in Ulster be regarded as a confrontation between alien cultures, for the bonds developed during the first millennium A.D. and sustained through the mediaeval period provided a common basis in folklife. In two important respects, however, they did differ. Most of the Scots who came to Ulster in the seventeenth century were English-speaking, although many must have been able to speak some Irish as well; and in religion the great majority were of the Reformed faith. The latter was to prove the more durable barrier, whose significance increased as time went on.

PLANTER AND NATIVE: COLONISATION AND ASSIMILATION

Cultural exchange is facilitated when people from different cultures are in frequent contact through living in close proximity. This was the situation following the Plantation. In no county did the colonists form a majority, and although they outnumbered the Irish in the newly established towns, in the countryside they were a minority, thinly scattered among the indigenous population (Currie, 1973, p. 88; Macafee, 1977, pp. 72–75; Robinson, 1974, p. 350). In these circumstances some assimilation would be expected, and a new hybrid culture would be expected to emerge, containing elements donated by both cultures.

This hybridisation is perhaps best illustrated in vernacular housing. The English Planters' main innovation was the "cage-work" house, but apart from a few examples noted in towns in the last century, very few survived beyond the mid-seventeenth century (Robinson, 1979, p. 18). Many were destroyed in the 1641 rebellion, but the depletion of timber resources and the absence of a skilled carpentry tradition probably contributed to their disappearance. One Irish house-type also disappeared during the same period, the hipped-roof, post-and-wattle dwelling. Already at the time of the Plantation this archaic method of building seems to have been used mainly for temporary houses (Robinson, 1979, pp. 1–4), and its demise may be associated with the more permanent settlements which were a consequence of the changes in land-holding and farming initiated at the Plantation.

By the end of the seventeenth century, the typical farmhouse in Ulster was a small, rectangular dwelling, its walls of mud or stone and with a thatched, gabled roof. In appearance it closely resembled the Irish "coupled" house described by the surveyors of the Plantation, and in this respect it could be said that the colonists had conformed to the Irish cultural tradition. In the case of the Scots, however, this involved little or no adjustment, since the Irish house was essentially the same as their own. But there were structural innovations which may be ascribed to the Planters, in some roofing techniques (Gailey, 1974; McCourt, 1973), the provision of chimneys and of internal partitions between the rooms, and walls built of stone and sometimes of brick. All these features were found in the house styles introduced by the Planters; they were virtually unknown in Irish houses before the Plantation, but were commonplace by the end of the seventeenth century (Robinson, 1979, p. 23). Only in one respect is there any hint of ethnic differentiation in the house-types of the eighteenth and nineteenth centuries, that is, in the explanations advanced by ethnologists to account for the distinction between the "outshot" and "jamb-wall" variations of the traditional dwelling. The former is thought to be derived from a long-established native house-type, whereas the latter may have been introduced to Ulster from east Leinster, its diffusion encouraged by the economic and social changes which followed the Plantation, in the seventeenth and eighteenth centuries (McCourt, 1973).

Differences in forms of settlement between Planter and native are almost impossible to distinguish. Initially most of the colonists seem to have lived in scattered farmsteads, each located on its own holding; but there are instances where single farms expanded into clachans within a few generations, in Planter as well as in Irish districts (Proudfoot, 1959, p. 118; Currie, 1973, p. 152). Apparently any ethnic component in settlement soon disappeared, as it did also in land-holding, for there are examples of farms originally held by Planters in severalty being leased as joint tenancies (Macafee, 1977, p. 84; Currie, 1973, p. 150; Frey, 1979); and in some instances these were farmed in rundale. Here ethnic differences were subsumed in what Desmond McCourt (1971, p. 134) has described as:

> ... a single flexible scheme of settlement and land-holding within which nucleation and dispersal, joint or individual ownership were alternative and often co-existing developments ... the predominance of either at a given time depending on changing social and economic factors.

In material culture, similar tools and implements seem to have been used by the descendants of native and Planter, with differences evident in relatively minor aspects of detail or design. For example, a type of flail found in Ireland only in the north is probably of Scottish origin, the distinctive feature being the method of joining the section known as the "striker" to the handstaff (Danachair, 1970, pp. 53–55). A similar origin is indicated for the Ulster form of the "thrawhook", a tool used in making straw rope (Gailey, 1962a). A more significant difference is in the type of spade used in Ulster which differs from the traditional spade used in southern Ireland by having a hand-grip to its shaft, and a two-eared blade. The southern one-eared spade is the older of the two, and although formerly used in Ulster it has been steadily supplanted by the two-eared spade, notably during the last century (Danachair, 1957, pp. 116–117; Gailey and Fenton, 1970, p. 46). The two-eared spade may have been used in Ireland before the Plantation (Evans, 1970, p. 12), but the one-eared type has clear Irish associations, perpetuated in a phrase commonly applied to Roman Catholics by Protestants: "They dig with the wrong foot". The explanation is that the right foot is normally used in digging with the one-eared spade, and the left foot with the two-eared. In these three examples the distinctively Ulster variation of tools and implements found in Ireland may pre-date the Plantation; but, whatever their origin may be, the Scottish connection is clear. Indeed it is reaffirmed in the spread of innovations in farming in the nineteenth century, in the introduction from Scotland of the improved plough, the Scots cart and the threshing-machine. In this movement, Alan Gailey (1975, pp. 19–20) sees "a cultural receptiveness to innovations from Scotland, operating in advance of factors like economic viability or proximity to centres of supply". The Ulster Presbyterians' educational link with Edinburgh and Glasgow, where ministers were mostly trained, must have been an important element in this continuing interchange in people and ideas between the two areas.

Initially differences in language must have placed a major barrier between native and Planter, although relations between the English and Scottish immigrants were similarly inhibited by their respective dialects. For long after the Plantation, Irish remained a majority language, and was still spoken even in the vicinity of Belfast at the end of the eighteenth century (Adams, 1964, p. 141). But English advanced steadily, and from the early nineteenth century Irish experienced a rapid decline: by 1851 monoglot Irish speakers were found only in Donegal, and, within the area that was to become Northern Ireland, Irish survived only in scattered communities in the Sperrin Mountains, west Tyrone and Fermanagh, south Armagh and north-east Antrim, including Rathlin (Adams, 1970, 1973, 1974). In this respect the Gael was absorbed by the Planter, and yet Ulster English is still strongly influenced by the language it supplanted. Many Gaelic loanwords are used in everyday speech (Adams, 1964), and the place-names of Ulster are overwhelmingly Gaelic.

In folk custom and belief, the native Irish were regarded as "more superstitious" than the descendants of the Planters, but in practice the range of belief, from ghosts and fairies to witchcraft and divination, was much the same in both groups. Likewise the observance of the "quarter-days"—i.e. St. Brigid's Day, May Day, Lammas and Hallowe'en—as the major events of the secular calendar were common to all sections of the rural community. This indicates that the English Planters in particular must have abandoned some of their own festivals when they settled in Ireland. Whitsun and Shrove for example were major events in the English rural calendar, but in Ulster they were of little consequence. Only on May Day, and then only in the towns, did certain English customs make an impact, for example the erection of May Poles, public dancing and the crowning of a May Queen (Buchanan, 1962, 1963). In contrast, Scottish colonists had fewer adjustments to make, for only in the celebration of Hogmanay did their seasonal calendar differ markedly from that followed in Ireland. Only a few specifically Scottish customs associated with Hogmanay have been recorded in

Ulster, in east Antrim and Down (Gailey, 1975, p. 15). On a general point it should be noted that the seasonal festivals observed in Ulster and their associated customs differ little from those of the rest of Ireland, and where regional variations do occur, for example on St. Martin's Day, they are unlikely to have been a consequence of the cultural influence of the Planters.

The adoption of Irish secular festivals by the Planters is an example of the way in which assimilation did take place, but no such adjustment was possible in religion, for the division between the Roman Catholic and Reformed Churches was much too great in matters of faith, doctrine and religious practice. Religious differences formed the greatest single barrier at the Plantation, and they have remained so ever since, sustained by the vested interests of the clerical establishments. For clerical attitudes and clerical intransigence have had an important influence on secular life, and it is not surprising that religion became a potent symbol of ethnic identity, with social concomitants of far-reaching consequence. By far the most important were the sanctions on intermarriage between Protestant and Roman Catholic. No legal sanctions were imposed by the civil code, but the Churches ensured that such unions were rare indeed, and condoned only if one partner was prepared to accept the religion of the other. In practice neither group was totally endogamous: marriages did occur between the groups (Woodburn, 1914, pp. 26–27), more commonly perhaps than has been assumed, and there were conversions on both sides (Adams, 1976, p. 83; Robinson, 1974, p. 347; Macafee, 1977, p. 85). But the individuals who "turned" were always a minority. Most people did remain true to their own faith and for this reason the descendants of the native Irish are today identifiable as members of the Roman Catholic Church, and the Planters as Protestants.

The change from ethnic to religious terms as a means of identifying the two main groups seems to have occurred in the course of the eighteenth century. As late as 1830, a field-worker for the Ordnance Survey in County Londonderry wrote:

> The Roman Catholics, instead of being as elsewhere called "Irish" are here called Papists. They possess most of the Irish character, but have at times exhibited some of that sturdy independence so characteristic of their Presbyterian fellow townsmen. (Ordnance Survey Memoirs, 1835)

It was in the attitudes that this writer summed up in the word "character", and in religion that the ethnic differences between colonist and native were to be recast and even accentuated in the course of the nineteenth century. In folklife the change is typified by the growing popularity of two seasonal festivals, neither of which had been given much recognition previously (Buchanan, 1962, pp. 21, 33). These were the celebration of St. Patrick's Day on 17 March, the day commemorating the national saint being used increasingly to promote an Irish identity; and the equally significant celebrations on 12 July, when northern Orangemen celebrated the victory of the Protestant King William over the Roman Catholic King James at the Battle of the Boyne in 1690. These are now the two major secular festivals in Northern Ireland: both have a sectarian character which was almost totally absent from the folk festivals of earlier times.

CONCLUSION: THE TWO CULTURES IN HISTORY

In a review of recent literature on family life in Ireland, the anthropologist John Blacking (1979, p. v) wrote: "Protestant and Roman Catholic in the North have too much in common to be defined as separate sub-cultures". Within the context of cultural anthropology this is undoubtedly true: both groups today live in the same types of houses, eat similar food, speak the same language and work at the same jobs. This is to be expected, for the urbanising processes of modern industrial society tend towards cultural uniformities, and the eradication of many of the cultural traits which distinguished different groups in the past. Yet the reality is that people in Northern Ireland today are strongly aware of group differences, and the fact that these are regarded as more than religious was indicated in the comments quoted at the beginning of this chapter. The most usual explanation is that the two groups belong to different traditions, those of the Planter and the Gael.

The purpose of this chapter has been to show that in the context of folkculture the concept of the two traditions cannot be substantiated. The deep cultural divide between Planter and native Irish which is said to have existed at the time of the Plantation cannot be demonstrated from the available evidence. Instead there is every indication that the Scottish colonists, who formed the majority of the Planters, had relatively few adjustments to make to the folkculture they found in Ireland. In its essentials it was very similar to that of their homeland, which of course had been in close contact with Ireland for more than a thousand years. For the English colonists the contrast in culture would have been much greater, but as a minority among the settlers it was they who adjusted to the prevailing pattern. The one exception was in speech, for English was the language of law, government and politics, of trade and the market-place, and in the face of this pressure Irish was bound to decline.

If elements of a common folkculture existed at the time of the Plantation, and accommodation between existing differences was largely achieved within a century, how is it possible for people today to feel that they still belong to two different traditions? The reason is that the original division was between the native and the immigrant, but as this distinction began to lose its relevance with each new generation born in Ulster, the old divisions were expressed in different form, that of the religious denominations of Protestant and Roman Catholic. In fact the transition was relatively easy, for at the time of the Plantation religion and language were the two main cultural differences separating the colonist from the native Irish, and of the two religion proved the more intractable. Deeply rooted divisions in matters of faith and doctrine ensured that denominational integrity was preserved intact, but even more important in maintaining divisions between the groups was the all-pervasive influence of religion in social life, in values, attitudes and relationships. This point has been made succinctly by Rosemary Harris (1972, p. xi) in the following comment on social life in a rural community: "Because of the separation of the social fields of Protestant and Roman Catholic, even neighbours belonging to different sides remain in some sense strangers".

There is a further reason why denominational labels became so closely identified with the concept of the two traditions, although the links are too complex to be examined here except in summary form. The explanation lies in the cultural and political history of nineteenth century Ireland, and the expansion of formal education which came to be organised on denominational lines. Roman Catholic emancipation in 1829 was an event of critical importance, for the formal recognition of the Church and the granting of civil rights to its adherents gave a new sense of group identity which was later to be used as an important political weapon. Coincidentally, a growing interest in the Irish language and its literature, and in Irish antiquities, provided the scholarly basis for a romantic nationalism which could proclaim the achievements of Ireland in the past. For the Roman Catholic Church this also provided an important Irish dimension in its teaching, by emphasising the central role of Celtic Christianity in the evolution of Irish culture and the Irish nation. To be Irish was no longer to suffer humiliation and scorn at the hands of a superior English culture: rather it was to take pride in the history of an ancient, civilised and Catholic people. In this history Protestants could find little of themselves or their own past, except as alien intruders and usurpers. Such roles are rarely acceptable even at a distance of several centuries; and so Protestants came to see their past in terms of the history of the larger island whence their ancestors had come, and to identify their present with the Empire as a symbol of British political power and achievement. These stereotypes were promulgated by two strongly contrasting and incompatible Church establishments—one autocratic and paternalistic, the other democratic and individualistic—each with a vested interest in stressing their differences.

In the recent past, therefore, formal education through denominational schools has reinforced the awareness of differences between Protestant and Roman Catholic, and has done much to foster the idea that each has inherited a cultural tradition fundamentally different from the other. In Northern Ireland schools today there may be a common syllabus for teaching and examinations, but only Roman Catholic children learn the Irish language and play Gaelic games; and in history lessons about the same period in time, events and personalities may be interpreted in one way in Roman Catholic classrooms, and in a very different way in those in which Protestant children are taught. John Magee (1970, p. 5) has put this in perspective:

> Many of the facts learned in the history lessons at school will in time be forgotten, but attitudes, enthusiasms and prejudices will remain. If those of us who teach history can persuade our pupils to accept a more critical attitude to what they hear and read, bring them to realise that there is generally more than one side to an argument ... they will have rendered a great service to the community without sacrificing in any way the legitimate aims of history teaching.

The concept of the two traditions has provided sectarian politicians in Northern Ireland with material for some of their more emotive slogans. Such individuals have a vested interest in maintaining divisions, and they are unlikely to be swayed by an academic statement which emphasises that Roman Catholic and Protestant share a common heritage in a folkculture which long pre-dates the seventeenth century Plantation. But through the processes of education, ordinary people may come to view their problems more objectively, and see the common ground wherein the real grass-roots are to be found, and which, with suitable nourishment, may be allowed to grow.

REFERENCES

Adams, G. B., ed. (1964). "Ulster Dialects." Ulster Folk Museum, Cultra.
Adams, G. B. (1970). Language and Man in Ireland. *Ulster Folklife* **15–16**, 140–171.

Adams, G. B. (1973). Language in Ulster, 1820–1850. *Ulster Folklife* **19,** 50–55.

Adams, G. B. (1974). The 1851 Language Census in the North of Ireland. *Ulster Folklife* **20,** 65–70.

Adams, G. B. (1976). Aspects of Monoglottism in Ulster. *Ulster Folklife* **22,** 76–87.

Alcock, L. (1973). "Arthur's Britain." Penguin, Harmondsworth.

Beckett, J. C. (1972). "Confrontations." Faber and Faber, London.

Blacking, J. (1979). Introduction to Aspects of Family Life in Ireland. *Journal of Comparative Family Studies* **10,** i–viii.

Bowen, E. G. (1972). "Britain and the British Seaways." Thames and Hudson, London.

Braidwood, J. (1964). Ulster and Elizabethan English. *In* "Ulster Dialects" (G. B. Adams, ed.), pp. 5–109. Ulster Folk Museum, Cultra.

Buchanan, R. H. (1957). Thatch and Thatching in North-East Ireland. *Gwerin* **1,** 123–142.

Buchanan, R. H. (1962). Calendar Customs, 1. *Ulster Folklife* **8,** 15–34.

Buchanan, R. H. (1963). Calendar Customs, 2. *Ulster Folklife* **9,** 61–79.

Buchanan, R. H. (1970). Rural Settlement in Ireland. *In* "Irish Geographical Studies" (N. Stephens and R. E. Glasscock, eds.), pp. 146–161. Department of Geography, Queen's University, Belfast.

Buchanan, R. H. (1973). Field Systems of Ireland. *In* "Studies of Field Systems in the British Isles" (A. R. H. Baker and R. A. Butlin, eds.), pp. 580–618. Cambridge University Press, Cambridge.

Caird, J. B. (1964). The Making of the Scottish Rural Landscape. *Scottish Geographical Magazine* **80,** 72–80.

Chadwick, H. M. (1949). "Early Scotland." Cambridge University Press, Cambridge.

Chadwick, N. K. (1963). "Celtic Britain." Thames and Hudson, London.

Crawford, W. H. (1975). Landlord–Tenant Relations in Ulster, 1609–1820. *Irish Economic and Social History* **2,** 5–21.

Currie, E. A. (1973). "The Reconstruction of the Geography of the Southern Part of County Derry, in Particular the Moyola Valley, in the Eighteenth and Nineteenth Centuries." Unpublished M.A. Thesis, Queen's University, Belfast.

Danachair, C. Ó (1957). Some Distribution Patterns in Irish Folklife. *Béaloideas* **25,** 108–123.

Danachair, C. Ó (1959). The Quarter Days in Irish Tradition. *Arv* **15,** 47–55.

Danachair, C. Ó (1970). The Flail in Ireland. *Ethnologia Europaea* **4,** 50–55.

De Paor, L. (1970). "Divided Ulster." Penguin, Harmondsworth.

Dodgshon, R. A. (1973). The Nature and Development of Infield-Outfield in Scotland. *Institute of British Geographers, Transactions* **59,** 1–24.

Dunbar, J. G. (1971). The Peasant-House. *In* "Deserted Medieval Villages" (M. Beresford and J. G. Hurst, eds.), pp. 236–244. Lutterworth, London.

Edwards, R. D. (1938). Letter-Book of Sir Arthur Chichester, 1612–14. *Analecta Hibernica* **8,** 74.

Evans, E. E. (1957). "Irish Folk Ways." Routledge and Kegan Paul, London.

Evans, E. E. (1970). The Personality of Ulster. *Institute of British Geographers, Transactions* **51,** 1–20.

Evans, E. E. (1973). "The Personality of Ireland." Cambridge University Press, Cambridge.

Fairhurst, H. (1960). Scottish Clachans. *Scottish Geographical Magazine* **76,** 67–76.

Fenton, A. (1976a). Thatch and Thatching. *In* "Building Construction in Scotland" (Scottish Vernacular Buildings Working Group), pp. 39–51. Scottish Vernacular Buildings Working Group, Dundee and Edinburgh.

Fenton, A. (1976b). "Scottish Country Life." John Donald, Edinburgh.

Frey, J. (1979). "An Analysis of Rural Settlement Change in the Barony of Kinelarty during the Nineteenth Century." Unpublished B.A. Dissertation, Department of Geography, Queen's University, Belfast.

Gailey, R. A. (1962a). Ropes and Rope Twisters. *Ulster Folklife* **8,** 72–82.

Gailey, R. A. (1962b). The Peasant House of the South-West Highlands of Scotland: Distribution, Parallels and Evolution. *Gwerin* **3,** 227–242.

Gailey, R. A. (1968–1969). Cultural Connections in North-West Britain and Ireland. *Ethnologia Europaea* **2–3,** 138–143.

Gailey, R. A. (1974). A House from Gloverstown, Lismacloskey, County Antrim. *Ulster Folklife* **20,** 24–41.

Gailey, R. A. (1975). The Scots Element in North Irish Popular Culture. *Ethnologia Europaea* **8,** 2–22.

Gailey, R. A. and Fenton, A. (1970). "The Spade." Ulster Folk Museum, Cultra.

Greeves, J. R. H. (1955–1956). Robert I and the De Mandevilles in Ulster. *Transactions of the Dumfriesshire and Galloway Natural History and Antiquarian Society* **34,** 59–73.

Greeves, R. (1957–1958). The Galloway Lands in Ulster. *Transactions of the Dumfriesshire and Galloway Natural History and Antiquarian Society* **36,** 115–121.

Gregg, R. J. (1964). Scotch-Irish Urban Speech in Ulster. *In* "Ulster Dialects" (G. B. Adams, ed.), pp. 189–190. Ulster Folk Museum, Cultra.

Harris, R. L. (1972). "Prejudice and Tolerance in Ulster: A Study of Neighbours and 'Strangers' in a Border Community." Manchester University Press, Manchester.

Harrison, J. (1882). "The Scot in Ulster." Blackwood, Belfast.

Hayes-McCoy, G. A., ed. (1964). "Ulster and Other Irish Maps c. 1600." Stationery Office, Dublin.

Heslinga, M. W. (1962). "The Irish Border as a Cultural Divide." Van Gorcum, Assen.

Hewitt, J. and Montague, J. (1970). "The Planter and the Gael." Northern Ireland Arts Council, Belfast.

Hill, G. (1879). "The Montgomery Manuscripts." Archer, Belfast.

Jackson, K. (1951). Common Gaelic: The Evolution of the Goedelic Language. *Proceedings of the British Academy* **37,** 71–97.

Jope, E. M. (1958). Castlecaulfield, Co. Tyrone. *Ulster Journal of Archaeology* **21,** 101–106.

Laing, L. (1975). "The Archaeology of Late Celtic Britain and Ireland." Methuen, London.

Lorrimer, W. L. (1949). The Persistence of Gaelic in Galloway and Carrick. *Scottish Gaelic Studies* **6,** 114–136.

Macafee, W. (1977). The Colonisation of the Maghera Region of South Derry during the Seventeenth and Eighteenth Centuries. *Ulster Folklife* **23,** 70–91.

MacQueen, J. (1973). The Gaelic Speakers of Galloway and Carrick. *Scottish Studies* **17,** 17–33.

Magee, J. (1970). "The Teaching of Irish History in Irish Schools." Northern Ireland Community Relations Commission, Belfast.

McCourt, D. (1964–1965). The Cruck Truss in Ireland and its West-European Connections. *Folkliv* **28–29,** 64–78.

McCourt, D. (1971). The Dynamic Quality of Irish Rural Settlement. *In* "Man and his Habitat" (R. H. Buchanan, E. Jones and D. McCourt, eds.), pp. 126–164. Routledge and Kegan Paul, London.

McCourt, D. (1973). Innovation Diffusion in Ireland: An Historical Case Study. *Proceedings of the Royal Irish Academy* **73,** (C, 1), 1–19.

Moody, T. W. (1957). The Social History of Modern Ulster. *In* "Ulster since 1800" (T. W. Moody and J. C. Beckett, eds.), pp. 224–235. British Broadcasting Corporation, London.

Moody, T. W. (1974). "The Ulster Question, 1603–1973." Mercier Press, Cork.

O'Rahilly, T. F. (1932). "Irish Dialects Past and Present." Browne and Nolan, Dublin.

Ordnance Survey Memoirs (1835). "County Londonderry: Drumachose Parish" (Box 38 MS, Public Record Office of Northern Ireland, Belfast).

Perceval-Maxwell, M. (1973). "The Scottish Migration to Ulster in the Reign of James I." Routledge and Kegan Paul, London.

Proudfoot, V. B. (1959). Clachans in Ireland. *Gwerin* **2,** 110–122.

Robinson, P. (1974). "The Plantation of County Tyrone in the Seventeenth Century." Unpublished Ph.D. Thesis, Queen's University, Belfast.

Robinson, P. (1977). The Spread of Hedged Enclosure in Ulster. *Ulster Folklife* **23,** 57–69.

Robinson, P. (1979). Vernacular Housing in Ulster in the Seventeenth Century. *Ulster Folklife* **25,** 1–28.

Rose, R. (1971). "Governing without Consensus: An Irish Perspective." Faber and Faber, London.

Sellar, W. D. H. (1971). Family Origins in Cowal and Knapdale. *Scottish Studies* **15,** 21–37.

Simpson, W. D. (1968). "The Ancient Stones of Scotland." Hale, London.

Sinclair, C. (1953). "Thatched Houses of the Highlands." Oliver and Boyd, Edinburgh.

Stell, G. (1972). Two Cruck-Framed Buildings in Dumfriesshire. *Transactions of the Dumfriesshire and Galloway Natural History and Antiquarian Society* **49,** 39–48.

Stewart, A. T. Q. (1977). "The Narrow Ground." Faber and Faber, London.

Walton, J. (1957). Cruck-Framed Buildings in Scotland. *Gwerin* **1,** 109–122.

Whittington, G. (1973). Field Systems of Scotland. *In* "Studies of Field Systems in the British Isles" (A. R. H. Baker and R. A. Butlin, eds.), pp. 530–579. Cambridge University Press, Cambridge.

Whyte, I. D. (1975). Rural Housing in Lowland Scotland in the Seventeenth Century: The Evidence of Estate Papers. *Scottish Studies* **19,** 55–68.

Woodburn, J. (1914). "The Ulster Scot." Allenson, London.

CHAPTER 4

THE DEMOGRAPHIC DIMENSION OF INTEGRATION AND DIVISION IN NORTHERN IRELAND

Paul A. Compton

INTRODUCTION

This book sets out to examine whether the distinctive attributes of Roman Catholics and Protestants in Northern Ireland complement each other, thereby creating cohesion and unity, or whether they are of a divisive nature leading to separation. Expressed in another way, the question under examination is whether the natural affinities of Protestants lie more with the British of Great Britain and those of Roman Catholics more with the Irish of the Irish Republic than they do with each other. Could it be that the only significant bond is the fact that the two communities inhabit the same geographical slice of territory? While no definitive answers to these questions can exist, the evidence of history and the events in Northern Ireland since 1969 would certainly appear to suggest that the forces of division are considerably stronger than those of integration.

Although such questions of unity or division lie firmly in the arena of political science they also possess a significant demographic dimension which we shall seek to examine in this chapter. A summary glance at the basic demographic characteristics of the constituent parts of the British Isles would seem to suggest that there exists a distinctive Northern Ireland demography, the area forming a sort of demographic half-way house between Great Britain on the one hand and the Irish Republic on the other. Three examples will suffice to illustrate this point. During most of this century the population of Great Britain has grown at a moderate pace, that of Northern Ireland has expanded but

slowly, while the population of the Irish Republic has actually declined.[1]
Again, as regards fertility, families are smallest in Great Britain and
largest in the Irish Republic, with Northern Ireland again occupying
an intermediate position. The same also applies to marriage, for celibacy
continues to remain high in the Irish Republic, is currently low in
Great Britain, with Northern Ireland again lying somewhere between
the two.

Such distinctiveness, however, is not a product of a unique Northern
Ireland demography common to both Protestants and Roman Catholics
but, on the contrary, is a function of the fact that the British and Irish
realms overlap in Northern Ireland, the population characteristics of
Protestants being much more akin to those seen in Great Britain and
those of Roman Catholics to the demographic features of the Irish
Republic than they are to each other. Indeed, as a demographic
differentiator of the population of Northern Ireland, religion is much
more significant than socio-economic attributes, particularly in the
areas of fertility, emigration and rate of population growth. Moreover,
it can be argued that the religious differentials are in themselves highly
divisive and create tensions in Northern Ireland that would otherwise
not exist. For example, the higher Roman Catholic growth rate creates
fears amongst Protestants of eventually becoming a minority in Northern
Ireland; the intransigent attitude of the Roman Catholic Church to
mixed marriages and the decimation of the Protestant population of
the Irish Republic since 1920 serves to reinforce such fears. It is also
clear that the high marital fertility of the Roman Catholic population
has been a major factor generating a high rate of Roman Catholic
emigration from both Northern Ireland and the Irish Republic. It has
also been shown to be implicated in the high level of Roman Catholic
unemployment and overcrowded housing conditions. It may even be
associated with the lower than average educational attainment of
Roman Catholics in Northern Ireland.

This chapter therefore seeks to set out the principal demographic
contrasts between Protestants and Roman Catholics in Northern Ireland and to point to the more significant of the implications that arise
from these. It therefore addresses itself to geographic distribution,
disparities in rates of growth and differentials in population composition. It amounts to a macro-study of the demographic features of the
population of Northern Ireland and therefore relies heavily on general
census data and on the summaries of vital statistics contained in the
Annual Reports of the Registrar General for Northern Ireland (1926–
1977).

In the United Kingdom demographic data are not usually available by religious denomination, primarily because religion is not viewed as so significant a differentiating feature of the population as occupation, educational attainment, and socio-economic position, but also because religious affiliation is regarded as a personal matter into which outside bodies should not probe.

Religious persuasion has, however, traditionally been enumerated in Irish censuses both north and south of the Border and, although the usable data are rather limited in scope, reliable information exists on the size and geographical spread of each denomination, while for the major persuasions age, sex and marital composition are also recorded. By contrast, the recording of religious denomination is not part of the process of birth and death registration and accordingly birth and death rates by denomination cannot be directly calculated. On the other hand, marriages are tabulated by method of solemnisation and some insight into nuptiality trends by religious affiliation can thus be obtained.

Religion is, of course, the crucial differentiator in Northern Ireland, much more so than social class, because it is around the former that the population has for long been polarised. Interestingly its supposed contentiousness prompted a move to drop the religion question from the 1981 Census of Northern Ireland on the presumption that the less there is known about religious affiliation the weaker the resulting polarisation will become. But as is apparent from other societies, such as the Lebanon, where strong disparities in demographic rates of growth exist, the very lack of definitive quantitative data heightens rather than diminishes tensions. It is therefore gratifying that better counsels eventually prevailed in Northern Ireland and the question on religious denomination was included in 1981 as in previous censuses.

THE ENUMERATION OF RELIGION AT THE 1971 CENSUS

A particular problem with the 1971 Census, an important data source for this chapter, concerns the implications of the 9% non-response rate to the voluntary question on religion, and possible methods of correcting for this. It should be emphasised that those not stating a religious persuasion are not to be confused with persons of no religion. It follows, therefore, that the numbers of Roman Catholics and Protestants enumerated in 1971 were significant underestimates of the correct totals. Since Northern Ireland-wide changes in the Roman Catholic–Protestant proportion have recently been of the order of 1–2% per decade, an assessment of the religious breakdown of the not-stateds becomes of critical significance when evaluating the changing religious structure of the population between 1961 and 1971. It also has a fundamental bearing on the calculation of rates of emigration and natural increase. Viewed geographically, the problem is even more complex, for the rate of non-response varied widely from area to area, ranging from 1·7% in Moss-side Ward in Moyle District to over 25% in Washing Bay Ward in Dungannon District.

The assignment of the not-stateds to a denomination would be simple if one were able to assume an equal rate of non-response among Roman Catholics and Protestants. But since the Roman Catholic population was under some pressure to ignore the question on religion, and indeed completely to boycott the census, it is reasonable to assume a higher rate of non-response among Roman Catholics than Protestants. This proposition is supported by the fact that the non-response rate varied directly with the proportion of Roman Catholics in each area.

No post-census survey was undertaken to ascertain the religious affiliation of the not-stateds and any method of assigning these people to their denomination is therefore open to error and criticism. However, the spatial covariation between non-response and the distribution of Roman Catholics suggests a linear regression technique of assignment and in the absence of anything superior this method has been used to adjust the 1971 figures. Revised estimates have been made for Northern Ireland and for the new administrative districts. Although the regression models only provide a best estimate, where the fit is good the correction can be accepted with some confidence for the figures relating to Northern Ireland as a whole and for the districts of Ards, Belfast, Down, Antrim, Ballymena, Ballymoney, Cookstown, Larne, Magherafelt, Moyle, Armagh, Banbridge, Craigavon, Dungannon, Limavady and Londonderry. The results of the correction suggest that, of the 135 000 people not responding to the question on religious affiliation, 82 500 or 61% were Roman Catholics and 52 500 or 39% were Protestants. The non-response rate was thus some three times higher amongst Roman Catholics, an estimated 14·6% of all Roman Catholics not responding, compared with 5·5% of Protestants. Among the districts there was considerable variation around these average values, and the adjustments suggest that, while 20% of the Roman Catholic population failed to respond in Antrim, Magherafelt and Dungannon Districts, the figure was down to around 10% in Larne, North Down and Fermanagh. Although Protestant non-response was lower in each district, substantial variability is again indicated, from almost 100% response in Moyle and Banbridge to 7% non-response in North Down and Fermanagh.

The apportionment of the not-stateds naturally makes a significant difference to the Northern Ireland and district totals of Protestants and Roman Catholics. Thus while the Census records that 34·7% of the population of Northern Ireland who stated a religious denomination in 1971 were Roman Catholics, a small drop compared with 1961, the adjusted figure suggests that 36·8% is a better estimate, i.e. a significant increase over 1961. Again the enumerated data show Roman Catholics comprising a clear majority in four districts only—Newry and Mourne (62·6% Catholic), Londonderry (57·2%), Omagh (52·3%) and Strabane (50·6%). By comparison the adjusted data show Roman Catholics comprising a majority of the population in nine districts—Newry and Mourne (71%), Londonderry (64%), Omagh (62%), Strabane (57%), Magherafelt (55%), Down (54%), Dungannon (52%), Fermanagh (52%) and Limavady (52%). In addition, the population is evenly balanced in the districts of Cookstown and Moyle. Unless otherwise stated it is always the revised estimates that are used in this chapter. A fuller discussion of the technique of adjustment together with non-response rates by District Council areas can be found in "Northern Ireland: A Census Atlas" (Compton, 1978, pp. 80–81).

POPULATION DISTRIBUTION AND CHANGE

Unlike Great Britain, which has experienced steady population growth throughout the nineteenth and twentieth centuries, the population of the six counties that now comprise Northern Ireland attained a maximum of 1 649 000 persons in 1841, i.e. 113 000 more than the 1 536 000 enumerated at the 1971 Census of Population. The Famine of the late 1840s and its aftermath heralded a long phase of population decline which only came to an end in 1891. For most of the twentieth century the population has shown a tendency to increase at an accelerating rate due to the combined effect of falling net emigration and a rising rate of natural increase. It seems likely, however, that this trend has recently been reversed. Natural increase has been declining since 1964 while the rate of emigration has again tended to rise, partly in response to the conflict of the 1970s. Although we only have estimates for the late 1970s, there is strong evidence that the population of Northern Ireland is now in a condition of zero growth.

The distribution of population is very uneven. Over 809 000 people or 52·7% of the total live within the Greater Belfast region, defined as the area stretching from the Ards Peninsula and Larne in the east to Lisburn and Antrim in the west, at a density of 359 persons per square

TABLE 4.1. Northern Ireland Distribution of Population 1971.

District Council areas	No.	Distribution (%)	Density per km²	Urban proportion (%)	Roman Catholics (No.)	Roman Catholics (%)	Protestants (No.)	Protestants (%)	% Roman Catholics in total population of each district and region
Belfast:[a]									
Belfast	416 679	27·1	2981	100·0	141 250	25·1	272 950	28·3	34·1
Total	416 679	27·1	2981	100·0	141 250	25·1	272 950	28·3	34·1
Belfast Fringe:[a]									
Antrim	33 998	2·2	60	55·7	10 450	1·9	23 100	2·4	31·1
Ards	46 778	3·0	127	64·9	7500	1·3	39 300	4·1	16·0
Carrickfergus	27 044	1·8	311	92·0	4400	0·8	22 650	2·3	16·3
Castlereagh	64 406	4·2	760	96·4	6500	1·2	57 900	6·0	10·1
Larne	29 897	1·9	88	66·6	8000	1·4	21 900	2·3	26·8
Lisburn	70 694	4·6	159	88·7	11 500	2·0	57 900	6·0	16·6
Newtownabbey	66 915	4·4	441	97·1	11 950	2·1	54 450	5·6	18·0
North Down	52 611	3·4	719	88·1	5900	1·0	46 350	4·8	11·3
Total	392 343	25·5	185	84·2	66 200	11·8	323 550	33·5	17·0
Fringe-Bann:									
Ballymena	48 998	3·2	77	53·7	8650	1·5	40 200	4·2	17·7
Ballymoney	21 920	1·4	52	26·0	6500	1·2	15 450	1·6	29·6
Banbridge	28 688	1·9	65	43·3	8950	1·6	19 750	2·0	31·2
Coleraine	44 608	2·9	93	62·8	10 650	1·9	33 950	3·5	23·9
Craigavon	67 718	4·4	177	70·3	26 100	4·6	41 400	4·3	38·7
Down	46 951	3·1	73	49·5	25 150	4·5	21 350	2·2	54·1
Moyle	13 979	0·9	28	30·0	6800	1·2	7150	0·7	48·7
Total	272 862	17·8	78	54·1	92 800	16·5	179 250	18·6	34·1

TABLE 4.1. (*continued*)

District Council areas	No.	Distribution (%)	Density per km²	Urban proportion (%)	Denominational distribution				% Roman Catholics in total population of each district and region
					Roman Catholics		Protestants		
					(No.)	(%)	(No.)	(%)	
West of Bann:									
Armagh	46 449	3·0	69	37·6	20 450	3·6	25 400	2·6	44·6
Cookstown	26 070	1·7	42	31·2	12 850	2·3	13 250	1·4	49·2
Dungannon	42 606	2·8	55	30·3	22 300	4·0	20 300	2·1	52·3
Fermanagh	50 979	3·3	27	24·7	26 750	4·8	24 200	2·5	52·5
Limavady	23 809	1·6	41	41·5	12 150	2·2	11 050	1·1	52·4
Londonderry	84 901	5·5	226	82·6	54 000	9·6	29 950	3·1	64·3
Magherafelt	31 460	2·0	57	25·3	17 200	3·1	14 250	1·5	54·7
Newry and Mourne	72 368	4·7	81	52·7	51 650	9·2	20 700	2·1	71·4
Omagh	41 175	2·7	37	38·3	25 300	4·5	15 450	1·6	62·1
Strabane	34 364	2·2	40	41·3	19 550	3·5	14 800	1·5	56·9
Total	454 181	29·6	54	45·6	262 200	46·6	189 350	19·6	58·1
Northern Ireland	1 536 065	100·0	109	70·8	562 450	100·0	965 100	100·0	36·8

[a]Belfast and the Belfast Fringe together comprise the Greater Belfast region.
Source: Adapted from Compton (1978, pp. 10, 80).

kilometre. Within the region, 775 000 people live approximately twenty-five kilometres or less from the centre of Belfast alone. Outside this highly peopled zone, population is much sparser and tends to be concentrated in the medium-sized towns of Londonderry, Armagh, Craigavon, Omagh, Enniskillen, Coleraine, Strabane and Newry. The distribution of population for 1971 is summarised in Table 4.1, according to District Council area. In addition Fig. 4.1a shows the District

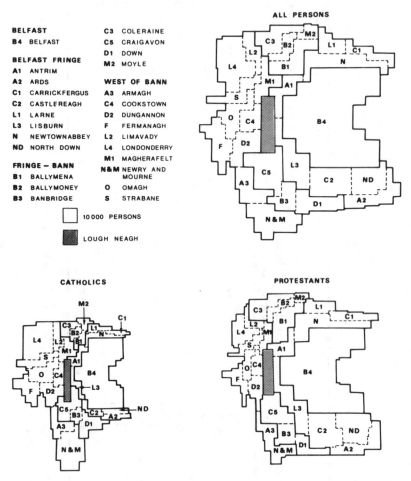

FIGURE 4.1. Northern Ireland Population Distribution by District Council Area, 1971: (a) All Persons; (b) Protestants; (c) Roman Catholics. Source: Constructed by J. A. E. Orr and F. W. Boal from data in Compton (1978, p.80). Each District Council area is drawn in proportion to its population size.

Council areas redrawn schematically so that the size of each area is proportional to resident population total rather than to area in square miles or kilometres. This establishes the importance of the population concentration in Belfast and its fringes.

Distribution of Population by Religious Denomination

The distributions of the two main denominations (Protestant and Roman Catholic) do not accord exactly with the overall population pattern. On the one hand Roman Catholics are quite widely dispersed throughout Northern Ireland and are comparatively more peripheral in their distribution. Protestants, on the other hand, are highly concentrated in the east-central area, and almost two-thirds of their total number reside in the Belfast region alone (Table 4.1; Fig. 4.2). This pattern is difficult to appreciate from a conventional map such as Fig. 4.2 but can be effectively depicted by transforming the conven-

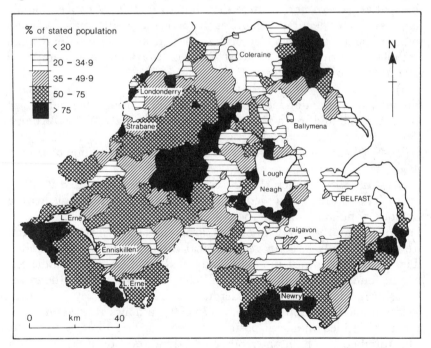

FIGURE 4.2. Northern Ireland Percentage Distribution of Roman Catholics in 1971.
Source: Compton (1976, p. 435). The spatial units employed are urban areas and rural electoral wards.

tional map in the same way as was done for Fig. 4.1a. This transformation has been carried out for the distribution of Protestants and Roman Catholics by District Council area in Figs 4.1b and 4.1c, thereby highlighting the broad regional contrasts. Protestants comprise the overwhelming majority (83%) of the Belfast Fringe population and about two-thirds of the population of the Fringe-Bann area. Belfast itself also weighs very heavily in their overall distribution. Roman Catholics, by contrast, form a majority in the West of the Bann area, but their proportion in this region (58%) is not nearly so dominant as the Protestant proportion east of the Bann. Compared with Protestants, however, they predominate in the districts of Newry and Mourne and Londonderry. On the other hand their apparent concentration in the extensive territories of north-east Antrim and the Sperrin Mountains where the population is sparse (Fig. 4.2) is greatly diminished and shown in a more realistic manner in Fig. 4.1c.

Broad regional comparisons naturally gloss over the complexity of the spatial pattern and relative distribution in 1971 is conventionally mapped in finer detail in Fig. 4.2 as the percentage of Roman Catholics in the population of each electoral ward. The areas with large Roman Catholic majorities (i.e. at least 75% of the total population) fall essentially into four clusters:

(i) The Border zone with the Irish Republic, stretching discontinuously from Londonderry in the north-west through Fermanagh to south Armagh and south Down, where approximately 100 000 Roman Catholics were enumerated at the 1971 Census.

(ii) North-east Antrim, with a Roman Catholic population of around 5000.

(iii) Mid-Ulster, where 12 000 Catholics were enumerated in 1971.

(iv) The southern and western peripheries of Lough Neagh, with a Catholic population also of about 12 000.

The principal Roman Catholic majority areas of Northern Ireland are thus generally large in geographical extent but sparsely inhabited (Fig. 4.1c). By contrast the main body of Roman Catholic population is to be found in the built-up area of Belfast, taken to include the towns of Lisburn, Holywood, Carrickfergus and Newtownabbey as well as Belfast itself. Here approximately 175 000 Catholics resided in 1971, but in a decided minority position comprising less than 30% of the total number of inhabitants. But any delimitation of areas based on denominational majorities must take note of scale, for within the major urban centres religious residential segregation is observed at the micro-level (see Chapters 10 and 11), best exemplified in Belfast itself, where at least half the Roman Catholic population lives in an exclusive area on the west side of the city. The geographical complexity of the religious pattern is further complicated by the numerous areas of Northern Ireland where the religious mix lies within the 45–55% range.

It is therefore clear that no easy unravelling of the religious-ethnic map of Northern Ireland is possible. A redefinition of the boundary in order to transfer into the Irish Republic those majority Roman Catholic areas contiguous with the existing international boundary would only reduce the size of the Catholic minority in Northern Ireland by between 70 000 and 90 000 (see Chapter 5). Geographical separation could therefore be achieved only through wholesale transfers of population.

As far as temporal change in the religious denomination of the population is concerned, the Census indicates that the number of Roman Catholics declined from 40·9% of the total population (572 000 persons) in 1861 to 33·5% (420 000 persons) in 1926, followed by a slight upswing to 34·9% (498 000 persons) in 1961 and subsequently a more rapid rise to 36·8% (562 500 persons) of the population of Northern Ireland in 1971. The post-1971 trend cannot be estimated accurately and will have to await the results of the 1981 Census of Population, but indirect evidence suggests that the increase in the proportion of Roman Catholics has continued, although at a slower pace. It is, however, interesting to note that, despite the recent upsurge, the 1971 Catholic total was still below that recorded in 1861. Temporal change in the relative size of the Protestant community has obviously followed an obverse course. The highest proportion, 66·5% of the total population (836 000 persons), was enumerated in 1926, declining to 63·2% (965 000 persons) in 1971. Summarising the changes over the forty-five year period 1926–1971, it is found that the size of the Protestant population rose by 124 000 persons, an increase of just under 15%, compared with a jump of 140 000 in the Roman Catholic total, a rise of 33%.

Significant regional variations, however, occur around this average trend. In the western counties of Fermanagh, Londonderry and Tyrone, religious composition has remained generally stable. By contrast, in County Down the proportion of Roman Catholics has fallen consistently since 1937, but in County Antrim has risen strongly over the same period, both trends being related to the selective suburbanisation of the population of Belfast. As such, the county figures can give a misleading impression of the areal extent of this change, which is essentially limited to the periphery of Belfast. Conversely, although redevelopment has generated a steep decline in the population of inner Belfast (the former County Borough area), the percentage of Roman Catholics has markedly increased there since 1961 because of a slower rate of suburbanisation (see Chapter 10) and a higher birth rate. The high level of non-response to the census question on religious persuasion makes it impossible to analyse recent changes in the distribution of the two groups in more spatial detail, but the evidence strongly suggests that the long-term trend towards the regional equalisation of the population by religious composition, which emerged just before the outbreak of the Second World War, is being maintained. Its main mechanism is the continuation of the steady rise of the proportion of Roman Catholics in the east, notably around Belfast, but also in some of the other large towns, e.g. Antrim and Craigavon.

Birth Rates, Death Rates and Natural Increase

From the creation of Northern Ireland in 1920 to the beginning of the 1930s the area's birth rate generally declined but eventually settled down at around 20 per 1000 population and remained thereabouts until the early years of World War II (Fig. 4.3). Thereafter it rose in three consecutive years to a peak of 24·2 per 1000 population in 1943, an all-time high for this century, and again peaked four years later in 1947. While the peak in 1947 marks the immediate post-war baby boom, the high level achieved in 1943 was closely related to an upsurge in marriages which began in 1937 and also peaked in the early 1940s. After 1947 the birth rate followed a broad cyclic swing, reaching a low point in the early 1950s and thereafter rising to a post-war maximum of 23·6 per 1000 population in 1964, slightly above the rate achieved in 1947. Since then a steep and unprecedented decline has occurred and by 1977 the rate had dropped to 16·5 per 1000 population, although the returns for the first three-quarters of 1978 suggest that the decline is now flattening out. Viewed in the United Kingdom context, the birth rate in Northern Ireland has been consistently higher than in the rest of the country, although in all its essential elements the post-war trend has closely followed the Great Britain pattern. The death rate has not fluctuated to the same extent as the birth rate. It generally fell, although in a rather erratic fashion, until the early 1950s, but since then has hovered around 11 per 1000 population (Fig. 4.3).

Natural increase remained quite low up to 1940–1941, fluctuating on either side of 6 per 1000 population per annum. Between 1941 and 1943, however, it quickly rose and settled down on a higher plateau of just over 10 per 1000 per annum for about ten years, only to rise again in the mid-1950s to a peak of 13·1 per 1000 in 1964. Subsequently, natural increase has followed the same course as the birth rate and by

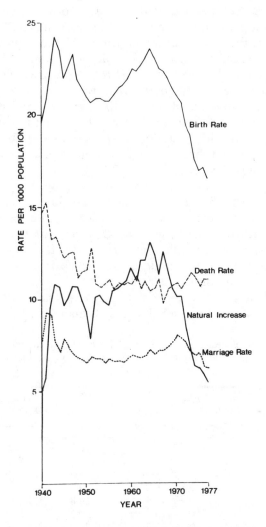

FIGURE 4.3. Northern Ireland Vital Statistics, 1940–1977.
Source: *Registrar General for Northern Ireland: Annual Reports 1940–1977.*

1977 had dropped to 5·4 per 1000 population, a decline of around 60% in the thirteen years from the 1964 peak (Fig. 4.3).

Because of the data limitations already alluded to, birth and death rates by religious persuasion can only be derived indirectly by combining vital statistical and census information. It is assumed that the application of the denominational proportion of infants under one year of age, as enumerated at the Census, to total live births gives a reasonable estimate of the number of births to Roman Catholics and Protestants in the year in question, from which denominational crude birth rates are easily obtained. In addition, annual denominational birth rates can be derived from the 1971 Census records which list the year of birth of the children of married, widowed and divorced women who were under the age of sixty at the time of the Census. Although subject to certain biases, these records can be used to calculate annual general marital fertility rates for the period 1960–1971 and these can be converted into robust estimates of denominational crude birth rates by simple interpolation.

Crude death rates were estimated by assuming that each denomination was subject to the Northern Ireland schedule of age-specific death rates. Applying these rates to the age composition of each group as enumerated at each Census gave an expected number of deaths from which the respective denominational crude death rates were calculated. Annual denominational estimates for the years 1960 to 1975 could then be derived by simple interpolation.

Looking first at the estimates for the Census years 1937, 1951, 1961 and 1971 (Table 4.2), we see that the Roman Catholic birth rate was

TABLE 4.2. Birth Rates, Death Rates and Rates of Natural Increase by Religious Denomination (per 1000 Population) (1937, 1951 and Annual Estimates 1961 to 1975).

	Roman Catholics			Protestants		
	Birth rate	Death rate	Natural increase	Birth rate	Death rate	Natural increase
1937	22·8	15·0	7·8	18·7	15·0	3·7
1951	25·7	12·2	13·5	18·2	13·3	5·1
1961	28·2	9·9	18·3	19·3	12·0	7·3
1962	29·0	9·2	19·8	19·5	11·3	8·2
1963	29·0	9·6	19·4	19·8	11·8	8·0
1964	29·8	9·1	20·7	20·5	11·3	9·2
1965	29·0	9·1	19·9	20·0	11·5	8·5
1966	28·5	9·5	19·0	20·0	12·1	7·9
1967	27·5	8·3	19·2	19·2	10·7	8·5
1968	27·0	8·8	18·2	18·7	11·6	7·1
1969	26·9	8·9	18·0	18·4	11·9	6·5
1970	25·9	8·9	17·0	18·3	12·1	6·2
1971	25·5	8·6	17·9	18·0	11·8	6·2
1972	23·9	9·0	14·9	16·6	12·2	4·4
1973	23·2	9·2	14·0	16·2	12·8	3·4
1974	21·6	9·0	12·6	15·1	12·6	2·5
1975	20·9	8·4	12·5	14·6	12·1	2.5

consistently the higher of the two and indeed climbed at each successive Census up to 1961, from 22·8 per 1000 population in 1937 through 25·7 per 1000 in 1951 to 28·2 per 1000 in 1961, although by 1971 it had fallen back below the 1951 level. By contrast, the crude birth rate of Protestants moved within the narrow limits of 18·0 and 19·3 per 1000 population. Because we have assumed identical age-specific mortality schedules, the crude death rate of Roman Catholics is shown as being lower than that of Protestants, the gap widening as we move from 1937 to 1971, due to the younger average age of the Catholic population. Real mortality disparities of any significance are, however, unlikely to have existed between the two groups, especially since the advent of the National Health Service, and differences in age composition are rightly taken as the main factor determining denominational differences in the crude death rate. On translating these birth and death rates into differential natural increase, it is clear that the rate of increase of the Roman Catholic population was some two and a half times greater than that of Protestants in each of the years in question. In terms of absolute numbers, the annual increment of Roman Catholics to the population of Northern Ireland through the balance of births and deaths is therefore shown to have been consistently greater than that of Protestants since 1937, although they comprised little more than one-third of the population during the period under consideration.

The post-1960 annual results are also of considerable interest as they provide the best estimates we have of recent demographic trends. The Roman Catholic crude birth rate is seen to have remained substantially higher than that of Protestants throughout the period, although a tendency for the gap to narrow is detectable after 1964 (Table 4.2; Spencer, 1979). The rates of both groups followed the general Northern Ireland pattern, rising to a peak of 29·8 per 1000 Catholics and 20·5 per 1000 Protestants in 1964, whereafter a steep decline set in, the Roman Catholic and Protestant rates falling to an estimated 20·9 and 14·6 per 1000 respectively by 1975. As for natural increase, the Roman Catholic rate of growth never dropped below 1·2% per annum and was as high as 2·1% in 1964. By comparison, the annual rate of Protestant increase was always below 1%, falling to as little as 0·2% in 1975. The most significant fact to emerge from this set of figures, therefore, is the very rapid widening of the denominational disparity in natural increase after 1970 as the Protestant birth rate rapidly approached the general level of the death rate. Viewed quantitatively, the relative disparity widened from a Roman Catholic rate of growth two and a half times greater than that of the Protestant population in the early 1960s to one six times higher in the early 1970s. Translating this into absolute numbers, the rates of natural increase imply a Roman Catholic growth increment of just over 9000 in 1961 and around 10 000 in 1971, compared with a Protestant increase of just under 7000 in 1961 and 6000 in 1971. This widening of the natural increase differential seems to have continued subsequently for although our 1975 estimates suggest a dramatic fall in the annual growth rates of both denominations, the Roman Catholic increment dropping to 7000 and the Protestant to a very low 2500, the differential accordingly widened to 4500 persons.

Emigration

Natural increase constitutes but one of the two factors determining overall population change, and a complete picture is only obtained when migration is introduced into the discussion. As has already been demonstrated, migration is indeed crucial because emigration has long been a traditional part of Northern Ireland life. Some notion of the magnitude of population outflow over the decades is conveyed by the fact that the present population of Northern Ireland is still less than that recorded in 1841. Emigration is even more striking when examined regionally: for instance, the 1971 population of Fermanagh is but one-third of the total enumerated in the county at the time of the 1851 Census.

However, we are not so much concerned with overall migration trends as with variations in migration by religious persuasion and here the strong denominational differential in net emigration that has existed for many decades is central to the discussion. Clearly, the Roman Catholic rate of emigration more than counterbalanced any higher rate of natural increase up to 1926 and thus accounted for the declining proportion of Roman Catholics in the Northern Ireland population that occurred up to that date. Since then, however, it is equally clear that the denominational differential in emigration, although remaining of very significant proportions, has not been of sufficient magnitude to outweigh the disparity in natural increase, partly because this has grown, and as a consequence the Roman Catholic proportion of the population has been rising steadily since around 1930.

The intercensal differential in net emigration can be estimated using a modified version of the residual technique. This involves computing the denominational populations expected from natural increase during the intercensal period, and then comparing these with the populations actually enumerated at the subsequent census. If the actual populations are found to be smaller than the expected, the difference is caused by net emigration; if larger the difference is explained by net immigration.

Using this method Barritt and Carter (1962, p. 108) estimated that 58% of net out-movement (67 300 persons) from Northern Ireland between 1937 and 1951 was composed of Roman Catholics, while calculations made by the author for the intercensal period 1951–1961 suggest that, of the 92 000 net emigrants, around 60% (55 000 persons) were Roman Catholics, a proportion not greatly different from that obtained by Barritt and Carter for the earlier period. In an earlier publication containing migration estimates for the most recent inter-censal period, it was concluded that the years 1961–1971 witnessed a clear break with the traditional emigration pattern, not only because the overall rate of emigration was lower than 1937–1951 or 1951–1961, but also because the religious differential had narrowed considerably, the proportion of Roman Catholics in the total apparently falling to just over 50% (Compton, 1976). However, the calculation of emigration rates for 1961 to 1971 is open to greater possible error than previously and these conclusions must now be modified in the light of subsequent refinements to the statistical data base. First, the size of the net outflow of population published in the 1971 Census has since proved to be an underestimate because no allowance was made for the presence of those sections of Her Majesty's armed forces stationed in Northern Ireland to meet the growth in terrorism; the Registrar General's authoritative correction was only published as recently as 1976 (Registrar General for Northern Ireland, 1976, p. 42). Secondly, a problem of crucial importance to the derivation of reliable emigration estimates by religion is the apportionment of the 9% who failed to state their religious per-suasion. Since the earlier estimates were computed, the method of correction has been refined and the modified results thus obtained can be accepted with more confidence. Thirdly, more accurate estimates of denominational natural increase for the intercensal period can now be derived from the annual birth and death rate data discussed above.

Taking these three factors into account, the revised computations suggest a total net outflow of 69 000 from Northern Ireland between 1961 and 1971, a lower emigration figure than between 1951 and 1961 but higher than between 1937 and 1951. Of this outflow 64·5% or 44 500 were Roman Catholics and 35·5% or 24 500 persons were Protestants (Table 4.3). Far from the denominational disparity narrow-ing, this revised calculation suggests that the differential has in fact widened and, moreover, would appear to have done so for each inter-censal period since 1937. Of course, these estimates are only as robust as the assumptions regarding denominational rates of natural increase and the apportionment of not-stateds on which they are based, and it should be stressed that very small errors in these figures can generate large differences in the emigration estimates.

TABLE 4.3. Denominational Net Emigration Estimate 1961–1971.

Protestants		
Population 1961	918 000	(64·4% of total population)
Population 1971	966 000	(63·2% of total population)
Change 1961–1971	48 000	(equivalent to an annual rate of increase of 5·6 per 1000 population)
Natural increase 1961–1971	72 500	(equivalent to an annual rate of natural increase of 7·6 per 1000 population)
Net emigration 1961–1971	24 500	(equivalent to 35·5% of all emigration: annual rate of outflow 2·6 per 1000 Protestant population)
Roman Catholics		
Population 1961	507 000	(35·6% of total population)
Population 1971	563 000	(36·8% of total population)
Change 1961–1971	56 000	(equivalent to an annual rate of increase of 10·5 per 1000 population)
Natural increase 1961–1971	100 500	(equivalent to an annual rate of increase of 18·2 per 1000 population)
Net emigration 1961–1971	44 500	(equivalent to 64·5% of all emigration: annual rate of outflow 8·5 per 1000 Roman Catholic population)

One can only speculate about denominational trends in emigration since 1971. The most recent estimates from the Registrar General suggest that during the seven years June 1971 to June 1978 the net outflow from Northern Ireland amounted to 72 500 persons. If correct (these estimates are derived from the transfer of National Health Service records) more people have, therefore, left during the seven years since 1971 than during the whole of the intercensal period 1961–1971. But it should be remembered that this intercensal period marked a phase of comparatively low emigration and that the latest estimates suggest a ten-year outcome up to 1981 not dissimilar from that for 1951–1961. While an upturn in emigration is a predictable consequence of ten years of sporadic civil disturbance, political uncertainty and economic recession, it might well be argued that the recent increase in outflow is somewhat less than might have been anticipated in view of the seriousness of the problems facing Northern Ireland at present. It is, however, important to realise that emigration is influenced not only by conditions at home but also by circumstances at places of potential destination and quite clearly these have not offered much inducement to move of late. Great Britain remains the most important destination for Northern Ireland migrants, but the recent high levels of unemployment experienced there must have curbed many potential movers— skilled and unskilled, white collar and blue collar workers alike. Nor are the opportunities of moving overseas to North America and Australia as great as they have been in the past.

Regarding the denominational differential, it has been argued that the Roman Catholic rate of emigration may well have declined and the Protestant rate risen during the early 1970s (Browne, 1978). This view is not based on quantitative evidence but rather on the hypothesis that during times of general economic recession it is only those with a skill or a profession who are able to emigrate with any ease. Since it is Protestants who are predominant in these groups in Northern Ireland, so the argument runs, recent emigration from Northern Ireland must have involved a higher proportion of Protestants than previously was the case, contrasting markedly with earlier periods when the typical emigrant was an unskilled Roman Catholic. While there may be some truth in the argument, for instance the outflow of Protestant students to universities in Great Britain has clearly risen during the last decade, the general conclusion cannot as yet be supported by any concrete statistical fact. Indeed, arguments about aggregate behaviour based on isolated impressions can be wildly wrong; we might with equal validity assert that it is the skilled Roman Catholic who is now leaving because of the growing economic attractiveness of the Irish Republic. But rather than adopt this stance, it seems more sensible, in view of the long-standing nature of the emigration differential and its tendency not to narrow, to assume that the denominational disparity has been carried forward largely unchanged into the 1970s although allowing for a slight rise in the proportion of Protestant emigration. It would therefore seem reasonable to posit that around 60% of the net outflow from Northern Ireland since 1971 has involved Roman Catholics, i.e. around 43 000 of the 72 500 emigrants between 1971 and 1978.

Family Size

We have already demonstrated that the crude birth rate of Roman Catholics is significantly higher than that of Protestants. The crude birth rate is, however, a poor measure of comparative child-bearing performance and tells us little about the precise nature of the fertility differential. In this section we therefore explore the question of denominational differentials in fertility in more detail through an examination of family size.

TABLE 4.4. Family Size by Religious Denomination 1971.

	Northern Ireland		Belfast Urban Area	
	All marriage durations	20 or more years of marriage	All marriage durations	20 or more years of marriage
Roman Catholic	3·64	5·31	3·47	4·73
Protestant	2·37	3·04	2·18	2·66
Jewish	2·02	2·15	2·02	2·15
Other religions	—	—	1·91	3·19
No religion	—	—	1·84	2·81
Religion not stated	—	—	2·72	3·73
All	2·70	3·55	2·49	3·10

Source: *Northern Ireland Census of Population 1971* (Fertility Tables and unpublished data).

The broad relationships in 1971 between family size and religious persuasion in the Belfast Urban Area[2] and in Northern Ireland are summarised in Table 4.4 for uninterrupted marriages of all durations and for uninterrupted marriages lasting twenty years or more, a reasonable estimate of completed family size. Not unexpectedly Roman Catholic families were markedly larger than those of Protestants in both situations. For all marriage durations, Roman Catholics averaged 1·3 more children per family than Protestants in both Northern Ireland and the Belfast Urban Area, rising to 2·3 more children per family in Northern Ireland and 2·1 more children per family in the Belfast Urban Area after twenty or more years of marriage. In relative terms, Roman Catholic families were therefore about 55% larger than those of Protestants for all marriage durations, the gap being slightly greater in the Belfast Urban Area than in Northern Ireland as a whole, and 75% larger after twenty or more years of marriage, the gap again being slightly wider in Belfast than in Northern Ireland.

Although the two are not strictly comparable because the family size data relate to the development of fertility over a number of years while the birth rate is an annual measure, the fertility differential as measured by family size is considerably larger than that suggested by the crude birth rate. Although this is not the place to go into technicalities, it can be demonstrated that the difference between the two is primarily a function of the differential marriage patterns of Protestants and Roman Catholics whereby, until very recently, a comparatively large number of Roman Catholics remained celibate and those who married did so at a comparatively high age, i.e. they exemplified the traditional Irish marriage pattern *par excellence*. By contrast, more Protestants married and married younger. Moreover these differences are still detectable today although not to the same extent as in former years. The effect on fertility is quite clear. The Roman Catholic marriage pattern reduced the number of Catholic births below what it would otherwise be if the marriage rate was the same as among Protestants. Indeed this is the intention as the traditional Irish marriage pattern is interpreted as a cultural device to control growth in a population rejecting family planning. The result is a crude birth rate also lower than it would otherwise be. On the other hand, family size within marriage remains unaffected—hence a denominational family size differential greater than the difference between the crude birth rates.

Regarding change in family size over time, we have data on the completed fertility of the 1931 to 1951 marriage cohorts for Northern Ireland as a whole, the Belfast Urban Area, Londonderry, the West and the East. In all five divisions, Roman Catholic families were consistently the larger of the two and, although completed fertility generally diminished for each successive cohort, the relative gap between the two denominations tended to widen because the size of Roman Catholic families declined at a slower pace. Thus for marriages contracted between 1931 and 1933 (Northern Ireland data), Roman Catholic families on completion were larger than those of Protestants, but were 77% larger for marriages contracted between 1949 and 1951. The gap was widest in Londonderry and in Belfast because in the former Catholic families were significantly larger and in the latter Protestant families significantly smaller than the Northern Ireland averages. Protestant families were largest in the West and smallest in Belfast, but were of similar size in the East and in Londonderry. Extending the comparison to marriages of ten years' duration enables us to examine temporal changes in family size between 1952 and 1961. These would suggest that the fertility gap continued to widen up to the mid-1950s but thereafter began to narrow. Although one cannot be categorical, the evidence suggests that this process has continued to the present.

It has been postulated in some quarters that Roman Catholic families are large for socio-economic reasons. This argument states that Catholics are over-represented in the lower socio-economic groups where family size also happens to be large, and that standardisation for socio-economic structure would remove the family size differential between the two groups. This hypothesis is emphatically fallacious: Roman Catholic families are always larger than Protestant for corresponding socio-economic groups regardless of marriage duration. Standardisation of Protestant family size on the socio-economic distribution of Roman Catholics clinches the case, for although Protestant family size would thereby be increased the denominational disparity would still remain greater than two children for marriages of twenty or more years' duration and around 1·2 children for all marriage durations.

Information for the Belfast Urban Area adds the further dimension of the actual socio-economic position of women to the question of family size and religious denomination. The discussion in the previous paragraph centred on socio-economic groups determined by the position of the husband. Women in employment, by contrast, have a socio-economic status in their own right conferred by their occupation, and some differences in the family size correlates of this group compared with all women might be expected. This is indeed confirmed, for not unexpectedly the family sizes of women in employment at the time of the Census are consistently smaller than those of housewives regardless of marriage duration. Moreover, although the families of both Roman Catholic housewives and Roman Catholic women in employment are again larger than those of their Protestant counterparts, the denominational differential is considerably smaller for women in employment. An interesting point that emerges is that during the first ten years of marriage the families of Roman Catholic women in employment are smaller than those of Protestant housewives of corresponding marriage duration, and this constitutes the only significant circumstance in which Protestant families are larger than those of Roman Catholics.

In summary, Roman Catholic families are significantly larger than those of Protestants and the difference in size is not explained by either demographic (age at marriage and duration of marriage) or socio-economic factors. The argument of Day (1968) that Roman Catholic fertility in Northern Ireland is high because of their position as a large minority cannot be sustained either, in view of the equally high fertility in the Roman Catholic-dominated Irish Republic. There is, however, evidence that the differential in family size is now diminishing and is likely to continue to do so. It has been shown that the disparity is comparatively small amongst women in employment, Roman Catholic working women having even smaller families than Protestant housewives during the first ten years of marriage. The fact that an increasing proportion of married women is likely to remain in employment during family building in the future is, therefore, a strong pointer to the continued narrowing of the fertility gap.

REPLACEMENT AND FUTURE POPULATION GROWTH

The number of Roman Catholics as a proportion of the total population of Northern Ireland has risen steadily since 1937. While this trend is unlikely to persist indefinitely, it is nonetheless true that, of the two communities, the Roman Catholic population has much the higher growth potential, which is well exemplified in the two contrasting levels of replacement, i.e. the implications of current fertility for generation replacement as opposed to the annual rate of growth. Thus in 1971 the net reproduction rate for Roman Catholics was 1·90 as opposed to a Protestant rate of 1·27, i.e. the next generation of Roman Catholic women of reproductive age would be 90% larger than the current generation, in contrast to a 27% expansion in the same group of Protestant women if the birth and death rates current in 1971 had remained unchanged. Since 1971, however, the reproduction rates of both communities have plummeted in line with the falling birth rate but, whereas the potential for generation growth among Roman Catholics still remains considerable (the 1977 estimate of the net reproduction rate was 1·66), for Protestants generation growth has come to an absolute halt (their net reproduction rate in 1977 was marginally above 1·00).

Another way of viewing essentially the same question is to examine the vital statistics of the respective stable populations, i.e. the populations that would obtain if the existing fertility and mortality schedules were to remain unchanged in future years. Not unexpectedly this yields similar findings. Thus, the intrinsic birth rate of both denominations fell quite sharply between 1971 and 1977 (from 28·6 to 22·4 per 1000 for Roman Catholics and from 18·8 to 13·6 for Protestants), but the Roman Catholic intrinsic rate of natural increase, although also falling sharply from 22·7 in 1971 to 14·5 in 1977, nevertheless remained high in absolute terms. On the other hand the Protestant rate dropped from a moderate 9·0 per 1000 to 0·12 in 1977; the underlying tendency among Protestants is for the development of a stationary population in about forty-five years' time. This evolutionary path is, of course, based on the supposition that fertility will remain unchanged at the existing level, and, although in the strictest sense an improbable event, it is nevertheless the case that demographers throughout western Europe are now taking seriously the likelihood of actual stationary populations emerging in most parts of the region. The demographic features of Northern Ireland Protestants thus fit into this overall pattern. The prognosis must therefore be one of continuing low Protestant fertility, although rises in the birth rate in the future cannot be ruled out.

The natural increase of the Roman Catholic population remains very much higher than in most of the rest of Europe: while being virtually identical to that of the Irish Republic, it is only in Albania that the rate of natural increase is currently higher. However, the achievement of very low fertility in the other Roman Catholic countries of Europe, plus the continuing diminution of family size in the Irish Republic, suggests that the present decline in the rate of natural increase of Roman Catholics in Northern Ireland is likely to continue (Guilmot, 1978). It is, however, still true that Catholic Ireland forms the last outpost of "traditional" west European demographic behaviour, composed of high marital fertility and low nuptiality, although this is now undergoing considerable transformation.

The time-scale over which the Roman Catholic rate of natural increase may be expected to decline to general European levels is not easy to assess, although if the present fertility trend continues it could be as short as ten to fifteen years. However, one incontrovertible fact is that, if the current natural increase differential between the two communities were to remain unchanged, *and in the absence of emigration*, the percentage of Roman Catholics in the population would continue to increase until they eventually formed a majority. Assuming these circumstances, our calculations based on 1971 fertility and mortality rates suggest a simple Roman Catholic majority by 2010 and a majority of the population of voting age by 2025, just under fifty years from now. The effect of the continuing decline of fertility since 1971, however, is not to bring forward the time of Roman Catholic majority, paradoxically in view of Protestant fertility falling to replacement level, but to delay the achievement of a simple majority to 2020 and a majority of the population of voting age to 2035. This projection is based on the birth and death rates of 1977 and suggests that, although the fertility and natural increase differential between the two groups is of significance in determining the speed of convergence of the two populations, of greater importance are the absolute levels of fertility and natural increase at any time.

These two projections provide estimates of the likely minimum time that must elapse before Roman Catholics can form a majority of the population, for two reasons. First, while Protestant fertility rates are unlikely to fall much below the present level, there is every possibility that Roman Catholic fertility will undergo a further significant decrease during the next decade or so. Secondly, the important effect of the religious selectivity of emigration has been ignored and to assess the impact of this on the inter-community balance three further projections have been made. In each the denominational breakdown of emigrants is assumed to remain constant at 60% Roman Catholic and 40% Protestant in view of the stability of this ratio since 1937. Moreover, fertility and mortality are also assumed to hold constant at rates for 1977. Only the volume of net emigration is therefore assumed to vary as follows:

(i) To hold at the level estimated for 1971–1977.

(ii) To rise 30% above the 1971–1977 level by the mid-1980s.

(iii) To fall 40% from the 1971–1977 level by the mid-1980s.

If emigration were to hold at the 1971–1977 level, a Roman Catholic majority could be expected by the middle of the next century, a result very similar to those obtained by projecting forward the natural increase and emigration current during the 1950s and 1960s. A certain underlying stability between the components of population change and their implications for the inter-community balance in the future would therefore seem to exist. On the other hand, were emigration to rise significantly, the date of Roman Catholic majority would be delayed indefinitely, but, as opposed to that, a fall in emigration as large as 40% would only hasten the time of likely majority by ten to fifteen years. Clearly, we cannot foretell the future and projections such as these indicate what would happen if certain sets of assumptions were realised. On the basis of current trends, however, one would have to conclude that the likelihood of a Roman Catholic majority in Northern Ireland would appear less probable now than at any time during the last twenty years. The reason for this conclusion is that Roman Catholic fertility in Northern Ireland, although rather belatedly, now seems to be susceptible to the same influences that have brought about fertility decline throughout Europe. The reversal of this process appears an unlikely event and one would therefore expect Roman Catholic birth rates to continue to fall until they are not significantly different from the Northern Ireland average. Indeed the ironing out of fertility differentials by ethnic group and religion is occurring throughout the developed world (Andorka, 1978).

AGE COMPOSITION

Age structure both reveals and reflects the basic demographic processes under which populations have evolved. For instance, because of the traditionally higher birth rate, the Roman Catholic community is composed of a significantly younger population than the Protestant community, and in 1971 38% of Roman Catholics were under the age of sixteen, whereas only 28% of Protestants fell into the same age range. These proportions are, of course, reversed for the elderly population, the 1971 position recording 13% of Protestants over the age of sixty-five, compared with 9% of Roman Catholics. The impact of emigration is similarly visible as a significant decrease in the size of successive age groups for the ten or so years after the passing of school leaving age. However, reflecting their higher incidence of emigration, the process is more marked amongst Roman Catholics (in 1971 the 20–24 age group was a full 25% smaller than the 15–19 age group) than amongst Protestants (the 20–24 age group being less than 10% smaller than the 15–19).

It follows from these differences that the ratio of Roman Catholics to Protestants, according to age group, varies widely around the average value for the whole population. Thus compared with an overall mean of 37–38%, we would estimate that 45–47% of the population under the age of sixteen in 1971 were Roman Catholics, but in contrast to this Roman Catholics made up only 33–34% of the population of voting age and less than 30% of the population aged sixty-five and over. The global ratios for Northern Ireland also hide important spatial differences and wherever we compare areas of similar socio-economic composition, we find that predominantly Roman Catholic areas are always possessed of the younger age structure.

The significance of these denominational differences in age structures would be slight in a more homogeneous and integrated society. But in Northern Ireland, with its two polarised communities, a situation is created in which the Roman Catholic community, because of its large numbers of young people, needs a greater share of educational provision, creates a greater public housing need because of a higher rate of family formation, and demands a higher level of new job creation than indicated by its overall demographic position within the population. By contrast, the age structure of Protestants creates a relatively greater need for the services used by the elderly.

Let us take jobs and education as two examples and look at the implications of current demographic trends in more detail. If the average denominational rates of natural increase for the years 1971–1977 were to continue unchanged in the future, the annual number of sixteen year old Roman Catholics leaving school and coming on to the labour market would be over 2000 greater at the end of the century than in 1980, whereas the number of Protestant school-leavers would fall by around 2500. In terms of the balance between those entering and those leaving the job market, the continuation of natural increase at the level of the 1970s would therefore mean a rise of 110 000 in the number of Roman Catholics seeking work between 1980 and 2000 compared with an increase in the number of Protestants of around 50 000. A similar disparity would also arise within the school population. For instance, the number of Roman Catholic five year olds in the year 2000 would be 7000 larger than in 1980, whereas the Protestant total would only be around 1000 greater. The overall effect would be an increase in the Roman Catholic school sector of 60 000, whereas the Protestant sector would only rise by about 8000.

Clearly these estimates represent the maximum likely disparity in future demand for jobs and school places, but they do serve to highlight the quite startling implications of the wide denominational differential in age structure generated by the different birth rates. More realistically, of course, the selective impact of emigration must also be brought into play when discussing these questions and assuming this to continue at the same general level as during the 1970s the outcome would be as follows. The number of sixteen year old Roman Catholics entering the job market would remain steady between 1980 and 2000 but the number of Protestant sixteen year olds might be expected to fall sharply by around 4000 from the 1980 level. The overall demand for new jobs generated within the Roman Catholic population would, however, still rise but by slightly less than 5000, compared with a decline of around 30 000 within the Protestant community.

As regards the demand for schooling, the number of Roman Catholic five year olds would grow by about 1000 between 1980 and 2000, and the total number receiving full-time education up to the age of sixteen expand by 5000 over the same period. The corresponding data for Protestants indicate a decline in the number of five year olds of around 1000 and a decrease in the school population up to the age of sixteen of between 10 000 and 15 000. In other words, the decline in the Protestant school population generated by the falling birth rate since 1964 would not be halted by a stabilisation of fertility at the present level and a reversal of this downward trend will only be brought about by a significant increase in Protestant fertility. On the other hand, stabilisation of the present Roman Catholic fertility rate is not only sufficient to halt the present downward trend in numbers but would ensure a rising school population up to the end of the century.

If migration continues at the present level, the changing balance of job and educational requirements is likely to take place within the context of an overall stationary population. It would, therefore, seem that a straightforward reallocation of resources would solve any difficulties that might arise from the growing denominational disparities within the field of education, assuming this to be politically feasible. The problem of jobs, however, is not such a simple trade-off and would appear to be more intractable. There remains a strong regional bias in unemployment and rates are generally much higher outside the economic heartland around Belfast (see Chapters 8 and 9). It is also the case that unemployment is highest in the least favourable peripheral parts of Northern Ireland which also happen to be the areas of majority Catholic representation. Although it has been shown that this fact of geography cannot entirely explain the higher overall level of Roman Catholic unemployment (Osborne, 1978), it must nevertheless be a significant contributory factor and the chances of such areas attracting new sources of employment in competition with Belfast must be slim. It would, therefore, seem that any significant lowering of Roman Catholic unemployment, at least in areas such as these, could most easily be achieved by the demographic strategy of further out-migration and in the longer term by lower natural increase.

SUMMARY AND CONCLUSIONS

This chapter has set out to describe the demographic contrasts between Roman Catholics and Protestants in Northern Ireland. The two areas of greatest difference are fertility and emigration which, in turn, are fundamental in determining the future religious balance of the population. During the first three decades of this century the high rate of Roman Catholic emigration more than offset their higher fertility level and, as a consequence, the proportion of Roman Catholics in Northern Ireland actually declined. Since then the combination of a rising Roman Catholic birth rate, a declining Protestant birth rate and some narrowing of the emigration differential has led to a resurgence of the Roman Catholic element and this is certainly viewed by many Protestants as a threat to the majority Protestant position. Although it has been argued by some that the inevitability of a Roman Catholic majority should encourage Protestants to attach themselves to the Irish nation, on balance the rising proportion of Roman Catholics in Northern Ireland is clearly divisive rather than a force for unity.

Because of its higher birth rate, the Roman Catholic community is composed of a larger proportion of school-age population and young adults than is the Protestant population. There is thus a built-in demographic disparity creating differential denominational demand for the provision of employment, housing, education and the social services which generates at the same time accusations of preferential treatment, levelled by Protestants against Roman Catholics, and of discrimination, made by Roman Catholics. The differences in age composition clearly form, therefore, a fundamental element underpinning the present tensions and are certainly divisive in nature. In addition, we would put forward the view that there is a direct link between rapid natural growth and the high rate of Roman Catholic migration from Northern Ireland through the mechanism of differential unemployment levels. The necessity of emigration is clearly a source of resentment within the Roman Catholic community in Ireland as a whole because of its disruptive influence on family life and corrosion of social cohesion and confidence (Commission on Emigration, 1955).

Each demographic disparity can be traced back to the marked fertility differential. Its elimination would immediately remove the natural increase disparity between the two groups and thereby help stem the higher rate of Roman Catholic emigration. Moreover, the growth rates of the Protestant and Roman Catholic communities could be expected rapidly to equalise and the age composition disparity eventually to disappear. The removal of the inter-community demographic differentials in Northern Ireland would clearly be of positive and beneficial value and would go a long way towards the creation of community harmony. It is to be hoped that Roman Catholic fertility and birth rates in Northern Ireland will quickly decline to the level now seen almost everywhere else in the western world.

NOTES

1. It should be noted that the population of the Irish Republic, rather perversely, is now increasing at a faster rate than that of any other country of Europe with the worthy exception of Albania. This fundamental change of demographic behaviour has been evident since the early 1970s.

2. The Belfast Urban Area is a more restricted area than the Belfast region. It basically is composed of the continuously built-up area focussed on the city of Belfast (see Compton, 1978, pp. 8–9).

REFERENCES

Andorka, R. (1978). "Determinants of Fertility in Advanced Societies." Methuen, London.

Barritt, D. P. and Carter, C. F. (1962). "The Northern Ireland Problem: A Study in Group Relations." Oxford University Press, London.

Browne, B. (1978). Emigration Shifts Balance in the North. *Hibernia* **42** (16), 10.

Commission on Emigration and Other Population Problems, 1948–1954 (1955). "Reports." Stationery Office, Dublin.

Compton, P. A. (1976). Religious Affiliation and Demographic Variability in Northern Ireland. *Institute of British Geographers, Transactions* **1** (New Series), 433–452.

Compton, P. A. (1978). "Northern Ireland: A Census Atlas." Gill and Macmillan, Dublin.

Day, L. H. (1968). Natality and Ethnocentrism: Some Relationships Suggested by an Analysis of Catholic–Protestant Differentials. *Population Studies* **22,** 27–50.

Guilmot, P. (1978). The Demographic Background. *In* "Population Decline in Europe" (Council of Europe), pp. 3–49. Edward Arnold, London.

Northern Ireland Census of Population 1971. Her Majesty's Stationery Office, Belfast.

Osborne, R. D. (1978). Denomination and Employment in Northern Ireland. *Area* **10,** 280–283.

Registrar General for Northern Ireland: Annual Reports 1926–1977. Her Majesty's Stationery Office, Belfast.

Spencer, A. E. C. W. (1979). The Relative Fertility of the Two Religious Ethnic Communities in Northern Ireland, 1947–1977. *In* "Sociological Association of Ireland, Transactions 1977–1978" (A. E. C. W. Spencer, ed.), pp. 122–131. Department of Social Studies, Queen's University, Belfast.

CHAPTER 5

NORTHERN IRELAND: SPATIAL FRAMEWORKS AND COMMUNITY RELATIONS

J. Neville H. Douglas

INTRODUCTION

In all states political structures and their spatial frameworks[1] give expression to the political system. Structure and framework control the relationship between governor and governed and between communities within the state area. While research on political structure is voluminous, much less work has been directed towards identifying ways in which spatial frameworks affect community relations either by reinforcing pluralist cleavages or by encouraging integrative processes. The aim of this chapter is to consider this aspect of the political system in the context of Northern Ireland.

At the outset, it will be helpful to clarify the links between political structure and spatial framework. Political structure can be recognised by such indicators as the hierarchical organisation and concentration of decision-making power within the political system; the degree of accountability to others of decision makers; the amount of organised political opposition tolerated and the amount of political influence exercised upon the leadership group by other segments of society (Jacob and Toscano, 1964). Where accountability and recognition of opposing views are indicated, the structure is labelled "democratic" and is thought to be conducive to group cohesion and political integration. Where political power is concentrated and intolerance of opposing views is found, the structure is usually labelled "authoritarian" and is thought to encourage cultural cleavages and political dissidence (Lijphart, 1977). Whatever the validity of these views, the political structure is given reality throughout the state by the creation and delimitation of administrative and electoral spatial frameworks. Accountability becomes much more important when electoral frameworks ensure widespread competition among viable alternative candidates at national and local elections. Tolerance is implemented when the same frameworks recognise the existence of cultural minorities in an attempt to give them a voice in the decision-making process. Spatial frameworks thus give expression to the political structure: they provide an important means of spreading political power, political accountability and tolerance throughout the state and of ensuring fair representation. Equally, they provide the means whereby such aims may be curtailed and the concentration of power in one area or in one group may be achieved.

The study of spatial frameworks in Northern Ireland requires investigation at both the regional and the local level. At the regional level there is the spatial framework of Northern Ireland itself. This framework, created by Partition in 1920, established a distinct set of territorial, cultural and political parameters. With a population of 1 250 531 (*Census of Ireland 1911*) and comprising 65·6% Protestant (overwhelmingly unionist) and 34·4% Roman Catholic (overwhelmingly nationalist) the framework enclosed two distinct communities, with the smaller community being large enough to maintain its cultural identity and to be perceived in political terms as a significant opposing force by the majority community.

Recent political theory has established a range of possibilities within which the "democratic" model can be successfully applied in plural societies (Neuman, 1976). The most favourable situation for the "democratic" model is that in which all distinct communities form minorities: here, political power can be achieved only by coalitions of communities working together and establishing cultural and political contacts. The least favourable is found in a two segment majority–minority society where the minority is sizeable. Such a situation lies at the limits of consociational democracy[2] and is found in Northern Ireland. In this case, the so-called "Law of Contradiction" (Rabushka and Shepsle, 1972) is constantly at work, i.e. where two communities exist with contrasting politics, the preferences of both groups can never be met simultaneously. Thus, pressure is put on the state administration and many issues, which in other societies remain outside the political arena, crowd in on political decision makers and cause further aggravation. The hegemony of the majority alienates the minority who, with increasing urgency, question the legitimacy of the political system and, as in the Northern Ireland framework, all situations appear to favour the process of segregation and alienation.

Northern Ireland's internal spatial frameworks which make up the local level are also set in difficult conditions. In any area where two communities show strong spatial segregation at a macro-level, spatial frameworks can be delimited easily in relation to community boundaries and community conflict passes from the nature of the framework to the nature and distribution of delegated power within it. However, as in Northern Ireland, where communities are intermixed in space or segregated only at a micro-level, the spatial frameworks themselves and the size, shape and precise limits of their constituent units become the focus of heated conflict. Accepting the argument (Morrill, 1973) that non-partisan spatial frameworks cannot be achieved where such complex community intermixing exists, the regional problems resulting from the spatial framework of Northern Ireland itself are repeated at the local level within the administrative and electoral frameworks.

The regional and local frameworks can now be considered in more detail.

THE REGIONAL FRAMEWORK—THE NORTHERN IRELAND BORDER[3]

The Border, as set out in the Government of Ireland Act, 1920, was established by the British Government to separate two groups who, because of diverging national aspirations, could no longer live together. As Irish Nationalists waxed strong on the prevarications of Westminster, their Unionist counterparts in Ulster matched them stride for stride towards polarity. The general election of 1918 swept away the moderate Irish Nationalist Party (reduced from seventy-three to six seats) and replaced it with the more militant Sinn Fein Party (Walker, 1977). In the north-east of Ireland the Unionists held firm, etching out the area from which Northern Ireland was to emerge (Fig. 5.1).

Partition brought little satisfaction to any of the groups involved. The Unionists in the north-east were much attracted to a nine-county Northern Ireland, so making the new political unit co-terminous with the historic province of Ulster. Such a spatial framework, however, would have left the Unionists in a minority in large areas of the new unit and would have resulted in an overall Roman Catholic minority of 43·7%—much too large for comfort. The Nationalists in the south, preoccupied with the war of independence, saw Partition as a purely temporary measure and signed the 1920 Act to give themselves a breathing space. Inability to grasp the probable permanent reality of Partition also led to the signing of the Anglo-Irish Treaty in 1921 by

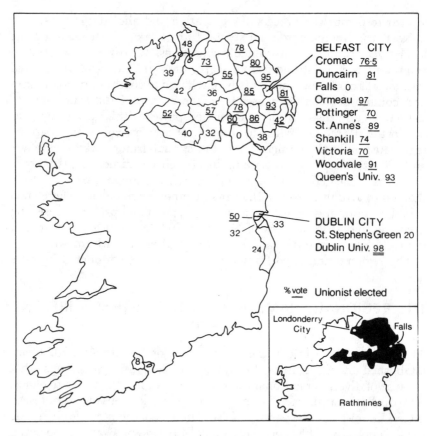

FIGURE 5.1. British General Election, 1918: Pattern of Unionist Support in the Area that Became Northern Ireland, and the Unionist Vote Elsewhere in Ireland. Inset: Constituencies Represented by Unionist M.P.s after the Election.
Source: Walker (1977).

the new Irish Free State leaders. This treaty included the important Article XII which established the Irish Boundary Commission and stated that: "The Commission shall determine, in accordance with the wishes of the inhabitants, so far as may be compatible with economic and geographic conditions, the boundaries between Northern Ireland and the rest of Ireland" (Hand, 1969, p. xii). To southern Nationalists it seemed inevitable that "recognition of the wishes of the inhabitants" would ensure transference of most of Counties Fermanagh and Tyrone, and large parts of Armagh, Down and Londonderry from North to South. Northern Ireland would then be of unrealistic size and shape and would lack enough economic viability[4] to ensure permanence. Figures 5.1 (inset) and 5.2(c) give some possible indication of the Nationalist view of the size and shape of the post-Commission Northern Ireland.

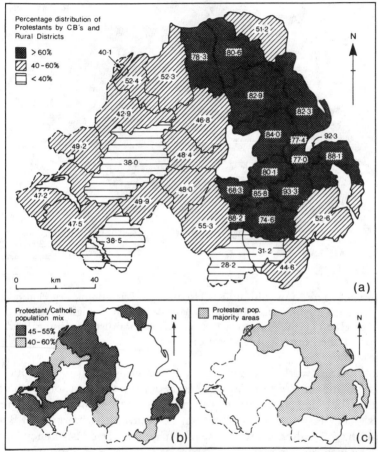

FIGURE 5.2. Northern Ireland: (a) Distribution of Protestant Population, 1926; (b) Areas with an Evenly Balanced Population Mix, 1926; (c) Areas with a Protestant Population Majority, 1926.
Source: *Northern Ireland Census of Population 1926.* The populations of urban districts have been included with the appropriate rural district data for the compilation of the percentage distribution.

The complicated intermixing of Roman Catholic and Protestant settlement within the zone where the Border was to be located made the delimitation of a mutually exclusive boundary impossible (Fig. 5.3).

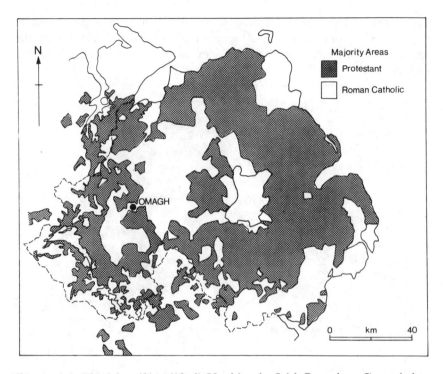

FIGURE 5.3. The Map (Simplified) Used by the Irish Boundary Commission, Showing the Distribution of Population by Religion, 1911.
Source: Hand (1969). The distribution is shown for district electoral divisions except in the Border zone where the distribution is shown for townlands.

Yet the framework of county boundaries appears to have loomed so large in the thinking of those concerned with the location of the new Border that the possibility of utilising alternative boundaries already in existence received scant attention. For example, what kind of Border would have resulted from the use of parliamentary constituency boundaries or local government boundaries as a basis for delimitation?

The parliamentary constituency boundaries set out by the Redistribution of Seats Act (Ireland), 1917 would have provided a much finer spatial mesh upon which to delimit the line of partition. Leaving aside county borough constituencies, the six counties in the north-east were sub-divided into nineteen constituencies. Had the drafters of the 1920 Act or the Boundary Commissioners located the partition line around those constituencies in which Unionists had been elected in 1918, Northern Ireland would have assumed a very different character. Accepting that delimitation must prevent the creation of territorial

enclaves and exclaves then, in this case, the Unionist exclave of Rath-
mines would have gone to the Irish Free State while the Falls (Nationalist) and Londonderry City (Sinn Fein) constituencies, enclaves
within the North, would have been included within Northern Ireland
(Fig. 5.1). This delimitation would have considerably reduced the
territorial extent of Northern Ireland, with the constituencies of South
Down, South Armagh, South Fermanagh and North West and North
East Tyrone being awarded to the new Irish State (Fig. 5.1 inset). It
would not, however, have removed Northern Ireland's minority
problem: the Roman Catholic community would have comprised
28·4% of the total population instead of 34·4%—still a sizeable minority.
There are two factors which help explain this relatively small decline
in minority group size, despite the significant territorial difference:

(i) The intermixture of Roman Catholic and Protestant in the five
constituencies which would have been excluded from Northern Ireland
was such that, although a large number of Catholics (129 971) would
have been located south of the Border, a significant number of Protestants (90 907) would also have been excluded from the North.

(ii) By far the greatest concentration of Roman Catholic population
was in Belfast and not in the Border zone. In 1911, 93 000 Catholics
lived in Belfast, comprising 32% of the total Catholic population of the
area that was to become Northern Ireland in 1920 (*Census of Ireland
1911*). Border relocations could, therefore, alter territorial extent
significantly and yet have little effect on the relative size of the minority
group.

Partition based on local government rural district boundaries would
also have reduced the territorial extent of Northern Ireland. Including
only districts with a majority Protestant population, Northern Ireland's
spatial framework would have been similar but not identical to that
based on parliamentary constituencies (Fig. 5.2c). The further contraction in territorial extent would have reduced the Roman Catholic
minority size only slightly to 26%—again illustrating that in most of
the west and south of Northern Ireland the population balance was so
fine that partition following any boundary location within the Border
zone would produce significant numbers of nationally dispossessed
political dissidents (Fig. 5.2b).

Figures 5.1 and 5.2 show that the result of the partition process is
controlled by the nature of the spatial mesh upon which it is based. It
can therefore be postulated that the most effective partition (i.e. that
which creates the smallest minorities on each side of the dividing line)
will be based on the finest and most detailed spatial mesh available.
Such a mesh, in the form of distribution of population by religion by

townlands[5] for 1911 was available to the Irish Boundary Commission and transferred to their working map for the Border zone (Fig. 5.3). The map illustrates that, by paying painstaking attention to local majority distributions and requiring territorial contiguity, a partition could have been achieved which would have minimised minorities. However, the resulting Border would have been so bewilderingly sinuous that it would have created insuperable administrative and customs control problems.

In practice the Boundary Commission chose a restricted interpretation of Article XII and recommended only limited change in the six-county spatial framework of Northern Ireland set out in the 1920 Act. It stated that a bare religious majority was insufficient to justify Border change and argued that no spatial framework should be so delimited as to render the territory it encloses incapable of political and economic survival. The Commission's Report (Hand, 1969) would thus have guaranteed the territorial future of Northern Ireland by recommending only small realignments of the Border in which fewer than 25 000 Catholics were to be transferred from North to South (Fig. 5.4). As a result, the Roman Catholic minority in Northern

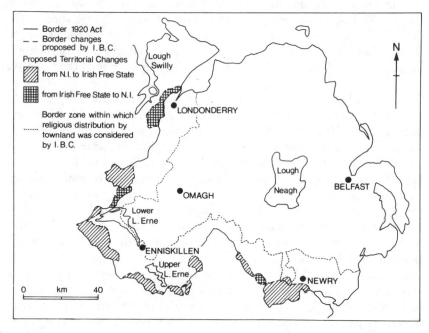

FIGURE 5.4. Irish Boundary Commission Proposals, 1925.
Source: Hand (1969).

Ireland would have fallen by less than 1% (Douglas, 1976). However, in October 1925, before publication of the Report, a substantially accurate forecast of the award appeared in the *Morning Post* newspaper. The detail and the map contained in the article gave rise to political turmoil throughout Ireland. The Irish Free State Commissioner resigned, the Commission was dissolved and its proposed award suppressed. In December 1925, in return for certain financial considerations, the Irish Government signed an agreement with the Great Britain and Northern Ireland Governments which established the legality of the Border as set out in the 1920 Act (Andrews, 1968).

This agreed Border followed the line of the county boundaries and enclosed the six-county territory of Northern Ireland. There was no special logic in the use of county boundaries as their location bore more relation to clan and family fortunes throughout centuries of Irish social history than to any readily recognisable principle of territorial division. The county boundaries were used, it must be suspected, because they were already delimited on maps, so giving some perceived authoritative backing to the deliberations of the Westminster decision makers in 1920 (Fig. 5.5). The new Border cut across agricultural holdings, through settlements and individual houses and across at least 180 roads on its 412 kilometre length from Newry in the south-east to Londonderry in the north-west. Because of its complexity, the Border has never been fully demarcated, a state of affairs which leaves ample scope for genuine confusion as well as deliberate abuse (Douglas, 1976).

With the wisdom of hindsight it might be argued that Northern Ireland was territorially overbounded by the 1925 agreement, particularly in the case of three areas—south Down and south Armagh, south and south-west Fermanagh and central Tyrone. South Down and south Armagh contains the largest concentration of Roman Catholic population contiguous with the Irish Republic. The Boundary Commission gave partial recognition to this in its proposal to award a large part of south Armagh, containing 14 000 Catholics and only 800 Protestants, to the Irish Free State. South Armagh remains strongly nationalist and has never been fully integrated nor has it wished to integrate within the political structure and framework of Northern Ireland, and since 1969 it has provided a heartland for terrorist activity (see Chapter 12) and a place of refuge.

South and south-west Fermanagh also contains a significant Border zone Roman Catholic population: however, the religious distribution is extremely uneven and scattered and the delicate balance between Catholic and Protestant makes the case for/against overbounding less clear cut. Nevertheless, areas south of Lower Lough Erne around

Garrison and Belcoo and south-west of Upper Lough Erne have always had strong *de facto* links towards the South and poor integrative relations with the rest of Northern Ireland (Jones, 1960).

THE KINDEST CUT OF ALL.

WELSH WIZARD. "I NOW PROCEED TO CUT THIS MAP INTO TWO PARTS AND PLACE THEM IN THE HAT. AFTER A SUITABLE INTERVAL THEY WILL BE FOUND TO HAVE COME TOGETHER OF THEIR OWN ACCORD—(*ASIDE*)—AT LEAST LET'S HOPE SO; I'VE NEVER DONE THIS TRICK BEFORE."

FIGURE 5.5. A Contemporary View (1920) of Lloyd George's Solution to the Irish Problem.
Source: Jones (1971, p. 231).

Central Tyrone is a region of considerable interest to the student of spatial organisation. Centred on Omagh town, it is a large upland area containing a sparse population. In the 1920s it was a distinct Nationalist area with over 60% of its population Roman Catholic, but also containing a sizeable Protestant minority. Although territorially large, the area is an enclave surrounded almost completely by Protestant majorities, from the Foyle lowlands in the north and west to the Erne and Blackwater lowlands in the south (Fig. 5.3). Because spatial frameworks should be economically and politically viable, central Tyrone posed problems. Its transfer to the Irish Free State could have been achieved only by the inclusion of Protestant areas to allow territorial contiguity and ensure a "corridor" link with the South. Such an arrangement would have led to problems of administration and security which could have become acute in times of civil unrest.

Finally, it is noteworthy that the Commission considered Northern Ireland underbounded in the north-west, despite the presence of the Catholic enclave of Londonderry city (Fig. 5.4).

With two new independent political systems eager to establish their own priorities, economic, social and administrative policies rapidly diverged north and south of the Border and the new division began to etch into the lives and minds of the people it now separated. The problems of pluralism which Northern Ireland had to face were undoubtedly emphasised by the unfortunate history of the Irish Boundary Commission. The failure of the Commission to relocate the Border was seen by the Roman Catholic population as treachery and blatant capitulation to the "not an inch" philosophy of the Northern Unionists. Irish Nationalist disbelief in the permanence of Partition in the 1920s, and indeed their implacable opposition to it subsequently, stems to an important degree from the view of Ireland as a natural territorial unit (an island) set apart by a natural boundary (the sea). The viewpoint that Ireland is geopolitically indivisible is illustrated in James Connolly's (1916) statement that:

> . . . the frontiers of Ireland, the ineffaceable marks of the separate existence of Ireland, are as old as Europe itself, the handiwork of the Almighty, not of politicians. And as the marks of Ireland's separate nationality were not made by politicians so they cannot be unmade by them. (MacAonghusa and Ó Réagain, 1967, p. 193)

From this viewpoint Partition ravaged the laws of nature for the short-sighted and subjective purposes of man (Heslinga, 1962). This view formed the cornerstone of much anti-Partition literature (Gallagher,

1956). That this geopolitical argument has held such sway in Ireland throughout the twentieth century, despite the growing emphasis on boundaries related to human desires and wishes begun at the Versailles Conference, testifies to the obduracy of the Border problem and the Irish inability to accept non-Irish precedents.

Partition, therefore, left Nationalists with a sense of injustice, doubly felt in the Border areas within Northern Ireland. The Northern Roman Catholic minority turned in upon itself in the search for self-sufficiency and abstention became, for its members, an honourable political course. It was perhaps not until 1949 when the Irish Free State became the Irish Republic and left the Commonwealth that the permanence of Partition was finally recognised in the South (Magee, 1974).

INTERNAL FRAMEWORKS (1): LOCAL GOVERNMENT

The importance of local government in any society is found in the control it has over the functions which have been delegated to it. In a divided society the power to allocate scarce resources in such areas as housing, education and welfare has increased significance. Local political control ensures "security" for the community which gains power and in the use (or misuse) of local powers are found strong forces for community integration or division.

In 1920 Northern Ireland inherited a well-established local government structure and framework: the structure of county boroughs and county councils (first-tier units) and urban and rural districts (second-tier units) was identical to that of the rest of the United Kingdom. The franchise was also similar, as was the general delegation of services between first- and second-tier units. Only the electoral method differed since the Westminster Government had introduced a form of proportional representation into Ireland in 1918 in an effort to ensure the best possible representation for unionist minorities throughout the island as a whole (Chubb, 1974).

The spatial framework of local government was established by the Local Government (Ireland) Act, 1898 and its pattern of urban and rural areas continued to form the basis for administration after 1920. The major characteristic of this framework was its continuity between 1920 and 1973 when reform took place; during this period the only changes were the removal of three small rural districts and the establishment of a number of urban districts. These changes were not controversial and provided no basis for community conflict. However, other changes in local frameworks, altogether more controversial, did take place. In 1922 the Northern Ireland Unionist Government passed the Local Government (Northern Ireland) Act. This act:

(i) Replaced proportional representation by the simple majority method of election, so returning to the British practice at local elections.

(ii) Altered the franchise by incorporating property ownership as a qualification for the vote. Later in the 1920s the franchise was changed again to introduce a company or business vote. This new franchise permitted all limited companies to nominate up to six electors, one for every £10 valuation of its premises.

(iii) Set out the means by which electoral redistricting could take place within the existing local government spatial framework. The electoral areas within county boroughs and urban districts were wards and, within counties and rural districts, district electoral divisions. These areas were to be investigated and, where deemed necessary, replaced by a new electoral spatial framework. To accomplish this task a Commissioner, appointed by the Northern Ireland Minister of Home Affairs, requested views and plans from interested local bodies, held hearings in local areas and subsequently announced his findings and recommendations.

Each of these changes produced an adverse reaction from the Roman Catholic minority. The removal of proportional representation was labelled a plot against minority rights; to the Unionists it was simply a matter of getting back into line with the rest of the United Kingdom. Bitterness was aroused by a new requirement that local councillors sign an oath of allegiance to the Crown. To the minority it was seen as a means of excluding from elections those opposed to the regime; to the Unionists, still in a grave state of constitutional insecurity, it seemed sensible to draw some sign of acceptance of the new system from those who wished to gain power in it.

In the new franchise regulations the property requirement and the company vote were believed by the minority to favour the Protestant community and certainly these regulations excluded a large number of potential voters, e.g. in 1924 registered local government electors (483 484) made up only 77% of registered Northern Ireland parliamentary electors (*Ulster Year Book 1926*). Lack of data makes it impossible to establish the extent, if any, to which franchise limitations discriminated against one or other community. Table 5.1 (a numerical reflection of Figs 5.2a and 5.2b) shows, however, that small changes in franchise could significantly affect the struggle for local political control. Data available for Londonderry city 1936–1937 (Table 5.2) show that limiting franchise regulations are most likely to depress the size of the majority vote, e.g. in South, West and Waterside Wards

TABLE 5.1. Northern Ireland: Population Characteristics in Marginal Local Government Areas, 1937.

	Roman Catholic population	Protestant population	Roman Catholic population over 21	Protestant population over 21	Numerical difference (over 21 populations)	Number of electoral divisions
Co. Antrim:						
Ballycastle U.D.	1348	861	732 (54·9%)	601	131	2
Ballycastle R.D.	4353	4618	2790 (47·6%)	3069	279	14
Co. Armagh:						
Armagh U.D.	4316	2928	2353 (56·1%)	1839	514	3
Co. Down:						
Downpatrick U.D.	2063	1310	1133 (57·1%)	851	282	1
Downpatrick R.D.	14 360	15 260	8895 (47·2%)	9948	1053	21
Newcastle U.D.	1139	1289	690 (42·1%)	950	260	1
Kilkeel R.D.	8535	6515	5201 (55·9%)	4109	1092	19
Co. Fermanagh:						
Enniskillen U.D.	2780	2100	1693 (54·4%)	1420	273	3
Enniskillen R.D.	8577	8499	5399 (50·1%)	5376	23	26
Irvinestown R.D.	6813	5944	4434 (53·1%)	3914	520	18
Co. Londonderry:						
Limavady R.D.	7392	7206	4247 (48·6%)	4499	252	23
Londonderry R.D.	7733	8138	4263 (46·0%)	5001	738	13
Magherafelt R.D.	16 688	14 405	10 314 (53·4%)	9004	1310	26
Co. Tyrone:						
Castlederg R.D.	5027	4778	3123 (51·8%)	2901	222	16
Clogher R.D.	5742	5832	3634 (49·1%)	3768	134	16
Cookstown R.D.	8244	7405	5001 (47·0%)	5638	637	16
Dungannon U.D.	2068	1862	1273 (51·6%)	1192	81	3
Dungannon R.D.	12 860	11 674	7852 (52·1%)	7223	629	19
Strabane R.D.	8730	8411	5255 (50·6%)	5126	129	28

Source: *Northern Ireland Census of Population 1937.*

TABLE 5.2. Londonderry: Population and Local Electoral Characteristics, 1936–1937.

Ward		Roman Catholic		Protestant		Majority	
East Ward	(a) Total Roman Catholic population	1798		(a) Total Protestant population	2964 $\frac{(b)}{(a)}=64\cdot6\%$	(i) Population majority over 21	819 (P)
	(b) Roman Catholic population over 21	1096 $\frac{(b)}{(a)}=61\cdot0\%$		(b) Protestant population over 21	1915	(ii) Electoral majority	831 (P)
	(c) Roman Catholics on local electoral register	643 $\frac{(c)}{(b)}=58\cdot7\%$		(c) Protestants on local electoral register	1474 $\frac{(c)}{(b)}=77\cdot0\%$	(iii) Difference	+12 (P)
North Ward	(a)	6752 $\frac{(b)}{(a)}=60\cdot0\%$		(a)	6230 $\frac{(b)}{(a)}=67\cdot9\%$	(i)	184 (P)
	(b)	4048 $\frac{(c)}{(b)}=53\cdot3\%$		(b)	4232 $\frac{(c)}{(b)}=62\cdot6\%$	(ii)	492 (P)
	(c)	2159		(c)	2651	(iii)	+308 (P)
South Ward	(a)	7072 $\frac{(b)}{(a)}=51\cdot4\%$		(a)	2365 $\frac{(b)}{(a)}=60\cdot8\%$	(i)	2195 (C)
	(b)	3633 $\frac{(c)}{(b)}=59\cdot3\%$		(b)	1438 $\frac{(c)}{(b)}=67\cdot0\%$	(ii)	1189 (C)
	(c)	2153		(c)	964	(iii)	−1006 (C)
West Ward	(a)	9087 $\frac{(b)}{(a)}=54\cdot7\%$		(a)	232 $\frac{(b)}{(a)}=71\cdot6\%$	(i)	4806 (C)
	(b)	4972 $\frac{(c)}{(b)}=62\cdot8\%$		(b)	166 $\frac{(c)}{(b)}=89\cdot8\%$	(ii)	2971 (C)
	(c)	3120		(c)	149	(iii)	−1835 (C)
Waterside Ward	(a)	4612 $\frac{(b)}{(a)}=55\cdot5\%$		(a)	6701 $\frac{(b)}{(a)}=60\cdot4\%$	(i)	1487 (P)
	(b)	2559 $\frac{(c)}{(b)}=52\cdot1\%$		(b)	4046 $\frac{(c)}{(b)}=56\cdot8\%$	(ii)	964 (P)
	(c)	1334		(c)	2298	(iii)	−523 (P)

Source: *Northern Ireland Census of Population 1937*; Curran (1946, p. 43).
(P) Protestant; (C) Roman Catholic.

where one community had a clear numerical majority. In the North and East Wards where the two communities were more evenly balanced, the limiting franchise favoured the Protestant vote. The advantage was marginal in East Ward, however, and while it was altogether more significant in North Ward, it is noteworthy that in neither instance did the franchise turn a population minority into an electoral majority. Table 5.2 does tend to show that, in Londonderry city at least, marked socio-economic differences in class necessary to give one community a persistently clear electoral advantage based on limitation of franchise did not exist.

Equally important in the voting struggle was the differential age structure of the two communities. In Limavady and Cookstown Rural Districts (Table 5.1) and in Londonderry North Ward (Table 5.2) a Roman Catholic population majority translated into an over twenty-one population minority because of a much younger age structure. Indeed, throughout Northern Ireland, the younger age structure served to reduce the size of the Catholic vote (Table 5.1).

The electoral redistricting which created the spatial framework within which all subsequent county and district government elections took place was by far the most significant piece of legislation resulting from the 1922 Act. It is doubtful if any other single legislative or political act during the early years of Northern Ireland's existence contributed so much to the distrust that increasingly separated the two communities. The Catholic minority has always viewed the 1922 local government redistricting as a widespread and blatant gerrymander which enabled the Unionists to take over power at local level, so supplementing control in the Northern Ireland Parliament and establishing an un-shakeable hegemony over the total territory of Northern Ireland (Figs 5.6a and 5.6b).

Gerrymandering occurs when electoral boundaries are drawn deliberately to favour one group at the expense of others. Boundaries can be located so that the group discriminated against cannot poll more than 49% in any two-group contest. In its ultimate form, this method can result in one party winning all constituencies with only 51% of the vote. A second method is to enclose one group into a small number of constituencies. This group will then win a few seats with massive majorities while the favoured group, with a larger number of constituencies, wins more seats with smaller majorities. Both methods frequently result in unusually shaped areas and contrived boundary locations (Osborne, 1977; Johnston, 1979).

In Northern Ireland there were real possibilities for partisan re-districting; clear-cut allegiances and residential segregation by religious

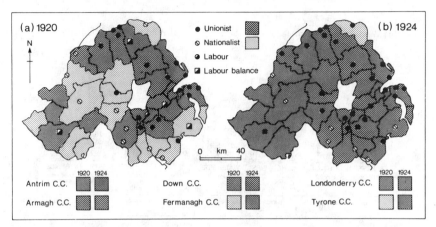

FIGURE 5.6. Political Control of Local Government: (a) 1920; (b) 1924. Results of early local government elections are widely scattered or lost–these maps have been compiled from data contained in: Elliott (1971); Gallagher (1956); Curran (1946); McCann (1974).

community in both urban and rural areas provided the ideal environment. That an electoral spatial framework with some degree of bias resulted from the 1922 reform is now generally accepted (Cameron, 1969) and Londonderry city, with its Nationalist and Unionist symbolism, is the clearest example of the gerrymander. Figure 5.7a shows the voting position within the five electoral wards in 1936; three wards (East, North and Waterside) had Unionist majorities and two wards contained Nationalist majorities (South and West). As each ward returned eight councillors, the Unionists controlled the city council with twenty-four seats to the Nationalists' sixteen. It was a biased electoral framework which ensured that a Nationalist electorate of 9409 was worth less than a Unionist vote of 7536. In 1936 this framework was removed and a new spatial pattern was introduced which reduced the wards from five to three and the number of seats on the city council from forty to twenty; however, with two Unionist wards (North and Waterside) and one Nationalist ward (South) the Unionists retained control of the council until 1969 (Fig. 5.7b). Nationalists saw the 1936 electoral reform as a refinement of an existing gerrymander, made necessary by the dangerously narrow and declining Unionist majority in North Ward (Curran, 1946; Table 5.2). This gerrymander employed the second method outlined above; by packing the Catholic Nationalist vote in one ward—South—the framework permitted the Unionists to gain control of two wards and win a majority in the council. In 1966, for example, 10 274 votes elected twelve Unionist representatives while 20 102 votes elected eight anti-Unionist councillors.

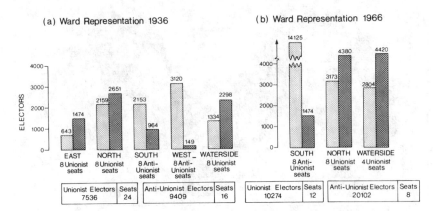

FIGURE 5.7. Local Government Representation in Londonderry, 1936 and 1966.
Source: Curran (1946); Campaign for Social Justice in Northern Ireland (1969).

Londonderry city is the classic case, oft quoted and easily translated in the Roman Catholic community mind to the rest of Northern Ireland. The exact extent of gerrymandering by the 1922 reform is not so easily established, however, as a detailed region-wide analysis of partisan representation is not possible. Population figures by religion for wards and district electoral divisions are not available after 1911, neither are age structures by religion, while figures for electorates are lost or scattered beyond recall. In the absence of such a study, strong suspicions of gerrymandering must be recognised in the critical areas of Fermanagh, Tyrone, south Armagh and south Down. These are the areas within which local authorities refused to recognise the legitimacy of the Northern Ireland Government in 1921 and 1922.[6] Figure 5.6b shows a definite extension of Unionist control after the 1923–1924 local elections; however, as the anti-Unionist literature often fails to note, the Nationalist Party in precisely these critical areas boycotted the elections and so could not have gained control whatever the spatial framework. Thus the exact extent to which Fig. 5.6b reflects the result of a Protestant gerrymander as opposed to a Catholic boycott will never be fully clarified; however, what is clear is that Unionist control of local government in the 1920s was facilitated greatly by the abstentionist policy of the Nationalist opposition. With unjustified confidence, the minority leaders sat back[7] and waited for the Irish Boundary Commission to fulfil the desired task of destroying the new Northern Ireland.

In the Unionist-controlled and inflexible local government political structure which resulted from the reform of the electoral framework the Nationalists perceived a co-ordinated anti-Roman Catholic strategy. Local government controlled public sector housing and provided important employment opportunities; such housing created local votes and employment led to a better standard of living. Houses built in properly selected areas could provide electoral security while job provision for the proper group could help maintain the population. Lack of housing and employment opportunity would encourage emigration, and differential emigration would help maintain the religious population balance in danger of being upset by a faster Catholic population growth rate (see Chapter 4; Compton, 1978). Inevitably, strong stereotyped images emerged: for example, the stereotyped Catholic view of Protestants is overwhelmingly that of power holders (O'Donnell, 1977).

The question, still familiar in Northern Ireland today in the search for power-sharing arrangements, was "How could a community which professed no allegiance to the political system and actively desired its removal be entrusted with power?" No state contributes knowingly to its own downfall and, to Unionists, the price of the Union was eternal vigilance against the anti-Partitionists. Such vigilance extended even to constant surveillance over and action against those within Unionist ranks who might "weaken" to the extent of placing socio-economic problems ahead of the constitutional issue. As is shown below, it was the fear of such a trend that led to the Unionist Government decision to reform the Northern Ireland (Stormont) electoral system in 1929 (see also Osborne, 1977).

Catholic community reactions against the inflexible political structure took several forms, the most important of which were:

(i) Emigration—made easy by long-standing, well-worn trails to North America and the larger cities of the United Kingdom (Barritt and Carter, 1962; Compton, 1978).

(ii) Opting out of the system—politically, this led to a large number of uncontested seats and a policy of abstention by successful Roman Catholic candidates (see Chapter 6). It also gave rise to a positive growth of many self-help organisations which were often focussed on the Roman Catholic Church (Griffiths, 1978).

(iii) Reaction against the system—since 1920 protest outside the law gave rise to civil unrest and, until 1969 when the present terrorist campaign began, sporadic terrorist activity. Peaceful protest has a less prominent history and came to the fore as a popular mass movement only in the 1960s with the Campaign for Civil Rights (Northern Ireland Civil Rights Association, 1978).

In the 1960s the local government structure came under increasing pressure. The civil rights campaign, aimed largely against local government practices, became allied to a growing recognition of the inefficiency of an outmoded administrative spatial framework which attempted to satisfy the twentieth century requirements of public service provision within a nineteenth century territorial pattern. Plans for the reform of local government, at first under the Northern Ireland Government and later under the control of Westminster, and the associated heated debate ran from 1966 to 1973 when a new spatial framework of twenty-six districts, based on the recommendations in the Macrory Report, 1970, was implemented (Fig. 5.8a). The new framework gave rise to few complaints of gerrymandering and local government elections since 1973 (a new electoral framework for the twenty-six districts was included in the reform) have resulted in revitalised electoral competition based on proportional representation and universal adult suffrage.

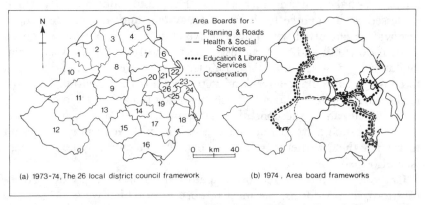

FIGURE 5.8. Administrative Areas in Northern Ireland. Local Government Districts: 1, Londonderry; 2, Limavady; 3, Coleraine; 4, Ballymoney; 5, Moyle; 6, Larne; 7, Ballymena; 8, Magherafelt; 9, Cookstown; 10, Strabane; 11, Omagh; 12, Fermanagh; 13, Dungannon; 14, Craigavon; 15, Armagh; 16, Newry and Mourne; 17, Banbridge; 18, Down; 19, Lisburn; 20, Antrim; 21, Newtownabbey; 22, Carrickfergus; 23, North Down; 24, Ards; 25, Castlereagh; 26, Belfast.

Is it possible that at last a spatial framework for local government, acceptable to both communities and defying the "Law of Contradiction" has been established? Unfortunately, such a conclusion is too simple. The spatial reorganisation was accompanied by a radical structural reform which effectively removed all important functions from the new districts. The tendentious issues such as housing provision, planning development and control, education and other social services, were taken from local control and centralised at Belfast, to be administered either by *ad hoc* bodies such as the Northern Ireland Housing Executive or by the former Northern Ireland government departments at Stormont. Thus the problems of conflict in local government were not solved by the implementation of a new, impartial spatial framework —rather, the solution was to remove administrative power from the local level and leave councillors with little about which to disagree.

It was soon apparent, however, that concentration of administrative functions at Stormont was creating problems of overcentralisation. Northern Ireland as a single unit was found to be too large for service provision and so a degree of administrative decentralisation took place as each department created a new spatial framework composed of units known as Area Boards (Fig. 5.8b). In this neat manoeuvre, traditional local government and its long-standing animosities were effectively by-passed. Under reform, however, Area Boards were composed predominantly of appointed individuals and not elected representatives; local interests were thus more easily controlled and professional administrators gained greater freedom in decision making. As the departments formulating overall administrative policies at Stormont have not been subject to scrutiny by elected regional representatives, i.e. the former members of the Stormont Parliament, since the implementation of Direct Rule from Westminster, it is clear that the community power struggle at local as well as regional level in Northern Ireland has not been solved but simply held in abeyance by the centralisation of decision making (Mitchel and Douglas, 1978).

Between 1922 and 1973 a carefully established spatial framework of local government electoral areas underpinned the narrow and inflexible political structure within which the Unionist majority safeguarded the constitutional position of Northern Ireland. The framework and the structure, however, added to the already deep feelings of antipathy in the Roman Catholic community, and prevented co-operation and integrative experiences between the two communities as part of the local administrative process. Social distance, more effective than any physical separation, encouraged the growth of stereotyped derogatory images and all local government activity became judged in terms of its consequences for each community. It was this situation which led to the limitation of representative local government in 1973. The partisan use of spatial frameworks in the past does perhaps indicate that the return of administrative power to a more local level in Northern Ireland at some future date, no matter how acceptable the spatial framework, will more easily encourage division than integration.

INTERNAL FRAMEWORKS (2): NORTHERN IRELAND (STORMONT) PARLIAMENTARY CONSTITUENCIES

The Government of Ireland Act (1920) provided Northern Ireland with a set of devolved powers and a regional parliament. The major components of the new system were a fifty-two member House of Commons, elected by proportional representation, and an electoral framework of multi-member constituencies based on the existing Westminster constituency framework. The vote was based on universal adult suffrage with a six-month Northern Ireland residence qualification. Second votes were given to occupiers of business premises and to graduates of the Queen's University, Belfast.[8] The system was guaranteed for three years after which the Northern Ireland Government, if it wished, could alter the electoral method and spatial framework, but not the number of seats.

Elections on this original basis were held in 1921 and 1925 and on each occasion the Unionists gained a clear majority (see Chapter 6, Table 6.1). Despite their majority, which was larger than expected (Colvin, 1936), the Unionist Government implemented major changes in the electoral method and framework prior to the 1929 election. Proportional representation was replaced by the simple majority voting system within a new spatial framework of forty-eight single-member constituencies (Chapter 6, Fig. 6.1). Predictably, the reform brought strong reaction from anti-unionist groups (Curran, 1946; Gallagher, 1956). Criticism was on three main grounds: the removal of proportional representation discriminated against nationalist minority representation; the procedure by which the reform was carried out was underhand and aimed at ensuring unionist parliamentary advantage; the new electoral spatial framework comprised a series of biased territorial units which amounted to a widespread gerrymander.

The electoral changes certainly had effects upon the 1929 election results (Chapter 6, Table 6.2). Their nature, however, hardly supported the nationalist minority claims of a widespread gerrymander; rather, the main losers were the smaller groups with socialist-inclined policies, e.g. the Independent Unionists and the Northern Ireland Labour Party. The 1929 reform was aimed primarily at wayward Unionists who were willing to give priority to matters other than the constitutional position. Single-member constituencies and majority voting reduced flexibility in voting choice and placed the constitutional position of Northern Ireland as the persistent and overwhelming issue (see Chapter 6).

Because the new constituency framework was created, not by inde-

pendent commission and public participation but by the Unionist
Cabinet, strongly led by Prime Minister Craigavon, formal principles of
redistricting are not to be found. However, it is clear that the boundaries
of the new constituencies were drawn to accord with county and
Westminster constituency boundaries. In each county single-member
constituencies were delimited to meet the population quota for that
county. Thus the distribution of seats reflected the existing allocation
of seats by county before reform—except in the west of Northern Ireland
where, prior to 1929, the counties of Fermanagh and Tyrone formed one
multi-member constituency with eight seats. In the reform, these two
counties were separated, Tyrone being awarded five seats and Fermanagh three. It is concerning the spatial arrangement of the three
Fermanagh constituencies that the strongest claims of gerrymandering
occur.[9]

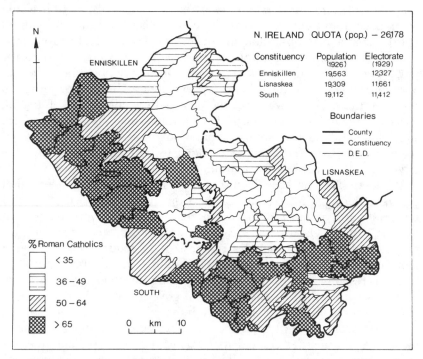

FIGURE 5.9. Northern Ireland Parliament Electoral Reform, 1929: Fermanagh Constituencies.
Source: Osborne (1979)·

Redistricting created one constituency, South Fermanagh, which
covered the south and south-west of the county and enclosed the areas

of Catholic majority population. The other two constituencies comprised the remainder of the county and were delimited by a north-south boundary which separated Enniskillen constituency in the west from Lisnaskea constituency in the east (Fig. 5.9). This redistricting was based on a "packing" gerrymander whereby South Fermanagh became a Nationalist seat with a large majority while Enniskillen and Lisnaskea became Unionist seats with relatively slender majorities[10] (Osborne, 1979). Other areas in which the objectivity of the 1929 redistricting have been questioned are County Armagh, Londonderry city and County Antrim. County Armagh, with a population which was 54·5% Protestant in 1926, was redistricted to give one Nationalist and three Unionist seats. In County Antrim the Nationalist population lost its representation because of its scattered nature. Ballycastle Urban and Rural Districts had the largest concentration of Catholic population (11 433) but with a county constituency quota of 27 378 it would have been impossible to create a Nationalist constituency without massive spatial discrimination and distortion of shape. In Londonderry, a number of district electoral divisions (D.E.D.s) were added to the city and two constituencies were set out. One, Foyle, became a Nationalist constituency and the other, City, enclosed a Unionist majority. In this case the problem was that the city, with a population of 45 159, was too large to form one constituency but too small on its own to form two, the Londonderry county population quota being 26 558. Consequently the extra D.E.D.s were added to both east and west of the city to give the required population.

While in the one specific instance of Fermanagh it is clear that gerrymandering occurred and in others the quality of redistricting may be questioned, it must be accepted that, as recent work has shown (Elliott, 1971; Osborne, 1977), no widespread gerrymander was perpetrated in 1929. Nationalist response to the redistricting was based more on emotion than objective calculation (Chapter 6, Table 6.2). Such a response is perhaps not surprising in the environment of suspicion bequeathed by the 1923 local government redistricting.

More serious for inter-community interaction was the effect of the new system on electoral behaviour. Simple majority voting in single-member constituencies created a rigid and entirely predictable electoral system. Nationalist and Unionist heartlands were quickly recognised (Chapter 6, Fig. 6.3); voting strengths and weaknesses became clear in every constituency and intervention by the voting minority ceased. In the elections between 1929 and 1969, seldom more than half the constituencies experienced an electoral contest; the high points in activity occurred in 1945 and 1949 when twenty-eight of the forty-eight territorial constituencies were contested. Overall, only nineteen of the forty-eight constituencies were contested more than five times in ten general elections. In these ten elections the Unionist Party won an average of thirty-four seats and never less than thirty-one seats (see Chapter 6). Small parties ceased to be of any significance and the scope for political change was non-existent.

In the Roman Catholic community view, regional government and local government were the means whereby Unionists maintained a hegemony of dubious legitimacy over Northern Ireland. In the Unionist view, it was right and proper that the majority should hold the reins of power. The "Law of Contradiction" held firm and regional government provided few opportunities for inter-community contact and integrative experience in decision making.

INTERNAL FRAMEWORKS (3): THE UNITED KINGDOM (WESTMINSTER) PARLIAMENTARY CONSTITUENCIES

The spatial framework of Northern Ireland's twelve Westminster constituencies lost much of its importance when the Stormont Parliament was established. The powers reserved by Westminster—such as defence, foreign affairs, customs and excise and direct taxation—were either far removed from the ordinary citizen or spatially undifferentiated and therefore beyond specifically regional and sub-regional reaction. Also, as the framework has hardly altered since 1920, conflict has not been aroused by the problems of redistricting. With simple majority voting in single-member constituencies the electoral returns have consistently paralleled the rigidity of the Stormont elections. Religious majorities meant electoral majorities and, with few marginal constituencies, the greatest conflict arose within each community about the choice of candidates. Two candidates from within the same community causing a split vote usually meant handing the seat to the unified opposition. Not unexpectedly, a majority of Unionist M.P.s[11] has always been returned to Westminster, their primary duty being to watch over and defend Northern Ireland's constitutional position.

The demise of the Stormont Parliament and the onset of Direct Rule in 1972 increased greatly the attention and interest given in Northern Ireland to Westminster matters as the twelve Westminster M.P.s, of necessity, took on the added task of dealing with local and sub-regional affairs. The establishment of the Northern Ireland Parliament in 1920 had been accompanied by the principle of reduced representation at Westminster as a counterbalance to increased regional representation:

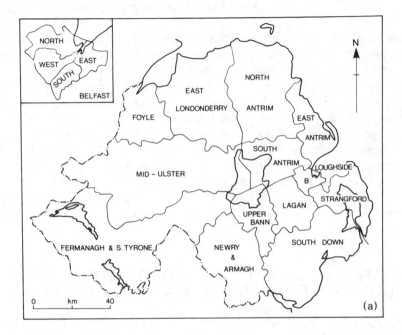

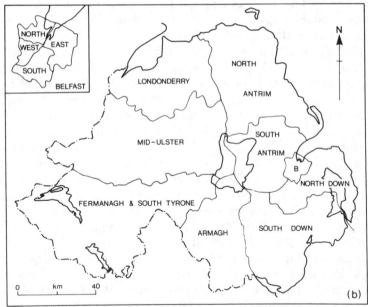

FIGURE 5.10. Westminster Constituencies: (a) The Seventeen-Constituency Framework Proposed by the Boundary Commission for Northern Ireland, 1980; (b) The Existing Twelve-Constituency Framework, 1980.

Northern Ireland was awarded twelve seats instead of the eighteen which it would have had if the United Kingdom population constituency quota had been applied. The removal of the Stormont Parliament, therefore, also removed the basis for the principle of reduced Westminster representation and, in a considered response to the Unionist call for increased representation, the Speaker's Conference on Electoral Law (Prime Minister's Office, 1978) recommended that Northern Ireland should have seventeen seats. The spatial framework containing the seventeen proposed constituencies was set out by the Boundary Commission for Northern Ireland, 1980. Whereas the twelve-constituency framework breaks down to give four western, four eastern and four Belfast constituencies, the seventeen-unit framework proposes five western, eight eastern and four Belfast constituencies (Fig. 5.10), thereby giving recognition to the continued growth and concentration of population in the Greater Belfast region (see Chapter 4).

Recent analysis of the proposed seventeen-constituency framework (Douglas and Osborne, 1981) indicates that the minority community would be likely to win five of the seventeen seats (i.e. three seats in the west, one seat in the east and one seat in Belfast), so increasing its relative level of representation. However, as Fig. 5.2b suggests, all five western constituencies will be marginal in terms of inter-community voting. The proposed framework has aroused some hostile reaction, particularly from the Democratic Unionist Party; however, tests for malapportionment and equality of representation reinforce the view that the Boundary Commission, given its terms of reference, carried out the redistricting exercise in an objective manner. The effects of the proposed framework, which will probably be implemented in 1981, will be variable at different political levels. At Westminster, the arrival of five extra Members of Parliament from Northern Ireland will have negligible significance: in Northern Ireland, however, the new framework will further increase the political interest and activity already aroused by the demise of Stormont. Given the marginality of a number of constituencies in the proposed framework, the redistricting will not remove but may reinforce traditional voting behaviour and group electoral rivalry which reflect and sustain the deep political cleavage found in Northern Ireland.

CONCLUSION

As this chapter shows, spatial frameworks in Northern Ireland have influenced greatly the political structure of the region. The minority community has complained consistently that the administrative and electoral frameworks established by the Unionist Government, primarily in 1923 and 1929, created a closed political structure, reduced accountability and limited minority participation in the decision-making process. This view has had direct effects upon minority group attitudes and behaviour towards local and regional government.

The question remains, however, of whether and to what extent frameworks perceived as more objective would have led to greater inter-community interaction and integration. This is a hypothetical question, yet important to consider in terms of possible future devolution of power back to a regional or sub-regional level in Northern Ireland. It is not clear what the effect of wider minority representation in government would have been in the 1920s, given the already soured political climate and the unhappy history of the Irish Boundary Commission. More acceptable frameworks could have removed specific grievances but it is unlikely that they would have reversed national values and the desire for the removal of Partition by the minority. Nationalist control in the peripheral local government areas of Northern Ireland could well have led to increased tension as local government–regional government conflict would have made necessary the more widespread removal of dissident local councils and their replacement by Unionist-appointed Local Government Commissioners. Such a likelihood exposes the limitation of using spatial frameworks as a means of encouraging inter-community integration.

Spatial frameworks can provide the opportunities for participation and interaction; communities decide whether such opportunities are grasped and used positively. In a two-segment society, both communities must accept and work within the spatial frameworks if a basis for consociational democracy is to exist. Political integration is composed of many strands and achieved by toleration of differences over a wide range of human activities and, with the "Law of Contradiction" at work in Northern Ireland, it is unlikely that electoral and administrative frameworks which did provide opportunities for participation by the minority would have led, on their own, to integrative interaction. Without doubt, however, the electoral and administrative frameworks established in Northern Ireland between 1923 and 1973 did much to create an environment in which cultural and political divisions prospered at the expense of inter-community understanding and tolerance.

NOTES

1. In this chapter the term "spatial framework" is used to refer to the many territorial units into which the area of the state is sub-divided for the purposes of administration and electoral representation.

2. Consociational democracy is a political state in which the centrifugal tendencies inherent in a plural society are counteracted by the co-operative attitudes and behaviour of the leaders of the different segments of the population (Lijphart, 1977).

3. Boundary is the correct political term; in this chapter, however, "Border" is substituted, being the term used in Ireland as a whole to describe the line of partition.

4. The use of the concept of economic viability in Article XII of the Anglo-Irish Treaty shows the extent to which the Treaty makers, both north and south of the partition line, were thinking of Northern Ireland as a separate territory. If Northern Ireland had been viewed as an integral part of the larger United Kingdom, its economic viability would have been related to the overall economic viability of the total country. The view of Northern Ireland as a place apart remains to the present, despite the removal of the principle of separate economic viability by the favourable flow of financial aid from the United Kingdom Government.

5. Townlands are amongst the most ancient divisions in Ireland and originally comprised a number of ploughlands. They are the smallest recognised territorial units in rural areas.

6. The local governments which refused to recognise the authority of the Northern Ireland Government were: Fermanagh County Council, Armagh Urban District, Downpatrick Rural District, Lisnaskea Rural District, Cookstown Rural District, Magherafelt Rural District, Strabane Rural District, Warrenpoint Urban District, Newry No. 1 Rural District, Newry No. 2 Rural District, Newry Urban District, Keady Urban District, Kilkeel Rural District and Downpatrick Town Commissioners. These local governments were thus dissolved and each placed under the control of a Commissioner. Tyrone County Council, Armagh Rural District and Strabane Urban District at first repudiated the authority of the Northern Ireland Government, but subsequently reversed their decision (Elliott, 1971).

7. The extent of Nationalist inaction is shown very clearly by the lack of contemporary literature and detailed analysis on the nature and consequences of the 1922 reform. Only Omagh Rural District Council set out statistical evidence which was then used to claim a gerrymandered electoral redistribution (Elliott, 1971).

8. The business vote, unlike the company vote, at local government level produced little reaction during its existence. It never reached as much as 2% of the total vote and there is evidence to suggest that it never significantly altered the result of an election in any constituency (Osborne, 1977).

Between 1921 and 1938 the University electors consistently returned Unionists to the four seats. From 1945 to 1968 each election produced one or two Independents to accompany two or three Unionist members.

9. The award of three seats to Fermanagh was highly contentious in the first place. Strict application of the Northern Ireland population quota would have given Fermanagh two seats, with the other seat going to either

Antrim or Londonderry, both of whom had a larger population surplus in excess of seats awarded.

10. In 1926 the Catholic community made up 56·1% of the total population of Fermanagh. It is not possible to break down the population by age as well as religion from the 1926 Census of Northern Ireland; however, given the younger age structure in the Catholic community, it is likely that Nationalist voters made up rather less than 56·1%.

11. In Westminster general elections between 1922 and 1970 the most frequent breakdown in Northern Ireland was ten Unionist and two Nationalist/anti-Unionist M.P.s (Craig, 1971).

REFERENCES

Andrews, J. H. (1968). The Papers of the Irish Boundary Commission. *Irish Geography* **5,** 477–481.

Barritt, D. P. and Carter, C. F. (1962). "The Northern Ireland Problem: A Study in Group Relations." Oxford University Press, London.

Boundary Commission for Northern Ireland (1980). "Third General Review: Provisional Recommendations." Her Majesty's Stationery Office, Belfast.

Cameron, Lord (1969). "Disturbances in Northern Ireland: Report of the Commission Appointed by the Governor of Northern Ireland" (Cmd. 532). Her Majesty's Stationery Office, Belfast.

Campaign for Social Justice in Northern Ireland (1969). "The Plain Truth." Campaign for Social Justice in Northern Ireland, Dungannon.

Census of Ireland 1911. His Majesty's Stationery Office, London.

Chubb, B. (1974). "The Government and Politics of Ireland." Oxford University Press, London.

Colvin, I. D. (1936). "The Life of Lord Carson," III. Gollancz, London.

Compton, P. A. (1978). "Northern Ireland: A Census Atlas." Gill and Macmillan, Dublin.

Craig, F. W. S. (1971). "British Parliamentary Election Statistics 1918–1970." Political Reference Publications, Chichester.

Curran, F. (1946). "Ireland's Fascist City." Derry Journal, Londonderry.

Douglas, J. N. H. (1976). The Irreconcilable Border. *Geographical Magazine* **49,** 162–168.

Douglas, J. N. H. and Osborne, R. D. (1981). Northern Ireland: Increased Representation in the Westminster Parliament. *Irish Geography* **14** (forthcoming).

Elliott, S. (1971). "The Electoral System in Northern Ireland since 1920." Unpublished Ph.D. Thesis, Queen's University, Belfast.

Gallagher, F. (1956). "The Indivisible Island." Gollancz, London.

Griffiths, H. (1978). Community Reaction and Voluntary Involvement. *In* "Violence and the Social Services in Northern Ireland" (J. Darby and A. Williamson, eds.), pp. 165–200. Heinemann, London.

Hand, S. J. (1969). "Report of the Irish Boundary Commission 1925." Irish University Press, Shannon.

Heslinga, M. (1962). "The Irish Border as a Cultural Divide." Van Gorcum, Assen.

Jacob, P. E. and Toscano, J. V. (1964). "The Integration of Political Communities." Lippincott, Philadelphia.

Johnston, R. J. (1979). "Political, Electoral and Spatial Systems." Clarendon Press, Oxford.

Jones, E. (1960). Problems of Partition and Segregation in Northern Ireland. *Conflict Resolution* **4**, 96–105.

Jones, M. W. (1971). "The Cartoon History of Britain." Tom Stacey, London.

Lijphart, A. (1977). "Democracy in Plural Societies." Yale University Press, New Haven, Connecticut.

MacAonghusa, P. and Ó Réagain, L., eds. (1967). "The Best of Connolly." Mercier Press, Cork.

Macrory, P. A. (1970). "Review Body on Local Government in Northern Ireland: Report" (Cmd. 546). Her Majesty's Stationery Office, Belfast.

Magee, J. (1974). "Northern Ireland: Crisis and Conflict." Routledge and Kegan Paul, London.

McCann, E. (1974). "War and an Irish Town." Penguin, Harmondsworth.

Mitchel, N. C. and Douglas, J. N. H. (1978). Devolution and the U.K.: The Northern Ireland Paradox. *Geographical Magazine* **51**, 113–117.

Morrill, R. L. (1973). Ideal and Reality in Reapportionment. *Annals of the Association of American Geographers* **63**, 463–477.

Neuman, S. G., ed. (1976). "Small States and Segmented Societies." Praeger, New York.

Northern Ireland Census of Population 1926. His Majesty's Stationery Office, Belfast.

Northern Ireland Census of Population 1937. His Majesty's Stationery Office, Belfast.

Northern Ireland Civil Rights Association (1978). "We Shall Overcome . . ." Northern Ireland Civil Rights Association, Belfast.

O'Donnell, E. E. (1977). "Northern Irish Stereotypes." College of Industrial Relations, Dublin.

Osborne, R. D. (1977). "The Political System, Voting Patterns and Voting Behaviour in Northern Ireland 1921–1974." Unpublished Ph.D. Thesis, Queen's University, Belfast.

Osborne, R. D. (1979). The Northern Ireland Parliamentary Electoral System: The 1929 Reapportionment. *Irish Geography* **12**, 42–56.

Prime Minister's Office (1978). "Mr. Speaker's Conference on Electoral Law" (Cmnd. 7110). Her Majesty's Stationery Office, London.

Rabushka, A. and Shepsle, K. A. (1972). "Politics in Plural Societies: A Theory of Democratic Instability." Merrill, Columbus, Ohio.

Ulster Year Book 1926. His Majesty's Stationery Office, Belfast.

Walker, B. M. (1977). "Parliamentary Election Results in Ireland, 1801–1922." Royal Irish Academy, Dublin.

CHAPTER 6

VOTING BEHAVIOUR IN NORTHERN IRELAND 1921-1977

Robert D. Osborne

INTRODUCTION

All governments seek the voluntary acquiescence of citizens to political decisions and activity. The most frequent means adopted to secure such acquiescence and to legitimate the political system are mass elections. Elections, when held under fair rules, enable members of a polity to endorse the formal political structure and to articulate demands to government. No political system is, however, socially homogeneous; rather each is characterised by conflict between groups and areas with the conflict manifested as cleavages within the political community. In this situation, political parties can be viewed as both the reflectors of past cleavages and the representation of current conflicts. Scrutiny of election results enables measurement of the level and distribution of the acceptance of the political system and the nature and salience of cleavages. The measurement of political party performance through the mapping of election results and the analysis of the basis of electoral behaviour can therefore provide an important method of evaluating the degree of integration or division in the system.

Voting can be seen as a process involving information gathering, perceptions, attitudes and values leading to decisions about whether to vote or abstain, and the partisan destination of the vote. Once voting is complete, however, the aggregate pattern of results becomes more than a passive reflector. It sets in motion actions and interactions which are strongly integrative or divisive and provide a new political balance in which new strategies and decisions evolve.

The primary concern of this chapter is to focus on voting behaviour as an indicator and reflector of the degree of integration in Northern

137

Ireland. This aim is pursued through the mapping of aggregate voting patterns and transfer analysis and the evidence is then used to construct an "ideological space" model for Northern Ireland. The second part of the chapter concentrates on the period 1965–1977 and charts events associated with the political turmoil of the 1965–1969 period and the attempts of the British Government to derive a "solution" to the conflict. Central to these events have been the use of the ballot box and the role of elections.

THE EARLY YEARS: 1921–1925

The Government of Ireland Act of 1920 provided that the six counties of north-east Ireland should remain within the United Kingdom and politically separate from the rest of Ireland. Northern Ireland retained representation at Westminster (Osborne, 1976) and a devolved legislature was set up in Belfast.

The first election to the new parliament in Belfast was held in 1921 and, as provided for in the Government of Ireland Act, was conducted by proportional representation (single transferable vote)—hereinafter P.R. (stv)—on the framework of the existing nine territorial and one university Westminster constituencies. These constituencies acted as multi-member constituencies with a total of forty-eight territorial and four university seats. The first election was fought virtually as a referendum on the right of Northern Ireland to exist as a political entity separate from the rest of Ireland. The Unionists crystallised the election as a "plebiscite of the people of the Six Counties . . . who is for the Empire and who for a Republic?" (*Belfast Newsletter*, 26 April 1921), whereas the Nationalists emphasised the moral character of their campaign "to rescue north-east Ulster" (*Irish News*, 11 May 1921) and held to a belief that Northern Ireland could not be economically self-sufficient and so Partition would be a temporary phenomenon. The intensity of the concentration on this issue forced most Labour and Independent candidates with other political priorities to withdraw. The partisan distribution of first preference votes is shown in Table 6.1.

The Unionist Party, by capturing two-thirds of first preferences and a majority of votes in all constituencies except in Fermanagh-Tyrone, clearly demonstrated the existence and size of the majority wishing to retain the link with Great Britain. This first election also demonstrated that the new political entity contained a substantial minority, capable of obtaining one-third of the total vote, which both rejected the British link and the political entity designed to maintain that link. This basic pattern underpins the electoral history of Northern Ireland.

TABLE 6.1. Results of the 1921 and 1925 Northern Ireland General Elections.

Party	First preferences		Percentage		Uncontested territorial seats		Total territorial seats		Q.U.B. seats	
	1921	1925	1921	1925	1921	1925	1921	1925	1921	1925
Unionist	341 622	211 852	66·9	55·0	—	6	36	28	4	4
Independent Unionist	—	34 716	—	9·0	—	—	—	4	—	—
N.I.L.P.	—	18 114	—	4·7	—	—	—	3	—	—
Independent Labour	3075	—	0·6	—	—	—	—	—	—	—
Nationalist	60 577	91 152	11·8	23·8	—	1	6	10	—	—
Sinn Fein	104 617	—	20·5	—	—	—	6	—	—	—
Republican	—	20 615	—	5·3	—	1	—	2	—	—
Independent	926	8286	0·2	2·2	—	—	—	1	—	—

Q. U. B.: Queen's University, Belfast. Source: Calculated from Elliott (1973).

By 1925, Partition was a less immediate issue although the Irish Boundary Commission, set up in 1924, had commenced its work considering the future spatial extent of Northern Ireland (see Chapter 5). Many nationalists in Northern Ireland and the authorities in the Irish Free State believed that the Boundary Commission would recommend the transfer of so much of Northern Ireland to the Free State that the rump could not survive as an economic unit. The Border, however, remained an important political issue, particularly in the western areas where unionists and nationalists were of roughly equal strength. The Nationalist Party sought to defeat Republicanism and become the sole party representing anti-Partitionists in Northern Ireland. In the Free State, Sinn Fein had split into pro- and anti-Treaty forces and in the North the anti-Treaty position was represented by the Republicans.[1] For the unionists, however, the pattern of opposition included the newly formed Northern Ireland Labour Party (N.I.L.P.),[2] with candidates in three of the Belfast seats, Independent Unionists in each of the four Belfast seats and two independent Tenants' Association candidates. This opposition which sought to present a variety of socio-economic issues to the electorate was strong enough to resist Unionist Party calls for a united front.

The results shown in Table 6.1 indicate that, although the Unionists were still the dominant party, eight seats were lost. Three of these were taken by the N.I.L.P., four by the Independent Unionists and one by a Tenants' Association candidate. The seats lost were, with a single exception, in the Belfast constituencies (the T. A. candidate was elected in Antrim). The results of the 1925 election were regarded by the Unionists, if not as a defeat, at least as a dangerous trend. The growth of Labour and Independent parliamentary representation, emphasising socio-economic issues, was assisted by the P.R. (stv) electoral system. Thus the alteration of the electoral system already carried out for local government (see Chapter 5) came to the forefront of Unionist thinking.

The change from P.R. (stv) and multi-member constituencies to the plurality system with single-member constituencies was undertaken in 1929. This framework, which consisted of forty-eight territorial constituencies (and four university seats elected by P.R. (stv)), provided the basis for elections until marginally altered for the 1969 election (Fig. 6.1). The pattern of constituencies created is examined for gerrymandering in Chapter 5, and although the constituencies in Fermanagh seem to have been designed to further partisan advantage (see also Osborne, 1979), there is no convincing evidence of widespread gerrymandering or malapportionment. Significantly, however, the belief that the new framework was gerrymandered entered into the everyday political language of the Nationalists (Gallagher, 1957). Thus the change of electoral system primarily aimed at restricting the Independents and Labour groups became part of the grievances held by the Nationalists against the Unionist Government. In this sense the change in electoral system acted to sustain and deepen the political cleavage. Moreover, the potential offered by P.R. (stv) for blurring the cleavage, by promoting cross-voting through transfers, was removed, in order to provide a system which, as the Prime Minister, Lord Craigavon, stated, would display "where men are for the Union on the one hand or against it and want to go into a Dublin parliament on the other" (*House of Commons Debates (Northern Ireland)* 8 (1927), 2275).

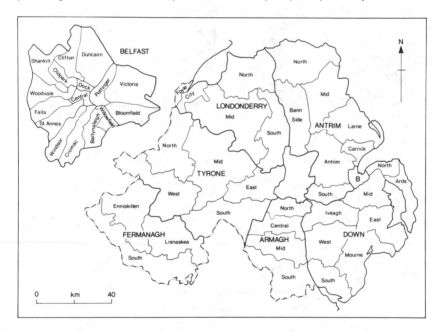

FIGURE 6.1. Northern Ireland (Stormont) Parliamentary Constituencies, 1929–1969.

The first election held on the new framework was in 1929. Anti-Partition groups were opposed to the abolition of P.R. (stv) and considered the new framework to be gerrymandered. They were nevertheless anxious to test their organisation in the new constituencies. The Unionists were still experiencing dissatisfaction from their supporters over education policy and temperance and the Independent Unionists were keen to represent these and other issues of dissent (Akenson, 1973).

TABLE 6.2. Results of the 1929 Northern Ireland General Election.

	Votes	Percentage	Uncontested seats	Total territorial seats	Q.U.B. seats
Unionist	147 099	50·6	16	34	3
Independent Unionist	41 336	14·3	—	2	1
N.I.L.P.	23 333	8·0	—	1	—
Independent Labour	2442	0·8	—	—	—
Nationalist	37 663	13·0	6	11	—
Independent	16 677	5·8	—	—	—
Liberal	21 645	7·5	—	—	—

Source: Calculated from Elliott (1973).

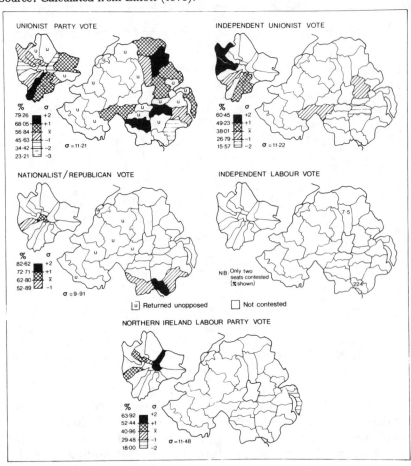

FIGURE 6.2. Northern Ireland (Stormont) Parliamentary Election, 1929: Distribution of Votes by Party.

The distribution and pattern of votes cast can be seen in Table 6.2 and Fig. 6.2.

There were three important features of this election. The first was the high proportion of uncontested seats. No less than twenty-two of the forty-eight territorial constituencies returned unopposed candidates, sixteen taken by the Unionists and six by the Nationalists. The second feature was the decline in turnout in contested seats from 76% to 67%. The final feature concerned the disproportionate share of seats gained by Unionists compared to their share of the vote, while the N.I.L.P. and Independent Unionists won fewer seats than their share of the total vote indicated. This increase in the disproportionality of the election is reflected in the difference index (D.I.) (Loosemore and Hanby, 1971). The scores shown in Table 6.3 demonstrate that distortion in the votes–seats relationship increased with the change to a plurality system.

TABLE 6.3. Distortion in Votes–Seats Relationship, 1929–1938
(the Difference Index).[a]

Election	D.I.
1921	0·101
1925	0 083
1929	0·301
1933	0·302
1938	0·293

[a]The difference index is a summary measure of distortion with higher scores indicating greater distortion.

Thus by removing P.R. (stv) and replacing it with the simple plurality system the Unionists achieved their aim of disadvantaging the smaller political groupings.

1929–1965

The 1929–1965 period involved nine general elections which can be conveniently considered *en bloc*. While each election produced some distinctive issues of its own, none were sufficiently overriding to alter the main characteristics of the electoral pattern across Northern Ireland.

In terms of vote shares and seats the Unionists and Nationalists remained the dominant parties throughout this period. The former was never challenged for supremacy in terms of seats (including those taken unopposed) and the latter was consistently the second largest party. The important characteristics of the electoral pattern are its stability through time showing two virtually discrete territories (Fig. 6.3).

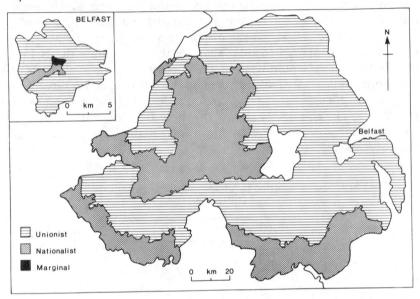

FIGURE 6.3. Northern Ireland (Stormont) Parliamentary Elections, 1929–1965: Unionist and Nationalist Pattern of Support.

Only in the Mourne constituency did the two territories overlap. Here the Unionists persistently opposed the Nationalists although never winning the seat. In the 1949 election which coincided with the Irish Government's world-wide anti-Partition campaign, both Unionists and Nationalists intervened in the other party's territory but this was not repeated in subsequent elections. On the other hand, in 1938, the abstentionist policy of the Nationalists meant that the party's pattern of intervention was curtailed. In rural areas, excluding the Mourne constituency, the Unionist pattern of support ($>50\%$) is co-terminous with that of electoral intervention. In Belfast, Unionist intervention included fourteen of the sixteen constituencies (Falls and Central were omitted) and in these support varied quite substantially between elections. In Woodvale the Unionist share of the vote varied between $33\cdot1\%$ and $54\cdot7\%$ and in Willowfield from $35\cdot5\%$ to $87\cdot5\%$. South Belfast as a whole produced consistently high Unionist support with

Ballynafeigh, Cromac, Windsor, St. Anne's and Bloomfield returning a Unionist at each election. Less consistent support was evident in the Clifton and Duncairn constituencies in the north of the city while Pottinger and Victoria in the east and Oldpark in the north all recorded several Unionist defeats. Shankill in the west was solidly Unionist from 1953 onwards although Woodvale was never a safe Unionist seat.

The Nationalist pattern of intervention is also easily demarcated. In rural areas the constituencies of South Armagh, South Down, Mourne, South Fermanagh, Foyle, Mid Londonderry and East, West and Mid Tyrone formed the normal pattern of intervention. This pattern, reflecting strong Nationalist support, is spatially fragmented and peripheral to the Unionist "core". Until 1945 the Nationalists also intervened in the Falls and Central seats in Belfast but conceded them to anti-Partitionist Labour groups after that date. Thereafter it became an exclusively non-Belfast party with its support showing close spatial coincidence with the distribution of religious affiliation (Chapter 4, Fig. 4.2).

The unshakeable characteristics of this basic pattern are revealed by the fact that in 111 constituency elections in rural areas only thirty-five (31·5%) involved Unionist–Nationalist contests. More revealing, however, is that these thirty-five contests represent only 12·1% of the total possible contests in rural areas.[3] These patterns of intervention and support contrast strongly with the British two-party system of the period where the parties competed over the entire electoral space, with areas of particular party dominance. In Northern Ireland, areas of partisan strength were recognised and intervention was tailored accordingly. The stability of these patterns in the 1929–1965 period demonstrates the extent to which political attitudes and preferences were regarded as fixed and immutable by the two main parties.[4] Frequency distributions of the vote shares of the two parties underline the characteristics of the patterns (Fig. 6.4). For the Nationalists the distribution is U-shaped with the overwhelming feature being the high number of seats left uncontested, reflecting the failure to regard the entire electoral space as valid for intervention. The modal vote share is 50–55%. The Unionist vote pattern is also U-shaped although the returned unopposed "tail" is more significant. The Unionist modal category is 60–65% although there is a broad plateau from 45% to 70%.

While both main parties tended to avoid each other electorally, both were challenged by smaller parties and groups. This was particularly so in Belfast where the Unionists were opposed by two main groups: Independent Unionists and the N.I.L.P. The Independent

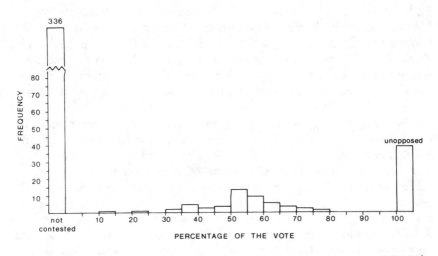

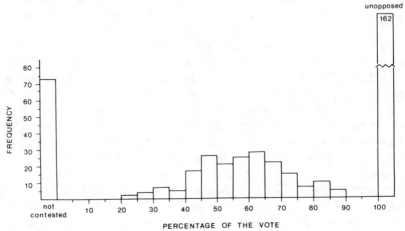

Figure 6.4. Northern Ireland (Stormont) Parliamentary Elections, 1929–1965: (a) Frequency Distribution of Nationalist Vote Shares (above); (b) Frequency Distribution of Unionist Vote Shares (below).

Unionists, who supported the political link with Britain, did not form a political party but attained coherence through their opposition to the Unionist Party on a range of socio-economic issues. Independent Unionist activity was limited geographically, the most widespread electoral intervention being that of the Progressive Unionists who gained 12·9% of the vote in 1938 but won no seats. The most consistent Independent Unionist areas of strength were in Protestant working-class west Belfast where Henderson held Shankill from 1929 to 1953 and Nixon Woodvale from 1929 to 1949. Elsewhere, Independent Unionists were variously represented by advocates of reform in social policy; their spatial intervention is restricted to areas of Unionist domination and the group never sought to act as surrogates for Unionists in Nationalist constituencies. Thus only a limited section of the electoral space was considered valid for intervention.

The Labour movement in Northern Ireland during this period suffered from internal conflict over Partition which culminated in a formal split into the pro-Partition N.I.L.P. and the anti-Partition Labour groups in 1949. In the pre-war period the N.I.L.P. fought in both pro- and anti-Partitionist areas, tending to nominate candidates of appropriate constitutional views in each constituency. Although it strove to put social and economic issues before the electorate, the party was constantly required to make sectarian calculations. The N.I.L.P. was almost exclusively a Belfast-based party (it never won either of the two Londonderry urban constituencies, never contesting Foyle and contesting the City constituency only once) and after 1949 contested only Unionist areas of the city. Despite the large number of uncontested seats, the N.I.L.P. never secured a "safe" seat. The party's best electoral performance came in 1958 and 1962 with four members returned at each of these two elections; this representation was halved in 1965. This fundamental weakness of a main section of the Labour movement tended to stifle the emergence of radical social policy and criticism.[5] (The performance of the N.I.L.P. in 1958 and 1962 is examined below but it is worth noting that under P.R. (stv) the N.I.L.P. could have taken twelve or thirteen seats.)

The formal acceptance of Partition by the N.I.L.P. in 1949 led to the formation of anti-Partition Labour groups. These groups were characterised by factionalism and developed numerous party labels built around relatively minor policy and personnel issues. From 1949 onwards the various Independent Labour groups fought out the destination of the Falls and Central constituencies in Belfast. From 1953 Dock, which until this time had been won by both Unionist and N.I.L.P., was added to this pattern of intervention and Independent Labour groups periodically contested Nationalist-held rural seats. The withdrawal of the Nationalists from Belfast seats was a recognition of the difficulties of reconciling urban working-class interests with those of small farmers and rural professionals (lawyers, teachers, etc.) who dominated Nationalist organisations (Rumpf and Hepburn, 1977). The final groups are the Republicans and Sinn Fein. These two parties largely rejected participation in Northern Ireland electoral politics but influenced Nationalist politics over policies of abstention.

In the 1929–1965 period Northern Ireland electoral politics can be summarised as being separated into two discrete spatial components. The larger of the two, the Unionist pattern of intervention, saw electoral competition from the Independent Unionists and the N.I.L.P. The Nationalist component was both smaller and generally peripheral to the Unionist core. The two components were virtual mirror images in terms of internal party competition: a dominant party challenged by a Labour group and Independents. The electoral history of the period suggests that pro- and anti-Partitionists evolved a relatively stable *modus vivendi.*

While the depiction of the essential spatial characteristics of electoral behaviour in the period provides an important introduction, a greater clarity can be gained by placing electoral behaviour in a more rigorous descriptive framework. One such framework is the model of party competition established by Downs in 1957. The basic premise of this model is that all electors and parties can be placed on a central ideological dimension and that political preference can be ordered from left to right in a manner which would be largely agreed upon by all electors. In many west European states the liberal/social democratic–conservative dimension is dominant. In Northern Ireland the ideological ordering dimension for electors and parties has been the constitutional issue. The strength and salience of this issue is not hard to demonstrate as the declared aims of the two most important parties consistently asserted opposing positions with regard to it. The N.I.L.P. was eventually forced to "make a decision" on the constitutional issue and the Labour movement was irrevocably split by the decision. Although at times socio-economic issues were of considerable electoral significance they never became the central ordering dimension of political life. The ideological dimension and its end points can be designated as in Fig. 6.5 (Laver, 1975).

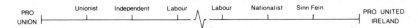

FIGURE 6.5. Northern Ireland: Model of Ideological Space for Voting Behaviour, 1929–1965.

It is evident, however, that the electoral behaviour discussed does not suggest a continuum on the constitutional position but rather a polarisation between those supporting the British link and those aspiring to a United Ireland. Rather than a single ideological space there are two sub-spaces with a "zone of dislocation" between them.

The sub-space structure of the Northern Ireland electoral space suggests that few electors would "jump" from one sub-space to the other. Analysis of the admittedly small number of transfers in the 1921 election shows this to be the case (Table 6.4).

TABLE 6.4. Average "Interim" Transfers in the 1921 General Election.

From: To:	Unionist	Indepen-dent	Labour	Nationa-list	Sinn Fein	N.T.V.	No.
Unionist	0·980	0·006	0·005	0·006	0·007	—	20
Independent	—	—	—	—	—	—	—
Labour	—	—	—	—	—	—	—
Nationalist	—	—	—	0·804	0·196	—	1
Sinn Fein	0·014	—	—	0·006	0·929	0·073	6

N.T.V. Non-transferable votes. Source: Calculated from Elliott (1973).

The accumulated evidence from the first two general elections of 1921 and 1925 and from the 1929–1965 period reveals a dominant cleavage fundamentally shaping and dividing electoral behaviour. Focussing on the legitimacy of Northern Ireland as a political entity, each election was conducted as a reaffirmation of the continuation of Partition on the one hand and an equally ritualistic restatement of the anti-Partition case on the other. Each election evidenced a tacitly stable distribution in this ideological space. Electoral behaviour in this period reveals two stable groups in a divided society with a characteristic territorial pattern of voting behaviour displaying "where men are for the Union on the one hand and against it and want to go into a Dublin parliament on the other".

1965–1969

Captain Terence O'Neill succeeded Lord Brookeborough as Prime Minister in 1963 and took over a system in which the traditional animosities between Protestants and Roman Catholics remained largely unchanged, providing the characteristic basis of social and political life. O'Neill saw his task as trying to "modernise" Northern Ireland and bridge the communal gap (O'Neill, 1969). Also of political importance was the electoral challenge being mounted by the N.I.L.P., which had increased its share of the vote from 16% in 1958 to 26% in 1962, although being largely restricted to Belfast and taking only four seats at both elections. This increase in the vote was primarily a product of contesting twice as many constituencies (fourteen) as in 1958. Bew *et al.* (1979) suggest that it was the political necessity of countering the N.I.L.P. challenge which underlay the innovations of the O'Neill period. While this challenge of the N.I.L.P., based on Protestant working class, obviously underlay the political calculations of O'Neill, the concern with the primary cleavage in Northern Ireland was a priority. The reforms introduced by O'Neill can be viewed in terms of both these political priorities. O'Neill set out to reorganise the administrative machinery of government in order to facilitate economic development which was to be the vehicle for modernisation and change. The Northern Ireland Committee of the Irish Congress of Trade Unions was recognised as the official trade union body previously denied on the grounds of being Dublin based. Exchange visits took place between the two Prime Ministers in Ireland and O'Neill was to be seen visiting Catholic schools. Economic growth and prosperity was to be shared between both Roman Catholic and Protestant with the hope that it would result in greater Catholic allegiance to the state. The stimulation of the economy could also reduce unemployment which was thought partially to underlie the rising N.I.L.P. vote.

It was ironic that O'Neill's strategy should have these implicit political goals while envisaging little action on traditional Roman Catholic grievances. These grievances became the main issues for the Civil Rights Association (C.R.A., founded in 1966) which campaigned for an end to what it saw as discrimination in public housing allocations and jobs and also the gerrymandering of local authority electoral boundaries. The C.R.A. was a predominantly Roman Catholic grouping which initially experienced support from liberal Protestants.

Public reactions within Northern Ireland to O'Neill's actions were generally favourable although hostile elements were evident within the Unionist Party. In 1965 O'Neill called a general election and the Unionist Party increased its total share of the vote and won two seats from the N.I.L.P. This result was regarded as an endorsement of O'Neill's strategy. On the fringes of Unionist politics, however, the fundamentalist religious leader, Rev. Ian Paisley, Moderator of the Free Presbyterian Church and bitterly anti-ecumenical, regarded any *rapprochement* with Roman Catholics as subversive to the Protestant cause. He moved to a more overtly political position with the formation of the Ulster Defence Committee and the Protestant Unionist Party in 1966. Although the weight of public opinion seemed to be behind O'Neill, opposition increased within the Unionist Party. While pressure on O'Neill to curtail his actions was being exerted from within his own party as well as by Paisleyites, the C.R.A. was holding rallies and demonstrations and demanding specific changes in policy which were far in excess of anything countenanced by O'Neill. The first serious disturbance came in October 1968 when a C.R.A. march in London-derry, called to protest at the social and economic plight of Northern Ireland's second (and predominantly Catholic) city, was banned by Craig, Minister of Home Affairs. The march took place, however, but ended in bloody confrontation between police and demonstrators. In the aftermath, a programme of reforms, designed to meet C.R.A. demands, was announced by the Government and included a points system for the allocation of public housing, the appointment of an ombudsman, and the abolition of the company vote in local elections. These were regarded as inadequate by the C.R.A. and further marches were planned, particularly by the radical student-based People's Democracy (Arthur, 1974).

The changes initiated by O'Neill and the resulting turmoil drove the Prime Minister to try to reassert his position in the Unionist Party. An election was called in February 1969. This election was perhaps the most critical in the history of Northern Ireland. In retrospect it marks the end of O'Neill's attempts to "modernise" Northern Ireland and bridge the gap between Protestant and Roman Catholic through cautious reform. In the view of Boal and Buchanan (1969) "the 1969 election was the first in Northern Ireland since 1921 in which the Border was not the principal issue". Yet this was not a time of political trans-formation for traditional rivalries and animosities underlay the cam-paign. While O'Neill sought to reassert his position within the Unionist Party, the election was fought amid increasingly strident demands by disenchanted younger Roman Catholics whose expectations had been aroused by the tenor of O'Neill's approach but who saw many of the promised changes not materialising. Moreover, O'Neill's initiatives had

aroused latent Protestant fears of Roman Catholic encroachment, especially among the working and lower middle classes and those in the "border" areas who feel especially vulnerable to Roman Catholic competition for jobs and housing under prevailing conditions of high unemployment and high Roman Catholic birthrates. (Boal and Buchanan, 1969, p. 78)

The election marked the first fragmentation of the "old monolith"—the Unionist Party. The timing of the election was such that many of the Unionist moderates had not secured positions of authority in local constituency associations which were virtually autonomous in candidate selection. In every constituency where an anti-O'Neill candidate secured the nomination, however, an independent pro-O'Neill Unionist

candidate stood in opposition. The Protestant Unionist Party nominated
five candidates, all in Unionist-held seats, with Paisley standing in the
Prime Minister's constituency of Bann Side. This fragmentation of the
Unionist Party did not imply an attempt to seek support across the
"zone of dislocation" although pro-O'Neill candidates hoped that
Catholics in Unionist areas would support them rather than abstain.

The anti-Partition parties also showed considerable disarray. The
Nationalists put up nine candidates within their "normal" pattern
of intervention. The National Democratic Party (N.D.P.) put up
seven candidates (McAllister, 1975, 1977), nearly all outside the areas
of anti-Partition intervention—a strategy born of a desire to promote a
"socialist" rather than a pan-Catholic party and an overall aim to form
a responsible, constructive and viable opposition to unionism. The
People's Democracy nominated eight candidates—six of which, once
more for ideological reasons, were in Unionist seats. In South Down
and South Fermanagh, People's Democracy candidates formed the
only opposition to the Nationalists. Civil Rights leaders stood for four
seats, all of which were anti-Partitionist.

The N.I.L.P. made one of its largest electoral challenges with ten
seats contested in Belfast and six in rural areas and for the first time

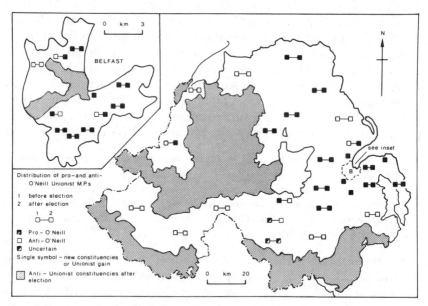

FIGURE 6.6. Northern Ireland (Stormont) Parliamentary Election, 1969:
Distribution of Party Support.
Source: Boal and Buchanan (1969, p. 82).

since 1949 the party contested Nationalist-held seats. The scene was thus set for a trial of strength and a testing of attitudes and positions on all sides.

Turnout at 71·9% was the highest since the 1921 and 1925 elections and, with only seven seats returned unopposed, electoral activity was at a peak. Before the election (Fig. 6.6) the anti-O'Neill Unionists had been located in the south and west with "outliers" in Larne and Carrickfergus. In Belfast the anti-O'Neill group was largely restricted to the western part of the city. This pattern changed only slightly with the election. The Larne-Carrickfergus anomaly was reduced from two seats to one while the anti-O'Neill outlier in east Belfast was eliminated. With the exception of North Tyrone, Unionist areas in the west and south remained anti-O'Neill. West Belfast remained anti-O'Neill to which St. Anne's was added, while Clifton, in the north of the city, switched to the pro-O'Neill camp. Overall, the pro-O'Neill vote was higher in a zone extending twenty-five kilometres out from Belfast—an area from which twenty M.P.s were returned. O'Neill was particularly disheartened by the result in his own constituency where he was returned with 47·3% of the vote and with a majority of only 1400 over Paisley. The N.I.L.P. polled poorly, taking seats only in Oldpark and Falls, and suffered from the seeming irrelevance of its manifesto to the issues of the times. The Nationalists suffered a setback with candidates in the safe seats of Foyle, Mid Londonderry and South Armagh being defeated by Civil Rights candidates. The People's Democracy polled moderately well in anti-Partitionist areas but failed, with the N.D.P., to take a seat.

The election did not provide the widespread support sought by O'Neill for his policies. Roman Catholics had not backed pro-O'Neill candidates to any degree and, by promoting independent candidates against official party nominees, O'Neill had antagonised further sections of the Unionist Party. The liberals in the parliamentary party had not been strengthened and O'Neill's personal standing had been reduced. Although obtaining parliamentary party agreement for a universal local government franchise, O'Neill felt his position to be untenable and he resigned in April 1969.

The election marked the end of an era. Over the forty years since the inception of Northern Ireland, electoral behaviour had lapsed into traditional areas of Unionist and Nationalist dominance representing a stable ideological distribution closely related to religious affiliation. O'Neill's attempts to alter this *status quo* and create a unified ideological space altered the face of politics while changing little of the underlying fundamentals.

1969–1977

O'Neill was replaced as Prime Minister by his cousin Major James Chichester-Clark but in August 1969 widespread rioting, initially in Londonderry and then in Belfast, led to the deployment of British troops at the request of the Northern Ireland Government. The British Government took a belated interest in Northern Ireland (Callaghan, 1973), and under British pressure the Northern Ireland Government pushed through further reforms, at the expense of increased resistance within the Unionist Party. The introduction of British troops gave rise to difficulties as constitutional authority for law and order lay with the regional parliament while British troops remained under the control of Westminster. Violence increased dramatically during 1970 and 1971 and Chichester-Clark resigned in March 1971, having been severely criticised by his own party for failing to force the British Government to react more firmly against the developing I.R.A. campaign. He was replaced by Faulkner. Internment without trial was introduced in August 1971. The continuing increase in violence, the need to speed further the pace of administrative reform, particular events such as "Bloody Sunday" and the division of responsibility in relation to the troops led to the British Government assuming responsibility for law and order in March 1972. The Unionist Government immediately resigned and the Northern Ireland Parliament was prorogued. The British Government took powers as from 30 March 1972 to govern Northern Ireland by Order in Council, and Direct Rule, seen as a temporary measure, was thus introduced.

The British (Conservative) Government based its ensuing policy on two points: one was that Northern Ireland should remain part of the United Kingdom if a majority so desired; the other was a need for some form of provincial government that would command the allegiance of both sections of the population. The first question was to be "settled" by a Border Poll, held on 8 March 1973 when electors were given the opportunity to vote for one of two choices:

(i) Do you want Northern Ireland to remain part of the United Kingdom?

(ii) Do you want Northern Ireland to be joined with the Republic of Ireland outside the United Kingdom?

Some 57·8% of the total electorate voted for the first choice (591 820) and 0·6% (6463) for the second. Although it is likely that the majority of Roman Catholics abstained, the absence of a spatial breakdown precludes a realistic assessment of either votes or abstentions. Nevertheless, the results of the Border Poll showed that the basic division in

Northern Ireland politics was as salient as ever. The British Government's belief that a clear democratic statement of public opinion on the existence of the Border would reassure Unionists that their status was safe and also demonstrate unequivocally to Catholics that this issue was now settled was naive. Through conceiving of the Border as an autonomous issue open to rational argument, debate and decision, a basic misconception of the bases of Northern Ireland politics was revealed. By attempting to force a clear delimitation of pro- and anti-Partition voting strengths little was done to promote forces of integration.

The issue of devising an acceptable provincial government was tackled with the publication of a series of proposals (Northern Ireland Office, 1973), as a result of which legislation was initiated at Westminster. The Northern Ireland Assembly Act (May 1973) provided for an Assembly of seventy-eight members to be elected under P.R. (stv); the elections took place on 28 June 1973. The Northern Ireland Constitution Act (July 1973) abolished the Northern Ireland Parliament and provided a constitutional framework for future government, which envisaged executive/cabinet level power-sharing.

These major constitutional changes took place amid bitter controversy and violence (see Chapter 12), causing dramatic alterations in party structure: alterations which were accelerated by the possibilities of representation afforded to small groupings under P.R. (stv). From 1968 new alignments had begun to emerge; the 1969 election had demonstrated the major splits in the Unionist Party. By early summer 1973 the stress of the previous four years had produced further conflict over policy and between individuals who sought to control the Party and represent the "true spirit of Unionism". Division arose in acute form over the Government's constitutional proposals which envisaged a coalition-based regional executive and a Council of Ireland.

Four main groups of Unionists and Loyalists contested the election. The Protestant Unionists had become the Democratic Unionist Party (D.U.P.), still led by Paisley, and they formed an electoral coalition with the Vanguard Unionist Party (V.U.P.), led by Craig. These two groups with a variety of independent loyalists formed a major challenge to the Unionist Party. Within the Unionist Party there was a major split over the White Paper proposals and this situation was further confused by the autonomy of local constituency associations, a number of which selected anti-White Paper candidates despite official party support for the proposals. The Unionist Party was represented therefore by pro- and anti-White Paper factions.

On the anti-Partition side the Nationalist Party had been superseded by the Social Democratic and Labour Party (S.D.L.P.), created in 1970 as an avowedly anti-sectarian party with "left of centre" principles. The party was formed primarily around Civil Rights leaders and individuals from the Nationalist and Independent Labour groups and led by Fitt. The S.D.L.P. is anti-Partitionist, advocating the unification of Ireland through achieving the consent of a majority of the electorate in Northern Ireland (McAllister, 1977).

Finally the Alliance Party had been formed, also in 1970, as a non-sectarian party supporting integrative policies (see below). The ideological space is depicted in Fig. 6.7.

PROTESTANT ULSTER REGARDLESS | VULC DULC AWPU OU | AP | NILP | NILP | AP | SDLP | Nat. | R Cl | UNITED IRELAND REGARDLESS

FIGURE 6.7. Northern Ireland: Model of Ideological Space for Voting Behaviour at 1973 Assembly Election.
Source: Adapted from Laver (1975, p. 27). VULC: Vanguard Unionist Loyalist Coalition; DULC: Democratic Unionist Loyalist Coalition; AWPU: Anti-White Paper Unionist; OU: Official Unionist; AP: Alliance Party; NILP: Northern Ireland Labour Party; SDLP: Social Democratic and Labour Party; Nat.: Nationalist; R. Cl.: Republican Clubs.

The N.I.L.P. does not fit easily into this depiction of the ideological space, being a social democratic party which attempted to ignore the central divide by emphasis upon economic and social issues. The election was fought on the electoral framework of the existing twelve Westminster constituencies assigned multi-seat magnitude for this election. The results of the election are shown in Table 6.5.

TABLE 6.5. Results of the 1973 Assembly Elections.

	First preferences	Percentage	Seats in proportion to votes	Seats
V.U.L.C.	75 759	10·5	8·2	7
D.U.L.C.	78 228	10·8	8·4	8
A.W.P.U.	89 758	12·4	9·7	10
Other Loyalist	11 660	1·6	1·2	2
Official Unionist	191 729	26·5	20·7	23
Alliance	66 541	9·2	7·2	8
Northern Ireland Labour Party	18 675	2·6	2·0	1
S.D.L.P.	159 773	22·1	17·2	19
Republican Clubs	13 064	1·8	1·4	—
Other Nationalist/ Republican	10 020	1·4	1·1	—
Others	7033	0·9	0·7	—

V.U.L.C. Vanguard Unionist Loyalist Coalition. D.U.L.C. Democratic Unionist Loyalist Coalition. A.W.P.U. Anti-White Paper Unionist. Source: Calculated from official returns.

Agreement between those parties prepared to work within the White Paper framework was secured during October 1973 and a meeting of the British and Irish Governments and the Northern Ireland political representatives took place at Sunningdale early in December 1973, where the details of the power-sharing Executive were formalised. The Executive took office from 1 January 1974.

Elections and the ballot box were crucial in the strategy of the British Government during 1972–1974. Optimistically, the Border Poll was designed to "remove the Border from politics" on a ten-year basis. Elections held under P.R. (stv) were also critical in the attempt to create a power-sharing Executive. P.R. (stv), by allowing an ordinal ranking of candidates rather than a single categorical choice, would, it was hoped, encourage voters to transfer towards the centre and in particular to the Alliance Party. In this instance it is particularly interesting to examine the transfer of lower order preferences (Table 6.6).

The transfer analysis demonstrates that, although the ordinal ballot was designed to facilitate the movement of votes towards the centre, the extent to which this took place was small. The main characteristics of the transfers are:

(i) For most parties the largest portion of transfers remain with the original party.

(ii) The flow of votes to the centre (Alliance) is greater for anti-Partition parties than pro-Partition parties.

(iii) The limited movement of vote values from one sub-space to the other.

Of the 308 197 transfers only 848 or 0·28% crossed the "zone of dislocation". Some 305 transferred from the Unionist sub-space while 543 flowed in reverse. A more revealing analysis can be gained through the examination of terminal transfers. Terminal transfers take place when there are no members of the candidate's party still available to receive vote values, such members having been either elected or eliminated. Variations in party availability at transfer stages render realistic generalisation problematic. Some examples can be given. Taking the Unionists and Loyalists, the only terminal transfer which took place with no available candidate from that sub-space was at the twelfth transfer in the Mid Ulster constituency. Here 99% of the votes became non-transferable with only 1% transferring to the S.D.L.P. Perhaps the most interesting transfer was at the tenth stage in West Belfast. In this instance with Alliance, S.D.L.P. and Republican Clubs available, 56% of the votes of the anti-White Paper Unionist (A.W.P.U.) candidate transferred to Alliance and 42% became non-transferable. This enabled the Alliance candidate to be elected although having fewer votes than the S.D.L.P. candidate prior to the transfer.

TABLE 6.6. Percentage Distribution of Lower Preferences, 1973 Assembly Elections.

From: To:	1	2	3	4	5	6	7	8	9	10	11	N.T.V.
1. V.U.L.C.	32	32	3	—	12	3	1	—	—	—	—	16
2. D.U.L.C.	36	25	15	—	12	—	—	—	—	—	—	12
3. A.W.P.U.	13	4	46	1	25	4	3	—	—	—	—	4
4. Other Loyalist	26	34	4	—	28	1	3	—	—	—	—	3
5. Official Unionist	8	6	8	—	70	3	1	—	—	—	—	4
6. Alliance	1	1	3	—	7	56	1	15	—	—	2	13
7. N.I.L.P.	2	3	6	4	7	43	11	14	—	—	—	10
8. S.D.L.P.	—	—	—	—	—	24	4	57	1	1	—	12
9. Republican Clubs	—	—	—	—	—	3	2	43	15	2	3	32
10. Nationalist/Republican	—	—	—	—	—	8	1	51	—	12	4	24
11. Others	—	—	—	—	—	9	2	58	8	2	2	21

N.T.V. Non-transferable votes. V.U.L.C. Vanguard Unionist Loyalist Coalition. D.U.L.C. Democratic Unionist Loyalist Coalition. A.W.P.U. Anti-White Paper Unionist. Source: Calculated from official returns.

The transfer analysis reveals the extent to which voting behaviour was, in its basic elements, similar to that of previous elections. Despite the facility for cross-voting the sub-space configuration dominated transfer behaviour. In effect the ballot paper, although ordinal, was treated as categorical once candidates from the voter's sub-space of origin were not available to receive transfers. Thus, despite the major changes in the party structure in the previous few years, there was no evidence that major realignments in electoral preferences in terms of the main political cleavage were taking place.

The results of the 1973 elections provided a working majority for those prepared to co-operate in the construction of a majority-minority coalition. In two respects the election results were disappointing however, that is to the British Government and to the pro-coalition groups. First, they demonstrated that the moderate centre was not as large as had been hoped. The Alliance Party polled fewer first preferences than any one of the anti-White Paper groups and gained only 10% of the seats. Secondly, the pro-White Paper Official Unionists, although the largest single faction in the Unionist bloc, were smaller than the combined anti-White Paper Unionists in terms of votes and seats. Clearly only a minority of the main unionist-Protestant electorate supported pro-coalition candidates.

Although detailed cartographic analysis is precluded by the higher level of vote aggregation at this election, it is evident that the support for the Alliance Party and the pro-White Paper Unionists shows co-incidence with that of the pro-O'Neill vote in 1969, being particularly strong in the constituencies of South Antrim, North Down and South and East Belfast. Thus the spatial cleavage in pro-Union opinion initially demonstrated in 1969 was reaffirmed in 1973.

The formation of a power-sharing Executive was a momentous event. The Executive was led by Faulkner (Official Unionist) with the S.D.L.P. leader, Fitt, as Deputy. For the first time in Northern Ireland, elected members from the Roman Catholic minority were represented in the regional political authority. One element of the Sunningdale Agreement, however, was causing considerable discussion amongst all shades of unionism. The Council of Ireland, designed as a formal structure for political discussion between the two governments in Ireland, seemed to many Protestants to be the first step towards a United Ireland. The events of early 1974 in Britain—the confrontation between the miners and the Conservative Government—were largely extraneous to Northern Ireland. Nevertheless, the decision of Prime Minister Heath to call a general election intruded into the Northern Ireland political scene. Limited survey evidence collected in South

Belfast immediately prior to the Westminster election of February 1974 (Osborne, 1977) showed 46% of Protestants opposed to a Council of Ireland and 32% against power-sharing, with more extreme opposition evident from working-class Protestants. The election was fought on the British plurality system and called on issues of secondary significance to Northern Ireland. However, it resulted in a resounding success for the anti-White Paper groups who won 51% of the votes and eleven of the twelve seats. As Craig, leader of the V.U.P., stated:

> ... we must not prop up the undemocratic form of administration that now exists in Northern Ireland; there is not the necessary consent for the present constitutional formula. (*House of Commons Debates* 870 (Fifth Series) (1974), 737–738)

On 14 May 1974 the Ulster Workers' Council, a previously unknown loyalist grouping, announced a General Strike to coincide with the rejection of a motion in the Assembly demanding a renegotiation of constitutional arrangements. The events of the fourteen-day strike have been vividly described by Fisk (1975) and the role of local communities and community groups by Griffiths (1978). The strike forced the resignation of the Executive after five months in office. The fragile integrative coalition thus became the victim of "external" British political issues and the plurality electoral system as much as from Protestant resistance. For instance the success of the strike called by the miners in Britain may have provided a successful model for the U.W.C. in its fight against an elected government. It was ironic that the British Government's endeavours in Northern Ireland should be undermined by the intrusion of the British plurality system which as a result of the election created a new environment for political behaviour and, for some, the mandate for action in Northern Ireland.

The second phase of British attempts to resolve the Northern Ireland conflict was undertaken by the Labour administration returned in February 1974. This strategy also rested on the use of elections. The future structure of devolved government was to be decided by an elected Constitutional Convention again based on P.R. (stv). The deliberations of the Convention were to be tightly controlled with the Government indicating its preference for power-sharing and an "Irish dimension". Moreover, the Convention's proposals had to be acceptable to the Westminster Parliament (Rose, 1976; Osborne, 1975a). The elections to the Convention took place in May 1975 and showed that the party structure had altered once more, with the main anti-Sunningdale groups fighting under the electoral coalition of the United Ulster

Unionist Coalition (U.U.U.C.)[6] (Table 6.7). This group gained 54% of the first preference vote and forty-six of the seventy-eight seats. With this result, the potential for the Convention providing recommendations acceptable to the Government's wishes seemed unlikely. Once more the post-election situation produced an environment in which political action was unlikely to follow government aspirations. The first phase of the Convention's deliberations ended in November 1975 with proposals envisaging a return to the pre-1972 position with the exception that some powerful back-bench committees would have

TABLE 6.7. Results of the 1975 Northern Ireland Convention Elections.

	First preferences	Percentage	Seats	Percentage
Democratic Unionist Party	97 073	14·7	12	15·4
Vanguard Unionist Party	83 507	12·7	14	17·9
Official Unionist	169 797	25·8	19	24·4
Other Loyalist	10 140	1·5	2	2·6
U.P.N.I.	50 891	7·7	5	6·4
Alliance	64 657	9·8	8	10·2
N.I.L.P.	9 102	1·4	1	1·3
S.D.L.P.	156 049	23·7	17	21·8
Republican Clubs	14 515	2·2	—	—
Other	2430	0·4	—	—

U.P.N.I. Unionist Party of Northern Ireland. Source: Calculated from official returns.

had a minority party chairman (Osborne, 1975b). Craig, one of the U.U.U.C. leaders, had become convinced of the merit of a voluntary coalition during the "emergency". He failed, however, to convince the other U.U.U.C. members and was expelled from the coalition. The Convention was asked to reconsider its position during early 1976 but its final proposals were unacceptable to the Government and it was dissolved in March 1976.

The 1973 and 1975 initiatives by successive British Governments sought to resolve the Northern Ireland conflict through a devolved legislative structure to enable the Roman Catholic minority to have participation at cabinet/executive level. The use of the ballot box was central to both strategies and the use of P.R. (stv) was critical, the hope being that it would fracture the main voting blocs and bolster the centre. While P.R. (stv) can be seen as instrumental in formalising the splits, particularly in the Unionist bloc (and also forcing some electoral co-operation), it did not produce the anticipated result for the centre. In this situation, it is appropriate to consider in greater detail the development of the Alliance Party.

THE ALLIANCE PARTY

The Alliance Party is the political expression of "integrative" forces in Northern Ireland. Formed in 1970, the party's basic principles emphasise equality of treatment for all citizens and the maintenance of the political link with Britain as long as a majority desire it. It seeks to promote the breakdown of social and political barriers between Catholic and Protestant which leads it to support such policies as the integration of schools and the voluntary integration of housing areas.

A summary of the electoral performance of the Alliance Party

TABLE 6.8. Electoral Performance of the Alliance Party, 1973–1977.

	Votes: first preferences	Percentage	Seats	Percentage
1973[a]	94 474	13.6	63	12·0
1973[b]	66 541	9·2	8	10·3
1974[c]	22 660	3·1	—	—
1974[d]	35 955	5·1	—	—
1975[e]	64 657	9·8	8	10·3
1977[f]	80 011	14·4	70	13·3

[a]Local elections, P.R. (stv), 526 seats. [b]Assembly elections, P.R. (stv), 78 seats. [c]U.K. general elections, February 1974, plurality, 12 seats. [d]U.K. general elections, October 1974, plurality, 12 seats. [e]Convention elections, P.R. (stv), 78 seats. [f]Local elections, P.R. (stv), 526 seats. Source: Calculated from official returns.

(Table 6.8) shows that although the party has established itself as one of the four largest parties (alongside the Official Unionists, Democratic Unionists and the S.D.L.P.) it had not by 1977 become a dominant force in Northern Ireland politics. Two factors seem to underpin the limited development of the Alliance Party. These are:

(i) A clear east–west bias in the pattern of first preference votes.

(ii) Electoral support being apparently concentrated amongst certain socio-economic groups.

Figure 6.8 shows the spatial distribution of the Alliance share of the vote in the two local government elections of 1973 and 1977, both held under P.R. (stv). The strength of Alliance voting can be seen to be primarily in the east, and more particularly in south and east Belfast and suburban areas associated with the Belfast Urban Area. This spatial bias, evident at the 1973 election, led the party to avoid contesting several low-polling areas in the 1977 election. The spatial pattern of Alliance electoral strength resembles that of the pro-O'Neill vote in the 1969 election, providing evidence of the continuity in the

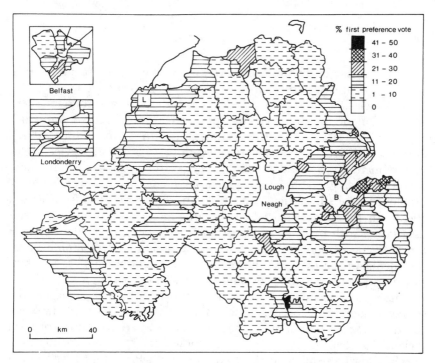

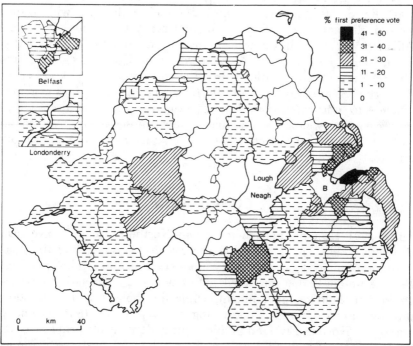

FIGURE 6.8. Northern Ireland Local Government Elections: Distribution of Alliance Party First Preference Votes by District Electoral Area: (a) 1973 (above); (b) 1977 (below).

spatial cleavage in the pro-Union voting surface: in very general terms a more liberal east and a hardline or more right-wing west.

A correlation exercise between census-derived variables and the distribution of the Alliance first preference vote in 1973 and 1977 suggested in 1973 a positive association with young adults (0·47), adults with high educational qualifications (0·56) and service sector employment (0·63), and a negative association with areas with poor quality housing (0·66), high unemployment (0·45), proportion of employed adults in agriculture (0·59) and linear distance from Belfast (0·42). In 1977 these associations became more marked and a positive association with percentage Protestant (0·53) becomes evident as does a negative association with percentage Catholic (0·57). To some extent the media image of the Alliance Party as "middle class" is substantiated and reinforces the geographical bias in support.

This evidence can be examined a little further with some limited survey evidence (Osborne, 1977). When Alliance respondents were asked to rank in order of preference six possible alternatives for Northern Ireland, a clear first preference is shown for "power-sharing in a devolved parliament" and this applies to both Protestant and Roman Catholic Alliance supporters. This unity tends to dissipate with second-ranked alternatives showing a split between Catholic and Protestant Alliance voters, with Catholics showing support for an alternative not favoured by Protestant Alliance voters—a United Ireland. Across all preferences there is little evidence of congruence in rankings (Kendall's coefficient of concordance 0·21, average r_s 0·19). This evidence, which is to some extent paralleled by rank ordering of parties, suggests that, even for Alliance voters, that is, those most favourably disposed to "integration", the deep sub-space characteristics of political life remain.

CONCLUSION

Since 1921 elections and their role in Northern Ireland have been distinctive. They have provided the means for reasserting the basic positions of majority and minority in a ritualistic and symbolic fashion. For the unionists they provided the democratic legitimation for their continuous hold on government, while for the nationalists elections provided a way of publicly reasserting their rejection of that legitimacy, and of the Northern Ireland political entity. The ideological space was fundamentally fractured between those who endorsed the existence of Northern Ireland and those who did not. O'Neill's attempts to restructure the ideological space through an "integrative" strategy based on a sharing of economic prosperity foundered on a socially and spatially distinctive Protestant resistance and a failure to satisfy Roman Catholic aspirations. The 1969 election gave clear spatial expression to these developments and marked not only the rapid deterioration in Catholic–Protestant interrelationships but also the emergent splits in the Protestant-unionist bloc.

The strategies employed by several British Governments, seeking to restore a devolved government with a substantial role for minority politicians at cabinet level, rested on the manipulation of the electoral system and the use of the ballot box to forge a new political reality. However the stubborn continuities of electoral behaviour in Northern Ireland, reflecting and sustaining the deep cleavage in the political community, have to date frustrated the integrative policies of successive British Governments.

NOTES

1. The "Treaty" refers to the settlement with Britain which included the partition of Ireland.

2. The Northern Ireland Labour Party was formed from the Belfast Labour Party in 1923.

3. Although the number of Unionist–Nationalist clashes was small such contests were regarded as the most significant. This is demonstrated by the significantly higher turnout evident at these contests compared to others. (Using the Kolmogorov-Smirnov two-sample one-tail test, the null hypothesis—Unionist versus Nationalist contests produce no higher turnout than other contests—is rejected at the 0·001 level.)

4. This is demonstrated by the large number of uncontested seats which only once fell below 40% of the forty-eight territorial constituencies in the 1929–1965 period.

5. See Probert (1978) and Bew *et al.* (1979) for a discussion of the introduction of "Welfare State" legislation in the 1945–1950 period in Northern Ireland notwithstanding the opposition of the Unionist Westminster M.P.s.

6. The significance of this coalition lay in the instructions to individual party supporters to vote for their party first but to give lower preferences to other parties in the coalition.

REFERENCES

Akenson, D. (1973). "Education and Enmity: The Control of Schooling in Northern Ireland, 1920–1950." David and Charles, Newton Abbot.

Arthur, P. (1974). "The People's Democracy 1968–1973." Blackstaff, Belfast.

Bew, P., Gibbon, P. and Patterson, H. (1979). "The State in Northern Ireland, 1921–1972." Manchester University Press, Manchester.

Boal, F. W. and Buchanan, R. H. (1969). The 1969 Northern Ireland Election. *Irish Geography* **6,** 78–84.

Callaghan, J. (1973). "A House Divided." Collins, London.

Downs, A. (1957). "An Economic Theory of Democracy." Harper and Row, New York.

Elliott, S. (1973). "Northern Ireland Parliamentary Election Results, 1921–1972." Political Reference Publications, Chichester.

Fisk, R. (1975). "The Point of No Return: The Strike which Broke the British in Ulster." Deutsch, London.

Gallagher, F. (1957). "The Indivisible Island." Gollancz, London.

Griffiths, H. (1978). Community Reaction and Voluntary Involvement. *In* "Violence and the Social Services in Northern Ireland" (J. Darby and A. Williamson, eds.), pp. 165–200. Heinemann, London.

Laver, M. (1975). Strategic Campaign Behaviour for Elections and Parties: The Northern Ireland Assembly Election of 1973. *European Journal of Political Research* **3,** 21–45.

Loosemore, J. and Hanby, V. J. (1971). The Theoretical Limits of Maximum Distortion: Some Analytical Expressions for Electoral Systems. *British Journal of Political Science* **1,** 467–477.

McAllister, I. (1975). "The Northern Ireland Convention Election." Occasional Paper 14, Survey Research Centre, Glasgow.

McAllister, I. (1977). "The Northern Ireland Social Democratic and Labour Party—Political Opposition in a Divided Society." Macmillan, London.

Northern Ireland Office (1973). "Northern Ireland Constitutional Proposals" (Cmnd. 5259). Her Majesty's Stationery Office, London.

O'Neill, T. (1969). "Ulster at the Crossroads." Faber and Faber, London.

Osborne, R. D. (1975a). Elections with a Difference. *Geographical Magazine* **47,** 651–653.

Osborne, R. D. (1975b). Proposals for Ulster. *Geographical Magazine* **48,** 178.

Osborne, R. D. (1976). Northern Ireland: Representation at Westminster and the Boundary Commission. *Irish Geography* **9,** 115–120.

Osborne, R. D. (1977). "The Political System, Voting Patterns and Voting Behaviour in Northern Ireland 1921–1974." Unpublished Ph.D. Thesis, Queen's University, Belfast.

Osborne, R. D. (1979). The Northern Ireland Parliamentary Electoral System: The 1929 Reapportionment. *Irish Geography* **12,** 42–56.

Probert, B. (1978). "Beyond Orange and Green: The Political Economy of the Northern Ireland Crisis." Academy Press, Dublin.

Rose, R. (1976). "Northern Ireland: A Time of Choice." Macmillan, London.

Rumpf, E. and Hepburn, A. C. (1977). "Nationalism and Socialism in Twentieth-Century Ireland." Liverpool University Press, Liverpool.

CHAPTER 7

POLITICAL PROCESSES AND BEHAVIOUR

Robert D. Osborne and Dale Singleton

This chapter examines government decision making and the processes involved in particular decisions. Its major concern is to analyse whether such decisions have been integrative or divisive over space and time. The case studies chosen are:

(i) The decision made in the mid-1960s to locate the New University of Ulster at Coleraine.

(ii) The decision made in the mid-1970s to build 2000 dwellings and ancillary facilities on the western outskirts of Belfast, at a site known as Poleglass.

The decisions were taken within contrasting political and administrative frameworks, although in both cases the essential social and environmental contexts remained the same. They illustrate the locational problems implicit in the allocation of scarce resources in a polarised society.

I The Lockwood Report and the Location of a Second University in Northern Ireland

Robert D. Osborne

INTRODUCTION

The succession of Captain Terence O'Neill to the leadership of the Unionist Party and hence the Prime Ministership of Northern Ireland in 1963 ushered in a novel period of political experimentation. O'Neill sought to stimulate economic growth in Northern Ireland which through allowing Roman Catholics an equal share in the new prosperity would increase their commitment to Northern Ireland as a political entity and thereby help to reduce the cleavage between Protestants and Roman Catholics (see also Chapter 6). Economic growth was to be planned through a series of programmes which had two overriding features:

(i) Their gearing to the interests of incoming foreign investment which was to provide the core of economic development.

(ii) Their spatial element.

It is not proposed to deal with the first feature but it is worth noting that the implementation of these programmes in their locational aspects was often geared to the specific demands of incoming investors (Oliver, 1978).

The spatial component of these programmes and in particular the location of a second university in Northern Ireland is the main concern of this section of the chapter. O'Neill's strategy, based on economic growth, can be seen to be closely aligned with the tenor of British political debate at the time, particularly as enunciated in Harold Wilson's speech to the Labour Party Conference in 1963 which linked the expansion of higher education to the production of skilled manpower. The Robbins Report of 1963 which recommended the expansion of higher education in Great Britain and its emphasis on the development of higher education as a means of promoting economic growth provided the model for the committee established by the O'Neill administration in November 1963. This committee was headed by Sir John Lockwood of Birkbeck College, London. The Committee's remit was to "review the facilities for university and higher technical education in Northern Ireland having regard to the Report of the Robbins Committee, and to make recommendations". The Robbins Report's emphasis on the untapped educational ability in lower socio-economic groups was not a theme of particular significance to the O'Neill administration, but the outline of the aims of higher education in the Robbins Report resonated satisfactorily with the tenor of O'Neill's strategy. Robbins outlined four main aims of higher education:

(i) It should provide instruction in skills suitable to play a part in the general division of labour. And in this regard "it must be recognised that progress—and in particular the maintenance of the competitive position depends to a much greater extent than ever before on skills which demand specific training".

(ii) What is taught should be taught in such a way as to promote the general powers of the mind.

(iii) It should encourage the advancement of learning.

(iv) It should assist in the transmission of a common culture and common standards of citizenship.

The first and fourth aims were particularly congruent with O'Neill's political and economic ambitions for Northern Ireland.

THE LOCKWOOD COMMITTEE REPORT

The Lockwood Committee reported in February 1965, after sixteen months' deliberation. The Report is derivative in terms of general principles from Robbins but geared to the specific situation in Northern Ireland. In two paragraphs the applicability of the Robbins suggestions on the reservoir of untapped ability in lower socio-economic groups is accepted. Stressed throughout is the significance of higher education to the economic situation in Northern Ireland. One particularly significant local feature was the movement in and out of Northern Ireland of students to take up undergraduate studies. The Report comments: "Student interchange, especially within the U.K. should be encouraged . . ." (para. 145), and "Any strengthening of the desire of students from Great Britain to seek university education in Northern Ireland must result in the enrichment of university life" (para. 146). Yet, as Table 7.1 demonstrates, the proportion of Northern Ireland undergraduates studying in the Republic of Ireland formed not only a larger proportion than those studying in Great Britain but the difference between the two destinations was growing. This flow, which included both Protestants and Roman Catholics, was not commented on in the Report.

TABLE 7.1. Destination of Northern Ireland Undergraduates[a] (Percentage of Total).

	N. Ireland	Gt Britain	Irish Republic	Other	Total
1957–1958	88·5	4·2	7·3	—	1033
1963–1964	82·3	5·1	12·6	—	3838

[a]This pattern altered with the onset of the "troubles" so that one in every three undergraduates left Northern Ireland for Great Britain in 1975.
Source: Lockwood Report (1965).

Using a similar forecasting technique to the Robbins Report, an estimated demand by 1980 was arrived at. The existing university in Northern Ireland, the Queen's University of Belfast, should cater for approximately 7000 places of which 6000 should be undergraduates.

The Committee, after examining a number of alternatives, including a federated Queen's University of Northern Ireland, opted for the creation of a new university, the establishment of which was regarded as a priority. The educational emphasis of the new university, it was suggested, should complement that of Queen's University rather than duplicate courses and it was recommended that concentration should be on four main subject areas:

(i) Biological and related pure and applied sciences.
(ii) Environmental and social sciences.
(iii) The humanities.
(iv) Teacher education.

In line with the recommendation to specialise in biological sciences the transfer of the Agriculture Faculty from Queen's University to the new university was advocated. The Committee also proposed the foundation of a regional technical college to provide technical-based courses to a level below degree standard. This new college was to be administratively grouped with several others in Northern Ireland to form a federated Ulster College.

The question of the *location* of new institutes of higher education has been generally shown to be of political importance. Stava (1973, p. 250), commenting on the development of higher education in Norway, has stated: "Unlike the decision to establish the colleges, the issue of location was debated at length, was the subject of considerable political activity and was a matter of considerable governmental attention". The reasons for the political activity surrounding such a location decision are readily appreciable. A new institute of higher education offers opportunities for new jobs and represents an injection of spending power into a local economy. It can also act as a "location factor" for investors seeking to locate new economic activity. The potential for cultural enrichment and the sheer "kudos" to be derived from becoming a university town are not inconsiderable. In Northern Ireland these factors were enhanced because of the probability that for the foreseeable future the issue of a third university would not be contemplated. From the appointment of the Lockwood Committee, speculation on the likelihood of a recommendation for a second university and, far more important, its location became a matter of intense debate and lobbying, primarily by the three locations which made submissions to the Committee: Armagh, Coleraine and Londonderry. Despite the interest of Coleraine and Armagh there was a tacit assumption that Northern Ireland's second city, Londonderry, would be the obvious and logical location for a second university. This assumption was based on two simple points: first, that as the second largest urban centre in Northern

Ireland it was "next in line" for an institute of higher education; secondly, that the existence of Magee University College[1] created the precedent and also the experience of university-level education which no other town could claim.

The question of the location of universities in Britain in the period of expansion was handled through a Government decision following confidential advice from the University Grants Committee. As noted in the Lockwood Report (para. 213) the U.G.C. considered the following factors when advising on issues of location:

(i) The proposed location, site and sponsorship to give confidence that the creation and growth of an academic institution would proceed smoothly and effectively.

(ii) Whether staff of quality and energy would be attracted in sufficient numbers.

(iii) Sufficient student lodgings to supplement university residential accommodation.

(iv) Adequate financial support.

(v) Whether locality offers associated research activities.

Strictly speaking the U.G.C. writ did not (and does not) extend to Northern Ireland although the body has acted in an advisory role to the political authorities. The decision on the location of a second university was the responsibility of the Northern Ireland Government but the Lockwood Committee was asked to consider location in the event of a recommendation for a second university.

The Lockwood Committee's Report dealt with the issue of location in fifteen paragraphs, noting that this issue had "already aroused much public interest throughout Northern Ireland and to which we devoted most careful consideration" (para. 211). The Committee did not regard the U.G.C. criteria for location as restrictive and suggested the following as appropriate for Northern Ireland:

(i) Of prime importance was the availability of an adequate site "to accommodate its proposed activities and to allow for future growth . . . It is of paramount importance in our view that, as the university develops, it should be able to do so within the boundaries of a single site" (para. 214).

(ii) Also regarded as significant was "the interaction between the university and its immediate environment" so that "it is certainly not right in our view to locate a university in a particular place chiefly for the good it may do to the location chosen" and furthermore "it is also essential that the development of a new university should be able to proceed smoothly and successfully through the planning and later stages unaffected by political considerations either at local or central government level".

(iii) The ability to attract good staff through the availability of good housing and schools.

(iv) An adequate supporting population to provide services and secretarial and technical staff.

(v) The existence of lodgings to supplement university student residences.

(vi) Good communications with the rest of Northern Ireland and Great Britain but sufficiently far from Belfast to permit separate development.

Having argued that these factors were those of relevance in Northern Ireland, the Committee did not argue the particular merits and/or disadvantages of the three major contending locations but stated that "in our concerted view, the Coleraine area satisfies our criteria better than any of the other areas we have considered and we are of the opinion that the new university will have the best opportunity of a good start and of ultimate success in that area" (para. 221). The failure to argue in detail the question of location is surprising in view of the acknowledged public debate and interest in the matter and the obvious care in discussing other issues. Following the choice of Coleraine the Committee recommended the phased closure of Magee University College in Londonderry.

REACTION TO LOCKWOOD REPORT

The Government published a Statement at the same time as the publication of the Report which accepted the main recommendations, the principal exception being Magee University College which was to be retained and brought into association with the new university in Coleraine. Public reaction in the wake of the publication of the Report and Government Statement was predictable in that most statements emanating from Londonderry reflected disappointment and criticism whereas those from Coleraine expressed satisfaction. A cavalcade was organised from Londonderry to Stormont as part of a programme to change the Government's mind with much being made of the presence of both Unionist and Nationalist community and political leaders from the city in the procession. The Government moved quickly to debate the issue in Parliament with O'Neill moving the endorsement of the motion "That the Report on Higher Education in Northern Ireland (Cmd. 475) be taken into consideration and that the Government statement thereon (Cmd. 480) be now endorsed" on 3 March 1965. The debate, lasting fifteen hours over two days, was one of the longest post-war debates in Stormont.[2] O'Neill, opening the debate, stressed the importance of the Report's proposals for the economic future of Northern Ireland, defended the process by which the locational decision was made and seemed to confirm that the vote at the end of the debate was to be "whipped".[3] Education Minister Kirk defended the Committee's integrity and also referred to the location of the new university at Stirling where other competing locations had accepted the Government decision without acrimony. Why could this not be the case in Northern Ireland? However, David Bleakley, Northern Ireland Labour Party member for Victoria, Belfast, indicated the future course of the debate when he rhetorically asked: "What is the shadow over Lockwood? The shadow is one of location". In perhaps the most comprehensive contribution to the debate, Bleakley commented on each of the Committee's remarks concerning location, asking what exactly was meant by the political considerations referred to by Lockwood, claiming that Magee University College provided the perfect basis for further expansion and concluded that "Going to Londonderry gives us the chance to revitalise a whole area without doing one whit of damage to the university". Other contributions suggested that: there was evidence of deliberate attempts to run down Londonderry as a location (Murnaghan, Liberal member for Queen's University); that the Coleraine Chamber of Trade supported Londonderry as a location and the new spirit of co-operation in Londonderry between Roman Catholics and Protestants deserved reward (Stewart, Independent member for Queen's University); that "the penalty [of this decision] will have to be paid. The people of Northern Ireland will have to pay that penalty" (Warnock, Unionist member for St. Anne's, Belfast); that passages in the Report concerning location made strange reading (McCoy, Unionist member for South Tyrone); the decision reinforced others which had disadvantaged the western counties of Fermanagh, Tyrone and Londonderry (Currie, Nationalist member for East Tyrone); the reasons for locating in Coleraine were unimpressive (Kelly, Unionist member for Mid Down); the feelings of the Unionists of Londonderry were similar to those of the "lost" three counties at Partition (Nixon, Unionist member for North Down); the failure to provide reasons for choosing Coleraine suggested a volte-face by the Committee (Boal, Unionist member for Shankill, Belfast). Of the two members for Londonderry city, McAteer (Nationalist) spoke against the motion while Jones (Unionist) did not speak. An amendment suggesting the location of the university in Londonderry was proposed by Bleakley and the division on the amendment reveals interesting features:

(i) The amendment was defeated by twenty-seven votes to nineteen.

(ii) The twenty-seven opposing the amendment were all Unionists. They included Jones, one of the two M.P.s for Londonderry city, and McCoy and Kelly who had both criticised the locational decision.

(iii) Two Unionists voted in favour of the amendment—Nixon and Boal. Boal, although having no constituency interest, was a native of Londonderry whereas Nixon had no connection with the city.

(iv) The nineteen members supporting the amendment included the four N.I.L.P. members (all from Belfast constituencies), eight Nationalists, three Independent Labour, the sole Liberal, one Independent and the two dissident Unionists.

(v) Two Unionists who had participated in the debate abstained— Little (West Down) and Warnock (St. Anne's, Belfast).

The pattern of voting demonstrated well the interaction of three powerful and interrelated influences. First, there was the pull of party, particularly amongst Unionists where the existence of a party "whip" on the vote seems to have forced some critical Unionists into the Government lobby. Secondly, there were the interests of constituency, with members surrounding Coleraine voting for that location. The third factor was the individual consciences and political sensibilities of some members.

In the wake of the debate and division the issue, far from being settled, received a further infusion of controversy with a statement from Nixon, Unionist member for North Down, which claimed that a Cabinet member had told him that "nameless faceless men from Londonderry had gone to Stormont and advised against the siting of Ulster's second university in the city or in settling industrial development there" (*Belfast Telegraph*, 7 May 1965). Nixon was supported by Alderman Austin, Unionist member of Londonderry Corporation, who asserted that "what Mr Nixon said was a repetition of what had been said by many for some time" (*Belfast Telegraph*, 7 May 1965). Criticism of Jones, Unionist member for the City of Londonderry constituency, came from a constituency Young Unionist group because "in voting with the Government he went against the wishes of the majority of the people he represents" (*Belfast Telegraph*, 7 May 1965). Gormley, Nationalist member for Mid Londonderry, claimed that the names of the "faceless men" were known and alleged that the Civil Service had facilitated their intervention (*Belfast Telegraph*, 26 May 1965). The names of the men alleged to have made the intervention were later published and included notable officials of the Unionist Party in the city and members of the Apprentice Boys of Derry. A petition was launched by the President of the Chamber of Trade in Londonderry, a Unionist, to demand an inquiry into the allegations, but on the following day announced his withdrawal from the proposal and alleged that threats against his life had been made. Nixon was expelled from the Parliamentary Unionist Party after repeating his allegations, and a censure motion was passed by his constituency association. The Government, however, stayed firm and action was taken to choose the site and prepare the building at Coleraine.[4]

CONCLUSION

Stava's (1973) assessment of the higher education programme and the location of new institutions in Norway concluded that the roles of values of social justice and equity were most important to an understanding of the decision processes concerned with their location. According to Stava these normative structures transcended over a considerable time the actions associated with individual processes of decision making. Such a temporal perspective is not possible in Northern Ireland, but the particular decision concerned with the location of a second university was not discernibly associated with egalitarian values. Indeed, the significance of directly political considerations is emphasised in the Lockwood Report's references to university development needing to be "unaffected by political considerations either at central or local government level". Although the superficial form of decision making in this instance was apparently fair—an independent review committee analysing issues and making recommendations to the political authorities—the question of location, already an issue before the publication of the Report, was clearly not regarded by individuals drawn from all political groupings as being handled in a fair and independent fashion. Perhaps most significantly there were splits within the Unionist Party, both in the parliamentary party and especially within unionist groupings in Londonderry. Whether the allegations about "faceless men" were entirely true or not there was a clear split between unionists who regarded the economic and educational development of Londonderry as a means of conquering the manifest social *malaise* in the city and a means of unifying the two communities there and those who rejected any moves to alter the *status quo*. There is no clear statement of the reasons underpinning the rejectionists' position. Two possible explanations are:

(i) The spatial structure of political power in Londonderry. As is shown in Chapter 5, there is fairly clear evidence that in the mid-1960s there was a careful gerrymander of the city council, designed to ensure Unionist domination. Any large-scale economic and educational development in or around the city could have promoted changes in the urban physical structure thereby endangering the gerrymander.

(ii) A second factor, which may have been particularly significant to unionists outside the city, concerned the potential role of a university in Londonderry. With the population of the city split 70% Roman Catholic and 30% Protestant, it was possible that the new institute, through acting as a focus for the north-west of Ireland (including perhaps Donegal and Sligo in the Irish Republic), would be a predominantly Roman Catholic institution and thus become an intellectual centre for anti–Partitionist political forces. Coleraine, a predominantly Protestant market town of 12 000 population, was unlikely to fulfil a similar role.

While the actual processes of the locational decision cannot be fully clarified, the results of the decision have been quite far-reaching. As indicated previously this particular locational decision was one of several associated with O'Neill's programmes for the development of Northern Ireland. Darby (1976) has suggested that the cumulative effect of decisions concerned with the initial choice of growth centres, which afforded Londonderry a secondary status, the closure of one of two rail links between Belfast and Londonderry, the location of the new city of Craigavon on the County Armagh towns of Lurgan and Portadown as well as that associated with the location of the second university gave rise to a sense of isolation and neglect in Londonderry and west of the Bann. As Birrell (1972) has noted, a sense of "relative deprivation" felt by Roman Catholics may well have helped to generate the disturbances in Londonderry in 1968. Certainly within Londonderry both Roman Catholics and liberal Protestants reacted together in deploring the choice of Coleraine. For many Catholics, however, and particularly for those outside the city, the evidence of Unionist splits was not obvious and certainly did not seem significant and some subsequent analyses have attempted to see the location of the second university as a further example of discrimination against Catholics (Farrell, 1977).

The location of the second university was undoubtedly regarded as divisive by most outside the Unionist Parliamentary Party and also by a number within it. It was divisive in two ways. First, it provided an opportunity for those in the Unionist Party who sought to maintain the *status quo* of forty years to question the merits of O'Neill's political strategy, a debate within the Unionist Party which culminated in O'Neill's resignation in 1969. Secondly, by seeming to bow to pressure from Unionists in Londonderry O'Neill did much to subvert his macro-political strategy in the eyes of Roman Catholics, who increasingly came to see it as consisting of fine sentiment but little substance. Finally, it was ironic that the programmes designed to facilitate O'Neill's political strategy, of which Lockwood was one, were substantially weakened by the spatial form of their implementation.

NOTES

1. Magee University College, originally opened in 1865, was not a degree awarding institute. It provided courses equivalent to the first year Arts Faculty in Queen's University and students transferred to complete their degrees. The College also provided part courses for Trinity College, Dublin with students transferring to complete their degrees. In 1963–1964 there were 245 full-time students.

2. See *House of Commons Debates (Northern Ireland)* 59 (1964–1965), 1338–1428, 1442–1658.

3. O'Neill's answer to a question on whether the vote was to be "whipped" was not entirely clear. He did not attempt, however, to correct subsequent suggestions that it was to be so.

4. Not all in Coleraine welcomed the new university. An Anglican clergyman speaking to his parishioners in Coleraine is reported to have said that "the university will bring to the area the big question of increased drinking, gambling and sex and other ancillary evils ... It will change the character of Coleraine and the other towns ..." (*Belfast Telegraph*, 5 May 1965).

REFERENCES

Birrell, D. (1972). Relative Deprivation as a Factor in Conflict in Northern Ireland. *Sociological Review* **20,** 317–343.

Darby, J. (1976). "Conflict in Northern Ireland: The Development of a Polarised Community." Gill and Macmillan, Dublin.

Farrell, M. (1977). "The Orange State." Pluto, London.

Government of Northern Ireland (1965). "Government Statement on the Report of the Committee Appointed by the Minister of Finance 1965" (Cmd. 480). Her Majesty's Stationery Office, Belfast.

House of Commons Debates (Northern Ireland) 59 (1964–1965).

Lockwood, Sir J. (1965). "Higher Education in Northern Ireland: Report of the Committee Appointed by the Minister of Finance" (Cmd. 475). Her Majesty's Stationery Office, Belfast.

Oliver, J. (1978). "Working at Stormont." Institute of Public Administration, Dublin.

Robbins, Lord (1963). "Higher Education: Report of the Committee under the Chairmanship of Lord Robbins" (Cmnd. 2154). Her Majesty's Stationery Office, London.

Stava, P. (1973). Theories of Public Policy Making and the Location of Norwegian District Colleges and Universities. *European Journal of Political Research* **1,** 249–264.

II   Poleglass:
a Case Study of Division

Dale Singleton

THE POLITICAL DECISION MAKING FRAMEWORK

In the context of Government decision making in Northern Ireland and its effect on the promotion of integration or division within the community, the Poleglass proposal, which dates from late 1973, is particularly significant as decisions relating to the scheme were made, unlike the Lockwood new university decision, after the introduction of Direct Rule and the reform programme in Northern Ireland. Those measures having a bearing on this case study and which to an extent conditioned reactions to the proposal are set out below:

(i) Following the recommendations of the Commission of Inquiry into Disturbances in Northern Ireland (Cameron, 1969) and what Chapman (1972) describes as "direct pressure from Whitehall", a central housing authority, the Northern Ireland Housing Executive, was established. It took over responsibility for the building, management and allocation of all public sector housing from the sixty-one local authorities, the Northern Ireland Housing Trust and the three New Town Development Commissions. A points scheme for the allocation of all public sector dwellings was also introduced.

(ii) In March 1972 the Northern Ireland Parliament at Stormont was prorogued and its powers were transferred to Ministers of State appointed by the Westminster Government.

(iii) In October 1973 the implementation of the report by the Review Body on Local Government in Northern Ireland (Macrory, 1970) led to the removal of planning powers from the former local councils. A central planning authority was established, headed by a Minister of State. Twenty-six new District Councils replaced the former local authorities, but they were endowed with few powers (see Chapter 5).

(iv) With the establishment of a central planning agency in 1973, it was considered that the appellate function of the Government Ministry responsible for planning was no longer consistent with the new situation and an independent body, the Planning Appeals Commission, was set up to carry out this function.

ORIGINS OF THE POLEGLASS DEVELOPMENT

The origins of the proposal date from 1973 when the Northern Ireland Housing Executive made crisis representations to the Department of the Environment (Northern Ireland) (hereinafter D.O.E.)[1] to designate a site or sites for housing in the Belfast area, to accommodate the large number of Roman Catholics on the waiting list. The reason why Roman Catholics formed such a large proportion of the waiting list at that time relates to the way in which the "religious geography" of the Urban Area developed from the date of the initial disturbances in August 1969. A massive internal population movement, triggered by intimidation and fear, took place within the Belfast Urban Area between 1969 and 1973 (Northern Ireland Community Relations Commission, 1971; Darby and Morris, 1974). It has been estimated that during this time more than 10 000 houses were abandoned and bricked up and some 60 000 people fled to the safety of Protestant and Roman Catholic enclaves (*Sunday Times*, 14 March 1976). In the process, most of the land in the Belfast suburbs which was earmarked for mixed (Roman Catholic and Protestant) public sector housing during the 1960s was taken up by Protestants, largely because of its geographical position in relation to existing majority Protestant areas. In parts of west and inner north Belfast, however, the reverse process occurred and several mixed housing areas became almost wholly Catholic (Fig. 7.1). Examples of these in the vicinity of the proposed Poleglass site are Twinbrook, a 1000 house scheme which in its early stages of development was 50% Protestant and 50% Roman Catholic and Suffolk, a 2000 house public sector estate, which is now 100% Roman Catholic, with the exception of a small Protestant exclave (Fig. 7.2).

It is important to add the rider that Community Relations Commission surveys subsequently established that many people who were obliged to move house from mixed areas were angry at being forced by general pressure from "outside elements", but simply felt that they

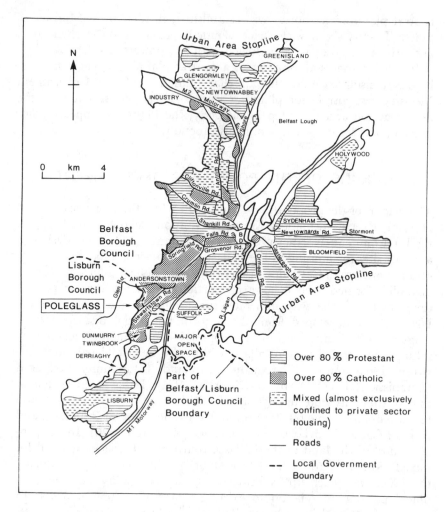

FIGURE 7.1. The Distribution of Protestants and Roman Catholics in the Belfast Urban Area in 1979, with the Location of the Poleglass Housing Development.

had no option[2] (Darby and Morris, 1974; see also Chapter 10). The process on a much reduced scale has continued up to the present. In simplistic terms the net result of this movement has meant that Roman Catholics have concentrated in the western sector of the Belfast Urban Area, consolidating their traditional territorial axis, while the main Protestant concentration is east of the River Lagan (Fig. 7.1). The historical territorial patterns of development of the two communities,

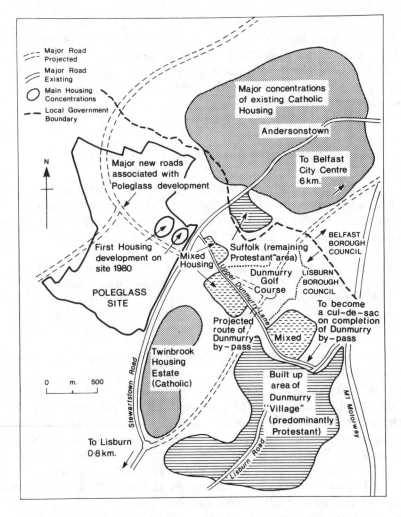

FIGURE 7.2. The Poleglass Housing Site and its Environs.

together with the results of the population movements from 1969 onwards, were an obvious constraint in the search for a new housing site for Roman Catholics.

The D.O.E. did initially consider locating the scheme in a Protestant suburb of the city, backed by blanket security, but eventually Poleglass, an extension of Roman Catholic west Belfast, was deemed to be the only realistic site in the Belfast Urban Area. Preliminary proposals, envisaging a development of up to 4000 dwellings, were published in 1974 (D.O.E., 1974). Designation of the site (Fig. 7.2) meant breaking the Belfast Stop Line which had been accepted by the Government in 1964 as part of the Regional Planning Strategy for Northern Ireland (Matthew, 1964). Both were means of limiting the growth of Belfast by creating a green belt around the city and moving the overspill to designated growth centres.

REACTIONS TO THE PROPOSAL

The proposal to build at Poleglass triggered predictable reactions. There was broad support from Roman Catholic politicians and the Catholic community and opposition by Protestant politicians and the Protestant community. Stewart (1977, p. 181) remarks that:

> The war in Ulster is being fought out on a narrower ground than even the most impatient observer might imagine, a ground every inch of which has its own associations and special meaning. The Ulsterman carries the map of this religious geography in his mind almost from birth.

Every Government locational decision is therefore scrutinised by sections of both communities in terms of how it might alter the existing territorial balance. The sectarian sorting process since 1969 had resulted in a loss of Protestant territory in the west Belfast-Dunmurry area. Although it may therefore have seemed logical to the D.O.E. that an extension to existing Roman Catholic territory in west Belfast was the only suitable "narrow ground" available for the scheme in the whole of the Belfast area, to many Protestants in the Dunmurry-Lisburn area the local spatial pattern was paramount and in these terms the proposal was viewed as an incursion into Protestant territory.

Some of the fiercest criticism of the proposal came from Lisburn Borough Council, the District Council area in which the scheme was to be built. The Lisburn Council area is predominantly Protestant (83%) and the balance of power in the council chamber rests with Unionist politicians (Table 7.2). However, as reorganisation of local government in Northern Ireland had removed housing and planning powers from local authorities, Lisburn Borough Council was to a large extent impotent in a situation where the D.O.E., headed by a Westminster-appointed Minister of State, had the final decision-making power.

TABLE 7.2. Political Composition of Lisburn Borough Council, 1979.

United Ulster Unionist Party	1 seat	(Anti
Official Unionist Party	10 seats	power-sharing
Democratic Unionist Party	6 seats	parties)
Alliance Party	3 seats	(Pro
Social Democratic and Labour Party	2 seats	power-sharing
Unionist Party of Northern Ireland	1 seat	parties)

While most of the initial opposition to the scheme was sectarian, in the sense that the development was seen as an extension of Roman Catholic (and therefore Republican and I.R.A.) territory in a largely Protestant Borough, there were others who criticised the scheme for more conventional planning reasons particularly on grounds of its sheer size and the inevitable social and other problems which large public sector estates often generate. Lisburn Borough Council also raised the question of squatting and the non-payment of rent and rates as objections to the Poleglass proposal. It argued that the experience of the neighbouring Twinbrook housing estate was a salient factor. Twinbrook (Fig. 7.2), comprising 1000 dwellings and almost completely lacking in community facilities, was built in the late 1960s and early 1970s. It has been the scene of considerable violence during the period of civil disturbance. The Council correctly claimed that the Housing Executive was unable to control house allocations in the estate, and that illegal tenants were subsequently given legal tenancies of dwellings in which they had originally squatted. Councillors contended, in spite of reassurances by the Minister of State for the Environment, that Poleglass would suffer the same fate.

The rents and rates issue has been a particularly divisive one since 1971 when Roman Catholics were encouraged to withhold payment as a protest against internment. Internment was phased out in 1975, but withholding of rents and rates continues in several areas throughout Northern Ireland. The Council was forecasting that, just as Twinbrook had a large payments deficit, Poleglass would also.

After this period of critical comment the D.O.E. re-examined waiting list and population data and revised proposals were published in May 1976 (D.O.E., 1976). The revised scheme for 2000 dwellings represented a cut by half in the original proposals. Rumours persisted that the real reason for such a fundamental reassessment had nothing to do with demographic or planning considerations. It was suggested that Unionist M.P.s had applied political pressure on the Northern Ireland Secretary of State, relating to the way they would vote in

crucial divisions at Westminster. At that time (1974–1976) the Labour
Government had a narrow and, following several by-elections in 1975
and 1976, no overall majority in the House of Commons. Although
this allegation was vigorously refuted, it is noteworthy that the possibility for such pressure did exist, notwithstanding the prorogation of
Stormont and the impotence of the local council. Therefore the ten
Unionist M.P.s at Westminster exerted a degree of influence much out
of proportion to their numbers in the 635 seat chamber.

Many objections were lodged to the proposals as amended and a
public inquiry was held to consider them, under the auspices of the
Northern Ireland Planning Appeals Commission.

THE INQUIRY

The inquiry took place in October and November 1976. The principal
objectors to the plan going ahead were: Lisburn Borough Council,
who employed independent planning consultants from London to
advise it, principally on the possibility of alternative sites for the
development; Belfast City Council; and Dunmurry residents. Dunmurry
is a predominantly Protestant suburb of Belfast just over one kilometre
from the Poleglass site (Fig. 7.2). Objecting for different reasons were
the Social Democratic and Labour Party and the Republican Clubs,
political parties which draw their support almost exclusively from
sections of the Roman Catholic population, who argued that the scheme
had been halved between 1974 and 1976 with no apparent justification.
In contrast, Rev. William Beattie, deputy leader of Rev. Ian Paisley's
Democratic Unionist Party, described the proposal as massive and
menacing, which would increase pressure on Protestants living in the
Dunmurry, Derriaghy and Suffolk areas. "Their present fear and
concern could reach panic level", he added. On several occasions
those objecting to the scheme described the proposed site as Protestant
territory which must not be violated.

Objectors on both sides challenged the D.O.E. statistics on housing
need and there was much debate concerning the size of the waiting
list for west Belfast and the birth, death, new household formation and
migration rates for the area. On several occasions the inquiry became
bogged down in a morass of disputed statistics. The Northern Ireland
Planning Appeals Commission, in its report on the inquiry (1978, p. 52),
criticised the D.O.E.'s presentation of statistical evidence on the
reasons why the scheme had been reduced from 4000 to 2000 dwellings:
"There can be no doubt that such a major policy change warranted a

more satisfactory explanation than was forthcoming from the Department's witnesses".

THE RESULT

Deliberations on the evidence presented at the inquiry lasted for more than a year. In November 1977 the matter was raised in the House of Commons when the Social Democratic and Labour Party member for West Belfast questioned what he called "the disgraceful and completely unjustified delay in producing the report".

In January 1978 the Minister of State for the Environment, having received the Planning Appeals Commission report on the inquiry, announced the Government's intention of proceeding with the development of housing and ancillary facilities at Poleglass. In its report to the D.O.E. the Planning Appeals Commission concisely summed up its view regarding objections to the scheme:

Members took the view that if fear were a relevant factor in favour of the scheme, then in all fairness, it had to be considered as an equally relevant objection to the scheme. The problem was that the need for the scheme had its roots in fear on the part of one section of the community whilst the proposed solution apparently created fear in another section of the community. (Northern Ireland Planning Appeals Commission, 1978, p. 5)

The D.O.E. in its subsequent statement (D.O.E., 1978) accepted the very real fears of the objectors, but maintained that it had also to take full account of the needs and aspirations of people in west Belfast for reasonable housing standards and for an easement of the social deprivation caused by overcrowding and poor housing conditions. The Department's statement also made the point that integration of the communities in housing would be encouraged "as the security situation improves" but that it would be unrealistic to assume that west Belfast housing demand could in the short term at least be satisfied to any significant degree by existing or new housing in north Belfast or elsewhere in the city.

PROBLEMS OF IMPLEMENTATION

The announcement by the Secretary of State did not diminish the protests. Several protest marches and other forms of lobbying have taken place, centred on the activities of the Anti-Poleglass Action Group and their "Stop Poleglass Campaign". The action group is composed of several Unionist Westminster M.P.s and Unionist councillors from Lisburn Borough Council.

It is difficult to gauge the extent of the Action Group's support. Several thousand people have turned up at protest marches and rallies, but it is likely that it also has support from a silent majority of Protestants in areas close to the designated site. Having failed in its attempt to either stop or divert the project to a site outside its boundary, Lisburn Borough Council subsequently voted to boycott meetings with the D.O.E. on the provision of open space and community facilities in the proposed development. These statutory functions remained with District Councils after reorganisation of local government in 1973.

Marches and rallies were the tactics used by the Civil Rights Movement in 1968 in an attempt to gain some of the levers of power, and abstentionist tactics by Roman Catholics on local councils have been used throughout the history of Northern Ireland. In a sense the wheel has come full circle with Unionists bereft of the levers of power in this instance being forced into "minority" tactics in an attempt to block the Poleglass proposal. One march, subsequently banned by the police, was planned to the site itself, passing within yards of the Twinbrook development, clearly a manifestation that the area was regarded as Protestant territory.

THE MIDDLE GROUND

Some reactions to the proposal did represent the narrow middle ground of opinion within each community. The three Alliance Party members (see Chapter 6) on Lisburn Borough Council supported Poleglass as an easing of the acute housing shortage in west Belfast, but reserved judgement on the environmental and social consequences of large housing estates.

The Alliance councillor for Dunmurry also spoke out against the road proposals associated with the development which he claimed would act as physical barriers between Protestants in Dunmurry and Roman Catholics in Twinbrook and Poleglass, and effectively destroy the mixed community at Upper Dunmurry Lane which he described as a stabilising force in the area (Fig. 7.2). The councillor was also concerned that the construction of roads associated with the development would require the removal of Dunmurry Golf Course. He described it as a valuable environmental amenity and an important meeting place for Roman Catholics and Protestants in the surrounding areas.

These statements pale somewhat against the weight of outright objections to the proposal. There has been no groundswell of moderate Roman Catholic and Protestant opinion in the Dunmurry and Lisburn areas welcoming the scheme in however qualified terms. Many owner occupiers in the Dunmurry and north Lisburn areas, from whom one might ordinarily expect such moderate attitudes, stand to suffer financially from falling property values as a result of the Poleglass scheme going ahead. There is already evidence of Protestants moving out of the Dunmurry area. The decision to proceed with Poleglass has therefore triggered a domino process of movement which will have ripple effects far beyond the actual development site.

A SAMPLE OF NEWSPAPER COVERAGE OF THE POLEGLASS ISSUE

Analysis of newspaper content in Northern Ireland is useful as an indicator of attitudes on a particular issue. The content can, of course, also condition attitudes. Roman Catholics and Protestants in Northern Ireland tend to read different newspapers. It has been estimated that 87% of the *Belfast Newsletter's* readership is Protestant and 93% of that of the *Irish News* is Catholic (Rose, 1971). They are both Belfast morning dailies. The former tends to represent the views of the Official Unionist Party and the latter propounds nationalist views of several shades. In contrast, the Belfast evening newspaper, the *Belfast Telegraph*, has a 68% Protestant readership (Darby, 1976) which is roughly *pro rata* for the percentage of Protestants in the total population of Northern Ireland. A content analysis of these newspapers, together with the *Andersonstown News* and the *Ulster Star*, was undertaken. The *Andersonstown News* is a weekly paper circulating in the west Belfast area, read by Roman Catholics. It has a "British withdrawal" editorial policy. The *Ulster Star* is a local newspaper circulating in the Dunmurry and Lisburn areas with a majority Protestant readership, reflecting their numbers in the circulation area. It had no editorial on Poleglass but reported the issue in detail, concentrating on the reactions of Lisburn Borough Council.

Before considering the newspaper coverage it is perhaps enlightening to repeat the apocryphal story quoted by Darby (1976) about the two Belfast morning newspapers:

A child fell into the crocodile pool at Belfast Zoo and a bystander, reacting quickly, jumped in, punched the reptile on the snout and pulled the child out. The *Belfast Newsletter* headlined the story "Protestant rescues boy". The *Irish News* headline was, "Protestant attacks dumb animal".

A content analysis of newspaper coverage of the issue, over the whole time period of the proposal, is impossible in the space available. Coverage of a particular aspect of the decision-making process, the inquiry and reactions to it, has therefore been selected to illustrate attitudes to the proposal.

Day to day coverage of the public inquiry was carried by the *Belfast Newsletter*, the *Irish News* and the *Belfast Telegraph*. The reporting was fairly objective although the underlying readership interests were apparent in the way that the Belfast morning dailies treated the subject. The *Belfast Newsletter* tended to concentrate on questions like "Who'll Enforce the Law inside Poleglass?" and "Orangemen Oppose Poleglass Scheme", whereas the *Irish News* headlines emphasised other aspects: "Poleglass the Only Suitable Site Says Planning Officer" and "Catholics Want to Live in the West of the City for Safety". The result of the inquiry received extensive coverage in all the newspapers scanned. The *Belfast Telegraph* editorial on the result of the inquiry was headlined "Hobson's Choice". The outcome was regarded as the least objectionable solution even though it meant creating another sectarian ghetto. The *Belfast Newsletter* leader titled "Not the Best Solution" argued that, while halving the number of houses was a step in the right direction, the situation then prevailing (January 1978) meant that Roman Catholics had much greater freedom of movement, allowing the possibility of their being housed in parts of north Belfast in houses which had been vacated by Protestants. The *Irish News* editorial described the result in very different terms:

> Because of the downright sectarian and intimidatory attitude of Protestant extremists, it was decided, two years ago, to cut by half a £50 million scheme for rehousing an estimated 18,000 people from West Belfast in 4,000 new houses in the townland of Poleglass on the outskirts of the city . . . Besides disappointing those who hoped for new houses, he [the Minister of State] has raised questions about the lack of courage of direct rule politicians in trimming down an admirable scheme because of the opposition of mean and bigoted men.

The *Andersonstown News*, in an editorial, raised the question of the description of the proposed scheme as sectarian, pointing to the fact that there were many Protestant-only estates in the Belfast area, and that few Roman Catholics in Belfast felt safe outside west Belfast. The *Ulster Star* reported reactions in the Lisburn area which were generally hostile, and contained calls to continue opposition to the scheme. Throughout 1978 the *Ulster Star* reported on the "Stop Poleglass Campaign" culminating in September when a march and rally was organised in opposition to the scheme proceeding. Reaction to the march and rally was carried in the *Andersonstown News* under the heading "Rally Tension Mounts". The organisers' estimate of those attending, reported in the following week's edition of the *Ulster Star*, was 10 000 people. The *Andersonstown News* estimated the turnout as 1500! The *Belfast Telegraph's* reaction to the march and rally under the title "Polarised" was that the Poleglass protest had descended into the realms of simple sectarian confrontation. The continuing opposition to the scheme, including in November 1978 the formation of a "War Cabinet" to stop Poleglass, has been regularly reported in the *Ulster Star*.

FURTHER BLOCKING TACTICS

The return of a Conservative administration in May 1979, pledged to cut public expenditure, gave the Lisburn Borough Council renewed hope that the scheme might be scrapped. It intensified its lobbying after the general election, but the Conservative Minister of State for the Environment announced in August 1979 that the scheme was to proceed. He did, however, warn that if there was any squatting in the first phase of 313 houses then further phases would be scrapped. He also gave an assurance that existing squatters in other housing areas and those with rent and rates arrears would not be housed at Poleglass.

The Lisburn Borough Council used blocking tactics on the three occasions when the planning application for the first phase was put to it for consultation. Eventually, in October 1979, the Minister's patience ran out, and planning permission was granted without the normal consultation procedure with the Council.

House building commenced in February 1980 with continuing protests from Lisburn Borough Council on the small amount of expressed demand for housing at Poleglass as reflected by the waiting list.

During the construction of the first phase, Lisburn Borough Council again came into conflict with the D.O.E., by deciding that it would not provide a refuse collection service to the estate when it was built. The Environment Minister warned the Council that the provision of a refuse collection service was its statutory duty. He made it clear that the

D.O.E. would make alternative arrangements to have the service carried out in the event of the Council's failure to do so, but that a levy for the cost of the operation would be payable by the Council. The Minister eventually made an order under the Northern Ireland Public Health Act making it mandatory on the Council to provide the service, at which point the leader of Lisburn Borough Council acquiesced, conceding that under the terms of the Northern Ireland Local Government Act the Council was duty bound to provide the service, and would do so.

The first thirty houses in the estate were completed and occupied towards the end of 1980, in what an "exclusive" report in a local Sunday newspaper described as: "a secret dawn occupation . . . in one of the biggest hush-hush operations ever mounted by the Housing Executive".

A few weeks later, despite massive cut-backs in public sector housing finance and a moratorium on all council house starts in Great Britain, plans were announced to commence building further phases of the Poleglass scheme.

CONCLUSIONS

There seems little doubt that the building of Poleglass will reduce the Roman Catholic waiting list and ease housing pressure in Catholic areas scheduled for redevelopment and housing action area treatment in parts of the inner city. This will enable clearance and improvement work to proceed, thus accelerating the Belfast inner city initiative.

The proposal was seen in 1973 as a reaction to a housing crisis during a period of civil strife. Nevertheless, normal peacetime procedures of housing and planning legislation were followed in the course of implementing the proposal. In the report on the public inquiry the D.O.E. was criticised by the Planning Appeals Commission for the way it presented its evidence on housing need. For the Planning Appeals Commission to insist on the niceties of elaborate and detailed statistical evidence in a highly dynamic war situation, when reliable data are so difficult to obtain, appears an over-ambitious requirement. The result of adopting peacetime procedures delayed a start to actual construction until 1980. The *Belfast Newsletter* and *Irish News* would interpret the reasons for this differently; it is certainly a very long response time.

Viewed at the time of writing (early 1981), a major question remains unanswered about events during the Poleglass decision-making process. The demand for housing among Roman Catholics in the Belfast Urban Area in 1973 was a problem of crisis proportions. More than eight years elapsed before the first houses at Poleglass were completed. How has the demand been met in the interim, as potential new households have continually added to the numbers requiring housing? Clearly part of the demand has been met by territorial expansion in inner north Belfast (see Chapter 10) and the "purification" process in Twinbrook. A small amount has been met by migration to growth centres outside Belfast, specifically Antrim, Craigavon and Downpatrick.

However, this is probably only a partial explanation of the way in which Roman Catholics solved their housing needs throughout the 1970s. It seems likely that many people who would have added to the number of potential households in west Belfast have migrated from Northern Ireland. This is a tentative conclusion as the establishment of the actual level of out-migration from west Belfast to other parts of Northern Ireland, and out of Northern Ireland altogether, must await the results of the 1981 Census.

A considerable demand still exists, measured by overcrowding in parts of west Belfast, and the need for overspill dwellings to facilitate redevelopment and action area treatment in the Roman Catholic inner city. Further housing need has been generated by the decision of the Northern Ireland Housing Executive to demolish a number of high density flat blocks in Catholic areas of Belfast, following pressure from community groups in these areas that their housing conditions were not fit to live in.

Viewed in terms of fostering integration or division, the decision to build Poleglass is divisive at most spatial scales and probably also over time. At the local level it creates a "ghetto" and the ripple effects may remove the "middle ground" in surrounding areas. The newspaper content analysis illustrates the fierce reactions of Protestants in the Lisburn Borough. These reactions in turn must be seen to have been at least partially provoked by the continuing I.R.A. bombing campaign and the loss of "Protestant territory" at Twinbrook and Suffolk. If it is accepted that newspaper coverage reflects and conditions attitudes, then, with the exception of the *Belfast Telegraph*, reporting of Poleglass has illustrated the polarised position and contributed to a further polarising of attitudes in the two communities.

The Poleglass decision can be seen as part of a process upsetting the existing territorial balance. The "flight" of population from 1969 onwards also created, in more stark form than previously, two public sector housing markets in the Belfast Urban Area, one Roman Catholic, the other Protestant. This in turn led to the designation of Poleglass which further polarised attitudes of the two communities.

Is the series of actions and reactions, therefore, a never-ending spiral of further polarisation and division? To some extent this must remain speculative. However, if by building Poleglass the Roman Catholic supply–demand equation for housing becomes more balanced, then it removes one motive for violence, namely the "lebensraum" mentality at other Roman Catholic–Protestant interfaces throughout the Belfast Urban Area.

Several authors have stressed the positive functions, including defence, which areas of ethnic residential segregation perform (see Deakin and Ungerson, 1973), and Rose (1973) has warned against social engineering gimmicks such as integration. Boal (1978, p. 91) makes the point that the actual process of creating a homogeneous area must take particular note of the nature of the urban spaces involved because in many instances "these spaces are profoundly territorial and the in-movement of 'alien' households will be viewed as invasion". The Poleglass proposal was seen by Protestants as invasion of their territory. Therefore any positive functions which such an area of ethnic residential segregation can claim have to be set against the polarising reactions generated during the process of its establishment and the possible removal of the middle ground in the surrounding area.

Finally, the Poleglass affair can be seen as a microcosm of the wider political "battle for territory" within the island of Ireland. Slogans such as "Not an Inch" were used in the micro-sense in relation to the land for the Poleglass scheme, just as they are used in the macro-sense in defence of the territorial boundaries of Northern Ireland as a whole. There is little doubt that the fierce reactions to the scheme, by Lisburn Borough Council in particular, reflected the growing disenchantment with the tenants of the neighbouring Twinbrook estate. Twinbrook tenants' behaviour, which included the withholding of rent and rates, the replacement of official street signs with professionally made alternatives printed in Irish, and the flying of tricolours (the flag of the Republic of Ireland) from several flat blocks within the estate, confirmed their disloyalty to the state in the eyes of the Council and the majority of its constituents. Obviously such "disloyal" behaviour could also occur in the Poleglass estate, and this was reason enough to resist the development all along the line.

In this sense the problems of integrated or segregated residential areas are secondary, as housing policy in west Belfast since the outbreak of violence in 1969 has been the hostage of the macro-political issue— the challenge to the legitimacy of the state itself.

NOTES

1. Between 1973 and 1976 the name of the Government Department responsible for housing and planning changed from the Ministry of Development to the Department of Housing, Local Government and Planning, then finally to the Department of the Environment. The term Department of the Environment has been used throughout the text to avoid confusion.

2. Based on survey work carried out in Belfast in 1966 before the onset of the present period of civil disturbance, Budge and O'Leary (1973) found that a majority of Belfast Catholics and Protestants, irrespective of class divisions, favoured integrated public sector housing estates. A survey of Housing Executive tenants throughout Northern Ireland carried out between April and November 1975 (Russell, 1980) found that in answer to the question: "If you were able to choose today would you decide to live in an area where you were surrounded by your own religion or where there were about as many Catholics as Protestants?" about two-thirds of all tenants interviewed were prepared to live in integrated estates. Almost half of those interviewed positively indicated that they wished to live in integrated housing areas. Disaggregating the analysis to the Belfast sample only, produced the following results. Two-thirds of the Belfast tenants interviewed demanded religiously segregated housing. In separating the Belfast responses by religion Russell found that one-half of Belfast Protestants wanted to live in segregated areas compared to four-fifths of Belfast's Catholics.

REFERENCES

Boal, F. W. (1978). Ethnic Residential Segregation. *In* "Social Areas in Cities: Processes, Patterns and Problems" (D. T. Herbert and R. J. Johnston, eds.), pp. 57–95. John Wiley, London.

Budge, I. and O'Leary, C. (1973). "Belfast—Approach to Crisis: A Study of Belfast Politics, 1613–1970." Macmillan, London.

Cameron, Lord (1969). "Disturbances in Northern Ireland: Report of the Commission Appointed by the Governor of Northern Ireland" (Cmd. 532). Her Majesty's Stationery Office, Belfast.

Chapman, P. (1972). Housing Reform in Northern Ireland. *Official Architecture and Planning* **35,** 171–174.

Darby, J. (1976). "Conflict in Northern Ireland: The Development of a Polarised Community." Gill and Macmillan, Dublin.

Darby, J. and Morris, G. (1974). "Intimidation in Housing." Northern Ireland Community Relations Commission, Belfast.

Deakin, N. and Ungerson, C. (1973). Beyond the Ghetto: The Illusion of Choice. *In* "London: Urban Patterns, Problems and Policies" (D. Donnison and D. Eversley, eds.), pp. 215–247. Heinemann, London.

Department of the Environment, Northern Ireland (1974). "Poleglass/ Lagmore Development Plan: Preliminary Proposals for Public Consultation." Her Majesty's Stationery Office, Belfast.

Department of the Environment, Northern Ireland (1976). "Poleglass Development Scheme." Her Majesty's Stationery Office, Belfast.

Department of the Environment, Northern Ireland (1978). "Poleglass Area Statement." Her Majesty's Stationery Office, Belfast.

Macrory, P. A. (1970). "Review Body on Local Government in Northern Ireland: Report" (Cmd. 546). Her Majesty's Stationery Office, Belfast.

Matthew, Sir R. H. (1964). "Belfast Regional Survey and Plan, 1962: A Report." Her Majesty's Stationery Office, Belfast.

Northern Ireland Community Relations Commission Research Unit (1971). "Flight: A Report on Population Movement in Belfast during August 1971." Northern Ireland Community Relations Commission, Belfast.

Northern Ireland Planning Appeals Commission (1978). "Poleglass Area Public Inquiry Report." Her Majesty's Stationery Office, Belfast.

Rose, R. (1971). "Governing without Consensus: An Irish Perspective." Faber and Faber, London.

Rose, R. (1973). Where Can People Live? *Community Forum* **3,** 15–17.

Russell, J. (1980). "Housing amidst Civil Unrest." Research Series No. 41, Centre for Environmental Studies, London.

Stewart, A. T. Q. (1977). "The Narrow Ground." Faber and Faber, London.

CHAPTER 8

PROBLEM REGION AND REGIONAL PROBLEM

Anthony G. Hoare

INTRODUCTION

Northern Ireland is a "problem region" with a "regional problem". To the Ulster[1]-watchers of the mainland United Kingdom and beyond, the first of these labels will be the more familiar. Even before 1969, when the "troubles" thrust it into the headlines of the world, Northern Ireland was universally accepted as the most unhealthy economic region of the United Kingdom. While the absolute level of this economic *malaise* varies with the state of the national, and, indeed, the world economy (Quigley, 1976, p. 15), the region's relative economic status has remained little altered since at least 1945.

TABLE 8.1. Northern Ireland: Some Regional Indicators.

	N.I.	U.K.	N.I. regional rank
Percentage unemployment	11·2	6·2	Highest
Weekly household income	£74·20	£87·67	Lowest
Percentage of households with weekly income under £20	11·2	4·7	Highest
Weekly expenditure per person	£21·5	£24·5	Lowest
Colour as a percentage of T.V. licences	50	61	Lowest
Two-car households	6·1	9·6	Lowest
Workers per household	1·18	1·35	Lowest
Percentage of workers in agriculture	7·3	2·9	Highest
Percentage of heads of household in professional and technical posts	4·1	6·5	Lowest
Percentage of heads of household in administrative and management posts	4·8	7·3	Lowest
Percentage of agricultural holdings more than thirty hectares	12·2	38·6	Lowest

Source: Central Statistical Office (1979). (The data refer to 1977 or to 1976–1977.)

Table 8.1, drawn from the latest available comparable set of regional statistics for the United Kingdom, bears witness to the deep-seated nature of Northern Ireland's economic problems. While its unemployment percentage is the most widely quoted statistic of regional distress, the data show the area also to be at the foot of the league table on a range of measures of economic structure, occupational status and family income and expenditure.

In fairness, it can be added that some other indices would show Northern Ireland in a happier light, but one has to search much harder for the favourable statistics than for the depressing ones. On balance, there is little doubt that, economically, Northern Ireland is the sick man of the United Kingdom.

Not surprisingly, there has been no lack of analysis of the past, present and possible future course of the region's economic woes. Diagnosis of their root causes, details of the remedial measures introduced, and of their success or otherwise are widespread in the literature (e.g. Black, 1976; 1977; Davies *et al.*, 1977; Houston, 1976; Isles and Cuthbert, 1957; Moore *et al.*, 1978; Quigley, 1976; Schiller, 1978; Simpson, 1971; Wallace, 1971). Even so, two general points must be borne in mind. First, as Northern Ireland is still the United Kingdom's problem region *par excellence*, regional policy at the broad scale has, at best, been a holding operation. Secondly, such broad-scale spatial analysis tells us nothing about the distribution of economic health and prosperity *within* Northern Ireland, which creates the internal "regional problem" of the Northern Ireland "problem region".

THE REGIONAL PROBLEM

Within any geographical area, "economic prosperity", whatever we mean by that term, is unevenly distributed in space. When these inequalities become intolerably large and persistent, we accept that a regional problem exists. By general consensus this holds true within Northern Ireland at the present time.

Unfortunately, intra-regional socio-economic data for Northern Ireland are not available for a common framework of areal subdivisions. Since 1972 unemployment statistics have been made public for so-called "Travel-to-Work Areas", designed to correspond to the journey-to-work structure of the region. Figure 9.3 (Chapter 9) shows the distribution of unemployment for these areas as of June 1978, and emphasises the east–west division most clearly. Comparison with the maps produced by Salt and Johnson (1975) for 1970–1973 shows that, despite a change of recording units, this spatial pattern is a well-established one. Analysis of the *duration* of unemployment (Chapter 9, Fig. 9.5) shows a very similar picture: not only is the chance of becoming unemployed less in the east than in the west, but the chance of finding a job quickly is greater, once unemployment has arisen.

The same Travel-to-Work Areas can be used to show the broad structural pattern of the employed population (Central Statistical Office, 1979). Since it is often taken as an index of comparative under-development, particular interest attaches to the pattern of agricultural employment, of which Northern Ireland as a whole has the highest regional proportion of the entire United Kingdom (Table 8.1). At the sub-regional level the same broad east–west divide recurs (Fig. 8.1): the dependence on agriculture as a source of employment is substantially higher in the west (with the exception of the Londonderry area) than in the east of Northern Ireland.[2]

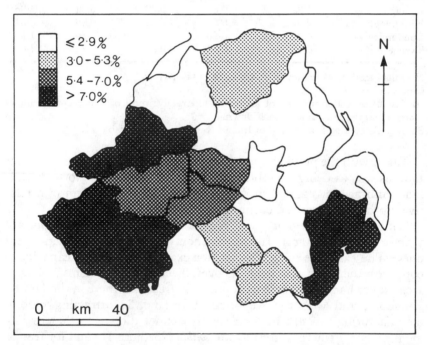

FIGURE 8.1. Employment in Agriculture by Travel-to-Work Area, June 1977.
Source: Central Statistical Office (1979, pp. 27–29).

Finally, another commonly used index of economic health is available at the county level from surveys of personal income conducted by the Inland Revenue. Table 8.2 shows a number of summary statistics, drawn from the 1969–1970 survey, the first one to record tax-payers by their county of residence rather than of their tax office. The distinction between the "wealthy" counties of Antrim and Down and the poorer western ones is obvious. This holds true for each type of taxable income identified, and for the proportion of resident populations paying the high-status category of investment income tax.

TABLE 8.2. Income Differences, 1969–1970.[a]

| | Net Investment Income | | | | |
| | Cases per 1000 population (1971) | Average taxable sum per case (£000)[b] | | | |
		Schedule D	Schedule E	Net Investment Income	Total
N. Ireland	5·15	0·94	0·99	0·36	1·14
Antrim[c]	5·50	1·12	1·01	0·35	1·16
Down[c]	6·13	0·96	1·05	0·43	1·19
Armagh	4·85	0·86	0·89	0·32	1·08
Fermanagh	2·97	0·59	0·89	0·20	1·01
Londonderry	4·30	0·98	0·92	0·30	1·05
Tyrone	4·13	0·79	0·85	0·24	1·00

[a]Results based on estimates from a sample of tax-payers.
[b]Sums are *pre*-tax.
[c]Belfast County Borough is not identified separately: most of it is recorded under Antrim and the remainder under Down.
Source: Calculated from Board of Inland Revenue (1972), Table 71.

Taken with the previous indices, there seems to be abundant evidence that, as well as being a problem region in its own right, Northern Ireland embraces a regional problem of its own—the problem of a relatively prosperous eastern economy set against a depressed west.

While "problem region" and "regional problem" are both important themes of the Northern Ireland economy they are not independent ones.[3] The existence of the former, for example, limits the capacity to cope with the latter. To tackle its overall economic problems Northern Ireland has had to compete with problem areas elsewhere in the United Kingdom, and with the Republic of Ireland, in attracting mobile manufacturing investment, and clearly cannot dictate to that investment precisely where it must locate *within* Northern Ireland for fear of frightening it away altogether. On the other hand, the existence of *some* internal spatial strategy is important to prepare suitable industrial locations as a lure to these footloose firms, so they can see themselves as part of some overall planning strategy and not as an *ad hoc* venture in a policy vacuum.[4]

The attack on regional inequalities within Northern Ireland, then, cannot be divorced from the attempt to revitalise the overall regional economy. Nevertheless, the whole issue of the internal geography of economic health in Northern Ireland, its causes, and its remedies, is even more convoluted than this introductory discussion would indicate.

"Planter" and "Gael"

The single most important reason for this, the *raison d'etre* for this book, is the schism of Northern Ireland society into two almost exhaustive[5] groups, commonly labelled "Roman Catholic" and "Protestant". Since 1969 the "troubles" have stimulated a vast literature on this divide, on the attitudes and fears of the two groups, the historical roots of the divide, the institutions that preserve it and the hopes for healing it. What has not yet been explored in any depth, though, is the extent to which this social divide correlates with the internal regional differences already noted in the economic geography of Northern Ireland.

Superficially, there seems good reason to expect that the two will interact. The consistent evidence from official population censuses before and after Partition is for the broad geographical patterns of Protestant and Roman Catholic respectively to accord with the economic distinction between prosperous east and depressed west. While the latest (1971) data must be treated with caution (Compton, 1976; 1978), Belfast County Borough and Counties Londonderry (exclusive of Londonderry County Borough), Down and Antrim have consistently contained Protestant majorities, and the remaining areas, other than Armagh, have consistently contained Catholic ones (see Chapter 4). Certainly, too, a substantial body of opinion links economic deprivation of all shapes and sizes, perceived and actual, with this same Catholic–Protestant divide (Birrell, 1972).

The remaining part of this chapter examines the interrelationships between inter-community geography on the one hand, and economic prosperity or deprivation on the other. First, it outlines a framework within which to examine these interrelationships and, secondly, it uses this same framework to analyse the recent history of some selected aspects of economic performance within Northern Ireland.

TWO MODELS OF ECONOMIC PROSPERITY

Consider the hypothetical spatial patterns represented in Fig. 8.2. In the diagram labelled "WHERE" the average level of attainment on some economic index does not vary between Protestant and Roman Catholic neighbours, wherever they live. There is, though, a geographical variation in prosperity levels such that the inhabitant of the west, be he Catholic or Protestant, attains only 60% of the wealth of the easterner, whatever his religion. However, given the persistent relative preponderance of Protestants in the east and Catholics in the west, these geographically rooted differences in prosperity will mean that, on average, Protestants will be more prosperous than Catholics. The differences, however, arise because of where the members of the different groups live—hence this will be referred to as the "WHERE" model.

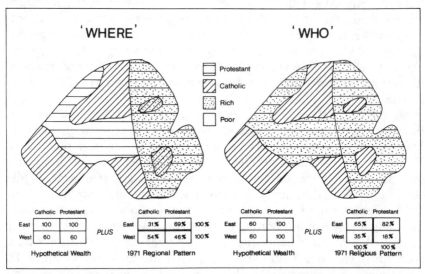

FIGURE 8.2. Two Models of Regional Economic Health.

The alternative (right-hand diagram in Fig. 8.2) is a "WHO" model. Here we assume for the sake of argument that a Protestant consistently is more prosperous than his Catholic neighbour, whether he lives in the east or the west. The key differences now arise because of *who* people are, rather than where they live. Overall, east–west differences will also arise because of the differential concentration of the favoured, Protestant, group in the east. In both models, then, both inter-community and spatial differences in economic health will result: in the "WHERE" model, though, the latter is the dominant partner, and in the "WHO" the former.

So far, so good. But any attempt to take these ideas much further as yet runs into some massive problems of data availability. This will be apparent both in the empirical testing of these models and in the immediately following discussion, where an attempt is made to identify more fully the underlying processes in each of them.

The "WHERE" Model

Here, an obvious starting point is with the family of centre–periphery models, beloved of economic geographers.[6] In the Northern Ireland context the eastern—Belfast—region would be seen as the "core", or "centre", and the west as the "periphery". Given the sharp intra-regional economic contrasts already identified it seems natural to ask in what ways the east could act as a "core region", emanating centralising forces of economic domination upon the west.

(a) Centralising forces

(i) *Market accessibility.* Perhaps the east's most telling economic advantage is its superior access to internal and external markets. The internal market supplied by the consuming public as a whole will vary geographically with population distribution, income levels, and a host of other socio-economic characteristics. A simple method of quantifying some of these factors is through the market potential concept,[7] in terms of which Northern Ireland is clearly dominated by the Belfast region (Fig. 8.3a).

Although income data are not available on a sufficiently fine spatial scale to be included in this model, evidence presented earlier leaves little doubt that such a modification would serve to increase the pull of the eastern "core" even more.

The potential model assumes that the market that can be served from a given point declines with distance, partly because of the effects of transport costs upon price and patronage levels. An alternative formulation, the minimum aggregate travel model, assumes that a producer wishes to serve the entire Northern Ireland market, absorbing all transport costs himself.[8] The corresponding map (Fig. 8.3b) is simpler than that for market potential, but is equally Belfast-centred.

(ii) *Industrial linkages.* In practice, most industrial firms sell, not to the general public, but to other industrial companies. Similarly, they depend on other manufacturers for a variety of inputs. Collectively, these supply and market ties are referred to as "industrial linkages". The market potential model can be modified to identify the geographical accessibility to these linkage opportunities, using 1971 Census data on workplace-based employment to replace the "population" term. The results (Fig. 8.3c) underline the dominance of the core, as does the "minimum aggregate linkage travel" version (Fig. 8.3d).

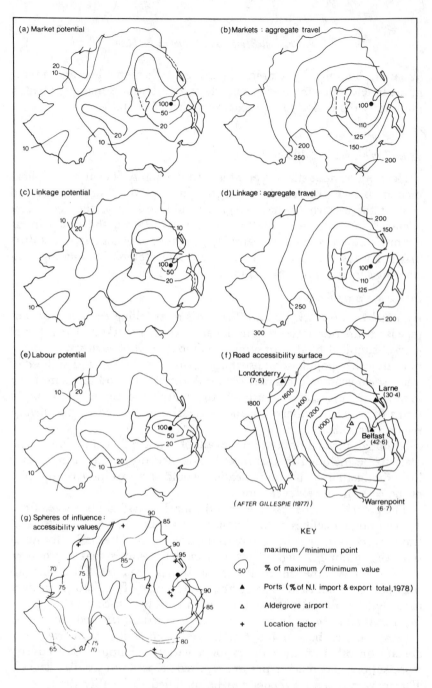

FIGURE 8.3. Centre–Periphery in Northern Ireland—Some Alternative Formulations.

(*iii*) *Labour availability.* 1971 Census data also record industrial employment by place of residence, allowing a further modification of the potential model to identify prime locations from the point of view of labour supply.[9] Labour supply is known to be a major force attracting manufacturing firms to Northern Ireland as a whole (Garnsey, 1965; Law, 1964; McGovern, 1965, p. 15; Murie *et al.*, 1973; Department of Trade and Industry, 1973), and the potential model again emphasises how the Belfast region dominates the rest of Northern Ireland in this respect (Fig. 8.3e).

(*iv*) *Attitudes to work.* Labour supply, as measured above, could be modified spatially by the attitudes towards work held by the potential labour supply. Miller's (1978) recent analysis has revealed that urban-based workers have more positive attitudes towards work than rural residents. As some 60% of the population of the eastern counties (Belfast County Borough, Antrim and Down) lived in "urban areas"[10] in 1971 compared to 45% in the west, his finding further emphasises the advantages of core over periphery.

(*v*) *Transport facilities.* Examination both of Northern Ireland's external and internal transport infrastructure also reveals a strong eastern bias. The area's major airport (Aldergrove) and leading ports (Belfast, Larne) are all "core"-based, while an accessibility index calculated for the internal major road network identifies the Belfast-Portadown corridor as the optimal part of Northern Ireland on this criterion (Gillespie, 1977; Fig. 8.3f).[11]

(*vi*) *Overall locational perception.* Finally, and in summary of some of what has gone before, Fig. 8.3g shows the overall response surface derived from a recent industrial location survey of 408 manufacturers. Each was asked to assess his location with respect to seventeen prompted location factors (Hoare, 1976). The overall score of different parts of Northern Ireland was based on the summation of their proximity to each of these factors, the extent to which the evaluation of each factor is distance-dependent, and the overall importance of each factor in the total survey.[12] The Carrickfergus area emerges as the prime attractive location and, again, the east–west distinction is very obvious.

In sum, there is overwhelming evidence from a number of sources of a centre–periphery distinction in the economic geography of Northern Ireland. Admittedly, the precise delimitation of the "centre" or "core" depends on the specific index adopted. Admittedly, too, the location of some of the centre's economic infrastructure was determined at Stormont, and so is subject to claims of political ("WHO") manoeuvring discussed later.

(b) Decentralising forces

Although less strongly developed, there are also certain counter-vailing "spread" forces to set against the pull of the centre.

(i) *Economic*. While evidence on this question is sketchy, there is some hint that the Belfast area in particular has been experiencing certain diseconomies of scale as an industrial location. These seem to be those typical of most western industrialised cities—a shortage of modern industrial premises, a lack of parking space, congestion problems and high rents and rates levels (Matthew, 1964; McGovern, 1965). More recently, the Quigley Report (1976, p. 84) has emphasised the shortage of labour supply in Belfast. Much of the resultant dispersion that has taken place has been to the outskirts of Belfast (Matthew, 1964, p. 110), or beyond the city but still within the economic "centre" (McGovern, 1965).

(ii) *Political planning*. Decentralisation of economic activity from the Belfast sub-region has also been encouraged as part of official planning policy. This has taken two forms. First, industrial planning, administered by the Department of Commerce, has been concerned with the location of new industrial enterprises within Northern Ireland, as well as bringing them to the area in the first place. While mindful of the limited pressures that can be applied to persuade firms to look beyond Belfast, successive Ministers of Commerce have claimed that, where practical, priority was given to peripheral, high unemployment areas.

The precise policy tools by which this can be achieved include maintaining a stock of industrial sites and advance factories, and the provision of industrially-related infrastructure (often in conjunction with other government departments). Particularly important too is the flexibility built into the negotiating process concerning the rates of industrial grants payable on new projects. Overall, these are the single most important lure that Northern Ireland can offer to the migrant factory (Department of Trade and Industry, 1973; Murie *et al.*, 1973) and *within* Northern Ireland, although no explicit zoning exists in this respect, the percentage grant attainable is higher in areas with high proportional unemployment, other things being equal. Although the majority of sponsored manufacturing remains in the east of Northern Ireland this relative concentration has certainly weakened through time. Between 1945 and 1959 23% of sponsored firms set up within Belfast County Borough, and 75% within fifty kilometres of the city; between 1960 and 1973 these figures had fallen respectively to 11% and 65% and the total number of sponsorships was double that of the earlier period.

Physical planning has also shown a progressive movement away from

Belfast, at least until the mid-1970s. Variously the responsibility of the Ministry of Development, the Ministry of Housing, Local Government and Planning, and the Department of the Environment (Northern Ireland), physical planning since 1960 has centred upon two major internal problems—the overwhelming concentration of population and employment in the immediate Belfast area, and the flagging fortunes of the west (Murie, 1973). Four major reports have focussed on these twin problems. The terms of reference of the first, the Matthew Report (1964), were confined to the Belfast sub-region, within which it instituted a "Stop Line" around built-up Belfast to restrict its further outward growth, and a series of "growth centres" partly designed to accommodate the surplus that this would release from Belfast.[13] The most important of these, the new city of Craigavon, was to serve also as a focus for growth in the south and west of Northern Ireland. While the Stop Line has been fairly faithfully preserved since, other aspects of the 1964 report have been less consistently observed. The three subsequent studies (Wilson, 1965; Matthew *et al.*, 1970; Department of

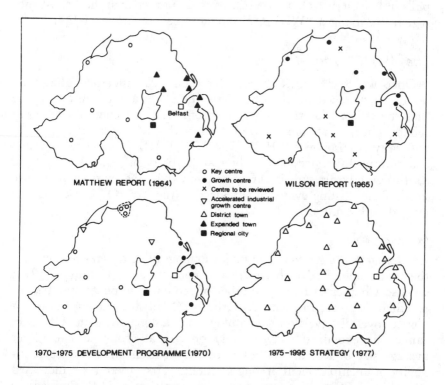

FIGURE 8.4. Regional Planning Strategies, 1964–1977.

the Environment, 1977) have extended physical planning to the whole of Northern Ireland, in the process altering the labels attached to the planned expansion centres, and modifying the locations so designated (Fig. 8.4).

Certainly, the attention given to the west has progressively increased, but beyond this little can safely be said about the strength of this "spread" process. While the locations actually designated as growth centres have been criticised on economic grounds (Gillespie, 1977) no comprehensive study has yet been made of their impact. The relationship between the actions of the industrial and physical planning agencies is also ill-defined. Recently, too, there has been a switch to concern with the problems of inner Belfast, and a major breach in the Stop Line has been opened up by the Poleglass housing scheme in west Belfast (see Chapter 7). All this must throw doubt on the capacity and desire of planning authorities to counteract the core attractions of the Belfast region.

On balance, there seems little reason to doubt that the relative spatial pulls in Northern Ireland are still strongly in favour of the Belfast sub-region, justifying a "WHERE" model of economic variability.

The "WHO" Model

Once we change tack to consider economic differences that arise because of who people are rather than where they are we must recognise that the reasons for this can come from within a community group (endogenous) or be imposed on it from without (exogenous).

Ideally, to isolate "WHO" from "WHERE", evidence of inter-community differences should be standardised for geographical area. As this standardisation is rarely attempted in the existing literature some of the existing evidence advanced in the "WHO" cause must be treated with caution.

(a) Endogenous

(i) *Demographic differences.* The major demographic differences between the two dominant Northern Ireland communities (Compton, 1976; see also Chapter 4) have a number of economic implications. Unemployment is a case in point. As Osborne (1978) has shown, the much higher overall levels of unemployment among Roman Catholics cannot be explained away merely on spatial grounds. The larger average size of Roman Catholic families in itself increases the probability of unemployment among Catholics. First, there is an increased probability of Catholics encountering unemployment in the immediate family, perhaps making them more likely to accept it as a way of life. Secondly, social security payments made to large families may reduce the perceived need to work (see Chapter 9). Thirdly, the younger age structure of Catholic families,[14] consequent upon high birth rates and large families, produces a high ratio of school-leavers to active workers, which may increase Catholic unemployment rates when jobs are scarce (Compton, 1976, p. 449). Large families, too, may mean fewer opportunities for "luxuries" such as a car, which in turn limits job-search and travel-to-work patterns, and thus job opportunities. Similarly, greater family commitments may prevent Catholic women seeking a job far from home, or seeking one at all: the 1971 proportion of Catholic females aged fifteen and over who were "economically active" was below the Northern Ireland average, despite the percentage of adult Catholic females who were single being above average. Conversely, the proportion of females in the 1971 total of employed Catholics (35·5%) was higher than for Protestants, again with implications for job-search and mobility. Finally, the persistently higher age-specific emigration rates of Catholics (Compton, 1976, p. 442; Walsh, 1970) should diminish the quality of the remaining labour force, assuming that one accepts the conventional wisdom that the most enterprising migrate first.

(*ii*) *Educational differences.* The very different school education structures of Roman Catholic and Protestant (Barritt and Carter, 1962, p. 77 *et seq.*) could produce variations in the character of the labour force. Table 8.3 summarises some of the important 1971 educational differences between the two communities. Overall, the proportion of qualified persons in the male population is higher for the Protestant community, whichever definition is used. The slightly higher Catholic female figure (at the "post-A level" definition) reflects the Roman Catholic tradition of nursing. In the science/technology category, more relevant to industrial needs, Protestants again clearly dominate. More detailed work on the distribution of A level passes also shows an under-representation of Catholics, at least until the mid-1970s, as well as at the O level stage (Osborne and Murray, 1978).

When subject areas are analysed, Catholics again are under-represented in "sciences". Analysis of these same General Certificate of Education results has explicitly eliminated the possibility of any centre–periphery ("WHERE") effect.[15]

(*iii*) *Income levels.* Data on inter-community income levels are more elusive. Even so, Rose's (1971, p. 289) "loyalty survey" showed a relative concentration of Catholics in lower income categories, while educated Protestants were likely to enjoy higher wages than educated

Catholics. More localised studies of farming communities have also shown Catholics as occupying more than their "fair share" of poor land (Darby, 1976, p. 148). Such income differences can both reflect existing, and encourage further, economic inequalities.

(*iv*) *Attitudes to work*. The relationship between resourcefulness, economic success and religious background has generated a vast and conflicting literature, although much of it is based on American experience (e.g. Datta, 1967; Glenn and Hyland, 1967). Within this debate, the concept of the "Protestant work ethic" has attracted academic approval (Hansen, 1963), although its particular relevance to Northern Ireland remains unclear. The most detailed research to date within Northern Ireland finds no convincing differences between Roman Catholics and Protestants over twenty-four different tests of attitudes to work (Miller, 1978). On the other hand, Rose (1971, pp. 284–285) discovered more favourable attitudes among Protestants than Catholics towards the Northern Ireland constitution generally (and thus, perhaps, to working to maintain its economic foundations?),[16] and, in particular, to the role of "big business" in the life of the area.[17]

TABLE 8.3. Qualified Persons, 1971.

| | Roman Catholics | | Protestants | |
	Males	Females	Males	Females
Percentage with post-A level qualifications	4·86	7·31	7·53	6·74
of whom				
Percentage qualified in:				
Education	28·3	37·4	16·3	39·2
Health	18·0	52·3	11·5	40·6
Technology	14·8	0·3	30·4	1·1
Science	6·9	1·3	9·9	2·9
Percentage with A levels, O.N.C. or equivalent	5·4	4·6	6·1	4·8

Source: *Northern Ireland Census of Population 1971*, Religion Tables.

(*b*) *Exogenous forces—discrimination in employment*

A commonly expressed view on this sensitive subject is that, while Roman Catholics can and do discriminate against Protestants, the opportunities are far greater for them to suffer job discrimination at Protestant hands. Some of these hands are those of private employers but the role of the formerly monolithic Unionist Party machine is also held to be important, this view being based on the almost universal and unchanging relationship in Northern Ireland politics between religion and party allegiance (Barritt and Carter, 1962, pp. 35–51; Birrell, 1972, p. 329; Budge and O'Leary, 1973, pp. 249, 363; Rose, 1971, p. 235; Wallace, 1971, p. 75). Given, too, the much-quoted statements of leading Unionists openly antagonistic to Catholic preferment in employment (e.g. Boyd, 1969, p. 192; Campaign for Social Justice in Northern Ireland, 1969, pp. 33–35) it is hardly surprising that the minority should feel the economic odds stacked against them (Rose, 1971).

But *proof* of discrimination is harder to come by. Employers are reluctant to release lists of employees, even to the Commissioner for Complaints (Darby, 1976, p. 146), and a volley of respectable reasons can be used to repulse any case of alleged discrimination (Utley, 1975, pp. 26–27). Even so, most commentators agree that job discrimination *does* exist, *does* favour Protestants on balance, and is tacitly accepted as such by all interested parties (Cameron, 1969, p. 60; Darby, 1976, p. 150). According to Barritt and Carter (1962, p. 93), "the interesting question is not the existence of discrimination, but how far it distorts the pattern of employment". These distortions can assume two forms. First, jobs with existing employers, public or private, may be made available selectively to members of one community. Such discrimination among private employers has been examined in detail by Boehringer (1971), Darby (1976, pp. 146–151) and Barritt and Carter (1962, pp. 93–108). The last emphasise how the type and degree of discrimination can vary widely in the private sector, and how it seems less strong among the newer industries brought in to cure the region's economic *malaise*.

Discrimination in public appointments has been the subject of even closer scrutiny, being seen as a greater sin than private discrimination. Roman Catholic underrepresentation in public employment is held to exist at both local and central government level, and to span the occupational spectrum from Stormont Permanent Secretaries and members of the High Court Bench to school bus-drivers in Fermanagh and hospital clerks in Lurgan. Chapter and verse are to be found in the literature (e.g. Campaign for Social Justice in Northern Ireland, 1969; Wallace, 1971, pp. 116–120).

The second "distortion" is the alleged discrimination against "opposition" areas exercised by the Unionist administrations of Northern Ireland, when locating new manufacturing employment. The claim that industrial investment has been used as a reward to the party faithful has been a consistent feature of Stormont's post-1945 economic debates. Certainly, the large inbuilt Unionist majority removes the "need" to use power to buy votes from opposition supporters, as may apply elsewhere (Johnston, 1977). The standard reply from the Unionist front benches has been that industrialists must be allowed to select their locations on profitability criteria, and that these generally pointed them towards the big urban centres, particularly Belfast, despite higher grants being available in the peripheries. Charge and defence became totally predictable, the protagonists resembling chess grand masters automatically playing through some familiar position. In both cases the result is stalemate (Hoare, 1981).

Thus we can see that many arguments can be, and have been, advanced in support of the "WHERE" and "WHO" models of economic performance. The evidence for some of them is stronger than for others, but all have an established place in the images of Northern Ireland, if not in its realities. The final section provides some preliminary evidence of their relative performance against these realities.

ECONOMIC REALITY: THE ROLE OF "WHO" AND "WHERE"

We argue, then, that it is important to examine the relevance of both geographical location and religious affiliation to economic performance. In practice, our ability to do so is severely limited by data problems: some data sets are suitable for a "WHO" analysis, some for a "WHERE" analysis, but few for both. This is especially so if we wish to examine the relative importance of these two models over time. Two topics that *can* be analysed in these terms are those of journey-to-work behaviour and employment accessibility. This final section examines some preliminary results drawn from the second of these two fields, although this involves consideration of the first as well.

Accessibility to Employment Opportunities

The evolving pattern of employment opportunities in Northern Ireland, and the relative accessibility of different parts of the region to them, depend not just on the locations of the employment centres themselves but also on the different journey-to-work mobilities of workers from their homes. The general model used is based on the premise that, for any one base location, employment accessibility varies directly with the employment available at all locations throughout Northern Ireland, and inversely with the distance of these locations from base, in that this affects journey-to-work mobility.[18] "Employment" can be defined in this context in five different ways:

(a) Total employment

The only spatial employment data in Northern Ireland available as a time series are those derived from the exchange of National Insurance cards. These are available for the twenty-six employment exchange areas for the period 1959–1972. These areas thus form the "j's" in the model.[18] The data include those insured workers who are unemployed, but as data on registered unemployed workers are also available for comparable dates and areas estimates can be made of insured employees *in work* at the twenty-six area level.[19] Even so, these data are estimates only. First, they exclude most agricultural workers. Secondly, they contain estimates of the geographical distribution of public service workers, who were not covered by insurance card exchange. Thirdly, certain employers exchanged cards at one central location for workers based in a range of different locations. Where this was known to occur the official data were adjusted accordingly. The data used in the analyses following relate to the terminal dates of 1959 and 1972, as they do for all four remaining cases of Ej.

(b) Manufacturing employment (1958 Standard Industrial Classification Orders III–XIX)

As the "card exchange" and "registered unemployed" data are both disaggregated to the S.I.C. Order level this subset of "total employment" can also be calculated, on the same basis as total employment.

(c) Growth employment

Given the structural weaknesses of the Northern Ireland economy, accessibility to employment in the expanding sectors of the economy is a very relevant issue. Between 1959 and 1972 overall employment grew by 9·2%, and estimates of job availability were determined, as before, for the fourteen Orders expanding at this rate or more.

(d) Sponsored manufacturing employment

The most generous employment-linked financial incentives made available to manufacturing investment in Northern Ireland are administered under the relevant Industries Development Act. Data on the subsequent employment experience of these same assisted firms, collected by the Department of Commerce, have been aggregated up to the twenty-six exchange area level, for June 1959 and June 1972.

(e) In-migrant sponsored manufacturing employment

This represents that subset of the previous heading relating to manufacturers who have moved into Northern Ireland, usually as branch plants from bases outside the region. They represent the most obvious way of restructuring the distressed local industrial base, and have hence been actively pursued by the Department of Commerce.

The formal testing of "WHO" against "WHERE" requires re-arranging Northern Ireland into two groups of mutually exclusive geographical subdivisions, one based on religious and one on locational criteria. The former is accomplished by means of population census data which for 1961 and 1971 recorded separately the religious affiliation of the residents of the sixty seven former local authorities in Northern Ireland. Each of these areas was thus classified as "Roman Catholic" or "Protestant" on the basis of which was the larger group of residents among those stating their religion[20] (Figs 8.5a and 8.5b). In the "WHERE" case the same sixty-seven areas were allocated to one of three sub-regions, an inevitably subjective exercise, given the several ways in which core–periphery relationships can be represented (see Fig. 8.3). The sub-regions derived are referred to as "Central", "Intermediate" and "Peripheral", and take the form shown in Fig. 8.5c.

Table 8.4 summarises the overall performance of Catholic and Protestant Northern Ireland on each of these employment access measures, based on the rank order of the sixty-seven local areas (rank 1 representing the most favoured area, and 67 the least). The pattern is remarkably consistent. Whichever measure is used, Protestant areas emerge as more favourably located than Catholic ones in job accessibility, and in all cases the differential has widened over the thirteen-year period surveyed.

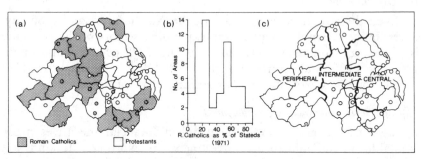

FIGURE 8.5. Subdivisions for "WHO" and "WHERE" Models.
FIGURE 8.5a. shows the sixty-seven former local government units classified as either Roman Catholic or Protestant. FIGURE 8.5b demonstrates the tendency for these local government units to have either a definite Catholic majority or a small Catholic minority. "Stateds" are those indicating membership of a religious denomination at the 1971 census. FIGURE 8.5c shows Northern Ireland divided into central, intermediate and peripheral sub-regions.

TABLE 8.4. Aggregate Employment Accessibility Ranks.

	Total		Manufacturing		Growth		All sponsored		In-migrant sponsored	
	1959	1972	1959	1972	1959	1972	1959	1972	1959	1972
Protestant areas	28·4	26·7	28·5	26·9	28·7	26·1	30·7	27·7	29·3	27·7
Roman Catholic areas	43·8	44·4	43·2	44·3	42·9	46·1	42·6	44·6	41·9	44·6

"WHO" and "WHERE" can be tested further via chi-square analysis, using the possible two-stage procedure outlined in Fig. 8.6.

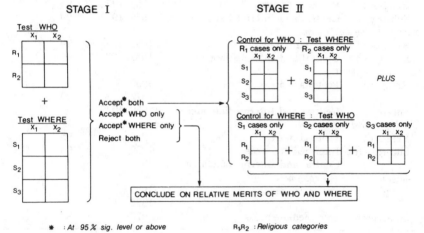

FIGURE 8.6. Testing "WHO" and "WHERE".

This was done first of all by representing X_1 by above median rank position for 1959 and 1972 and improving rank position for 1959–1972, and by representing X_2 by below median rank position for 1959 and 1972 and deteriorating rank position for 1959–1972. All the static cases proved significant at 99% requiring Stage II analyses (Table 8.5a). This tends to fall foul of the technical requirements of the chi-square test (see, for example, Siegel, 1956), particularly when controlling for sub-region. A clear "WHERE" dimension emerges when controlling for religion in the Protestant areas case (where the Central sub-region consistently performs better), though not for the Catholic one. Additionally, "WHO" can also claim some support, with Catholic areas consistently scoring less highly than Protestant. The fact that this inter-community difference is at least as strong in the "non-sponsored" as the "sponsored" measures argues that, whatever the causes of this pro-Protestant finding, there are no grounds for assuming that the "biased" direction of new firms by Ministry officials need be a potent factor here.

TABLE 8.5. Chi-Square Analysis: Employment Accessibility (Showing Significant Cases Only).

(a) Stage II results: Static cases		
Controlling for:	Date	Significance (%)
Total employment		
Religion: Protestant areas	1959, 1972	95
Sub-region: Central and Intermediate areas	1959, 1972	99
Manufacturing employment		
Religion: Protestant areas	1959, 1972	99
Sub-region: Central and Intermediate areas	1959, 1972	99
Growth employment		
Religion: Protestant areas	1959	95
	1972	99
Sub-region: Central and Intermediate areas	1959, 1972	99
Total sponsored employment		
Religion: Protestant areas	1959	95
Sub-region: Intermediate areas	1959	95
Central and Intermediate areas	1972	99
In-migrant sponsored employment		
Religion: Protestant areas	1959	95
	1972	99
Sub-region: Intermediate areas	1972	99

(b) Dynamic cases		
Stage I	Model	Significance (%)
Total employment	WHERE	99
Manufacturing employment	WHERE	99 ┐
	WHO	95 ┘ →Stage II
Growth employment	WHERE	95
Total sponsored employment	(WHERE	90)
In-migrant sponsored employment	WHERE	95
	(WHO	90)
Stage II	Controlling for:-	
Manufacturing employment	Religion (Protestant areas 90%)	

Given, though, that these static cases take no account' of the geography of *demand* for work it may be more relevant to examine the *changing* pattern of job accessibility. Here, assuming that this spatial pattern of demand is reasonably constant through time, we can identify those parts of Northern Ireland that have improved their relative job access status *vis-à-vis* job need. The results in the dynamic case are more emphatic. "WHERE" is more successful than "WHO" in all five measures (Table 8.5b). In each case, too, this is caused by a *widening* of intra-regional job access differences, with an improvement of the status of the Central sub-region and a worsening of the periphery, irrespective of religious status (Fig. 8.7).

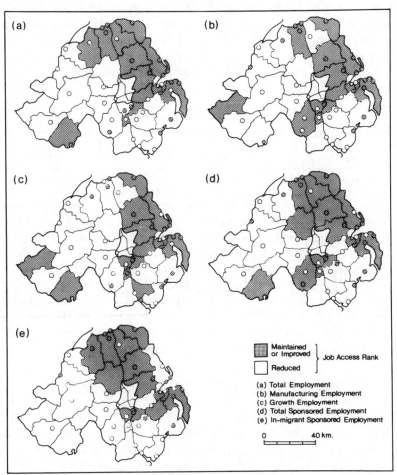

FIGURE 8.7. Changing Employment Accessibility, 1959–1972.

In addition, it is also important to consider the question of industrial diversity. Other things being equal, an area with access to 1000 jobs based on a single industry is in a weaker economic position than one with a similar number spread over a range of industrial sectors. By combining an index of diversification with the previous employment accessibility model a diversity access index can be determined for any base location i (DA_i), based on the extent to which the "accessible employment" is spread over different industrial sectors.[21] This index was calculated for 1959 and 1972, with both "total employment" and "manufacturing employment" as the "E" term.

Since the diversification index is sensitive to areal size, analysis should concentrate on dynamic changes. Aggregate data suggest a clear inter-community difference, with Protestant areas, on average, having more diversity than Catholic ones, and the differential widening over the study period for total employment, though narrowing in the "manufacturing" case (Table 8.6).

TABLE 8.6. Aggregate Diversity Access Values.

	Total		Manufacturing	
	1959	1972	1959	1972
Protestant areas	36·16	39·54	36·83	35·59
Roman Catholic areas	30·36	24·68	29·24	31·32

Chi-square analysis shows that these aggregate data cannot be taken at face value. Stage I examination of both the "total" and "manufacturing" cases provides support only for the "WHERE" model (at 99% and 95% respectively). In each case the relative diversity of the Central sub-region has increased while that of the Peripheral sub-region has deteriorated, compared to the Northern Ireland average. Again, the evidence not only supports "WHERE" over "WHO", but suggests that the trend within Northern Ireland is towards increasing intra-regional disequilibrium.

SOME ENDS AND SOME BEGINNINGS

The central argument advanced in this essay is that the internal economic geography of Northern Ireland is more complex than many have been prepared to recognise. Two very different sets of processes could be operating there. There is circumstantial evidence in favour of both, but little attempt has been made to date to isolate and compare them, despite their very different policy implications.

The analysis presented here is no more than a first step in this direction. Extending the arguments to, say, spatial variations in employment structure, economic activity rates, income levels, or industrial productivity and profitability requires a far better data base than is yet available. Moreover, even if location and religion could be isolated in these areas, this of itself need tell us nothing about the relative importance of the *specific* processes that together comprise the "WHO" and "WHERE" models. In other words, there is plenty yet to do!

But, within its own terms of reference, the evidence suggested here is not insignificant. At the aggregate level of data examination a superficial difference between Catholic and Protestant Northern Ireland consistently emerges in favour of the majority community. On the other hand, when geographical location is also taken into account this is generally of greater "explanatory" significance than the inter-community, aspatial dimension. More detailed analysis along the same lines using journey-to-work data (but not reported here) reinforces these results: such variations as are apparent in journey-to-work behaviour across Northern Ireland vary more strongly with spatial location than with religious affiliation insofar as the two can be separated for analysis. This dominance of "WHERE" over "WHO" should come as no surprise to those who recall Northern Ireland-type spatial variations in economic health and behaviour in other regions and nations lacking the area's social bipolarity. At times, we all need reminding that the geography of Northern Ireland is not merely that of the Planter and the Gael.

ACKNOWLEDGEMENTS

Part of the work reported here was supported by a research grant from the Social Science Research Council, and the industrial employment and unemployment data were supplied by the Northern Ireland Department of Commerce and the former Ministry of Health and Social Services. Helpful advice on the technical aspects of the paper was kindly supplied by Neil Wrigley and Edward Thomas, of the writer's department. To all of these, their assistance is gratefully acknowledged, and all parties are exonerated from any responsibility for the views expressed and any unforced errors.

NOTES

1. Despite forming historically a nine-county province of Ireland the term "Ulster" is used in its popular sense, as synonymous with the six counties of Northern Ireland.

2. Statistics on agriculture tend to under-estimate the overall importance of farm employment, by omitting family workers, which form an important component of farm employment in Northern Ireland (see Gillespie, 1977).

3. For discussion of the general interrelationships between national economic growth and regional problems, embodied in the "efficiency versus equity" debate, see King and Clark (1978).

4. Thus Brian Faulkner, as Minister of Development, addressed a Stormont debate on the Craigavon Commission on 17 February 1970: "We would not have had the Goodyear plant anywhere in Northern Ireland had we not been able to give the firm a clear undertaking that the new city would be developed where the factory was established".

5. In the 1971 Census only $5 \cdot 8\%$ of the population replying to the question on religion declared themselves to be other than Roman Catholic, Presbyterian, Church of Ireland or Methodist, and of these a substantial number belonged to offshoots of one of the main Protestant branches.

6. The best-known advocates of these models are probably Myrdal (1957) and Hirschman (1958). For a discussion of their application see Keeble (1967).

7. This calculates the market "potential" (or accessibility) of any place i (MP_i), thus

$$MP_i = \sum_{j=1}^{j=n} \left(\frac{P_j}{d_{ij}^{\beta}} \right).$$

The sixty-seven former local authority areas of Northern Ireland represent the i, j subscripts (i.e. $n = 67$), with P_j being the 1971 population of area j, and d_{ij} being the crow-fly distance between the centroids of each i-j pair. The β exponent is set arbitrarily at $2 \cdot 0$. In the case of "self-potential" (i.e. $i = j$) the convention of defining d_{ij} as $d_{in}/2$ was adopted (d_{in} being the distance from i to its nearest neighbour centroid, n). The program used to calculate d_{ij} took account of the water barriers of Lough Neagh and Belfast Lough: where crow-fly lines crossed these the "crow" was directed to take the shortest diversion over land.

8. Assuming these costs to be directly related to distance the producer seeks the location that minimises T_i (aggregate transport cost at location i in serving all n markets in Northern Ireland) when

$$T_i = \sum_{j=1}^{j=n} (P_j \cdot d_{ij}).$$

9. In this case, distance exponents were determined from a separate analysis of journey-to-work flows, not reported here.

10. Defined as "urban districts", "municipal boroughs" and "county boroughs" in the pre-1973 local authority structure of Northern Ireland.

11. Gillespie used the Shimbel index, which determines, for each base

point i, intra-Northern Ireland accessibility on the first class road network, thus

$$\sum_{n=1}^{n=25} d_{ij} \text{ (and i} \neq \text{j)}$$

when i, j are the centroid towns of the twenty-six employment exchange areas, representing in practice the largest towns in Northern Ireland.

12. The perceived attractiveness of any point x in Fig. 8.3g is given thus:

$$Ax = \sum_{f=1}^{f=17} [E_f (V_{fx} \cdot I_{mf})]$$

where E_f = the overall percentage of respondents evaluating factor f positively as a locational advantage

V_{fx} = the proportion of firms within the same distance-zone from f as x that evaluates it positively as a location factor

I_{mf} = the maximum distance zonal value for factor f

f = any industrial location factor.

13. In fact, despite its more restrictive terms of reference, the report also identified six "key centres" outside the Belfast sub-region.

14. This is one of the few demographic variables which is broken down in the 1971 Census Religion Tables by both religion and location. It is thus possible to see that this age structure difference persists throughout all parts of Northern Ireland.

15. R. Osborne, personal communication.

16. Gillespie (1977) suggests that industrialists may avoid Catholic areas because of uncertainty over their political attitudes, as a means of avoiding possible tension. His subsequent analysis confirms an association between the estimated percentage Unionist vote and certain indices of employment growth.

17. While this list of "endogenous" forces could be extended it becomes increasingly difficult to decide what is a "new" ingredient, and what merely the result of "WHO" and "WHERE" differences already outlined.

18. The formal model tested against "WHO" and "WHERE" was

$$A_i = \sum_{j=1}^{j=m} \left(E_j/d_{ij}\beta \right)$$

where E_j = employment based in area j

d_{ij} = distance between i and j

and m = 26.

As such, it is a *supply*-oriented model, measuring the relative attractiveness of location i (in practice, a local authority area) for employment access (A_i), independent of the demand for work existing at i. *Demand* for jobs, in this context, is much more difficult to measure, depending on a range of considerations that cannot easily be quantified from existing data.

The β exponents are derived independently from a study of journey-to-work mobility, with those derived from 1966 Northern Ireland Census tabulations being used for the 1959 access analysis, and those from the 1971 tabulations for the 1972 equivalent.

Assuming that spatial interaction parameters determined at one level of areal disaggregation apply also to another, as is done here, has been severely criticised by Openshaw (1978). However, given the impossibility of calculating journey-to-work mobilities specifically at the twenty-six area scale, and also the wide variations evident in the β values over the sixty-seven areas, it might be argued that they represent the best estimate available of interaction at the twenty-six area scale too.

19. The data do not record jobs as such, but persons in jobs. Thus one person holding two jobs will be counted only once. The annual Census of Employment, introduced in 1972, reverses this procedure and counts jobs rather than persons in employment. Data on reported vacancies were not incorporated in the calculation as these can misrepresent the number of actual vacancies in an area, both in a negative and in a positive direction.

20. The "Protestant" figure was taken as the sum of those recorded as Church of Ireland, Presbyterian and Methodist. In the few cases where 1961 and 1971 figures showed a different majority group the allocation was based on the 1971 figure.

21. The DA_i index, developed from that of Britton (1967), is measured thus:

$$DA_i = P_1{}^2 + P_2{}^2 + P_3{}^2 \ldots \ldots + P_n{}^2$$

when P_1 is employment in Industry 1 as a percentage of all the employment accessible from i being calculated thus:

$$P_1 = \left\{ \left[\sum_{j=1}^{j=26} \left(E_{ij} / d_{ij}\beta \right) \right] \Big/ \sum_{j=1}^{j=26} \sum_{k=1}^{k=n} \left(E_{kj} / d_{ij}\beta \right) \right\} \times 100$$

where $n = \Sigma_k$ = number of industrial categories k.

REFERENCES

Barritt, D. P. and Carter, C. F. (1962). "The Northern Ireland Problem: A Study in Group Relations." Oxford University Press, London.

Birrell, D. (1972). Relative Deprivation as a Factor in Conflict in Northern Ireland. *Sociological Review* **20**, 317–343.

Black, W. (1976). The Northern Ireland Economy—Problems and Prospects. *Irish Banking Review* (June 1976), 14–21.

Black, W. (1977). Industrial Development and Regional Policy. *In* "Economic Activity in Ireland: A Study of Two Open Economies" (N. J. Gibson and J. E. Spencer, eds.), pp. 40–78. Gill and Macmillan, Dublin.

Board of Inland Revenue (1972). "The Survey of Personal Incomes, 1969–1970." Her Majesty's Stationery Office, London.

Boehringer, K. (1971). Discrimination: Jobs. *Fortnight* **17**, 5–7.

Boyd, A. (1969). "Holy War in Belfast." Anvil Press, Tralee.

Britton, J. H. (1967). "Regional Analysis and Economic Geography." Bell, London.

Budge, I. and O'Leary, C. (1973). "Belfast—Approach to Crisis: A Study of Belfast Politics, 1613–1970." Macmillan, London.

Cameron, Lord (1969). "Disturbances in Northern Ireland: Report of the Commission Appointed by the Governor of Northern Ireland" (Cmd. 532). Her Majesty's Stationery Office, Belfast.

Campaign for Social Justice in Northern Ireland (1969). "The Plain Truth." Campaign for Social Justice in Northern Ireland, Dungannon.

Central Statistical Office (1979). *Regional Statistics*, **14.** Her Majesty's Stationery Office, London.

Compton, P. A. (1976). Religious Affiliation and Demographic Variability in Northern Ireland. *Institute of British Geographers, Transactions* **1** (New Series), 433–452.

Compton, P. A. (1978). "Northern Ireland: A Census Atlas." Gill and Macmillan, Dublin.

Darby, J. (1976). "Conflict in Northern Ireland: The Development of a Polarised Community." Gill and Macmillan, Dublin.

Datta, L. E. (1967). Family Religious Background and Early Scientific Creativity. *American Sociological Review* **32**, 626–635.

Davies, R., McGurnaghan, M. A. and Sams, K. I. (1977). The Northern Ireland Economy: Progress (1968–75) and Prospects. *Regional Studies* **11**, 297–307.

Department of the Environment, Northern Ireland (1977). "Northern Ireland: Regional Physical Development Strategy 1975–95." Her Majesty's Stationery Office, Belfast.

Department of Trade and Industry (1973). "Expenditure Committee (Trade and Industry Sub-Committee): Minutes of Evidence, 4 July 1973." Her Majesty's Stationery Office, London.

Garnsey, R. (1965). The Experience of Courtaulds Ltd. in Northern Ireland. *In* "Papers on Regional Development" (T. Wilson, ed.), pp. 54–61. Blackwell, Oxford.

Gillespie, A. R. (1977). "Growth Centres and Regional Economic Development in Northern Ireland." Unpublished Ph.D. Thesis, University of Cambridge.

Glenn, N. D. and Hyland, R. (1967). Religious Preference and Worldly Success: Some Evidence from National Surveys. *American Sociological Review* **32**, 73–85.

Hansen, N. M. (1963). The Protestant Ethic as a General Precondition for Economic Development. *Canadian Journal of Economic and Political Science* **29,** 462–474.

Hirschman, A. O. (1958). "A Strategy of Economic Development." Yale University Press, New Haven, Connecticut.

Hoare, A. G. (1976). Spheres of Influence and Regional Policy: The Case of Northern Ireland. *Irish Geography* **9,** 89–99.

Hoare, A. G. (1981). Why They Go Where They Go: The Political Imagery of Industrial Location. *Institute of British Geographers, Transactions* **6,** (New Series), 152–175.

Houston, J. (1976). The Northern Ireland Economy: A Special Case? *Politics Today* **16,** 274–288.

Isles, K. S. and Cuthbert, N. (1957). "An Economic Survey of Northern Ireland." Her Majesty's Stationery Office, Belfast.

Johnston, R. J. (1977). The Geography of Federal Allocations in the United States—Preliminary Tests of Some Hypotheses for Political Geography. *Geoforum* **8,** 319–326.

Keeble, D. E. (1967). Models of Economic Development. *In* "Models in Geography" (R. J. Chorley and P. Haggett, eds.), pp. 243–302. Methuen, London.

King, L. J. and Clark, G. L. (1978). Government Policy and Regional Development. *Progress in Human Geography* **2,** 1–16.

Law, D. (1964). Industrial Movement and Locational Advantage. *Manchester School of Economic and Social Studies* **32,** 131–154.

Matthew, Sir R. H. (1964). "Belfast Regional Survey and Plan 1962: A Report." Her Majesty's Stationery Office, Belfast.

Matthew, Sir R. H., Wilson, T. and Parkinson, J. (1970). "Northern Ireland Development Programme 1970–75: Report of the Three Consultants." Her Majesty's Stationery Office, Belfast.

McGovern, P. D. (1965). "Industrial Dispersal." Broadsheet 485 (*Planning* **31,** 3–39), Political and Economic Planning, London.

Miller, R. (1978). "Attitudes to Work in Northern Ireland." Research Paper 2, Fair Employment Agency, Belfast.

Moore, B., Rhodes, J. and Tarling, R. (1978). Industrial Policy and Economic Development: The Experience of Northern Ireland and the Republic of Ireland. *Cambridge Journal of Economics* **2,** 99–114.

Murie, A. S. (1973). Planning in Northern Ireland: A Survey. *Town Planning Review* **4,** 337–358.

Murie, A. S., Birrell, W. D., Hillyard, P. A. R. and Roche, D. J. D. (1973). A Survey of Industrial Movement to Northern Ireland between 1965 and 1969. *Economic and Social Review* **4,** 231–244.

Myrdal, G. (1957). "Economic Theory and Under-Developed Regions." Duckworth, London.

Northern Ireland Census of Population 1971. Her Majesty's Stationery Office, Belfast.

Openshaw, S. (1978). An Empirical Study of Some Zone-Design Criteria. *Environment and Planning (A)* **10**, 781–794.

Osborne, R. D. (1978). Denomination and Unemployment in Northern Ireland. *Area* **10**, 280–283.

Osborne, R. D. and Murray, R. C. (1978). "Educational Qualifications and Religious Affiliation in Northern Ireland: An Examination of G.C.E. 'O' and 'A' Levels." Research Paper 3, Fair Employment Agency, Belfast.

Quigley, W. G. H. (1976). "Economic and Industrial Strategy for Northern Ireland: Report by Review Team 1976." Her Majesty's Stationery Office, Belfast.

Rose, R. (1971). "Governing without Consensus: An Irish Perspective." Faber and Faber, London.

Salt, J. and Johnson, J. H. (1975). Recent Trends in the Level and Distribution of Unemployment in Northern Ireland. *Tijdschrift voor Economische en Sociale Geografie* **66**, 225–233.

Schiller, P. (1978). Companies Little Affected by "Troubles". *Business Location File* (April/May 1978), 40.

Siegel, S. (1956). "Nonparametric Statistics for the Behavioral Sciences." McGraw-Hill, New York.

Simpson, J. V. (1971). Regional Analysis: The Northern Ireland Experience. *Economic and Social Review* **2**, 507–529.

Utley, T. E. (1975). "The Lessons of Ulster." Dent, London.

Wallace, M. (1971). "Northern Ireland: 50 Years of Self-Government." David and Charles, Newton Abbot.

Walsh, B. (1970). "Religion and Demographic Behaviour in Ireland." Paper 55, Economic and Social Research Institute, Dublin.

Wilson, T. (1965). "Economic Development in Northern Ireland, Including the Report of the Economic Consultant Thomas Wilson" (Cmd. 479). Her Majesty's Stationery Office, Belfast.

CHAPTER 9

THE GEOGRAPHY OF UNEMPLOYMENT

Paul Doherty

INTRODUCTION

One of the principal indicators of Northern Ireland's economic difficulties is a persistently high level of unemployment. This unemployment produces consequent social problems, and as the division between employed and unemployed is at least partly concurrent with other social divisions, in particular the ethnic one, it has contributed to the *nexus* of difficulties known as "The Northern Ireland Problem". In seeking to identify the dimensions of unemployment, its causes, consequences and possible solutions, it is proposed to proceed at three scales. First, at a regional scale, the level of unemployment in Northern Ireland in relation to the rest of the United Kingdom will be examined. Secondly, the distribution within Northern Ireland will be considered, and finally attention will be focussed on variation within Belfast. As the unemployment of adult males is of greater economic and social consequence than that of adult females or juveniles, the discussion will largely be confined to adult male unemployment.

UNEMPLOYMENT IN NORTHERN IRELAND AS A REGION OF THE UNITED KINGDOM

The high level of unemployment in Northern Ireland in relation to the rest of the Common Market is illustrated in Table 9.1.

The table is ranked by worst region: only Italy and Belgium have regions with higher unemployment than Northern Ireland. Of Italy's twenty regions, five have unemployment above 9·7%, and three of

225

Belgium's nine provinces also exceed this figure. In other words, of the 112 administrative units in the European Economic Community, Northern Ireland ranks ninth in terms of unemployment, and it ranks first in the eleven standard regions of the United Kingdom.

TABLE 9.1. Unemployment in the European Economic Community, 1977, by Country and Worst Region of Each Country.[a]

Country/Worst region	Percentage unemployment	Relativity
European Economic Community	5·3	100
Italy	6·4	122
Campania	16·8	319
Belgium	7·6	144
Limbourg	11·8	225
United Kingdom	5·7	107
N. Ireland	9·7	184
Republic of Ireland	9·5	181
Germany	4·0	75
Aurich	8·3	157
Netherlands	4·2	80
Limburg	7·5	143
France	4·8	91
Languedoc-Roussillon	7·0	133
Denmark	5·8	111
Luxembourg	0·6	10

[a]Statistics are not available for subdivisions of the Republic of Ireland, Denmark and Luxembourg. Source: Eurostat (1979, pp. 110–111).

Historically, unemployment has been much higher, as shown in Fig. 9.1. In relation to the rest of the United Kingdom, Northern Ireland has been an unemployment "black spot" for at least fifty years, and has had a higher unemployment rate than any other U.K. region consistently from 1936 (Simpson, 1971). Figure 9.2 illustrates the disparity by plotting the unemployment relativities of the four U.K. regions against the overall United Kingdom figure which is given a base line value of 100. The unemployment level in England has been consistently better than in the U.K. as a whole, while the other three regions have been worse. The graph also shows the cyclical fluctuations which occur through time in unemployment statistics, with Northern Ireland generally lagging behind the other regions in up- and down-swings. Regions which have an unemployment rate higher than the national average tend to have wider cyclical movements, and between 1957 and 1966 Northern Ireland seems to have been the most sensitive U.K. region to cyclical variation (Black and Slattery, 1975). However, since 1966 this sensitivity has been substantially reduced, and in 1975 the Northern Ireland unemployment figure was for the first time ever less than twice the national average.

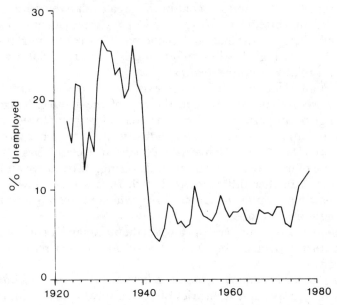

FIGURE 9.1. Average Annual Total Registered Unemployed for Northern Ireland, 1923–1978, as a Percentage of Registered Employees. Source: Department of Manpower Services.

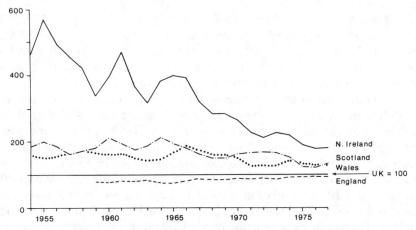

FIGURE 9.2. Unemployment Relativities, 1954–1977. Source: Central Statistical Office (1965–1979).

The two chief reasons for the relative improvement in Northern Ireland's position are an increased government intervention in the economy, and a substantial increase in emigration (Davies *et al.*, 1977). However, while the improvement in the area's relative position is to be welcomed, in absolute terms the level of unemployment is well over 10% and rising as the national economy faces continuing problems. Furthermore, a high level of emigration is a severe social cost to pay for such a relative improvement.

Important structural differences exist between the unemployment in Northern Ireland and that in the rest of the United Kingdom. A much higher proportion of Northern Ireland's unemployed are from agriculture and the construction industry, and a higher proportion are manual labourers. Conversely Northern Ireland has its lowest proportion of unemployed from manufacturing, distributive and service industries. A further difference is that there is a much lower level of female participation in the labour force, which represents a substantial untapped source of labour.

No single factor can account for Northern Ireland's continued high level of unemployment, but a number of interrelated reasons may be advanced:

(*i*) *The structure of industry.* There has been a substantial decline in the traditionally important industries of agriculture, textiles, shipbuilding and aircraft manufacture, related to world-wide changes in these industries. In 1948, 40% of employment in Northern Ireland was in these four industries. By 1968 this had fallen to 22%, and by 1977 it had fallen to 11%.

(*ii*) *The location of Northern Ireland.* Not only is the area peripheral in relation to the centres of population and manufacturing in the U.K., but it is also peripheral in relation to the E.E.C. super-core. It thereby incurs high transport costs for raw materials and manufactured products, making the area less attractive to industry.

(*iii*) *The distribution of the population.* According to the 1971 Census of Population, 78·2% of the population of England and Wales lived in urban administrative areas, compared with 70·8% in Scotland and 55·1% in Northern Ireland. Northern Ireland's more rural population distribution tends to militate against industrial development.

(*iv*) *The high rate of natural increase.* In 1976 the following rates of natural increase per 1000 population obtained: England −0·2; Wales −1·1; Scotland −0·1; Northern Ireland +6·1. Northern Ireland is thus the only U.K. region experiencing natural increase. A lower rate would mean fewer individuals entering the labour force and ease the unemployment problem (see Chapter 4).

(v) *The "troubles"*. From 1971 to 1975 over 800 jobs were lost through the permanent closure of sixteen companies as a direct result of civil disturbance. Against this must be set a short-term benefit to the construction and security industries. However, in the longer term a loss in business confidence outside Northern Ireland has led to a reduction in investment, which the Government is now seeking to rectify by means of a massive promotional drive. The "troubles" have served to increase emigration and an estimated 100 000 people have left Northern Ireland in the ten years since 1968 (*Belfast Telegraph*, 16 October 1978). Given this emigration, there is some justification for suspecting that those remaining in long-term unemployment are really unemployable, since migration tends to select the more skilled and enterprising from among the unemployed (Walsh, 1977).

(vi) *The link between the regional economy and the national economy.* Northern Ireland is very much affected by the economic circumstances of the United Kingdom as a whole. Cyclical variations in the national unemployment level are mirrored in variations at the regional level. From 1954 to 1976 the average annual unemployment rates in Northern Ireland and the United Kingdom had a positive correlation of 0·66, indicating that, over that period, 44% of the regional variation was related to national variation. If the lag of Northern Ireland behind the trend of the U.K. as a whole had been taken into account, this correlation would be higher.

Some of the causes of Northern Ireland's unemployment problem are more easily solved than others. Little can be done about the area's peripheral location and its link with the national economy, except to counter the effect of these factors by regional development incentives. The "troubles" have proved a particularly intractable problem, and a permanent solution is essential for the long-term economic future. The Quigley Report (1976) sought to provide an economic and industrial strategy for Northern Ireland, and indicated four conditions necessary for an economic turnround: (i) an end to the "troubles"; (ii) an upturn in the national economy; (iii) measures to retain the area's industrial competitiveness in terms of industrial incentives; (iv) means of releasing the dormant initiative of the people.

The persistence of high unemployment levels in Northern Ireland indicates that a reduction in these levels will not be easy. Even if new jobs were created for all of the 70 000 people without work in 1978, the problem would not be solved. Many of the unemployed are of such low skill, have been without work for so long and are of such an age as to be virtually unemployable (Doherty, 1977). Furthermore, the creation of these new jobs would stem the flow of emigration, and draw more women on to the labour market, so that still further jobs would be required. The reduction in the disparity between the Northern Ireland economy and the U.K. national economy has been achieved by a considerable increase in government spending: between 1971–1972 and 1974–1975 the rate of growth was over 14% per annum, an increase nearly two and a half times as great as that for the U.K. as a whole (Davies *et al.*, 1977). However, in view of the current national economic difficulties and the resultant cuts in public expenditure, Northern Ireland cannot expect these growth rates to continue. This means that the area will experience continued high unemployment in the immediate future, and an improved situation can only obtain regionally if there is a marked upturn in the national economy.

VARIATION IN UNEMPLOYMENT WITHIN NORTHERN IRELAND

While Northern Ireland as a whole experiences much higher levels of unemployment than other U.K. regions, internally there is very considerable variation. This is illustrated in Fig. 9.3, which shows the percentage male unemployed at 8 June 1978, by Travel-to-Work Area (the statistical unit used by the Department of Manpower Services).

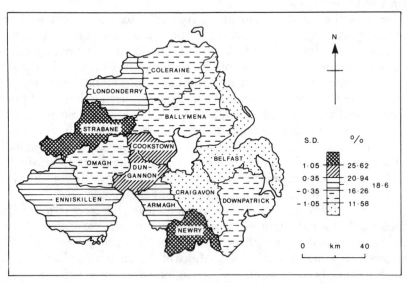

FIGURE 9.3. Male Unemployment, 8 June 1978.
Source: Calculated from data obtained from the Department of Manpower Services.

Two clear areas are apparent, one in the east, focussed on Belfast and Craigavon, with low unemployment, and one in the west and south with high unemployment, particularly in Newry and Strabane. This pattern has remained stable over time. The distribution of unemployment variability (Fig. 9.4) can also be examined by mapping the standard deviations from January unemployment means. Belfast not only has the lowest levels of unemployment but it also has the least variability. Strabane has high unemployment and a high variability, indicating a particularly weak and unstable labour market. Cookstown has experienced a greater worsening of its unemployment position than any other area, rising from 10·9% male unemployment in January 1974 to 25·6% in January 1978.

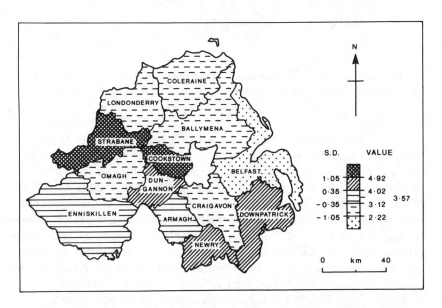

FIGURE 9.4. January Male Unemployment Variability, 1972–1978.
Source: Calculated from data obtained from the Department of Manpower Services.

A more significant picture of the economic stress caused by unemployment is obtained by looking at long-term unemployment. Figure 9.5 shows the percentage of the male unemployed who have been out of work for more than one year. The east–west division of Northern Ireland is again clear, as is the particular seriousness of the problem in Newry and Strabane, where 45·5% and 50·7% respectively of the male unemployed have been out of work for more than one year.

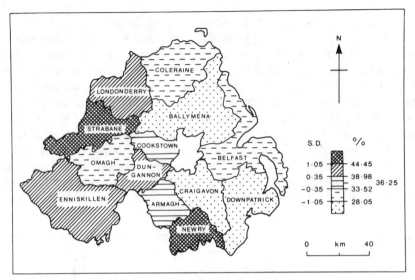

FIGURE 9.5. Males Unemployed More than One Year, 8 June 1978.
Source: Calculated from data obtained from the Department of Manpower
Services.

On the basis of these distributions, Northern Ireland can be divided
into three unemployment regions:
(*i*) *Belfast, Craigavon and Ballymena.* This constitutes the economic core
of Northern Ireland, and is characterised by persistent low levels
of unemployment, low variability and low levels of long-term unemployment. The Quigley Report (1976) commented that Northern
Ireland had virtually a dual economy: Belfast, Ballymena and Craigavon, and the rest of the area. This region has 70% of Northern Ireland's
male employees, and while the unemployment rates in this region are
low, it still has 57% of Northern Ireland's male unemployed (27 694
persons in June 1978). Thus, although in percentage terms the problem
is not great, in terms of absolute numbers it is in this core region that the
largest unemployment problem resides.
(*ii*) *Strabane and Newry.* In this region, which comprises two Travel-
to-Work Areas in peripheral locations, the numbers unemployed are
comparatively small, only 5053 males in June 1978. However this
represents almost one-third of the male employees in the two areas,
and 10·4% of Northern Ireland's male unemployed. Strabane and
Newry are characterised by persistent high unemployment rates, high
variability, and very high levels of long-term unemployment, indicating
severe economic stress in these areas with consequent social distress.

(*iii*) *The remainder of Northern Ireland.* While not experiencing the same levels as Strabane and Newry, the remaining eight Travel-to-Work Areas had an overall male unemployment rate of 19·3% in June 1978, and had almost one-third of Northern Ireland's male unemployed. Unemployment in these areas is largely rural, and the high proportion of long-term unemployed and the high average unemployment rates indicate that here too is a problem which is not easy to solve.

A SPATIAL MODEL OF UNEMPLOYMENT VARIATION

A model is now developed to account for the spatial variation in unemployment levels described above. The data used were derived from a special tabulation of the 1971 Northern Ireland Census of Population, provided by the Department of Manpower Services. The data were tabulated for the twenty-seven Local Office Areas of Northern Ireland, and this data source was used because these were the only areal units on which it was possible to obtain all the data required. Three sets of factors are advanced to explain spatial variation in unemployment: the geographical distribution of the population, the social characteristics of the population, and the industrial structure of the population.

The Geographical Distribution of the Population

(*a*) *Distance from Belfast*

The existence of a dual economy in Northern Ireland and the dominance of Belfast has been commented upon. In view of the core–periphery relationship which exists, it is hypothesised that, the greater the distance from Belfast, the higher the level of unemployment which may be expected.

(*b*) *The density of male workers*

High percentage unemployment figures do not necessarily indicate a good labour supply. Roche *et al.* (1973, p. 60) have suggested that "it is not the percentage of unemployment that matters, but the numbers available within a reasonable travel-to-work radius of the plant". In June 1978 ten Local Office Areas in Northern Ireland had over 1000 men registered as unemployed, but only three had more than 2000. Belfast was the only area with more than 10 000. Thus, despite the high unemployment rates which prevail, few areas in Northern Ireland can offer a good supply of labour to a large industrial concern. It is suggested that the availability of labour can be measured by the density of male workers per square kilometre, and hypothesised that, as the density of male workers decreases, the level of unemployment will rise.

The Social Characteristics of the Population

(a) Percentage in Social Class V

It has been shown that unskilled workers will tend *ceteris paribus* to have relatively high unemployment rates (Daniel, 1974; Hill *et al.*, 1973), because they have least to offer a prospective employer and because unskilled workers tend to be laid off before skilled workers. Social Class V consists of unskilled manual workers, and it is hypothesised that the level of unemployment in an area is positively related to the percentage of males in this class.

(b) Percentage Roman Catholic

Unemployment is two and a half times greater for Roman Catholics than for Protestants (Fair Employment Agency, 1978). Although Catholic men in 1971 comprised less than 21% of the economically active population, they represented 44% of the unemployed (Aunger, 1975). Osborne (1978) has discussed spatial aspects of this relationship but not in relation to other factors. This factor is included in this analysis, because of its obvious importance in relation to the Northern Ireland problem, and so that its importance might be assessed in relation to the other hypothesised factors.

The Industrial Structure of the Population

Percentage employed in agriculture

It has already been noted that one reason for Northern Ireland's high unemployment is the decline in the traditionally important industries of agriculture, textiles, shipbuilding and aircraft manufacture. Of these, only agriculture has been a substantial employer of labour throughout Northern Ireland. It is suggested that, if a high proportion of the labour force in an area is employed in this declining industry, that area will tend to have a relatively high unemployment rate.

Stepwise Multiple Regression

Stepwise multiple regression can now be used to demonstrate the nature of the links between male unemployment and these five variables.

Table 9.2 presents the results of this procedure, which orders the variables in terms of their statistical importance in the overall equation.

TABLE 9.2. Stepwise Multiple Regression on Male Unemployment in Northern Ireland.

Independent variable[a]	Simple R	Multiple R	Multiple R^2	Change in multiple R^2	B	Standard error of B	F[b]
Males: Social Class V (%)	0·833	0·833	0·694	0·694	0·099	0·025	15·6
Males: Roman Catholic (%)	0·825	0·878	0·771	0·077	0·006	0·003	3·4
Distance from Belfast (kms)	0·670	0·896	0·802	0·031	0·004	0·002	6·5
Density of male workers (Persons per km²)	−0·351	0·908	0·825	0·023	0·237	0·069	11·7
Males in agriculture (%)	0·507	0·935	0·874	0·049	0·023	0·008	8·2
					Constant: −0·272		

[a]Two variables, male unemployment rate and density of male workers, were transformed logarithmically to reduce skewness and improve the linearity of relationships.
[b]$F \geqslant 4·0$ is statistically significant at the 99·9% level.

The simple R values confirm the importance of the factors chosen, each having the relationship with the dependent variable as hypothesised. In combination, the five variables account for 87·4% of the spatial variation in male unemployment throughout Northern Ireland. While the social class variable is the most important, each of the others makes a statistically significant contribution to the overall equation. One variable, the density of male workers, changed the direction of its relationship with the dependent variable, from a negative simple R (as hypothesised) to a positive multiple R. It is likely that this change is due to interrelationships between the independent variables, and it is necessary to examine these to obtain a better understanding of the model. Table 9.3 shows that some particularly strong interrelationships are present.

The distance variable has the strongest correlations overall, the lowest value being 0·53. With increasing distance from Belfast, the density of workers decreases while the percentage in agriculture, the percentage in Social Class V and the percentage Roman Catholic all increase. This demonstrates the dominance of Belfast in the regional economy, and the consequent core–periphery effect. The highest correlation, -0.85, is between males in agriculture and worker density. There is also a high correlation (0.78) between males in Social Class V and Roman Catholic males. Aunger (1975) has demonstrated that, as the status of a social class declines, the number of Roman Catholics in the class increases, and the "typical" male Catholic worker is unskilled.

TABLE 9.3. Correlation Matrix of the Independent Variables in the. Regression Equation.

	S.C.V	R.C.	Distance	Density	Agriculture
Males: Social Class V	1·00				
Males: Roman Catholic	0·78	1·00			
Distance from Belfast	0·53	0·62	1·00		
Density of male workers	−0·36	−0·47	−0·65	1·00	
Males in agriculture	0·35	0·52	0·64	0·85	1·00

As the independent variables of the model are so strongly inter-related, this calls into question the meaning of their correlations with male unemployment. For example, is the correlation between male unemployment and Roman Catholic males due in some way to their religious affiliation, or is it due to the predominantly unskilled social status of Catholics, or is it due to the rural and peripheral location of Roman Catholics in Northern Ireland? Is the correlation between male unemployment and males in agriculture due to the declining agricultural employment, or is it due to the low density of workers in agricultural areas? To answer these questions, the effect of the inter-relationships between the variables must be removed. This can be achieved by calculating partial correlation coefficients, a statistical technique which identifies the relationship between two variables while taking out the effect of specified intervening variables. Fourth order partial correlations are presented in Table 9.4: these show the relationship between male unemployment and each of the other variables independently.

Examination of this table gives a clearer picture of the effect each of the five independent variables has on the distribution of male unemployment:

(a) *Males: Social Class V*

This variable has the strongest partial correlation with male unemployment. It is clear from this result that areas with high proportions of unskilled males will experience high unemployment. It follows that, if the level of skill of the workforce could be raised in such areas, there should be a consequent lowering in the level of unemployment.

TABLE 9.4. Fourth Order Partial Correlation Coefficients.

	Percentage in Social Class V	Density of male workers	Percentage of males in agriculture	Distance from Belfast	Percentage males Roman Catholic
Correlation with percentage males unemployed	0·65	0·60	0·53	0·49	0·37
Significance level	99·9%	99·9%	99·5%	99·0%	95·0%

(b) Density of male workers

This variable has a strong and significant partial correlation with male unemployment. However, as in the multiple regression, the direction of this relationship is positive, rather than negative as initially hypothesised. Thus, when the effect of the other variables is removed, in particular the high correlations with males in agriculture and with distance from Belfast, male unemployment in fact rises with increasing density of workers. This finding disproves the hypothesis that unemployment is related to availability of labour, and it is suggested that the high positive partial correlation obtained is indicating an urbanisation factor in the distribution of unemployment.

(c) Males in agriculture

A clear positive relationship with unemployed males is found, demonstrating the link between unemployment and a high level of dependence on this declining industry in an area.

(d) Distance from Belfast

Distance from Belfast is found to be significantly related to increasing unemployment, as hypothesised.

(e) Males: Roman Catholic

This variable has the weakest and least significant partial correlation with male unemployment. The high simple correlation between the two variables (0·82) is thus largely due to the relationship between Roman Catholic males and the other variables, as shown in Table 9.3. However, the fourth order partial correlation, though the weakest obtained, was still statistically significant, indicating that, even when the strong interrelationships with the other variables are removed, there is still a direct link between male unemployment and religious affiliation.

In summary, three sets of factors were advanced to account for the distribution of male unemployment: these were geographical, social and industrial. The analysis revealed that each contributed to explanation of the observed patterns of unemployment. One variable, the density of male workers, did not have the expected relationship with male unemployment: this result was explained by a possible relationship between urbanisation and unemployment.

VARIATION IN UNEMPLOYMENT WITHIN THE BELFAST URBAN AREA

The Belfast area is characterised by low unemployment rates in comparison with the rest of Northern Ireland. However, as this is the major centre of population, the number of unemployed persons is high: the Belfast Travel-to-Work Area had 19 000 men registered unemployed in June 1978. Furthermore, it has been pointed out that:

> The Belfast figures hide variations in the level of unemployment within the city. The percentage unemployed within certain residential areas in Belfast is probably as high as in the small towns of the west. In other words, there are problems of unemployment in eastern Northern Ireland just as grave as in the west of the Province, possibly made worse by the larger total of jobs required to solve the unemployment problem. (Salt and Johnson, 1975, p. 232)

Local surveys have indicated male unemployment rates of around 30% in parts of west Belfast (Weiner, 1972; Spencer, 1973). The variation in unemployment within Belfast is clearly an important aspect of the overall unemployment problem, but it is difficult to investigate as official data is only published for Local Office Areas and Travel-to-Work Areas: no official statistics are available on small areal units. This problem is circumvented in the present study by mapping data from the primary source, i.e. the live unemployment register.

The built-up area of Belfast is delimited by the "Matthew Stop Line" (Matthew, 1964), and, in 1971, had a population of 553 294. For the purposes of this analysis, the area was sub-divided into 166 one kilometre grid squares (Doherty, 1978). A 42% sample of the unemployed was drawn from the live registers in the Belfast and Lisburn Offices, during the period December 1971 to February 1972, and coded into this grid system. For each square, the number of unemployed males was divided by the number of economically active males aged 19–65, to give the male unemployment rate.

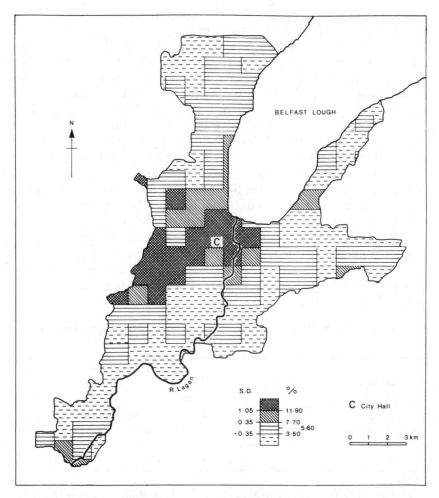

FIGURE 9.6. Male Unemployment in the Belfast Urban Area, December 1971–February 1972.
Source: Sample data from live register.

The map of these rates (Fig. 9.6) shows a wedge of continuous high unemployment running through central and west Belfast. Within the wedge are two cores of very high unemployment, one in the inner city with a peak of 30·1%, and one on the periphery with a peak of 37·7%. A mapping of male unemployment in 1966 had an almost identical distribution (Doherty, 1977). Outside the wedge of continuous high unemployment two other peaks occur, in the Catholic enclaves of Ardoyne and Ligoniel. Average male unemployment within the Belfast Urban Area as a whole was 7·7%.

What explanation can be offered for this pattern? At a regional scale, levels of unemployment are determined largely by economic and political factors. However, at a sub-regional scale, social factors become more important, as evidenced by the preceding examination of variation in unemployment within Northern Ireland. At the micro-urban scale, social factors can be hypothesised as being of equal or greater significance, and a model can therefore be developed which links the level of unemployment to the social geography of the city.

The social geography of Belfast in 1971 has been examined through a Principal Component analysis of twenty-two census variables (Doherty, 1978). The first three components accounted for 82·6% of the variance in the data set and were identified as Social Structure, Age Structure and Ethnic Structure. Social Structure and Ethnic Structure had sectoral distributions, while Age Structure was distributed concentrically. The relationship of the distribution of male unemployment to these patterns can be demonstrated using the technique of Regression on Principal Components (Massy, 1965). The regression is presented in Table 9.5; the procedures employed are more fully discussed elsewhere (Doherty, 1980).

TABLE 9.5. Principal Components Regression on Male Unemployment in the Belfast Urban Area.

Independent variable	Multiple R	R^2	R^2 change	B	Standard error of B	F
Social Structure	0·521	0·271	0·271	0·521	0·053	96·6
Ethnic Structure	0·727	0·529	0·248	0·508	0·053	91·8
Age Structure	0·755	0·571	0·042	0·204	0·053	14·9
			Constant: 0·000			

The regression was performed in a stepwise mode; this ordered the independent variables in relation to their statistical importance: Social Structure, Ethnic Structure, Age Structure. The equation may be stated as:

Male Unemployment = 0·52 Social Structure + 0·51 Ethnic Structure + 0·20 Age Structure.

It demonstrates, first, a positive relationship between the dependent variable and each of the independent variables. Each independent variable may be viewed as a continuum running from advantaged to disadvantaged in terms of the job market. The Social Structure variable ranges from those of high class, accompanied by high skill and educational attainment to those of low class, with low skill and educational levels. Ethnic Structure picks out the Protestant–Roman Catholic dichotomy; Aunger (1975) has demonstrated that this overlies a number of dimensions: skilled–unskilled, employed–unemployed, masculine–feminine employment and superordination–subordination. The Age Structure variable ranges from those who are young, and therefore attractive to employers, to those who are old and less attractive. The model demonstrates that the level of unemployment in an area will increase as the social class and skill level of the population become lower, as the Ethnic Structure becomes more Catholic, and as the Age Structure becomes older.

The model has an R^2 value of 0·57, indicating that it provides a fairly good explanation of the distribution of unemployment. The major contribution to the model is made by the Social Structure and Ethnic Structure variables, with Social Structure being the more important of the two. This links very clearly with the regression model developed to account for the distribution of unemployment across Northern Ireland. Age Structure has a significant, although less important, contribution to the model. One explanation for this is that social and ethnic residential segregation within the Urban Area is much stronger than segregation by age (Boal *et al.*, 1976).

CONCLUSIONS

The high unemployment in Northern Ireland is attributable to economic factors such as the structure of industry and the link with the national economy; to geographical factors such as the location of the area; and to social factors such as high natural increase and the "troubles". Within Northern Ireland, it was shown that 77% of the variation in unemployment levels was due to low social class and Roman Catholic religious affiliation. These two influences were also found to be important in accounting for the variation in unemployment within Belfast: 53% of the variation was found to be due to Social Structure (a factor consisting of social class measures) and Ethnic Structure (a factor consisting of religious affiliation measures).

The association between unemployment and low skill is to be expected, and has been demonstrated in a number of studies in Great Britain (Daniel, 1974; Hill *et al.*, 1973; Metcalf, 1975). The association of unemployment with religious affiliation is, however, slightly more unusual in the United Kingdom context and requires comment, particularly as the Catholic–Protestant cleavage is the fundamental dichotomy in Northern Ireland society. The study has demonstrated that while the distribution of Roman Catholics is strongly correlated with low social class, distance from Belfast, density of workers and agricultural employment, each of which is also related to unemployment, there is a significant relationship between Roman Catholic religious affiliation and male unemployment, when the effect of these intervening variables is controlled for. Within Belfast, 27% of the variation in unemployment is due to Ethnic Structure.

A number of explanations for this relationship have been advanced. Perhaps the most commonplace explanation is that discrimination in employment exists. To prove or disprove such a suggestion is, by its very nature, difficult. Discrimination in employment has never been proven in a court of law. While individual cases have been alleged, it has not been possible to show the existence of systematic discrimination on a scale sufficient to produce the demonstrated link between Catholic religious affiliation and unemployment. Barritt and Carter (1962), in their classic study of Northern Ireland society in the late 1950s, indicated that they had found some discrimination in employment on the grounds of religion, but this was on the part of both Protestants and Catholics. Furthermore, they provided no measure of the discrimination which they observed. Using survey data, Rose (1971) was unable to find evidence of systematic discrimination in public employment.

A series of research reports published by the Fair Employment Agency has provided useful insights. Analysis of 1971 Census data (Fair Employment Agency, 1978) demonstrated marked differences in the industrial and occupational profiles of Roman Catholics and Protestants. Catholics tended to be over-represented in low paid and declining industry, and in unskilled occupations. However the Agency pointed out that these figures do not of themselves prove or disprove discrimination. As Barritt and Carter (1962) commented, discrimination cannot be proved merely by statistics on the religion of the employed. What the figures demonstrate, if anything, is an absence of equality of opportunity.

It has been suggested that Catholics have a higher unemployment rate because they have a less favourable attitude to work. The "Protestant work ethic" is believed to make Protestants more ambitious and more positive in their attitude to work. Research into this topic by Miller (1978) has demonstrated that this is not so, and in fact only minimal differences in attitude to work were found between the two groups.

Given the generally lower social status of Roman Catholics, it may also be suggested that Catholic children will have a lower educational attainment than Protestants, which would place them in a disadvantageous position in a highly competitive job market. Investigation of G.C.E. results (Osborne and Murray, 1978) indicates that, while there is evidence of this in the past, Catholics tend to be catching up on Protestants, and in the future this factor should have lesser significance. This is, however, of some significance at present, because of its impact on people currently in the labour market.

The relationship between Roman Catholic religious affiliation and unemployment cannot be simply explained by a single factor. Discrimination by both communities has existed in the past, and Catholics, being the minority group with less political and economic power, have undoubtedly suffered most. Such practices are now illegal and Government has demonstrated its determination to eradicate them. However, the legacy of the past, in terms of individual attitudes, educational attainment, industrial and occupational structures, and self-segregation, cannot be erased simply by legislation. Time is required, together with a substantial change in community attitudes. Given the overall high level of unemployment in Northern Ireland, and the stagnant United Kingdom economy, it is a truism to state that this is no easy task.

Quite apart from the sectarian aspects of the unemployment problem, its social consequences are very severe, and in this respect the problem in Northern Ireland is not unique. The level of unemployment in a society has a direct bearing on its standard of living and unemployment is a key problem in the cycle of deprivation. Studies of multiple deprivation in Belfast have demonstrated that the areas of the city characterised by high unemployment (Fig. 9.6) also suffer from a variety of social problems such as low income, overcrowding, and poor housing (Boal *et al.*, 1974, 1978; Project Team, 1977). There is a high correlation between adult male unemployment and juvenile unemployment (Boal *et al.* 0·73, Project Team 0·75), and a correlation of 0·96 between adult male unemployment and long-term male unemployment (Project Team). This indicates that, as the level of unemployment in an area increases, so do its dimensions, and it suggests that in areas of high unemployment this has become an established feature of life, with high long-term unemployment and high juvenile unemployment.

The link between unemployment, low income, state benefits and family size is also worthy of comment. In 1975, *per capita* personal income in Northern Ireland was 83·1% of the figure for the United Kingdom (Central Statistical Office, 1979). This gap in incomes has been narrowing in recent years, but it remains substantial. Welfare benefits, in contrast, are the same in Northern Ireland as in the rest of the United Kingdom. It seems obvious, therefore, that unless there is a sufficient gap between earnings and social security, it is hardly worthwhile to work. At least 10% of manual jobs in Northern Ireland are paid at a rate where a man might be financially better off unemployed (*Belfast Telegraph*, 17 October 1978).

Insight into this aspect of the unemployment problem is provided by Doherty (1977), in a further analysis of the 42% sample of unemployed males in Belfast. The sample was divided into two groups: those who were receiving more money while unemployed and those who were receiving less. It was found that 23·1% of the male unemployed were financially better off unemployed, and that this group was characterised by an average of three child dependants, and a low level of skill. They were also characterised by very low wage levels while in employment. Given their low earning potential and their financial responsibilities towards their families, it would seem that these men prefer not to work so that they can obtain a higher income. Table 9.6 shows the length of time out of work for this group with comparative statistics for three English towns.

TABLE 9.6. The Percentage of Various Unemployment Lengths Receiving More while Unemployed than when Employed.[a,b]

Unemployment length	Coventry	Hammersmith	Newcastle	Belfast
Under 6 months	2	7	8	16
6 months to 1 year	4	13	12	29
Over 1 year	7	21	13	34

[a]The English statistics are from Hill *et al.* (1973), and refer to October 1971. The Belfast statistics refer to the period December 1971 to February 1972, and are derived from a sample drawn from the live register.
[b]The Belfast statistics include those unemployed less than four weeks, the English statistics do not.

This indicates that this group is out of work longer than those who experience a drop in income while unemployed: they have an average length of time out of work of 57·4 weeks, as opposed to 41·6 weeks for those whose income dropped. The much higher proportion of this group in Belfast in comparison with the three English towns confirms that this is due to the lower level of incomes in Northern Ireland. There is thus a classic "poverty trap" in existence, with substantial numbers of low paid workers who find it financially advantageous to be out of work. The problem is compounded by the larger average family size in Northern Ireland of 2·92 persons, compared with 2·76 in the United Kingdom as a whole (Central Statistical Office, 1979), which tends to increase the level of payments to families in Northern Ireland. As Roman Catholic marital fertility is 172% of Protestant marital fertility (Compton, 1978; see also Chapter 4), completed family size is significantly higher for Catholics. This suggests that a higher proportion of Roman Catholics than Protestants will be caught in the poverty trap, and is a further explanation of the link between unemployment and Catholic religious affiliation.

Unemployment is a major social evil, linked, as has already been noted, with a number of other social problems. The cleavage between employed and unemployed is a significant one, and the fact that it overlies the Protestant–Catholic cleavage has served to compound the tensions in Northern Ireland society:

> There can be little doubt that sustained unemployment and the sense of job insecurity of even those who are employed have contributed to sectarian conflict in Northern Ireland. If this is correct then the social cost of unemployment has surely been mammoth and must justify a radical approach to its amelioration and preferably elimination. (Gibson, 1973, p. 364)

Prospects for the future are not encouraging, particularly in view of Northern Ireland's vulnerability to economic trends in the rest of the United Kingdom. In a period of financial stringency, the area cannot continue to experience a high level of government funding. Unemployment would seem to be set to continue at a high level, and emigration must continue to be the solution for many, particularly the more highly skilled and the more highly motivated. The sectarian aspects of unemployment which have been identified are being tackled by Government; they also require a change of attitude within the community. Over half of all firms employing eleven or more persons have signed the Fair Employment Agency's Declaration of Principle and Intent, indicating their commitment to non-sectarian employment, although a number of employers, including some District Councils, have refused to sign. It will take time to erase the legacy of segregated employment and unemployment; but it is essential that this goal is attained if a solution is to be found to the wider Northern Ireland problem.

REFERENCES

Aunger, E. A. (1975). Religion and Occupational Class in Northern Ireland. *Economic and Social Review* **7**, 1–18.

Barritt, D. P. and Carter, C. F. (1962). "The Northern Ireland Problem: A Study in Group Relations." Oxford University Press, London.

Belfast Telegraph, 16 October 1978. The Hunt for Jobs, Part 1.

Belfast Telegraph, 17 October 1978. The Hunt for Jobs, Part 2.

Black, W. and Slattery, D. (1975). Regional and National Variations in Employment and Unemployment. Northern Ireland: A Case Study. *Scottish Journal of Political Economy* **22**, 196–206.

Boal, F. W., Doherty, P. and Pringle, D. G. (1974). "The Spatial Distribution of Some Social Problems in the Belfast Urban Area." Northern Ireland Community Relations Commission, Belfast.

Boal, F. W., Doherty, P. and Pringle, D. G. (1978). "Social Problems in the Belfast Urban Area: An Exploratory Analysis." Occasional Paper No. 12, Department of Geography, Queen Mary College, University of London.

Boal, F. W., Poole, M. A., Murray, R. C. and Kennedy, S. J. (1976). "Religious Residential Segregation and Residential Decision Making in the Belfast Urban Area." Final Report to the Social Science Research Council (Available from the National Lending Library, Boston Spa, Yorkshire).

Central Statistical Office (1965–1979). (*Abstract of*) *Regional Statistics*, **1–14**. Her Majesty's Stationery Office, London.

Compton, P. A. (1978). "Northern Ireland: A Census Atlas." Gill and Macmillan, Dublin.

Daniel, W. W. (1974). "A National Survey of the Unemployed." Broadsheet 546, Political and Economic Planning, London.

Davies, R., McGurnaghan, M. A. and Sams, K. I. (1977). The Northern Ireland Economy: Progress (1968–75) and Prospects. *Regional Studies* **11**, 297–307.

Doherty, P. (1977). "A Geography of Unemployment in the Belfast Urban Area." Unpublished Ph.D. Thesis, Queen's University, Belfast.

Doherty, P. (1978). A Social Geography of the Belfast Urban Area, 1971. *Irish Geography* **11**, 68–87.

Doherty, P. (1980). Patterns of Unemployment in Belfast. *Irish Geography* **13**, 65–76.

Eurostat (1979). "Regional Statistics—Main Regional Indicators 1970–1977." Office des Publications Officielles des Communautés Européenes, Luxembourg.

Fair Employment Agency (1978). "An Industrial and Occupational Profile of the Two Sections of the Population in Northern Ireland." Research Paper 1, Fair Employment Agency, Belfast.

Gibson, N. J. (1973). Economic Conditions and Policy in Northern Ireland. *Economic and Social Review* **4**, 349–364.

Hill, M. J., Harrison, R. M., Sargeant, A. V. and Talbot, V. (1973). "Men out of Work: A Study of Unemployment in Three English Towns." Cambridge University Press, London.

Massy, W. F. (1965). Principal Components Regression in Exploratory Statistical Research. *Journal of the American Statistical Association* **60**, 234–256.

Matthew, Sir R. H. (1964). "Belfast Regional Survey and Plan 1962: A Report." Her Majesty's Stationery Office, Belfast.

Metcalf, D. (1975). Urban Unemployment in England. *Economic Journal* **85**, 578–589.

Miller, R. (1978). "Attitudes to Work in Northern Ireland." Research Paper 2, Fair Employment Agency, Belfast.

Osborne, R. D. (1978). Denomination and Unemployment in Northern Ireland. *Area* **10**, 280–283.

Osborne, R. D. and Murray, R. C. (1978). "Educational Qualifications and Religious Affiliation in Northern Ireland: An Examination of G.C.E. 'O' and 'A' Levels." Research Paper 3, Fair Employment Agency, Belfast.

Project Team (1977). "Belfast: Areas of Special Social Need. Report." Her Majesty's Stationery Office, Belfast.

Quigley, W. G. H. (1976). "Economic and Industrial Strategy for Northern Ireland: Report by Review Team 1976." Her Majesty's Stationery Office, Belfast.

Roche, D. J. D., Birrell, W. D., Murie, A. S. and Hillyard, P. A. R. (1973). Some Determinants of Labour Mobility in Northern Ireland. *Economic and Social Review* **5**, 59–73.

Rose, R. (1971). "Governing without Consensus: An Irish Perspective." Faber and Faber, London.

Salt, J. and Johnson, J. H. (1975). Recent Trends in the Level and Distribution of Unemployment in Northern Ireland. *Tijdschrift voor Economische en Sociale Geografie* **66**, 225–233.

Simpson, J. V. (1971). Regional Analysis: The Northern Ireland Experience. *Economic and Social Review* **2**, 507–529.

Spencer, A. E. C. W. (1973). "Ballymurphy: A Tale of Two Surveys." Department of Social Studies, Queen's University, Belfast.

Walsh, B. M. (1977). The Labour Force and the Problem of Unemployment. *In* "Economic Activity in Ireland: A Study of Two Open Economies" (N. J. Gibson and J. E. Spencer, eds.), pp. 79–103. Gill and Macmillan, Dublin.

Weiner, R. S. P. (1972). "Unemployment in Andersonstown." Mimeographed Report to the Northern Ireland Research Institute and the Northern Ireland Community Relations Commission, Belfast.

CHAPTER 10

SEGREGATING AND MIXING: SPACE AND RESIDENCE IN BELFAST

Frederick W. Boal

SEGREGATION AND ASSIMILATION *describing*

Ethnic residential segregation is a feature of many cities. Insofar as we can classify Protestants and Roman Catholics in Northern Ireland as members of two ethnic groups, we can examine the degree to which ethnic residential segregation exists in Belfast. If we take an ethnic group to mean "any group which is defined or set off by race, religion or national origin or some combination of these categories" (Gordon, 1964, p. 27), where these categories have a common social-psychological function in that they serve to create a sense of peoplehood, and where there is an assumption of common origin, real or imaginary (Greeley, 1969, p. 40), then it seems reasonable to claim that Protestants and Roman Catholics do indeed form two ethnic groups.

Societies are said to be pluralistic when they are segmented into corporate groups that frequently, although not necessarily, have different cultures or sub-cultures and when their social structure is compartmentalised into analogous, parallel, non-complementary but distinguishable sets of institutions (van den Berghe, 1967, p. 34). The former state is called cultural pluralism, the latter social or structural pluralism. Northern Ireland is characterised by a *degree* of cultural pluralism and a *degree* of structural pluralism. The degree of pluralism displayed within a society may vary over time. Reduction in pluralism is referred to as assimilation, and just as there is cultural and structural pluralism, so there may be cultural and structural assimilation. Cultural

249

assimilation is said to take place where the cultural patterns of (say) an immigrant group change to those of the host society, while structural assimilation occurs when there is large-scale entry of members of the immigrant group into the institutions of the host society on the primary group level. A less asymmetrical view of assimilation would be one where two somewhat dissimilar groups converge *on each other* in terms of cultural characteristics and institutional participation.

A number of American sociologists have suggested that there is an inverse relationship between the degree of assimilation of two ethnic groups and the degree of residential segregation that exists between them (Duncan and Lieberson, 1959; Lieberson, 1961), that is, where segregation is high assimilation is low and vice versa. Thus, increasing assimilation will be accompanied by decreasing segregation. Recently some doubt has been cast on the validity of the correlation of low residential segregation with high assimilation, at least for certain groups (Lee, 1977, p. 71). However, it does seem incontrovertible that the existence of a high degree of residential segregation between two ethnic groups will be accompanied by, at the most, only limited assimilation.

Assimilation, when it occurs, takes place over time. For many immigrant groups in American cities it has been shown that assimilation has increased with length of residence. This leads to a possible assumption of unidirectional change. However, the differences between ethnic groups may not decline; indeed they may increase, particularly where ethnic difference is used as a basis for group organisation—"a great amount of attention may be paid to the revival of select traditional cultural traits, and to the establishment of historical traditions . . ." (Barth, 1969, p. 35). In addition, outbursts of conflict over political, economic or other issues may put a brake on trends towards the assimilation of ethnic groups, and, indeed, may reverse the process.

Residential segregation between two ethnic groups is likely to indicate some significant degree of difference between them. Indeed the physical separation of residence may contribute to and reinforce division. Equally, however, segregation between groups may act as an integrating force *within* each group—common residence permits the maintenance of ethnic cultural attributes and reduces the likelihood of dilution due to outside contact (Boal, 1978a).

Overall, then, we can suggest the following three sets of relationships. First, residential segregation between two ethnic groups will indicate that the two groups are relatively unassimilated, at least in terms of key criteria in the particular context being observed (for instance religious affiliation, political orientation and institutional structures in the Northern Ireland context). Secondly, decrease in segregation *may* indicate increasing assimilation, whilst increase in segregation may well indicate the elaboration of group differences. Thirdly, just as segregation may indicate and causally contribute to division between ethnic groups, so such segregation may indicate and contribute to significant levels of integration *within* each ethnic group. Although no study has been completed in Northern Ireland that attempts to establish the extent and nature of any relationship between the degree of ethnic segregation and the degree of ethnic assimilation, it does seem reasonable to suggest that the above generalisations will hold.

In consequence of these points, this chapter will attempt to establish the extent to which ethnic segregation has existed in Belfast at different points in time, and consider any temporal variation that has occurred. In addition, because ethnic residential mixing may indicate reduction of differences between groups, particular attention will be paid to those areas where such mixing can be observed, and to the households residing in such situations.

ETHNIC SEGREGATION IN BELFAST OVER TIME

Emrys Jones in his book "A Social Geography of Belfast" (1960) has suggested that residential segregation of Roman Catholics and Protestants may have been a characteristic of the city from its inception. He has argued that towns in Ireland were the gift of invading peoples and that, outside Ireland, there are many parallels to the exclusion of native peoples from towns when indigenous and intrusive cultures clashed. An early map of Belfast, published in 1685, may indicate a native (Catholic) housing cluster immediately outside the town walls (Jones, 1960, p. 48). Be that as it may, Jones (1960, p. 189) notes that relations between Protestants and Roman Catholics in Belfast during the latter part of the eighteenth century and the early part of the nineteenth appear to have been fairly amicable. What there cannot be any doubt about is the deterioration in these relationships as the nineteenth century proceeded. This deterioration seems to be related to the rapid growth in the number of Catholics, due, in large measure, to the considerable in-migration of rural dwellers into the growing industrial city. The deteriorating relationship was accentuated by outbursts of inter-ethnic rioting (Boyd, 1969; Boal and Murray, 1977). These conflict outbursts sharpened the growing segregation in that Catholics and Protestants living in situations where they perceived themselves to be vulnerable minorities moved house in search of the greater security provided by the ethnic cluster. Indeed, significant numbers were forced to make these moves. The existence of segregation in 1857 and its sharpening as a consequence of the rioting of that year are both described in the report of the Commission of Inquiry established by the Government:

> The Pound district has for many years been chiefly inhabited by a Roman Catholic population, while Sandy-row district has been chiefly inhabited by a population of Orangemen and Protestants. Until lately however, there was some intermixture, a few Catholics residing in the Sandy-row district and a few Protestants in the Pound district. Since the commencement of the late riots, however, the districts have become exclusive, and by regular systematized movements on both sides, the few Catholic inhabitants of the Sandy-row district have been obliged to leave it and the few Protestant inhabitants of the Pound district have also been obliged to leave that locality. (Commissioners of Inquiry, 1858)

Throughout the latter part of the nineteenth century and into the twentieth there was a sequence of periods of relative tranquillity punctuated by conflict outbursts, the latter frequently triggered by heightened political agitation associated with moves for and against "Home Rule" for Ireland, and more recently associated with the political division of the island and the continued conflict within the new political unit of Northern Ireland.

TABLE 10.1. Belfast County Borough: Percentage Distribution of Population in Five Levels of Ethnic Street Mixing, 1911, 1969 and 1972.

Street religious proportion (Percentage Catholic)	Catholics and Protestants			Catholics			Protestants		
	1911	1969	1972	1911	1969	1972	1911	1969	1972
0–9	49	53	60	7	6	3	62	69	78
10–29	28	21	16	20	15	11	31	23	18
30–49	6	8	4	9	12	8	5	7	3
50–90	7	4	3	23	12	9	2	2	2
91–100	10	14	17	41	56	70	*	*	*

* Rounds to zero.

Source: The 1911 data were obtained from manuscript records of the 1911 Census and refer to population. The 1969 data refer to the early part of that year and were obtained by the combined use of Roman Catholic parish records and electoral registers. The 1972 data are drawn from a sample survey.[1] The 1969 and 1972 data refer to households.

The first year for which it is possible to quantify the ethnic residential distribution in Belfast is 1911 (Table 10.1). If we take those streets where less than 10% of the population is Roman Catholic as segregated Protestant situations and those streets where the Roman Catholic proportion is over 90% as segregated Catholic, it can be seen that in 1911 41% of Catholics and 62% of Protestants were residentially segregated. The next year for which approximately comparable data are available is 1969. Here we are dealing with households rather than population and this may reduce the degree of street-level mixing observed, because households are classified on the basis of religion of head of household. Thus domestics or lodgers of a different religious affiliation will not be recorded. In addition it should be noted that the data for 1911 and 1969 (and 1972) refer to Belfast County Borough, a unit that approximated the built-up area in 1911, but which by 1969 underbounded the built-up area to a considerable degree. In other words the newer suburbs of Belfast in 1911 were located within the County Borough, but the newer suburbs of 1969 were, in the main, located outside. Thus to the extent that the suburbs in 1969 were less ethnically segregated than the inner, older parts of the city so the data will tend to overstate the amount of ethnic segregation. The same point applies to comparisons of the 1972 data with 1911, but not to 1969–1972 comparisons. However, bearing in mind these qualifications, it seems very likely that segregation had increased between 1911 and 1969, for by the latter year the proportion of Roman Catholic households resident in segregated (almost all Catholic) streets had risen from 41% to 56%, while the corresponding figure for Protestants had risen from 62% to 69%. Other evidence suggests that the sharp increase occurred somewhere during the intercensal period 1911–1926 (Boal, 1980).

When we compare 1969 with our third data period, 1972, a further sharp increase in segregation can be observed, for by then 70% of Roman Catholics were living in Catholic streets, with 78% of Protestants in Protestant streets.

Thus, overall, at an early phase of Protestant–Roman Catholic contact in Belfast quite high levels of segregation were established. More importantly it would appear that segregation since then has increased, suggesting a sharpening of difference between the two ethnic groups. It seems likely, therefore, that assimilation has not progressed with time—if anything the reverse being the case. Notwithstanding this trend a degree of ethnic residential mixing has always existed. As this mixing may indicate some degree of assimilation or integration of the two groups it is important to examine in detail the mixed areas and their constituent households.

ETHNIC RESIDENTIAL MIXING

At the end of 1972, within the area of Belfast County Borough, 23% of households were resident in streets where there was a significant degree of ethnic mixing (that is Roman Catholics *and* Protestants each formed at least 10% of the households). The wider Belfast Urban Area, with which we will concern ourselves from here on, had 30% of households resident in "mixed" streets. As we have already noted, some degree of ethnic residential mixing has been a feature of Belfast geography for a very long time. Nineteenth century evidence is almost

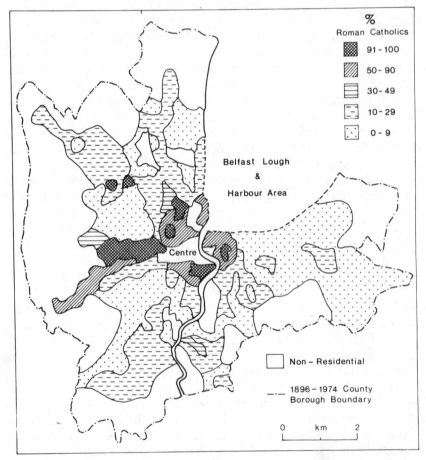

FIGURE 10.1. The Distribution of Roman Catholics in Belfast County Borough in 1911.
Source: Calculated from data extracted by Mrs. S. Gribben from the 1911 manuscript census of Ireland.

non-existent, but even the Riot Commission Report of 1858, quoted earlier, makes reference to the fact that "there was some intermixture" in the working-class Pound and Sandy Row areas. However, very firm evidence of ethnic residential mixing is provided in a map of religious distribution in Belfast in 1911. On this map (Fig. 10.1) we can see the very substantial areas of religious mixing particularly in two sectors, the one running north from the city centre (basically focussed on the Antrim Road), the other running south on the lines of the Malone and Ormeau Roads. The highly segregated areas are, of course, also evident.

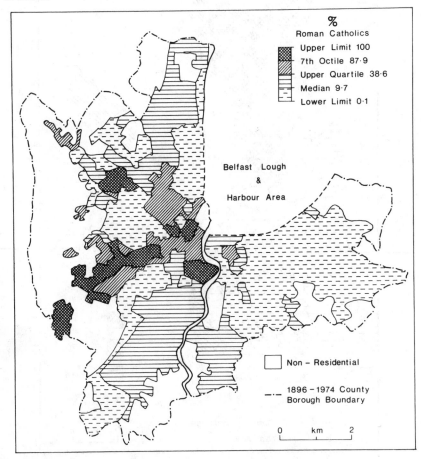

FIGURE 10.2. The Distribution of Roman Catholics in Belfast County Borough in 1951.
Source: Redrawn from Jones (1960, p. 196).

The next evidence on religious distributions is provided by Emrys Jones (1960, p. 196) with his mapping of Roman Catholics at the time of the 1951 population census (Fig. 10.2). Again, whilst the main segregated cores are no less evident than they were in 1911, the mixed sectors equally stand out, still basically in the same locations as was the case forty years earlier.

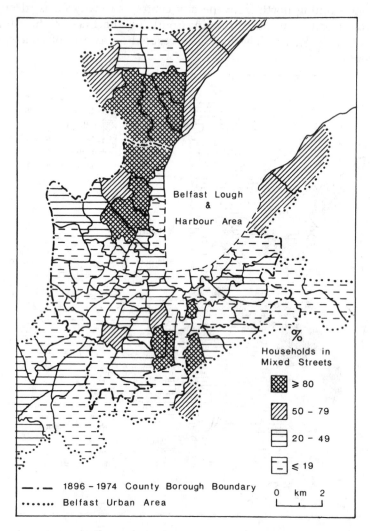

FIGURE 10.3. The Distribution of Households in Ethnically Mixed Streets in the Belfast Urban Area in 1972.
Source: Sample survey (footnote[1]).

The 1911 and 1951 maps are restricted to the area of the city of Belfast. Figure 10.3, however, based on a 1972 sample survey[1] provides an indication of the extent of ethnic residential mixing beyond the city boundary into the northern, eastern, southern and south-western suburbs. It will be seen most particularly that the northern mixed wedge extends into Newtownabbey and the southern mixed wedge out along the line of the Saintfield Road, whilst there is a detached area of mixing on the eastern shore of Belfast Lough at Holywood.

Thus throughout the present century ethnically mixed residential areas have persisted in Belfast. With this in mind, we will now turn to a detailed examination of households in mixed streets in 1972.[1]

HOUSEHOLDS IN MIXED STREETS

The data in Table 10.2 show that, in 1972, 29% of Protestant households resided in ethnically mixed streets (i.e. those streets 10–90% Roman Catholic), with 31% of Catholic households being similarly located. The similarity of the two groups becomes less marked when we note that 99% of Protestants in the Belfast Urban Area live in streets in which they are a majority, the equivalent figure for Roman Catholics being 75%. If we further consider only the households located in mixed streets we find that 96% of Protestants are in majority situations, whilst only 28% of Roman Catholics are similarly located.

TABLE 10.2. The Percentage Distribution of Protestant and Roman Catholic Households in Streets Classified by Religious Composition, Belfast Urban Area, 1972.

Street religious proportion (Percentage Catholic)	Households Protestant	Catholic	All (Including Others and Ethnically Mixed)
0–9	71	3	55
10–49	28	22	27
50–90	1	9	3
91–100	*	66	15

* Rounds to zero. Source: Sample survey.[1]

In addition to examining the households in the mixed streets purely on the basis of their ethnic/religious affiliation, it is considered desirable to disaggregate the streets in terms of the degree of ethnic mixing and to disaggregate the households according to a variable that attempts to combine social class and dwelling tenure characteristics. The basic division of the mixed streets is between those where Protestant households form a majority and those where Roman Catholics form a majority. However the Protestant majority mixed streets have been further sub-divided, since 90% of the households in mixed streets are located in Protestant majority situations. The division has been made into streets where Protestants are in a large majority (between 71% and 90%), and into streets where Roman Catholic households are significantly over-represented relative to their proportion in the Belfast area (which, in 1972, was 22%). This latter grouping is composed of streets where Protestants form between 51% and 70% of the households. Those streets which are 71–90% Protestant will be given the shorthand label MP (mixed, large Protestant majority), those that are between 51% and 70% Protestant will be labelled Mp (mixed, small Protestant majority). The Roman Catholic majority mixed streets are designated MC (mixed, Catholic majority).

The household classification is based on the type of housing occupied. It has been found (Poole, 1975) that, in Belfast, housing can be divided into two basic categories, the first category predominantly occupied by "non-manual" households, the second by households whose head has a manual occupation. The first housing category consists of all households in private tenure, whether owner occupied or rented, with the exception of small terraced houses.[2] This is referred to as the "Upper" category. The second category consists of all households in the public sector, together with small terraced houses in the private sector. This is referred to as the "Lower" category. Because public sector housing is so distinctive in its rules of entry, a further division is made within the "Lower" category between the private and public sectors. Overall, then, we have a system whereby households are classified as residing in "Upper" category (predominantly the larger owner occupied houses), "Lower Private" category (the small, predominantly terraced houses, both rented from private landlords and owner occupied) and "Lower Public" category. We can now proceed to examine Protestant and Roman Catholic households as they reside in the different house-categories located in streets of various religious compositions.

An examination of the data in Table 10.3 demonstrates that there is considerable variation between the house-category groups in the extent to which they are located in mixed streets. It will be seen that the Catholic Upper is the least segregated group (55% of such households being located in mixed streets), followed a considerable way behind (at 38% mixed) by the Protestant Upper group. Comparing these two groups, however, we see that 97% of the Protestant households in mixed streets are in *majority* situations, whilst 78% of Roman Catholic households are in *minority* situations. Thus the Upper house-category displays the greatest degree of residential mixing, but within

TABLE 10.3. Distribution of Protestant and Roman Catholic Households in the Belfast Urban Area, 1972, according to Street Religious Composition Level and Ethnic House-Category Group.

| Ethnic house-category group | Percentages in mixed streets Percentage Catholic | | | Percentage in mixed streets of all types | Percentage of those in mixed streets who are in majority situations | Percentage of those in mixed streets who are in minority situations | Percentages in segregated streets Percentage Catholic | |
	10–29 (MP)	30–49 (Mp)	50–90 (MC)				0–9	91–100
Protestant Upper	31	6	1	38	97	3	62	*
Protestant Lower Private	14	2	2	18	89	11	83	*
Protestant Lower Public	32	2	1	35	98	2	65	1
Catholic Upper	28	15	12	55	22	78	10	34
Catholic Lower Private	10	6	14	30	47	53	0	71
Catholic Lower Public	11	2	1	14	7	93	2	83

* Rounds to zero. Source: Sample survey.[1]

that category the experiences of Catholic and Protestant households are quite different.

If we next examine households located in public housing (Lower Public category), it will be seen that over one-third of Protestant households are in mixed situations with only 14% of Roman Catholic households similarly located. This latter figure makes public sector Catholic households the most segregated of all. A further examination of the public sector housing shows that, whilst 35% of Protestant households reside in mixed streets, an overwhelming 98% of these are in majority situations—indeed 91% are in streets that are more than 70% Protestant. The relatively small proportion of Roman Catholic public sector households located in mixed streets, in stark contrast to the "mixed" Protestants, find themselves overwhelmingly in minority situations (93% of such households). Indeed almost 80% of these households are located in streets where they form less than 30% of all households.

Finally we can look at the Lower Private category households. Here the Protestant–Catholic relationship is somewhat reversed from the situation prevailing in the public sector, because almost one-third of Roman Catholic households are in mixed streets, the equivalent figure for Protestants being only 18%. The Protestant–Catholic relationship is only partially reversed, however, because almost 90% of the Lower Private category Protestant households are located in majority Protestant streets, a situation only slightly less marked than that to be found with Upper and Lower Public Protestants. With Lower Private Catholics, on the other hand, we find that almost 50% of such households in mixed streets are in Catholic majority streets.

The evidence examined so far indicates that the three house-category groupings are quite distinctive in terms of religious residential mixing at street level. The evidence also stresses the fact that in the mixed situations Protestants experience environments where they form a majority, Roman Catholics environments where they form a minority, with the partial but very important exception of the Lower Private house-category.

PERCEPTION OF NEIGHBOURHOOD ETHNIC CHANGE

Ethnically mixed residential areas that are relatively stable in their ethnic composition suggest a degree of permanence. Mixed residential areas that are changing in the balance of their ethnic composition suggest impermanence. The stable areas indicate the possibility either for the reduction of inter-ethnic difference, or for the relative absence, to start with, of such difference for the particular households concerned. On the other hand mixed areas that appear to be in a state of ethnic transition seem likely to be poor environments for difference reduction to occur in. The extent to which stability or transition is perceived to exist will now be examined by analysing the responses of heads of households to a request to assess "the religious composition of their neighbourhood" on a seven-point scale running from "all Protestant" through "same number Protestant and Catholic" to "all Catholic".

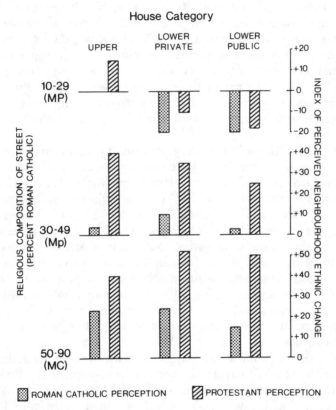

FIGURE 10.4. Perception of Change in Neighbourhood Ethnic Composition. The perception of change is shown separately for Roman Catholic and Protestant households. The households, in turn, are classified according to their house-category and according to the religious composition of the street in which they resided at the time of the survey in 1972. The index of perceived neighbourhood ethnic change may lie within the range +100 to −100. An index of +100 would mean that all households reported a shift in neighbourhood composition to more Catholic; an index of −100 would indicate that all households reported a shift to more Protestant.

Respondents were asked to assess the ethnic composition of their present neighbourhood as they perceived it on moving into their current dwelling, and as they perceived it to be at the time they were interviewed.

Figure 10.4 displays, in simplified form,[3] the perceived shifts in neighbourhood ethnic composition in the various mixed street situations. In the Upper house-category, for those households resident in large Protestant majority (MP) streets, only a small proportion perceive change. Indeed, on balance, Roman Catholic households do not perceive any change. In the large Catholic minority situations (Mp) and in the mixed streets with a Catholic majority (MC) a substantial proportion of Protestants do perceive a shift towards a more Catholic neighbourhood composition. Roman Catholics, being on average resident for a shorter time in their present dwelling than Protestants, tend to perceive less shift. However, they too note a significant amount of change towards a more Catholic situation in the Catholic majority (MC) streets.

In the Lower Private house-category a small proportion of Protestant households in the large Protestant majority streets (MP) perceive a change towards more Protestant. However, where Roman Catholics are currently a large minority (Mp) or in a majority (MC), a substantial shift towards a more Catholic neighbourhood composition is observed, the greatest shift of all being perceived by Protestants currently resident in the Catholic majority (MC) mixed streets. As with the Upper house-category, fewer Roman Catholics perceived change in neighbourhood ethnic composition. However, a proportion resident in the Protestant large majority (MP) streets note a shift towards more Protestant situations and those in the Catholic majority (MC) mixed streets confirm the Protestant perception of a shift towards a more Catholic composition.

In the Lower Public house-category, both Roman Catholics and Protestants in the MP streets observe a shift towards more Protestant neighbourhood ethnic environments. The situations in the Mp and MC streets (which, however, it should be noted, have only 10% of all public sector households resident in mixed streets) indicate a shift on balance towards more Catholic environments.

The observations made on neighbourhood ethnic environmental change suggest a division of the housing situations as follows:

(i) Streets 10–29% Catholic (MP): little change observed in the Upper house-category, some change towards more Protestant in the Lower Private category, and a more marked change towards more Protestant in public sector housing.

(ii) Streets 30–49% Catholic (Mp): generally display a perceived shift towards more Catholic environments.

(iii) Streets 50–90% Catholic (MC): major shifts towards more Catholic environments·observed for all three housing categories, the greatest shift of all being in the Lower Private situation.

Thus it is evident that the neighbourhoods of mixed streets in the Upper house-category with relatively small Catholic minorities (MP) display either considerable ethnic stability or only slow change. In the Lower Private and Lower Public categories the neighbourhoods of these same streets display shifts towards more Protestant environments (that is, they are Catholic "retreat" situations). Once the Catholic proportion in streets rises to over 30%, however, the ethnic change pattern becomes quite different. Here the shift is towards more Catholic environments (in other words they are Protestant "retreat" situations). The most marked of these retreat situations occurs within the Lower Private house-category where not only is there a larger degree of observed ethnic shift, but the actual numbers of households involved are considerably greater than is the case with the public sector. Figure 10.5 summarises the basic elements of neighbourhood ethnic change. Thus much of the ethnic residential mixing *at the time of the survey* at the end of 1972 was of a transitional nature.

HOUSE CATEGORY	STREET TYPE		
	MP	Mp	MC
UPPER	STABLE	+C	+C
LOWER PRIVATE	+P	+C	+C
LOWER PUBLIC	+P	+C	+C

+P: becoming more Protestant
+C: becoming more Catholic

FIGURE 10.5. The Basic Direction of Perceived Neighbourhood Ethnic Change.

ANALYSIS OF LOCALITIES

Up to this point we have examined the households as they have been located in broad categories of "types of street". However each household does not just reside in a "type of street" detached from a real-life location. Consequently we now intend to refer briefly to groupings of households in a series of specific spatial locations. These locations have been defined to encompass most of the principal locational clusters of our sample of mixed street households. The characteristics of households in the clusters can only be approximately sketched in since the sample was not originally designed to enable precise estimates to be made of small area attributes.

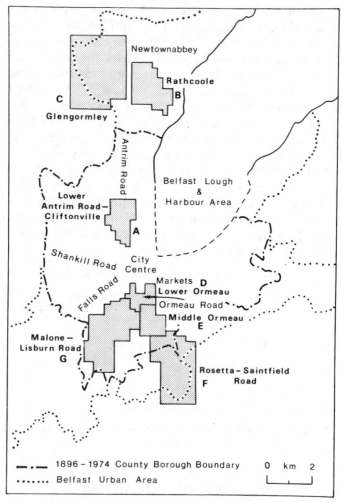

FIGURE 10.6. The Locations of the Ethnically Mixed Residential Areas Discussed in the Text.

Figure 10.6 shows the "gridded" limits of the locational clusters selected for analysis. It will be seen that they are located in both the northern (Antrim Road-Newtownabbey) and southern (Ormeau/Saint-field Road-Malone) mixed sectors. Clusters A and D are on the fringes of the inner city, C and F are relatively new suburban private housing areas, B is a suburban public sector estate while E and G are long-established, predominantly good quality private housing areas.

The inner mixed areas (Area A—Lower Antrim Road-Cliftonville and Area D—Lower Ormeau Road) are composed predominantly of Lower Private housing with between 30% and 40% of the streets in the MC category. There is a very marked contrast between Roman Catholic and Protestant households in length of residence at the present address, with the Protestants being much longer term residents. Roman Catholic households show a small numerical gain, Protestant households very substantial losses.[4] Both sets of households clearly perceive these changes as a major shift in ethnic population balance in the direction of more Catholic, this being most marked in the Lower Antrim Road-Cliftonville area. Inflows into this area suggest movement from two segregated Catholic areas—New Lodge on the cityward side and the Falls sector of south-west Belfast. Lower Ormeau displays inflows from its inner edge (the Catholic Markets) and more generally from the inner ring. Areas A and D are classics of ethnic change as it occurs in some situations of Lower Private housing with Catholic expansion and major signs of Protestant retreat.

The two outer housing areas, Glengormley (C) in the north and Rosetta-Saintfield Road (F) in the south, are predominantly Upper house-category in composition. Both areas are almost entirely Protestant majority with about 80% MP. Both ethnic groups show major numerical gain suggesting an ethnically fairly balanced flow into new suburban housing areas. Perception of ethnic change is slight with the possibility of a small shift towards more Catholic. However for both areas Protestant households have been earlier movers. The flow of households to Glengormley appears to be strongly from the northern parts of the Urban Area, drawing on a wide spectrum of mixed and segregated neighbourhoods. Flows to Rosetta-Saintfield Road are much more widely spread in origin, except that Roman Catholic in-movers show a tendency to have come from the cityward parts of the Ormeau sector. Overall these two suburban areas appear to represent examples of Upper house-category situations of ethnic residential mixing with a fairly high degree of stability in ethnic balance, though more substantial change may be occurring in limited areal segments. The two areas form a major contrast with areas A and D, not only in house-category and associated social class characteristics but more importantly, in this context, in degree of change in ethnic balance.

Rathcoole (B) is a relatively new public sector estate, with the mixed streets in the sample being almost entirely MP. Both Roman Catholics and Protestants show a very similar spread of time of moving to their present house (the flows, perhaps, having been regulated by the public housing authority?). Members of both ethnic groups moved into Rathcoole from a considerable variety of locations in the north Belfast sector. Many former locations were segregated and Rathcoole was clearly the creation of mixing Roman Catholic and Protestant inflows. Both groups show numerical gain, but this is more marked for Protestants. However, both groups perceive change to be quite strongly in the direction of more Protestant. This could reflect the differential inflow. However, it may also reflect a significant Roman Catholic outflow in the period between 1969 and the survey.

Rathcoole is an example, indeed one of the rare examples in the Urban Area, of an ethnically mixed public housing estate. However, the observed dynamics of the situation suggest that in the period immediately before 1972 there had been net Catholic outflow. The ethnic composition of the estate, therefore, cannot be described as having been stable.

Two other mixed areas may be briefly referred to—Middle Ormeau (E) and Malone-Lisburn Road (G). Middle Ormeau is predominantly Lower Private housing with about one-third of sample households located in streets where Roman Catholics form large minorities (Mp). Catholic households, on average, are more recent movers than Protestants and show a tendency to have come from the inner Markets area, the Falls Road area and several other Catholic locations. Protestant in-movers have fairly widely dispersed origins. Roman Catholic households show considerable numerical gain. This corresponds closely with the Protestant perception of an increasing proportion of Catholics. Overall Middle Ormeau displays Catholic gain in a situation of predominantly Lower Private housing, but the area has not changed ethnically as much as the mixed inner city areas. This may well be due to the fact that, unlike the two inner city areas discussed above, Middle Ormeau is not in juxtaposition with a segregated Catholic area.

Malone-Lisburn Road has a majority of its housing in the Upper category. Both Roman Catholics and Protestants perceive little ethnic change overall in a situation where almost all the streets sampled are MP. Despite this, however, Catholic households are later movers than Protestant, suggesting the possibility of some relatively minor ethnic composition shift towards more Catholic. The area is characterised by considerable internal population movement and also in-movement of households from outside Northern Ireland. These "immigrant" households present interesting possibilities for further study focussed round the question "where, and for what reasons, do such households locate in the Belfast ethnic-class housing matrix?" (For some discussion see Kennedy, 1973.) Malone-Lisburn Road presents an example of an area of relative ethnic composition stability, or, at the most, only slow change.

FURTHER ASPECTS OF MIXING

Our understanding of the ethnically mixed residential areas can be increased by an examination of three further aspects—the length of residence at the current address, the age of the head of household and a temporal perspective.

When we examine the date on which people moved into their current dwelling we find that, in the Upper and Lower Private categories of mixed streets, Roman Catholics, on average, are later movers than Protestants. This sets up a situation that has already been referred to, where Protestants are likely to be the "sitting residents" observing Catholics moving into dwellings in the same street, and, in consequence, concluding that their neighbourhood is shifting in ethnic balance.

The greatest contrasts in date of move between Roman Catholic and Protestant households occur in the mixed streets where Catholics are in a majority (MC) and where Catholics are a largish minority (Mp). In the Upper house-category we find that in the Catholic majority situations 36% of Protestant households moved into their current dwelling in 1964 or later, while this was true for 70% of Roman Catholic households. In the large Catholic minority situations 42% of Protestant households moved after 1964, as did 72% of Catholic households. The greatest time-of-move contrasts occur, however, in the Lower Private category. Here, in the Catholic majority streets (MC) only 13% of Protestant households moved in 1964 or later compared to 55% of Catholics. Indeed 72% of Protestant households moved to their present dwelling before 1945! In the substantial Catholic minority streets (Mp) a mere 8% of Protestant households had moved in 1964 or later (63% moved before 1945); 63% of Roman Catholic households occupied their present dwelling in 1964 or later. Thus, in these situations, a high proportion of Protestant households were very long-term residents. In contrast a high proportion of Catholic households were recent movers.

There is little difference in the length of residence of Roman Catholics

and Protestants in public sector housing, probably reflecting the administered nature of entry to such dwellings.

The fact that Roman Catholics in Upper and Lower Private housing
have moved into their current dwellings more recently than Protestants
would suggest the possibility of contrast in age of head of household
between households in the two ethnic groups. Inspection of the data
indicates that Roman Catholics, on average, are younger than Protestants, reflecting the Northern Ireland age structure differences
between the two groups (see Chapter 4). Age contrasts between Roman
Catholics and Protestants in mixed street situations increase as the
streets become more Catholic. This is at its most marked in the mixed
streets in the Lower Private house-category, and the contrast is at its
sharpest in the streets that are over 50% Catholic. Here, while half the
Roman Catholic heads of households are under fifty years of age, this
applies to only 11% of Protestants.

Overall a number of very important contrasts between Protestant
and Roman Catholic households in mixed streets are evident. Catholics
will tend to be younger than Protestants, and they are likely to have
larger numbers of children. Within the Upper and Lower Private
house-categories, Catholics are likely to have moved into their present
dwelling more recently than Protestants (they are incidentally more
likely to be owner occupiers). Protestant–Catholic contrasts are most
marked where Catholics form a majority, these contrasts being at their
sharpest in the Lower Private house-category, where the Protestant
population seems to form a small residual group—relatively elderly folk
who have resided in their present dwellings for a long time.

As we proceed the evidence is accumulating that, at least at the end
of 1972, many mixed areas in Belfast cannot be viewed as stable units
of ethnic integration. Instead transition is the dominant theme. At
the same time we have demonstrated earlier in this chapter that both
mixed and segregated residential areas have existed in Belfast from the
mid-nineteenth century onwards. On this basis it is possible to argue
that the patterns observable in the 1970s are a continuation of something
long established. Major outbursts of conflict have, from time to time,
sharpened segregation, followed by some relaxation and an expansion of
residential mixing (Boal, Murray and Poole, 1976, p. 98). Indeed Figs
10.1, 10.2 and 10.3 have shown that some of the mixed residential
areas have been locationally stable for long periods of time, perhaps
contracting during outbursts of open conflict and then growing
again during less stressful periods. This would suggest that the mixed
residential areas in the past were not merely transitional phenomena,
and therefore, possibly, provided residential arenas for meaningful and

positive ethnic interaction. However, the period from 1969 may, in a number of ways, represent something significantly different. The new factors that have emerged appear to be as follows. First, open ethnic conflict has continued for a longer period than ever before and patterns that developed in response to this conflict have consequently had a greater opportunity for consolidation. Secondly, previous outbursts were not contemporaneous with urban renewal and the widespread availability of public sector housing. The urban renewal process has itself tended to thrust many households into forced mobility. Most redevelopment areas have been reoccupied by members of the same ethnic group that occupied the particular site previously. However, redevelopment-related household mobility has also accelerated out-movement of population. The large-scale availability of public sector housing has been crucial here. Working-class sections of the population, both Roman Catholic and Protestant, who had been previously excluded by economic constraints, were able to participate in suburban-isation through access to peripherally located public sector housing. This has been particularly the case with Protestants who have had, because of the *spatial* structure of the Belfast housing market, a greater range of suburban opportunities than Catholics.[5] What this basically means is that inner city areas where Protestants would have previously been highly resistant to Roman Catholic in-migration have, in many instances, not responded in this way to the same degree in the 1970s. This suggests a parallel with Hirschman's concepts of exit and voice, where people dissatisfied with a particular circumstance can respond in one of two ways—by voice, whereby an attempt is made to end an objectionable state of affairs without leaving the situation, or by exit, where escape from the objectionable state of affairs is the strategy adopted. As Hirschman (1970, p. 83) says, "the willingness to develop and use the voice mechanism is reduced by exit". In our context this means that voice (resistance to entry of members of the other ethnic group) is less likely to be employed because the exit option (a move to housing elsewhere) is open. Thus the dynamic of the ethnic residential geography of Belfast in the 1970s is such that residential invasion is more likely, producing mixed areas. It also follows, however, that much of the mixing is likely to be of a short-term nature as the "invaded" group moves out. Our interpretation of earlier periods in Belfast is that such transitional mixed situations were less extensive than has been the case since 1969.

DISCUSSION

To this point we have observed that a degree of ethnic residential mixing exists in Belfast, but also that much of the mixing (as of 1972) tends to be of a temporary nature, with only limited segments of ethnic stability. We have also noted that there is variation in degree of ethnic mixing related to social class and dwelling tenure (house-category) characteristics. Why does the degree of mixing vary and why is transitional mixing a predominant feature? An attempt can be made to answer these questions through a series of observations.

The first observation is that middle-class (Upper house-category) areas tend to be less ethnically segregated than working-class areas, and, in some instances, to display stability in their ethnic composition balance. In other words a middle-class household is more likely to be located in a mixed street than a working-class household, and, in turn, its neighbourhood is less likely to be ethnically transitional. Three reasons for this can be suggested. First, it has been observed, at least in cities in western Europe and North America, that people like to live with others who belong to the same culture; share values, ideals and norms; understand and respond to the same symbols; agree about child rearing, interaction, density and lifestyle (Rapoport, 1977, p. 251). This can be associated with a further set of observations—that working-class areas have tighter-knit networks of social interaction within local areas and that the neighbourhood may be viewed as an extension of the home. Marc Fried has noted that with the middle class there is a relatively impermeable boundary between the walls of the dwelling and the street, whilst with the working class there is high permeability between the dwelling unit and the immediately environing area (Fried, 1973; Fried and Gleicher, 1961). The neighbourhood is an extension of the house (Willmott and Young, 1960). In these circumstances interaction within the local area will be intense and difficult to avoid. Thus ethnically incompatible neighbours will be undesirable. In the more privatised, lower density middle-class areas, however, local interaction is less intense, contact with ethnic incompatibles may be minimised, and social networks developed that are much less dependent on the residents of one's own street. Thus, in the middle-class context, provided basic middle-class behavioural norms are adhered to, the presence of members of the "other" ethnic group should not present too great a difficulty. In the working-class context this presence becomes much more important and the desired level of ethnic homogeneity will be raised significantly—and thus the levels of segregation increased over those pertaining in the middle-class areas.

A second factor contributing to the greater degree of ethnic segrega-tion between working-class households may be the greater degree of conflict between the two ethnic groups in Belfast experienced in the working-class context. This conflict is generated by situations of scarcity and competition—scarcity of working-class housing and competition for insufficient numbers of jobs.

The third factor may be related to the "reservoir hypothesis". This suggests that an ethnic group's reaction to the in-movement of a member of a different group will be partly conditioned by how large they per-ceive the reservoir of potential followers of that in-mover. If the in-moving group is perceived as growing numerically as well as being large to start with, it will be seen as a much greater "threat" than a small or numerically stable group. In Belfast, Roman Catholics are perceived as a growing group. More significantly in this context the class structure of the Catholic ethnic group is such that working-class Catholics comprise a significantly larger proportion of the working class than middle-class Catholics comprise of the middle class (Table 10.4). Thus it will be in working-class situations that Roman Catholic in-movement will be perceived as having a significant potential for accelerated growth, and where, consequently, it will be more strongly resisted or, alternatively, reacted to by accelerated out-movement by Protestants. Either way, segregation will be increased in everything but the very short term. In the American context Goering (1978, p. 76) has written: "future expectations about the fate of a neighbor-hood have appeared to play an important role in determining the rate at which neighborhoods may [racially] change".

TABLE 10.4. Roman Catholic Households as a Percentage of All Households in Three Social Class Groupings, Belfast Urban Area, 1972.

| | Social Class | | |
	Professional/Managerial and other White Collar	Skilled Manual	Semi-skilled and Unskilled Manual
Percentage of social class group that is Catholic	17	21	32

Source: Sample survey.[1]

It is of interest to note that not only is the greatest degree of residen-tial mixing present in the middle-class context, but that the greatest degree of ethnic integration in terms of party politics is also found with the middle class, through joint affiliation with the Alliance Party (see Chapter 6). This is not to suggest that residential mixing necessarily leads to political convergence, rather that the same basic "integrating" factors may be operative in both the residential and party political spheres.

The second observation we make concerns the very high level of ethnic segregation in the public housing sector. The reasons for this can only be hinted at. First, the class factor as outlined above will, in all likelihood, be operative. Secondly, most public housing areas tend to be architecturally distinctive. This clarity of image seems likely to work its way through to suggest homogeneity of occupancy within a well-defined territory (Reid, 1973, p. 119). Thirdly, the public housing authorities (now fused into the Northern Ireland Housing Executive) were given statutory responsibility for emergency housing—a scheme set up to provide alternative accommodation for households forced to move during the various outbursts of overt ethnic conflict in the city since 1969. Due to the nature of the circumstances of their moves these households are likely to have sought security amongst "their own people" —thus leading to further build-up of ethnic segregation in the public sector. An additional factor appears to have been the relative ease of movement in the public sector, due to all the stock being rental (with occupants consequently unconstrained by the tenure ties of owner occupation) and due to the system of transfer operated by the Housing Executive. Murray and Osborne (1977) have noted that the Executive's policy of "maximum freedom of choice", admirable in itself, can and has accelerated segregation in a situation of stress and open conflict. A final factor contributing to the high levels of segregation in the public sector derives from the urban renewal process. When households are required to move during clearance the public housing authority has a statutory obligation to rehouse them. If an already segregated old inner city area is being redeveloped it is likely, therefore, that the segregation will be reproduced in the new housing, both on the original site and in new estates. This is not inevitable—several outer Belfast estates were originally occupied as ethnically mixed—but in the circumstances prevailing over the past ten years it is very probable.

Public sector housing tends to have fairly high levels of segregation in part because of the operation of "working-class" factors as outlined earlier. In addition, characteristics of public sector housing such as architectural uniformity and features of access regulation tend also to increase ethnic segregation. Since public sector housing is overwhelmingly associated with the working class, this in turn contributes to the high levels of ethnic segregation within that class.

The third observation to be made is that the most marked change in ethnic composition seems to have occurred and to be occurring in certain segments of the Lower Private house-category. These areas are basically working class and consequently the factors discussed earlier regarding class variation in ethnic segregation will be operative. In this case the tendency towards high levels of segregation makes mixed areas unstable, with some degree of predictability that transition to a segregated state will take place. Lower Private category housing is economically open to the relatively large Catholic working class and the reservoir hypothesis seems relevant here. However, only limited segments of the Lower Private housing stock display features of ethnic transition. These areas are in close proximity to inner segregated Catholic areas and are within the same sector. Thus "invasion" seems to occur outwards within specific sectors (Antrim Road and Ormeau Road). Invasion across sector boundaries is rare (see Boal, 1969; 1978b for a discussion of one such enduring boundary). An additional factor to be considered as contributing to the ethnic transitivity of parts of the Lower Private stock is the spatially constrained pattern of the opportunity structure for housing for Roman Catholics.

The fourth observation relates to the fact that in the mixed streets, in most situations, Protestant households form substantial majorities. This is not surprising given the Protestant–Catholic balance of households in the Belfast Urban Area. For instance, within the area of the old Belfast County Borough, in 1969 about 25% of households were Roman Catholic. If all households were distributed randomly amongst the streets a distribution is generated whereby over three-quarters of all households are located in streets between 20% and 39% Catholic (Poole and Boal, 1973, p. 25). This random distribution would therefore be one with the overwhelming majority of households living in mixed but Protestant majority streets. In fact only a minority of households live in mixed streets, but these streets are indeed overwhelmingly Protestant majority situations. A further observation follows, however, based on the evidence derived from residents' perception of neighbourhood ethnic change. This evidence suggests that where Catholic proportions of households at street-scale level exceed something of the order of 30%, change in neighbourhood ethnic composition appears to be in the direction of more Catholic. On the other hand where Protestants are in excess of 70% (with the exception of the Upper house-category), change seems to be towards more Protestant. This suggests that Protestants are not particularly tolerant of situations where there is a large Catholic minority or where there is a Catholic majority, and that Roman Catholics do not favour situations where they are a small minority. The former interpretation is given some reinforcement by Fairleigh (1976, p. 11) in a study of personality and social factors in what he calls "religious" prejudice in Northern Ireland:

The main finding was that the Protestants felt significantly more social distance from Catholics than did Catholics from Protestants. And religion was the most important factor associated with the Protestant decision—high social status was relatively unimportant if the religion was different. For the Catholic group, religion was also an important consideration in the level of friendship envisaged, but slightly less than the other person's interests or jobs.

It also appears that a large number of Roman Catholics are not tolerant of minority situations. Whether this is due to inter-ethnic attitudes on their part, to perceived need for the security of segregation or to a combination of these factors remains unclear.

CONCLUSION

Ethnic segregation has been a feature of the geography of Belfast for a long time. There is no evidence of long-term decline in segregation levels—indeed the contrary is the case. Consequently it seems unlikely that the passage of time has led to increased assimilation between Roman Catholics and Protestants. Nonetheless a limited amount of ethnic residential mixing has been present, which has also, historically, displayed considerable locational stability. This mixing has had a relatively greater importance with the middle class, and some of it has survived because of sheer inertia—once an area becomes established as mixed many non-ethnic factors associated with residential decision making may help to perpetuate it. The presence in an area of ethnic institutions (particularly schools and churches) affiliated with both groups also aids continuity.

However, the mixed areas are particularly vulnerable to destabilisation due to the impact of ethnic conflict outbursts from time to time, due to a dynamic produced by relative shifts in group sizes and due to changes in housing provision and access to such housing. Vulnerability also appears to be generated by differences in ethnic tolerance levels between the two groups—Catholics being more accepting of numerical minority status in a neighbourhood than Protestants. These destabilising factors appear to have had their greatest impact in the period since 1969.

The limited amount of ethnic residential mixing present in Belfast in 1972 cannot be assumed to have much significance as an indicator of ethnic assimilation, first because of its limited extent and secondly because, at least in the circumstances of the early 1970s, much of it is of a transitional nature. The possibility of interpreting mixing as an indicator of assimilation/integration is further complicated by the demonstrable degree to which such mixing varies according to the social class and dwelling tenure characteristics of the households concerned. The only situations where mixing might have real assimilation/integration significance are where such mixing is reasonably stable—basically in some middle-class, owner occupation contexts, although even here the degree of assimilation/integration must remain uncertain, bearing in mind the looser nature of community interaction (see the discussion on this above).

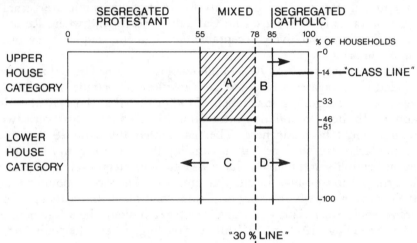

FIGURE 10.7. The Basic Components of the Ethnic Residential Geography of the Belfast Urban Area, 1972.
The diagram is sub-divided so that the proportions of households resident in segregated Protestant, segregated Catholic and ethnically mixed streets are shown. Each of these, in turn, is sub-divided along a "class-line" according to the proportion of households classified as Upper or Lower house-category. The households in ethnically mixed streets are further sub-divided according to whether they reside in streets more or less than 30% Catholic (on either side of the "30% Line"). The arrows indicate the direction of change of ethnically mixed areas.

Figure 10.7 attempts a summary of the basic elements of residential segregation and mixing in Belfast. Two large segregated categories provide the context for the existence of limited areas of mixing. The mixed areas can, in general terms, be disaggregated along social class (house-category) and ethnic balance lines. The ethnic balance disaggregation occurs at the "30% Line"—the approximate ethnic proportion Catholic, on one side of which mixed areas tend to be transitional towards more Protestant (where they are below 30% Catholic) and on the other towards more Catholic (where they are above 30% Catholic). Situation *C* (working class less than 30% Catholic) is transitional towards more Protestant. Situation *D* (working class more than 30% Catholic) is transitional towards more Catholic. Both situations have developed in the context of the relatively intense ethnic conflict evident among the working class. Situation *B*, which is middle class, is also an unstable one, due to the low Protestant tolerance of Catholic majority or large Catholic minority situations. *A* is the exceptional state of relative stability where Protestants tolerate a small or, at most, only slowly growing Catholic minority and where Roman Catholics find a relatively acceptable environment, despite being in a small minority.

The fact that, in 1972, 70% of households in the Belfast Urban Area resided in segregated streets indicates low levels of ethnic integration. We are also suggesting that much of the mixing that did exist then is also of limited assimilation/integration significance. However, two points should be made here. The first is that the early 1970s were particularly stressful and ethnic mixing that at other times might display stability and therefore have assimilation/integration significance was subject to well-nigh intolerable pressures. The second point is that the degree of segregation may be greater than many segregated house-holds would wish. This "excessive" segregation could be a function of what Schelling (1974, p. 49) calls unravelling, where the underlying motivation may be far less extreme than the observable patterns of separation. Here Schelling suggests that people may not want complete segregation but fear the prospect of becoming a small minority in a particular neighbourhood. Because of this they move house. This changes the residential environment for others of their own group who find themselves becoming more isolated. They, in turn, respond to this new situation by moving, and so on until the neighbourhood becomes completely segregated.

Russell, in an unpublished report (1977, p. 117) touches on another aspect. He refers to what he calls "hard core segregators" in public housing in Northern Ireland, who, wanting to live beside their own kind:

> Put their opinions more forcibly than those who prefer integrated [housing] estates ... In a discordant situation strong opinions count for more than single votes in an election. Because of the greater strength of feeling about community choices amongst segregationists it seems likely that many adaptables [those otherwise willing to live in mixed residential areas] will be drawn into joining movements towards religiously exclusive areas.

Millen (1973, p. 165) also refers, in the American context, to the possible influence of a small number of residents "who may guide the reaction of the hesitant majority . . .".

Overall, residential mixing in Belfast is a very delicate creation. It is much easier to understand why segregation exists. Indeed the dominance of segregation and the problems that may be associated with it are much easier to focus on than the dispersed process of mixing (Millen, 1973, p. 150). It is also true that in many western cities there seems to be a tension between the desires of many people to cluster and the values of politicians and planners who are opposed to such enclaves (Rapoport, 1977, p. 251). The notion that residential segregation is in itself a bad thing has meant that western urban society has been particularly inept at handling it in a positive way. In Belfast, which has to take the massive strains of the urban encapsulation of a national conflict, where perhaps no more than about 10% of households reside in stably mixed residential areas, a positive approach to segregation is fundamental. At the same time the relatively limited stable mixing that does exist should be handled with the greatest of care.

ACKNOWLEDGEMENT

The survey on which much of this chapter is based was financed by the Social Science Research Council.

NOTES

1. The data used were obtained by a household survey carried out in the Belfast Urban Area. The B.U.A. in this chapter includes all the area within the Regional Plan "Stop Line", with the exception of the town of Lisburn and its environs. Altogether 2203 households were interviewed, the sample selection employing a stratified random design. The stratification was based on the ethnic composition of the street, the ethnic (religious) affiliation of the household and the tenure of the dwelling. The survey was carried out during the last four months of 1972 and during 1973. The mid-point of data collection was the end of 1972. (See Boal, Poole, Murray and Kennedy, 1976.) Except where stated those households ethnically mixed (i.e. Protestant and Catholic) and those adhering to non-Christian faiths or none are excluded from the analysis. These comprised 3% of all households.

2. Small terraced houses are distinguished by being either two-storey with a frontage of up to 7·5 metres or three-storey with a frontage of up to 5·0 metres.

3. The simplification involves grouping the seven points on the original scale to form only three. All points indicating a Protestant majority in a neighbourhood (no matter what size the majority) form one group; all points indicating a Roman Catholic majority form a second. The third group is the original scale point "same number Protestant and Catholic".

4. Numerical gain or loss is based on a comparison of the inflow of households into the mixed area concerned with the outflow to all other locations in the Belfast Urban Area. Only those households changing residence are included—newly formed households living in their first dwelling are excluded. Households who may have moved right outside the Belfast Urban Area are also excluded from the calculation, as there are no data available on these in our sample. In any mixed area numerical gain by one ethnic group may not equate with loss by the other due to the influence of new household formation, demolition of property and vacant dwellings.

5. Interestingly the lesser degree of suburbanisation of Roman Catholics can partly be attributed to the fact that the earliest redevelopment took place in Catholic areas of the inner city (North Queen Street, Unity Flats and Divis). These areas were redeveloped with a fairly high replacement rate of population. This was due to two factors—the then current style amongst planners and architects for multi-storey urban housing development, and the pressure exerted by the Roman Catholic Church who did not wish the support for local religious institutions (churches and schools) to be weakened by geographical dispersal of population (Belfast Workers Research Unit, 1980, p. 28).

REFERENCES

Barth, F. (1969). Introduction. *In* "Ethnic Groups and Boundaries" (F. Barth, ed.), pp. 9–38. Universitets Forlaget, Oslo.

Belfast Workers Research Unit (1980). The Churches in Northern Ireland. *Belfast Bulletin* **8**, 1–51.

Boal, F. W. (1969). Territoriality on the Shankill-Falls Divide, Belfast. *Irish Geography* **6**, 30–50.

Boal, F. W. (1978a). Ethnic Residential Segregation. *In* "Social Areas in Cities: Processes, Patterns and Problems" (D. T. Herbert and R. J. Johnston, eds.), pp. 57–95. John Wiley, London.

Boal, F. W. (1978b). Territoriality on the Shankill-Falls Divide, Belfast: The Perspective from 1976. *In* "An Invitation to Geography" (D. A. Lanegran and R. Palm, eds.), pp. 58–77. McGraw-Hill, New York.

Boal, F. W. (1980). "Ethnic Residential Mixing in an Ethnic Segregation Context." Paper Read at Symposium on Ethnic Segregation, St. Antony's College, Oxford.

Boal, F. W. and Murray, R. C. (1977). A City in Conflict. *Geographical Magazine* **44**, 364–371.

Boal, F. W., Murray, R. C. and Poole, M.A. (1976). Belfast: The Urban Encapsulation of a National Conflict. *In* "Urban Ethnic Conflict: A Comparative Perspective" (S. E. Clarke and J. L. Obler, eds.), pp. 77–131. Comparative Urban Studies Monograph No. 3, Institute for Research in Social Science, University of North Carolina, Chapel Hill.

Boal, F. W., Poole, M. A., Murray, R. C. and Kennedy, S. J. (1976). "Religious Residential Segregation and Residential Decision Making in the Belfast Urban Area." Final Report to the Social Science Research Council (Available from the National Lending Library, Boston Spa, Yorkshire).

Boyd, A. (1969). "Holy War in Belfast." Anvil Press, Tralee.

Commissioners of Inquiry (1858). "Report of the Commissioners of Inquiry into the Origin and Character of Riots in Belfast in July and September 1857." Her Majesty's Stationery Office, Dublin.

Duncan, O. D. and Lieberson, S. (1959). Ethnic Segregation and Assimilation. *American Journal of Sociology* **64**, 364–374.

Fairleigh, J. (1976). Personality and Social Factors in Religious Prejudice. *In* "Sectarianism—Roads to Reconciliation: Papers Read at the 22nd Annual Summer School of the Social Study Conference, Dungarvan, 1974," pp. 3–13. Three Candles, Dublin.

Fried, M. (1973). "The World of the Urban Working Class." Harvard University Press, Cambridge, Massachusetts.

Fried, M. and Gleicher, P. (1961). Some Sources of Residential Satisfaction in an Urban Slum. *Journal of the American Institute of Planners* **28**, 305–315.

Goering, J. M. (1978). Neighborhood Tipping and Racial Transition: A Review of Social Science Evidence. *Journal of the American Institute of Planners* **44**, 68–78.

Gordon, M. M. (1964). "Assimilation in American Life." Oxford University Press, New York.

Greeley, A. M. (1969). "Why Can't They Be Like Us?" E. P. Dutton, New York.

Hirschman, A. O. (1970). "Exit, Voice and Loyalty." Harvard University Press, Cambridge, Massachusetts.

Jones, E. (1960). "A Social Geography of Belfast." Oxford University Press, London.

Kennedy, S. J. (1973). "Migrants in Belfast: A Sociological Perspective." Unpublished M.S.Sc. Thesis, Queen's University, Belfast.

Lee, T. R. (1977). "Race and Residence." Clarendon Press, Oxford.

Lieberson, S. (1961). The Impact of Residential Segregation on Ethnic Assimilation. *Social Forces* **40**, 52–57.

Millen, J. S. (1973). Factors Affecting Racial Mixing in Residential Areas. *In* "Segregation in Residential Areas: Papers on Racial and Socio-Economic Factors in Choice in Housing" (A. H. Hawley and V. P. Rock, eds.), pp. 148–171. Division of Behavioral Sciences, National Research Council, National Academy of Sciences, Washington, D.C.

Murray, R. and Osborne, R. (1977). Segregation on Horn Drive—A Cautionary Tale. *New Society* **40**, 106–108.

Poole, M. A. (1975). "Social Class and Housing Class." Paper Read at Institute of British Geographers Annual Conference, Oxford.

Poole, M. A. and Boal, F. W. (1973). Religious Residential Segregation in Belfast in Mid-1969: A Multi-Level Analysis. *In* "Social Patterns in Cities" (B. D. Clark and M. B. Gleave, eds.), pp. 1–40. Special Publication No. 5, Institute of British Geographers, London.

Rapoport, A. (1977). "Human Aspects of Urban Form." Pergamon Press, Oxford.

Reid, J. (1973). Community Conflict in Northern Ireland: Analysis of a New Town Plan. *Ekistics* **36**, 115–119.

Russell, J. (1977). "Motivation for the Use, Defacement and Destruction of Housing and Neighbourhood Facilities in Northern Ireland." Unpublished Report to the Centre for Environmental Studies, London.

Schelling, T. (1974). On the Ecology of Micromotives. *In* "The Corporate Society" (R. Marris, ed.), pp. 19–64. Macmillan, London.

Van den Berghe, P. L. (1967). "Race and Racism." John Wiley, New York.

Willmott, P. and Young, M. (1960). "Family and Class in a London Suburb." Routledge and Kegan Paul, London.

CHAPTER 11

RELIGIOUS RESIDENTIAL SEGREGATION IN URBAN NORTHERN IRELAND

Michael A. Poole

RELIGIOUS DIVISION AND RESIDENTIAL SEGREGATION

A divided society is, of course, considerably more newsworthy than an integrated one, especially when that division erupts into the kind of violent conflict which has characterised Northern Ireland since the end of the 1960s. Many commentators, too, apparently consider that a cleavage ostensibly between religious groups is a bizarre survival of an age long vanished elsewhere (Orme, 1970, p. 246; *House of Commons Debates* 874 (Fifth Series) (1974), 184), and consequently the Northern Ireland conflict has had a certain curiosity value. Whatever the source of interest, the persistence of the present "troubles" has stimulated an almost frenzied outpouring of narrative and analysis on Northern Ireland society (Whyte, 1978, p. 257).

Apart from violence itself, the main arena for conflict between these religious groups is probably politics, and, both before and since the start of the current "troubles", nearly all political parties have attracted votes from one or other of the two basic religious groups (Rose, 1971, p. 235; McAllister and Wilson, 1978, pp. 207–208; see also Chapter 6). Another obvious example of congruence with the religious division is the segmentation of the educational system, for it could be asserted, with very little exaggeration, that both the pupils and the teachers of almost every school are either wholly Catholic or wholly Protestant *Schools* (Darby *et al.*, 1977, pp. 25–28).

If politics and primary and secondary education are spheres of life in which religious segregation is almost total, this raises the question

281

of how much segregation occurs between the two religious groups in other aspects of life in Northern Ireland. This subject has been reviewed by Barritt and Carter (1962) and by Darby (1976b), while intensive research has been carried out in small geographical areas by Harris (1972) and by Boal (1969, pp. 36–47; 1970, pp. 383–391). However, Darby (1976b, p. 161) has emphasised the need for far more detailed research into the extent of segregation between Northern Ireland's two religious groups, and Whyte (1978, pp. 272–273) has stressed the need for more research into both its causes and effects. These pleas for further research appear to be totally justified, though this may seem ironic, in view of the frenzy of publication on the conflict referred to earlier. However, the intensity, spatial extent and change through time in each of the multitude of forms of segregation is still a subject about which very little is known or understood.

The purpose of this chapter is to narrow the gap in our knowledge of religious segregation. This will be attempted by concentrating on the all-important field of housing and, following a review of mostly unpublished research, a detailed analysis of residential segregation will be carried out. As is usual with studies of residential segregation, the analysis will be limited to urban areas, but this is not a particularly restrictive limitation in Northern Ireland, for two-thirds of the population live in settlements with more than 2500 people (*Northern Ireland Census of Population 1971*).

The analysis of religious residential segregation will fall into three sections. The first will have the objective of establishing just how much segregation of this type existed in Northern Ireland towns in the 1970s. More specifically, an attempt will be made to measure the intensity of this form of segregation and to discover the extent to which towns differ from one another in the degree to which they are characterised by religious segregation in housing. The second section of the empirical analysis is an attempt to explain the inter-urban variation in the intensity of religious residential segregation. It will seek to discover variables, descriptive of contemporary characteristics of the towns included in the analysis, which are correlated with the variation in segregation between towns. The third and final section will continue the search for explanation by examining certain past characteristics of the towns analysed, including the measurement of former segregation intensities. Attention in this historical section will be focussed, however, on the last century and a quarter rather than on any attempt to establish the more uncertain possibility of continuity throughout the three centuries since the Ulster Plantation.

THE LITERATURE ON RELIGIOUS RESIDENTIAL SEGREGATION

The justification for the presentation of the analysis in this chapter, apart from the intrinsic importance of the subject, is the poverty of the existing published literature on religious residential segregation in Northern Ireland. It is true that there has been a long history of published quantitative analysis describing the religious geography of Belfast (Evans, 1944, pp. 25–29; Jones, 1952, pp. 209–211; 1956; 1960, pp. 172–206; Poole and Boal, 1973; Boal *et al.*, 1976, pp. 99–110), and the type of work carried out by the earlier researchers on Belfast has been partially replicated in Londonderry and in the Brownlow segment of Craigavon (Robinson, 1969, pp. 56–58; 1970, pp. 213–215; Reid, 1973).

However, only one piece of work has compared the intensity of religious residential segregation in different Northern Ireland towns. This is the research of Hepburn (1978, pp. 90–92), who used the dissimilarity index (see below) to compare the intensity of segregation in the adjacent County Armagh towns of Lurgan and Portadown in 1911. Such comparative work requires the use of a single statistic, like Hepburn's employment of the dissimilarity index, to summarise the amount of segregation in a town. The only other Northern Ireland research which has done this, even for a single town, let alone for a number of towns, is the recent work of Poole and Boal (1973) on Belfast.

The result is that any analysis of the Northern Ireland conflict concerned with the extent of religious residential segregation amongst the whole set of towns has been presented with one of three possible courses of action. The first possibility has been to limit comment to a very small number of towns. For example, Freeman (1969, pp. 160–161) restricts his comments to Belfast and Londonderry, even though the context is one of discussing Northern Ireland as a whole. The second possible strategy has been to make sweeping statements on the basis of the very incomplete information available. By far the majority of these are assertions of the ubiquity of intense religious residential segregation, such as that of Barritt and Carter (1962, p. 53) that "in the towns, the two communities tend to live apart", or that of Easthope (1976, p. 432) that "within each village, town and city, where there is not complete homogeneity of religious membership, there are areas for Protestants and Catholics". However, the available evidence is so sparse that, not surprisingly, it has also been used to reach a totally different conclusion: thus Rumpf and Hepburn (1977, p. 165) assert that "the

Make a general comment

pattern of segregation has been sharpest . . . in the two largest towns, Belfast and Londonderry". The final sweeping statement quoted is from a more compromise stance: Darby (1976b, p. 161) suggests that "apart from Belfast, Derry and some other towns which have recognisable segregated housing, communities in most other parts of the province are essentially integrated in their . . . housing". The third of the three possible strategies is to adopt a position of ambiguity. Orme (1970, pp. 246–247) is an academic writer using this tactic, but the most frequent examples are in Annual Reports (1972, p. 18; 1973, p. 41; 1978, p. 15) of the Northern Ireland Housing Executive which leave the reader totally confused as to whether the comments are meant to apply to Northern Ireland as a whole or to Belfast only.

In view of this lack of evidence as to whether Northern Ireland towns differ from one another in the extent to which their housing is subject to religious segregation, it is hardly surprising that there is virtually no literature attempting to explain such differences. The only exception is found in the work of Hepburn (1978, p. 91). He suggested that the difference in segregation intensity between the two towns investigated was the result of their contrasting migration histories.

METHODOLOGY

In this research the measurement of residential segregation will be by means of the dissimilarity index. It is true that no single summary statistic can be a perfect measure of segregation, since the latter is a concept which can be defined in a number of ways (Duncan and Duncan, 1955, p. 217; Taeuber and Taeuber, 1965, pp. 205–207). There is now, however, a quite firmly established convention of employing the dissimilarity index (Poole and Boal, 1973, pp. 23–24; Peach, 1975, pp. 2–4), and, despite some recent controversy (e.g. Cortese *et al.*, 1976), this convention still appears well justified.

Interpretation of the dissimilarity index is facilitated by bearing in mind two fundamental points. First, it can vary from a maximum of 100 to a minimum of zero. The maximum value represents total segregation, while the minimum indicates a complete absence of segregation. Secondly, the index defines segregation between two religious groups in any one town as the deviation between the religious composition in the town as a whole and the religious composition in each of the sub-areas into which the town is divided for analysis.

To illustrate these points, imagine a town whose total population is 25% Roman Catholic and which is divided into four sub-areas with equal total populations. The dissimilarity index would be zero if all four sub-areas were, like the town as a whole, 25% Catholic. On the other hand, if three of the sub-areas had no Catholics, while the fourth was wholly Catholic, the dissimilarity index would attain the maximum value of 100.

The size of the sub-areas used in the empirical analysis in this chapter is guided by the suggestion that the most perceptually and behaviourally relevant scale-level for the study of segregation, from the point of view of the individual person or family, is the street or block (Lee, 1973, p. 478). Our preference therefore has been for analysis at this micro-level, and an attempt has been made to standardise scale-level as much as possible by using sub-areas averaging about forty households each.

In practice, however, such micro-level data are very difficult to obtain, and their use has been supplemented by employing what has been termed "meso-level analysis", involving sub-areas averaging about 200 households each. It is known that this scale-level is sufficiently larger than the micro-level to reduce substantially the practical difficulties of gathering data, but it is considered that the two scale-levels are not so distant that the meso-level sub-areas have no perceptual or behavioural relevance. The assertion of this latter point is influenced by Boal's (1978, p. 69) hypothesised hierarchy of areas possessing varying degrees of significance to the individual resident.

The work reported in this chapter has therefore been carried out at two distinct scale-levels, and no analyses have been conducted using a combination of dissimilarity indices at the two scale-levels. This rigid separation of analyses at the two scale-levels is made necessary by the well-documented effect of the size of sub-area on the magnitude of the dissimilarity index (Poole and Boal, 1973, p. 7).

QUANTITATIVE SOURCES FOR MEASURING CONTEMPORARY SEGREGATION

In adding to the literature currently available describing the prevalence of religious segregation in Northern Ireland's urban housing, it is clearly essential to provide quantitative data on individual towns far superior to those which have existed before. The most obvious potential source of such quantitative information is the population census. However data on religious composition in the 1970s for the micro and meso scale-levels described earlier are available only in the unpublished set of "small area statistics" based on 100 metre grid squares in urban areas. Unfortunately, inadequate funds have limited the purchase of these data. Nonetheless some data have been obtained at the micro-level together with more at the meso-level.

Non-census sources of information on the spatial distribution of religious affiliations are of two types. The first comprises data gathered from clergy, and its use was pioneered in the early 1960s by Kirk (1967, pp. 14–18, 60–61, 78) in Lurgan. The second type of non-census source of religious affiliation data is the household survey, usually involving sampling. The only published application of this method to a whole town is the work on Belfast by Boal *et al.* (1976, pp. 99–110, 115, 124–125) which has been used, in conjunction with clergy data, to help generate, in this chapter, a dissimilarity index for Northern Ireland's largest city. The author has also supervised household surveys in twenty other towns since 1973, some of them written up as under-graduate or postgraduate dissertations.

All but one of these household surveys involved sampling, and a decision on how many of the towns surveyed should be included in the analysis depends on an assessment of the sampling error incurred in each case. Unfortunately, very little indeed appears to be known about the sampling distribution of the dissimilarity index or, indeed, about the separate factors affecting the reliability of sample-derived indices (Morgan, 1975, p. 48; Musgrove, 1977, p. 367; Massey, 1978, p. 588; Cortese *et al.*, 1978, p. 591). Two factors can be singled out as of prob-able importance. These are, first, the average number of sample minority households per sub-area—this affects the extent to which the dissimi-larity index can, in practice, approach the minimum possible value of zero—and, secondly, the total sample size in each sub-area, which affects the reliability of the estimate of religious composition. In consequence of these considerations, five towns for which sample survey data were available were excluded from the analysis.

Overall, then, for the twenty-six towns finally examined in this chapter (Fig. 11.1), fifteen use household sample survey data, eight use unpublished population census data, two are based on clergy data only and one uses a combination of sample survey data and clergy-derived data. All but two of the twenty-six towns are defined in terms of their built-up area, the only exceptions being Holywood and White-abbey, which are inliers within Belfast. The latter is itself defined as an area stretching as far as Greenisland and Glengormley in the north, Suffolk and Twinbrook in the west, Seymour Hill and Belvoir in the south, and Dundonald and Cultra in the east.

It should be emphasised that not only are these twenty-six towns only a sample of towns in Northern Ireland, but also that they have not been selected as a random sample. The towns in which household

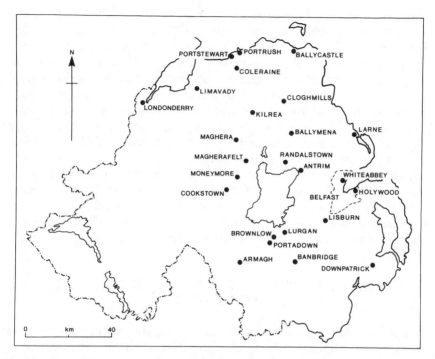

FIGURE 11.1. Northern Ireland: Towns Examined in Analysis of Religious Residential Segregation.

surveys have been conducted have been chosen in accordance with the locational convenience of the interviewers, and the choice of towns for which census data have been used was made in an attempt to ensure that the overall sample of towns was as representative as possible. Three possible sources of bias have been investigated: (i) town size; (ii) the ratio of Roman Catholic to Protestant households; (iii) geographical distribution. As regards town size, fewer than 10% of the towns with a population of between 500 and 2500 have been included in the sample, compared with one-quarter of towns with between 2500 and 5000 people and more than half the towns with over 5000 people. There is thus a bias towards larger towns, but, when the twenty-eight towns in this largest size-class are further divided into three categories on the basis of size, the proportion included in the sample lies between one-half and three-quarters for all three categories. No town size bias is therefore involved in the choice of sample from the largest and thus more important towns.

If these twenty-eight towns with over 5000 people are divided into three equal-spaced categories on the basis of their number of Roman Catholic households as a proportion of all households, it is found that between one-third and two-thirds of all towns in each category are included in the sample, though with a slight bias towards the more Protestant towns. Finally, analysis of the geographic distribution of towns in the sample shows that, at one extreme, all towns of over 5000 people in Counties Armagh and Londonderry are included while, at the other extreme, in Fermanagh and Tyrone such towns are hardly represented at all. Antrim and Down have about half of their towns of this size represented in the sample. Of the three aspects of bias investigated, this geographical one, with its underrepresentation of the two main Border counties of Fermanagh and Tyrone, is considered to be the most serious. However, even this bias should not be over-emphasised, since there are only five towns of over 5000 in these two sparsely populated counties, and one of these towns is in the sample.

THE INTENSITY OF RELIGIOUS RESIDENTIAL SEGREGATION

The empirical analysis begins by examining the extent to which the intensity of religious residential segregation varies between different Northern Ireland towns. The evidence available to answer this problem is contained in Tables 11.1 and 11.2, which present dissimilarity indices for thirteen and nineteen towns respectively, listed in each case in descending order of segregation intensity. The only difference between

TABLE 11.1. Contemporary Religious Residential Segregation at the Micro-Level.

Town	Dissimilarity index	Date	No. of households per sub-area	Type of data source
Belfast	76	1972	39	Clergy/Sample survey
Armagh	74	1971	56	Census
Londonderry	63	1971	57	Census
Whiteabbey	40	1970	35	Clergy
Antrim	35	1976	35	Sample survey
Kilrea	34	1973	23	Sample survey
Maghera	32	1971	48	Census
Ballycastle	31	1977	26	Sample survey
Coleraine	31	1975	49	Sample survey
Holywood	29	1971	36	Clergy
Cloghmills	27	1977	46	Sample survey
Magherafelt	26	1971	53	Census
Moneymore	24	1975	28	Population survey

the two tables is that the first is restricted to towns analysed at what was defined in the methodological section as the micro-level, while the second contains only towns analysed at what was referred to as the meso-level. It has been possible to include six of the towns in both tables, but the remaining twenty towns in the analysis have each had to be confined to one or the other.

Table 11.1 shows that, at the micro-level, the dissimilarity index ranges from a maximum of 76 in Belfast to a minimum of 24 in Moneymore. The corresponding meso-level range, illustrated in Table 11.2, is from a peak of 74 in Armagh to a low of 14 in Randalstown. Clearly, the first conclusion must be that there is a very wide variation indeed in segregation intensity, especially at the meso-level. Even the micro-level range, however, is greater than that in the only comparable research, the micro-level residential segregation of blacks and whites in 109 United States cities in 1970, where the range was from a minimum of 61 to a maximum of 98 (Sorensen *et al.*, 1975, pp. 128–130).

TABLE 11.2. Contemporary Religious Residential Segregation at the Meso-Level.

Town	Dissimilarity index	Date	No. of households per sub-area	Type of data source
Armagh	74	1971	204	Census
Lurgan	73	1971	202	Census
Londonderry	61	1971	206	Census
Downpatrick	48	1977	210	Sample survey
Brownlow	43	1975	198	Sample survey
Lisburn	43	1975	268	Sample survey
✗Portadown	37	1971	203	Census
Ballymena	35	1971	209	Census
Larne	32	1976	255	Sample survey
Cookstown	32	1974	200	Sample survey
Portrush	25	1974	187	Sample survey
Holywood	25	1971	195	Clergy
Limavady	25	1977	200	Sample survey
Coleraine	22	1975	212	Sample survey
Portstewart	22	1973	202	Sample survey
Magherafelt	21	1971	196	Census
Ballycastle	18	1977	238	Sample survey
Banbridge	18	1971	206	Census
Randalstown	14	1978	186	Sample survey

The entire array of dissimilarity indices in Northern Ireland is presented for easier visual inspection in Fig. 11.2, where they are graphed against the scale-level, which is measured as the average number of households per sub-area. It is apparent that, at the micro-level, there is a very clear division into two groups of towns. The first group, consisting of ten towns, has indices ranging between 24 and 40, while the second, containing only three, has indices varying between 63 and 76. There appears to be a dichotomising of towns into two clusters, separated by a very wide break.

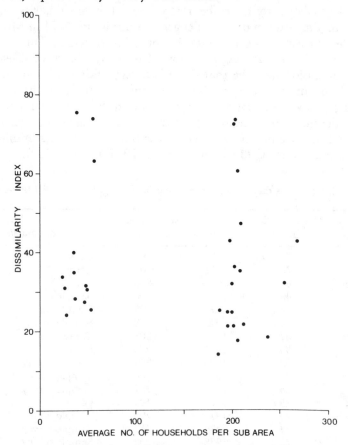

FIGURE 11.2. Dissimilarity Indices for Twenty-Six Towns Graphed against the Average Numbers of Households per Sub-Area Used in the Calculation of the Indices.

At the meso-level, this dichotomous pattern is much less clear cut. Sixteen of the nineteen towns have indices ranging from 14 to 48, while the second group of three towns has indices varying from 61 upwards to 74. The much less dichotomous structure in the set of meso-level indices results principally from the presence of three towns with index values of between 43 and 48 at this less detailed scale-level, and, significantly, for none of these three towns are micro-level data available.

This has implications for the certainty with which any conclusion can be reached about the existence of a dichotomy in the micro-level indices, because the nature of the dissimilarity index is such that spatial disaggregation into a larger number of smaller sub-areas cannot decrease the index, provided that none of the smaller sub-areas is created by combining part of one large sub-area with part of another. Therefore, the three towns with meso-level indices between 43 and 48 must have micro-level indices which are at least as high. It may therefore be that the thirteen towns for which micro-level data are presented in Table 11.1 are unrepresentative and that it is coincidental that the gap between the two clusters of towns is so great.

Whatever the verdict of future research on the existence of a dichotomy or a continuum in the set of dissimilarity indices, two conclusions appear inescapable from the evidence presented in the two tables and the graph when viewed in the context of the theoretical range of the index from zero to 100. First, despite the very wide variation in segregation intensity which does exist, there are no values near either of the two theoretical extremes. This is particularly true of the micro-level.

The second point is most simply illustrated by classifying towns according to whether their dissimilarity index is above or below 50. Only three of the thirteen towns for which micro-level data are available have indices above 50, while only three of the nineteen towns for which meso-level data exist have a segregation index over 50. However, before making a sweeping statement about the prevalence of low segregation intensities in Northern Ireland, it is pertinent to identify the specific towns with high dissimilarity indices. These are Belfast, Armagh, Lurgan and Londonderry.

The salient point about these four towns is that they were all amongst the fifteen largest towns in Northern Ireland in 1971 and that, above all, they include the two largest, Belfast and Londonderry. Belfast alone contained 54% of that part of Northern Ireland's population living in towns with over 2500 people, and these four towns together contained no less than 64% of the urban population. Therefore, even if none of the towns excluded from the sample of twenty-six used in the analysis in this chapter had dissimilarity indices for religious segregation exceeding 50, it could still be asserted that almost two-thirds of Northern Ireland's urban population lived in towns whose segregation index was closer to 100 than to zero.

What emerges from this study of religious segregation in housing is, in a sense, a paradox. On the one hand, it is highly probable that the great majority of Northern Ireland towns have a low level of this type of segregation. On the other hand, it is certain that a substantial majority of the urban population lives in towns that are characterised by a high level of segregation. However, the attainment of any firm conclusions on the prevalence of religious residential segregation from the evidence available is impeded not only by the fact that data exist for only a sample of Northern Ireland towns but also by the variation in the dates to which this sample of data refers. The main problem is that some indices pre-date the population movement associated with the present "troubles", while other indices post-date it. The problem is complicated further by the very limited literature which exists on this movement, but it seems likely that Belfast was most affected from 1969 to 1972, whereas those other towns which were affected did not suffer population movement much before the summer of 1971 or even before 1972 (Darby and Morris, 1974, pp. 66–69, a–c, k). Since 1973 intimidation appears to have declined again everywhere (Darby, 1976a, p. 139; Northern Ireland Housing Executive, 1978, p. 15; Kennedy and Birrell, 1978, p. 105). Of the twenty-six towns for which dissimilarity indices have been presented, sixteen are towns whose data definitely post-date any "troubles"-motivated population movement there may have been. The other ten include four towns which are reported to have suffered from this type of movement.

There are thus four towns whose quoted dissimilarity indices may be underestimates of the contemporary level of religious residential segregation because of the intensification which may have taken place after population movement associated with the "troubles". These are Armagh, Londonderry, Lurgan and Portadown (Darby and Morris, pp. 66–69, 114, f, k), the first three of which have been shown to belong to that small cluster of towns with a high level of segregation, while Portadown has a dissimilarity index placing it towards the upper end of the low segregation cluster.

It is now important to assess the effect of these four possible cases of under-estimated dissimilarity indices on the conclusions reached earlier on the extent of religious segregation in housing. First, the possibility of a dichotomy between towns with high and low levels of segregation is hardly affected at all, for only Portadown has an index which might possibly have been lifted into what is currently a gap between these two groups of indices. Secondly, the absence of very low dissimilarity indices will not be affected by these four under-estimated cases, but the absence of very high indices could be affected if segregation has intensified sufficiently, especially in Armagh and Lurgan. Thirdly, the fact that there are far more towns with segregation indices below 50 than above this critical mid-point is hardly affected at all by the possibility of underestimation in the four problem towns, because Portadown is the only one of the four whose quoted index is below 50 and is therefore capable of being switched from one side of this value to the other.

CONTEMPORARY CORRELATES OF RELIGIOUS RESIDENTIAL SEGREGATION

Given that there is such a wide variation in the intensity of religious residential segregation in Northern Ireland towns, the next problem is to try to explain it. This section of the chapter will attempt an explanation in terms of some of the contemporary characteristics of the sample towns. This is a style of explanation used both by Morgan (1975) to investigate socio-economic segregation in Great Britain and by Marshall and Jiobu (1975) to analyse the causes of racial segregation in the United States.

The presence of Northern Ireland's two largest towns amongst the set of four which have been found to be strongly segregated suggests an obvious hypothesis. This is that there is a positive correlation between town size and segregation intensity. This was a hypothesis tested and confirmed by Morgan in his work, but deliberately omitted by Marshall and Jiobu (1975, p. 451), partly because they could not propose a plausible *rationale* for the existence of such a relationship and partly for methodological reasons.

Morgan (1975, p. 51) justified his inclusion of this hypothesis by drawing on the suggestion of Wirth that, as settlement size increases and personal relationships become less close-knit, so the neighbourhood becomes a critical status symbol, thus encouraging residential segregation between different social strata. This type of reasoning is probably less salient as an explanation of ethnic residential segregation, though there may still be some anxiety to advertise ethnic identity by living in an appropriate neighbourhood.

Perhaps a more plausible reason, however, for suspecting a correlation between town size and residential segregation, whether of social classes or of ethnic groups, is that, the larger the town, the larger an individual neighbourhood of a particular social composition is likely to be. Thus, in the context of religious segregation in Northern Ireland, a small town and a large city might each be divided into separate Catholic, mixed and Protestant areas, but an individual neighbourhood which is, for example, entirely Protestant in the large city is likely to be much larger than an all-Protestant area in the small town and, indeed, it might even contain more people than the entire population of the small town.

Therefore, whenever analysis is conducted at a specific scale-level, such as the meso-level used in this chapter, there is likely to be a higher proportion of meso-level areas in the large city which are entirely Protestant than in the small town. This is because many of the areas of such a size in the small town will contain a mixture of very small areas, some of which may be all Protestant while others are of a different religious composition, but making the meso-level area as a whole relatively mixed in composition.

In testing the hypothesised relationship between the dissimilarity index for religious residential segregation and town size, the latter variable was measured in terms of the number of households present at the time to which the measurement of segregation refers. The testing was done by applying the Pearson correlation method three times at each of the two scale-levels, one using the untransformed town size and the other two employing logarithmic and square root transformations. The best result at both scale-levels was achieved with the logarithmic transformation of town size, and the actual coefficients of determination were 0·50 and 0·37 at the micro and meso scale-levels respectively, with the relationship being positive, as predicted. Both coefficients are statistically significant at the 0·003 level.

Clearly, the relationship is encouragingly close, but by no means so perfect as to suggest that a search for better correlates of segregation intensity would be fruitless. The work of Marshall and Jiobu (1975, pp. 450–451) can be drawn on at this stage, for they hypothesised that the size of the black population, both in absolute terms and relative to the total population, would affect the level of segregation between blacks and whites in United States cities. Their *rationale* for this hypothesis derived from two suggestions. First, they proposed that, the larger the black community, in either absolute or relative terms, the greater the perceived threat to the economic and social status of the white population. This threat would then trigger discrimination to counter it. Secondly, they suggested that, the larger the black community, the greater the number and variety of institutions and facilities catering specifically for that community which could be supported. In turn, the greater this number and variety of specialist facilities, the greater the encouragement for the black population to live close together to take advantage of them.

This pair of factors leading to a combination of voluntary and enforced segregation of the minority black population in American urban housing could equally be proposed as hypotheses to explain religious residential segregation in Northern Ireland. However, the demographic situation is such that the variable here analogous to the black community in the United States is not totally clear. This is mostly because of the complication introduced by the existence of the "double minority", with Roman Catholics being in a minority in Northern Ireland and Protestants being currently in a minority in Ireland as a whole and afraid of becoming a minority even in Northern Ireland in the future (Jackson, 1971, p. 4; Poole and Boal, 1973, p. 11; Whyte, 1978, p. 276).

Therefore, both the size of the Catholic community and the size of the Protestant community can be considered to be "minority" size measures and both can be hypothesised to affect the intensity of segregation. Moreover, it can be proposed that the more relevant variable is the size of the group that forms the actual numerical minority in a particular town, regardless of whether the group concerned is Catholic or Protestant. Consequently three concepts of the "minority" are provided and each of these can be measured in terms of absolute size. However, the relative size of the three possible "minority" communities can be measured using only two variables. This is because the number of Roman Catholic households, expressed as a percentage of the total number of households, is a simple function of the corresponding Protestant percentage, one being simply 100 minus the other. Overall a total of five "minority" size variables is produced.

TABLE 11.3. Coefficients of Determination for the Contemporary Relationship between Religious Residential Segregation and Each of Five "Minority" Size Variables, along with Town Size, at Two Scale-Levels.

Variable	Micro-level	Meso-level
Number of Catholic households (log)	0·62[a]	0·63[a]
Catholic percentage	0·08	0·23[c]
Number of Protestant households (log)	0·42[b]	0·11
Number of minority households (log)	0·61[a]	0·54[a]
Minority percentage	0·02	0·26[c]
Total households (log)	0·50[b]	0·37[b]

Key to significance levels: [a] 0·001; [b] 0·01; [c] 0·05.

The Pearson coefficients of determination for the relationship, at both scale-levels, between religious residential segregation and each of the five "minority" size variables identified are presented in Table 11.3. For comparison, the corresponding coefficients using town size (total households) as the independent variable are also included in this table. The three variables involving absolute "minority" size are, as for the earlier analysis of town size, transformed logarithmically, since, at both scale-levels and for all three of these variables, higher coefficients were achieved this way than by using either untransformed data or the square root transformation.

What is very clear from Table 11.3 is that both relative measures of "minority" size exhibit a very low correlation with segregation at both scale-levels. Even the highest of the coefficients of determination for these variables, 0·26, is much lower than all but the very lowest generated by the absolute measures of "minority" size. Apart from this very lowest coefficient (0·11, involving the number of Protestant households at the meso-level), the smallest coefficient of determination involving an absolute measure of "minority" size is 0·42.

It is less easy, however, to distinguish amongst the three absolute measures of "minority" size. True, the number of Protestant households is not highly correlated with segregation intensity, especially at the meso-level, but the other two variables do not differ much in their correlation with segregation. At the micro-level, the number of Roman Catholic households and the number of minority households yield coefficients of determination of 0·62 and 0·61 respectively when correlated against the dissimilarity indices. At the meso-level, Catholic community size gives rise to a coefficient of 0·63, compared with 0·54 for minority community size. Both these relationships with segregation intensity are significant at the 0·001 level at both scale-levels.

Part of the difficulty of distinguishing the separate effects of these two "minority" size variables upon segregation intensity is the fact that in only five of the twenty-six towns studied is the Roman Catholic community not the local minority. However, it is possible to be rather firmer in stating, from the evidence in Table 11.3, that both the number of Catholic households and the number of minority households are more closely correlated with segregation than is town size, especially at the meso-level. Moreover, the correlation coefficients measuring the relationship between these two most successful "minority" size variables and segregation are positive at both scale-levels, thus confirming further the original hypothesis that, the larger the "minority" community, the more intense the residential segregation.

Though Marshall and Jiobu (1975, pp. 458–459) did emphasise the particular significance of the absolute size of the black population as a correlate with residential segregation in the United States, they paid more attention to another pair of variables which are not analogous to any tested so far in this chapter. These are the income and occupational differentiation between the black and the white communities.

They postulated that, where this differentiation was high, residential segregation would be at its most intense, and subsequent analysis showed that these two variables were more successful predictors of segregation than any of the other independent variables tested (Marshall and Jiobu, 1975, pp. 450, 455–457).

These American writers did not elaborate a *rationale* for this relationship, except to suggest that, where income differentiation between blacks and whites is large, the two groups cannot compete equally for the more expensive housing and thus tend to live apart. This is simply a restatement of the poverty hypothesis of racial segregation in housing which Taeuber (1968, pp. 9–10) so conclusively disproved earlier for one not untypical American city. This finding of Taeuber, however, is not necessarily incompatible with the results of Marshall and Jiobu, for it is possible for income differences between blacks and whites to contribute very little to the total racial segregation in each individual city, but for the differences in such segregation between cities to be explicable in terms of this otherwise minor factor. Therefore, although a replication of Taeuber's analysis in Belfast, using occupation instead of income as the postulated determinant of segregation, showed that socio-economic differences between Roman Catholics and Protestants contributed very little indeed to an explanation of religious residential segregation in that city (Boal *et al.*, 1976, p. 115), it is still possible that differences between Northern Ireland towns in religious segregation in housing may be attributed to differences in the occupational profile of the two religious groups from town to town.

Data totally analogous to those used by Marshall and Jiobu are not available for any of the twenty-six towns analysed in this chapter. However, for twelve towns, cross-tabulations of religion against occupation are available. From these cross-tabulations the occupational differentiation between Catholics and Protestants is measured using, like Marshall and Jiobu (1975, pp. 453–454), the dissimilarity index. This index is applied to two separate dichotomous classifications of occupation. The first is the distinction between manual and non-manual households, while the second is that between households classified as professional, managerial or employers and all remaining households. These two divisions have generally been regarded as the most salient in British studies of social stratification (Rosser and Harris, 1965, pp. 100–101).

The reliability of the analysis involving these measures of occupational differentiation is rather greater at the meso-level than at the micro-level, for data are available only for five towns at the smaller scale-level, compared with the ten for which they exist at the meso-level.

The relevant coefficients of determination are presented in Table 11.4, along with the corresponding coefficients involving the most successful of the other variables tested so far for the two small samples of towns for which occupational differentiation data are available. It is clear from this table that, whatever the success of occupational differentiation as a correlate of racial segregation in the United States, neither of the two variables measuring the occupational differentiation between Roman Catholics and Protestants in Northern Ireland is of much value as a correlate of religious segregation here at either of the two scale-levels considered.

TABLE 11.4. Coefficients of Determination for the Contemporary Relationship between Religious Residential Segregation and a Number of Variables, Including Occupational Differentiation between the Two Religious Groups.

Variable	Micro-level (five towns)	Meso-level (ten towns)
Non-manual/manual differentiation	0·00	0·20
Professional, etc./other differentiation	0·03	0·11
Number of Catholic households (log)	0·59	0·66[a]
Number of minority households (log)	0·61	0·46[b]
Total households (log)	0·48	0·20

Key to significance levels: [a] 0·01; [b] 0·05.

This analysis of contemporary correlates of religious residential segregation in Northern Ireland towns must lead to a final conclusion, albeit preliminary because the relevant research is by no means yet concluded, that "minority" size, in absolute terms, is the best predictor of the intensity of segregation. Specifically, the number of Roman Catholic households and the size of the local minority (Protestant or Catholic) are the two most successful variables.

AN HISTORICAL EXPLANATION OF RELIGIOUS RESIDENTIAL SEGREGATION

Despite the high correlation between certain contemporary characteristics of Northern Ireland towns and religious residential segregation, care must be taken in interpreting this correlation as indicating a causal relationship in view of the truism that the explanation of the present must lie in the past.

In order to consider this, use has been made of the 1911 census enumerators' returns, available in manuscript form for individual households for the whole of Ireland (Royle, 1978, pp. 121–122). The choice of date is controlled by two factors. First, it was considered desirable to go reasonably far back into the past, at least to the period before Partition. Secondly, spatially detailed data on religious composition before 1911 are available only for extremely limited areas, except in the case of 1901.

These 1911 census enumerators' returns were used by Hepburn (1978, pp. 90–92) for his comparison of religious residential segregation at the street level in Lurgan and Portadown and by Baker (1973, p. 794) to produce a street map of religious composition in Belfast (see also Chapter 10, Fig. 10.1). The data employed by these authors have been obtained to present dissimilarity indices measuring religious segregation in housing at the micro-level, and the enumerators' returns have also been consulted to calculate corresponding indices for ten other towns in Northern Ireland. These ten other towns, like the three examined by Hepburn and Baker, are all amongst the sample of twenty-six settlements whose contemporary religious residential segregation has been analysed in preceding sections of the chapter.

TABLE 11.5. Dissimilarity Indices Measuring Religious Residential Segregation in 1911 and in the 1970s.

Town	Micro-level		Meso-level	
	1911	1970s	1911	1970s
Lurgan	83		77	73
Belfast	66	76		
Armagh	58	74	58	74
Londonderry	55	63	51	61
Portadown	54		47	37
Ballymena	38		27	35
Downpatrick	37			48
Coleraine	34	31	25	22
Whiteabbey	32	40		
Limavady	29			25
Kilrea	28	34		
Maghera	27	32		
Holywood	22	29		25

The resulting thirteen towns are listed in Table 11.5 in descending order of micro-level segregation intensity in 1911. Where possible, meso-level dissimilarity indices have also been calculated for 1911, and, where available, indices at both scale-levels for these thirteen towns in the 1970s have been added to the table.

At the micro-level, all but one of the eight towns for which indices are available at both time periods show an intensification of segregation. The one town whose segregation lessened over the period, Coleraine, had a fall of only 3 in its index, and six of the seven towns whose segregation increased had rises of between 5 and 10. The only town showing a substantial increase was Armagh, where the index rose by no less than 16. As a result, in particular, of the similarity of the trend in six of these eight towns, the coefficient of determination for the correlation between the 1911 indices and those for the 1970s in these eight towns is no less than 0·96. This is statistically significant at the 0·001 level.

The evidence at the meso-level is less clear cut, for, of the six towns for which indices can be presented at both points in time, three show an increase in segregation and three show a decrease. The most substantial changes are the fall of 10 in Portadown and the rises of 16 in Armagh and 10 in Londonderry. However, despite this significant divergence of trends, the correlation between the 1911 indices and the contemporary indices remains very high, the coefficient of determination being 0·78. True, this is rather below the extraordinarily high coefficient found at the micro-level, but it is still significant at the 0·01 level.

These two exercises correlating 1911 indices with contemporary indices at the micro and meso scale-levels have, between them, involved eleven of the thirteen towns featured in Table 11.5. The only towns which could not be included in either exercise were Downpatrick and Limavady. The limited evidence presented for these two towns in the table suggests that there must have been a fairly substantial increase in segregation in Downpatrick, but that Limavady showed very little change.

The most important conclusion to be drawn from Table 11.5 is neatly summarised in the very high coefficients of determination quoted. This is the marked stability over time in the differences in religious residential segregation between towns. The indices may rise a little in some towns, and they may fall a little in others, but it is clear that, if a town was highly segregated in 1911, then it remained so sixty or more years later. Similarly, if a town was weakly segregated at the earlier time, it still was in the 1970s.

This conclusion, in turn, has critical consequences for the attempt to explain differences between towns in the extent to which they are segregated. Specifically, any attempt to explain such differences in the 1970s solely in terms of other contemporary characteristics of these towns would be spurious. That is because these differences, with little modification, already existed in 1911, and segregation in 1911 could hardly have been caused by, for example, the size of the Roman Catholic community in 1971!

In order to understand differences between towns in their contemporary segregation intensity, it is therefore essential to try to explain those differences existing in 1911. The attempt to do this proceeds first by conducting an analysis identical to that presented in the previous section on contemporary correlates of segregation. The dissimilarity indices measuring religious residential segregation in 1911 are correlated with town size and "minority" size in 1911, using the same variables as were applied to the 1970s in Table 11.3. The analysis is conducted only at the micro-level, because, unlike the contemporary data, there are no towns for which meso-level indices alone are available.

The resulting set of coefficients of determination is presented in Table 11.6, and it is apparent that the findings are very similar to those emerging from the contemporary analysis. The two best correlates are the number of Catholic households and the number of minority households, with town size and the number of Protestant households also significant. The two measures of relative "minority" size again have very low coefficients indeed. Once again, a firm verdict about the relative importance of the other four variables as correlates of segregation is impeded by the very high intercorrelation amongst them. However, the fact that the number of Catholic households and the size of the local minority are yet again the best two correlates of segregation provides more evidence that there must almost certainly be a causal relationship at work here.

TABLE 11.6. Coefficients of Determination for the Relationship in 1911 between Religious Residential Segregation and Each of Five "Minority" Size Variables, along with Town Size, at the Micro-Level.

Variable	Coefficient
Number of Catholic households (log)	0·56[a]
Catholic percentage	0·00
Number of Protestant households (log)	0·41[a]
Number of minority households (log)	0·57[b]
Minority percentage	0·05
Total households (log)	0·47[a]

Key to significance levels: [a] 0·01; [b] 0·001.

It has been pointed out earlier that the only proposal made in the literature to explain why some towns are more segregated than others is Hepburn's suggestion that the contrasting migration histories of Lurgan and Portadown made these towns differ in intensity of religious residential segregation. Moreover, it was the 1911 segregation difference between these two towns that he was trying to explain, so it is particularly appropriate to test his hypothesis using the more extensive 1911 data presented in Table 11.5.

More specifically, Hepburn (1978, p. 91) observed that, between 1861 and 1911, the Roman Catholic population in Portadown grew by 39%, compared with no less than 149% for the Protestant population. The corresponding figures for Lurgan were the much more similar percentages of 67 and 58 respectively. The choice of 1861 for comparison was determined by the availability of census data on religious affiliation (Macourt, 1978). Hepburn's interpretation of these figures was that Lurgan experienced substantial immigration of both Catholics and Protestants, whereas Portadown's immigrants were overwhelmingly Protestant. It was suggested that both towns had residentially relatively mixed central business districts, and that the effect of this migration differential was that the proportion of Portadown's Roman Catholics living in this mixed area was much higher than the corresponding proportion in Lurgan. Consequently, it was argued, the housing of Portadown was subject to considerably less religious segregation than that of Lurgan.

One interesting point about Hepburn's hypothesis is that its numerical definition, though not its *rationale*, makes it identical to the only one of the hypotheses of Marshall and Jiobu which has not yet been tested in this chapter. Marshall and Jiobu (1975, p. 451) suggested that the "black–white growth differential", which is the percentage change in the white population subtracted from the percentage change in the black population, would be positively correlated with racial segregation in housing. They suggested that the causal links involved were "not entirely clear", but the rise in the black proportion of the urban population, which would be implied when the black–white growth differential was positive, would threaten white economic and social dominance, involving discriminatory behaviour in retaliation.

Hepburn's proposed correlate of segregation can, for convenience, be referred to as the Catholic–Protestant growth differential. If, as in Hepburn's work, this variable is defined with reference to population change between 1861 and 1911 (*Census of Ireland 1861*; *Census of Ireland 1911*) and is correlated with 1911 segregation, the resulting coefficient of determination is found to be a mere 0·20. Moreover, what little correlation exists is, in fact, negative. This is contrary both to the argument of Marshall and Jiobu in the United States context and to the reasoning of Hepburn in relation to Lurgan and Portadown. Clearly, what appeared plausible in the context of two Northern Ireland towns is firmly rejected when analysis is widened to thirteen.

Because of the complexity, discussed in an earlier section, of defining "minority" and "majority" in the Northern Ireland situation, a second variable measuring growth differential has been correlated with segregation. Called the minority–majority growth differential, this is based on the definition of the minority as whichever group is the local minority in each town considered. However, the results are even less encouraging than for the Catholic–Protestant differential, for the coefficient of determination is a mere 0·13 and the correlation is again negative.

TABLE 11.7. Coefficients of Determination for the Relationship between Micro-Level Religious Residential Segregation in 1911 and Each of Ten Variables Measuring Population Change between 1861 and 1911.

Variable	Coefficient
Catholic–Protestant growth differential	0·20
Minority–majority growth differential	0·13
Absolute Catholic population change	0·23[a]
Absolute Protestant population change	0·21
Absolute minority population change	0·23[a]
Absolute total population change	0·22
Percentage Catholic population change	0·09
Percentage Protestant population change	0·24[a]
Percentage minority population change	0·10
Percentage total population change	0·23

Key to significance levels: [a] 0·05.

Both these coefficients involving growth differential variables are presented in Table 11.7, along with coefficients of determination for the correlation between segregation and each of eight other variables. Four of these eight refer to absolute population change, again between 1861 and 1911, and the other four refer to percentage population change over this period. The four in each case involve respectively Roman Catholics, Protestants, the local minority, and the total population. Table 11.7 makes it clear, however, that none of these variables has a substantial correlation with religious residential segregation. True, all eight correlation coefficients are positive, but the highest coefficient of determination is only 0·24, and no coefficient is significant at the 0·01 level. The level of success in explaining 1911 segregation achieved by the variables measuring population change between 1861 and 1911, listed in Table 11.7, is thus considerably lower than that resulting from the employment of the four measures, listed in Table 11.6, of absolute population size in 1911 itself. In particular, the size of the local minority and the size of the Catholic community appear to be the best predictors of religious residential segregation in 1911, just as they were earlier found to be the best predictors of contemporary segregation.

CONCLUSION

The success of these two variables as predictors of the differences in religious residential segregation between towns in both 1911 and the 1970s is highly encouraging, particularly in view of the extremely high coefficients of determination calculated. However, it leaves unsolved the problem of precisely when the causal process which generated these relationships actually operated. For example, if the correlation is measured between 1911 segregation and the two predictor variables at their 1861 values, then the resulting coefficients of determination are still as high as 0·56 and 0·55 respectively. These are virtually no different from the corresponding coefficients of 0·57 and 0·56 when the values of these two predictor variables used are for 1911, contemporary with the residential segregation being measured.

It would therefore appear that 1911 differences in segregation between towns are determined at least partly by certain population characteristics of these towns fifty years before. This could be either because of a direct causal relationship or, more likely, because of a combination of two effects which could have been occurring simultaneously. The first of these would have been the existence of a relationship between one or both of the two critical population characteristics in 1861 and the residential segregation existing then. The second would have been the persistence of considerable stability between 1861 and 1911 in the level of segregation in each town, just as there was between 1911 and the 1970s. Certainly, there was a strong correlation between the 1861 and 1911 values of the two predictor variables, for the coefficients of determination are 0·94 for the size of the local minority and 0·95 for the size of the Roman Catholic community.

Unfortunately, no information on religious residential segregation in 1861 is available, so this hypothesis about differences between towns in the intensity of segregation at that time cannot be tested. Indeed, there is no research which has measured religious segregation in housing at any stage of the nineteenth century, and the only measurement available for any earlier date comes from the work of Wilson (1978, pp. 91–94). He found that the dissimilarity index for micro-level segregation in Armagh in 1770 was 52, which is not substantially different from the corresponding 1911 index of 58.

It would clearly be unwise, therefore, to infer too much about the stability of segregation before 1911. However, it can safely be concluded, from the evidence presented earlier, that there was substantial stability in the segregation differences between towns in the later period studied, that is, between 1911 and the 1970s. Moreover, this stability has survived through several periods of violent conflict and refugee movement, as well as having persisted through a period both of fundamental tenure shift and of substantial redevelopment and extension in Northern Ireland's urban housing stock.

This is one of the three principal conclusions to be drawn from this chapter. In addition, it is clear that, out of all the variables tested for their correlation with segregation differences, as they existed in either 1911 or the 1970s, the absolute measures of population size were the most successful. In particular, the size of the Roman Catholic community and the numbers in the local minority have invariably exhibited a remarkably high correlation with segregation. The historical evidence suggests, moreover, that these relationships existed in the nineteenth century and may have developed even earlier, so it is in the distant past that the explanation of the origin, though not the maintenance, of the segregation differences lies.

Finally, the very fact that considerable differences in segregation have been demonstrated to exist between towns must itself be regarded as a major conclusion, in view of the inadequacies in the published literature reviewed earlier. Northern Ireland towns, like those of any region, differ in many ways, but one difference not adequately recognised previously has been that, while some towns have very strong religious segregation in their housing, the majority are, in this respect, only weakly segregated.

This final conclusion has particularly important implications in the broad theoretical context in which the research investigation in this chapter was originally placed. It is clear that it can by no means be taken for granted that the religious segregation in the spheres of politics and primary and secondary education in Northern Ireland, which is virtually universal geographically and nearly total in intensity, is so strongly characteristic of other aspects of life. Nowhere is housing segregation as intense as the religious segregation in the schools, and rarely is it as strong as the religious cleavage in voting behaviour. Moreover, there are very many towns in Northern Ireland whose housing is, from the point of view of religious composition, very mixed, and this is a statement that could certainly not be applied to the spheres of politics and education.

REFERENCES

Baker, S. E. (1973). Orange and Green: Belfast, 1832–1912. *In* "The Victorian City: Images and Realities" (H. J. Dyos and M. Wolff, eds.), pp. 789–814. Routledge and Kegan Paul, London.

Barritt, D. P. and Carter, C. F. (1962). "The Northern Ireland Problem: A Study in Group Relations." Oxford University Press, London.

Boal, F. W. (1969). Territoriality on the Shankill-Falls Divide, Belfast. *Irish Geography* **6**, 30–50.

Boal, F. W. (1970). Social Space in the Belfast Built-Up Area. *In* "Irish Geographical Studies" (N. Stephens and R. E. Glasscock, eds.), pp. 373–393. Department of Geography, Queen's University, Belfast.

Boal, F. W. (1978). Ethnic Residential Segregation. *In* "Social Areas in Cities: Processes, Patterns and Problems" (D. T. Herbert and R. J. Johnston, eds.), pp. 57–95. John Wiley, London.

Boal, F. W., Murray, R. C. and Poole, M.A. (1976). Belfast: The Urban Encapsulation of a National Conflict. *In* "Urban Ethnic Conflict: A Comparative Perspective" (S. E. Clarke and J. L. Obler, eds.), pp. 77–131. Comparative Urban Studies Monograph No. 3, Institute for Research in Social Science, University of North Carolina, Chapel Hill.

Census of Ireland 1861. Her Majesty's Stationery Office, Dublin.

Census of Ireland 1911. His Majesty's Stationery Office, London.

Cortese, C. F., Falk, R. F. and Cohen, J. K. (1976). Further Considerations on the Methodological Analysis of Segregation Indices. *American Sociological Review* **41**, 630–637.

Cortese, C. F., Falk, R. F. and Cohen, J. K. (1978). Understanding the Standardized Index of Dissimilarity: Reply to Massey. *American Sociological Review* **43**, 590–592.

Darby, J. (1976a). Conflict and Conciliation in Northern Ireland: 1975. *New Community* **5**, 139–141.

Darby, J. (1976b). "Conflict in Northern Ireland: The Development of a Polarised Community." Gill and Macmillan, Dublin.

Darby, J. and Morris, G. (1974). "Intimidation in Housing." Northern Ireland Community Relations Commission, Belfast.

Darby, J., Murray, D., Batts, D., Dunn, S., Farren, S. and Harris, J. (1977). "Education and Community in Northern Ireland: Schools Apart?" New University of Ulster, Coleraine.

Duncan, O. D. and Duncan, B. (1955). A Methodological Analysis of Segregation Indexes. *American Sociological Review* **20**, 210–217.

Easthope, G. (1976). Religious War in Northern Ireland. *Sociology* **10**, 427–450.

Evans, E. E. (1944). Belfast: The Site and the City. *Ulster Journal of Archaeology* **7**, 5–29.

Freeman, T. W. (1969). "Ireland: A General and Regional Geography." Methuen, London.

Harris, R. L. (1972). "Prejudice and Tolerance in Ulster: A Study of Neighbours and 'Strangers' in a Border Community." Manchester University Press, Manchester.

Hepburn, A. C. (1978). Catholics in the North of Ireland, 1850–1921: The Urbanization of a Minority. *In* "Minorities in History" (A. C. Hepburn, ed.), pp. 84–101. Edward Arnold, London.

Jackson, H. (1971). "The Two Irelands: A Dual Study of Inter-Group Tensions." Minority Rights Group, London.

Jones, E. (1952). Belfast: A Survey of the City. *In* "Belfast in its Regional Setting: A Scientific Survey" (E. Jones, ed.), pp. 201–211. British Association for the Advancement of Science, Belfast.

Jones, E. (1956). The Distribution and Segregation of Roman Catholics in Belfast. *Sociological Review* **4**, 167–189.

Jones, E. (1960). "A Social Geography of Belfast." Oxford University Press, London.

Kennedy, S. and Birrell, D. (1978). Housing. *In* "Violence and the Social Services in Northern Ireland" (J. Darby and A. Williamson, eds.), pp. 98–116. Heinemann, London.

Kirk, T. (1967). "The Religious Distributions of Lurgan with Special Reference to Segregation Ecology." Unpublished M.A. Thesis, Queen's University, Belfast.

Lee, T. R. (1973). Ethnic and Social Class Factors in Residential Segregation: Some Implications for Dispersal. *Environment and Planning* (*A*) **5**, 477–490.

Macourt, M. P. A. (1978). The Religious Inquiry in the Irish Census of 1861. *Irish Historical Studies* **21**, 168–187.

Marshall, H. and Jiobu, R. (1975). Residential Segregation in United States Cities: A Causal Analysis. *Social Forces* **53**, 449–460.

Massey, D. S. (1978). On the Measurement of Segregation as a Random Variable. *American Sociological Review* **43**, 587–590.

McAllister, I. and Wilson, B. (1978). Bi-Confessionalism in a Confessional Party System: The Northern Ireland Alliance Party. *Economic and Social Review* **9**, 207–225.

Morgan, B. S. (1975). The Segregation of Socio-Economic Groups in Urban Areas: A Comparative Analysis. *Urban Studies* **12**, 47–60.

Musgrove, P. (1977). The Structure of Household Spending in South American Cities: Indexes of Dissimilarity and Causes of Inter-City Differences. *Review of Income and Wealth* **23**, 365–384.

Northern Ireland Census of Population 1971. Her Majesty's Stationery Office, Belfast.

Northern Ireland Housing Executive: Annual Reports 1972–1979. Northern Ireland Housing Executive, Belfast.

Orme, A. R. (1970). "Ireland." Longman, London.

Peach, C. (1975). "Urban Social Segregation." Longman, London.

Poole, M. A. and Boal, F. W. (1973). Religious Residential Segregation in Belfast in Mid-1969: A Multi-Level Analysis. *In* "Social Patterns in Cities" (B. D. Clark and M. B. Gleave, eds.), pp. 1–40. Special Publication No. 5, Institute of British Geographers, London.

Reid, J. (1973). Community Conflict in Northern Ireland: Analysis of a New Town Plan. *Ekistics* **36**, 115–119.

Robinson, A. (1969). "Geographical Field Work in an Irish Border Area: Londonderry and Moville." Department of Geography, Bishop Grosseteste College of Education, Lincoln.

Robinson, A. (1970). Londonderry, Northern Ireland: A Border Study. *Scottish Geographical Magazine* **86**, 208–221.

Rose, R. (1971). "Governing without Consensus: An Irish Perspective." Faber and Faber, London.

Rosser, C. and Harris, C. (1965). "The Family and Social Change: A Study of Family and Kinship in a South Wales Town." Routledge and Kegan Paul, London.

Royle, S. A. (1978). Irish Manuscript Census Records: A Neglected Source of Information. *Irish Geography* **11**, 110–125.

Rumpf, E. and Hepburn, A. C. (1977). "Nationalism and Socialism in Twentieth-Century Ireland." Liverpool University Press, Liverpool.

Sorensen, A., Taeuber, K. E. and Hollingsworth, L. J. (1975). Indexes of Racial Residential Segregation for 109 Cities in the United States, 1940 to 1970. *Sociological Focus* **8**, 125–142.

Taeuber, K. E. (1968). The Effect of Income Redistribution on Racial Residential Segregation. *Urban Affairs Quarterly* **4**, 5–14.

Taeuber, K. E. and Taeuber, A. F. (1965). "Negroes in Cities: Residential Segregation and Neighborhood Change." Aldine, Chicago.

Whyte, J. (1978). Interpretations of the Northern Ireland Problem: An Appraisal. *Economic and Social Review* **9**, 257–282.

Wilson, J. A. (1978). "The Residential Segregation of Catholics and Protestants in the Armagh Urban Area in 1971: A Measurement and Causal Analysis together with a Discussion of Future Policy Options." Unpublished M.Sc. Dissertation, New University of Ulster, Coleraine.

CHAPTER 12

POLITICAL VIOLENCE IN NORTHERN IRELAND 1969-1977

Russell Murray

INTRODUCTION

The national and international interest in Northern Ireland since 1969 is due to the violence which has occurred there; the underlying problems have been present for many years but it took the violence to draw the attention and concern of the outside world. Violence is the most dramatic and serious manifestation of the divisions within any society. An examination of these phenomena thus forms an integral part of any discussion of the Northern Ireland problem. This chapter attempts such an examination, chiefly from a geographic perspective. It is not the intention here to investigate the origins of the present violence. The background has been widely documented (e.g. by the Cameron Commission, 1969; the Scarman Tribunal, 1972; the Sunday Times Insight Team, 1972), and there has been considerable lay and academic discussion of possible explanations. This chapter is concerned with the form of subsequent events; what started as street rioting has developed over the years, with the involvement of the Irish Republican Army (I.R.A.), into a mixture of civil and guerilla war. These events have varied widely from area to area in both form and intensity; as Kirk (1978, p. 383) has pointed out, however, geographers have paid little attention to "the study of war as an expression of the spatial behaviour of human groups".

Any study is immediately faced by data problems arising from the duration, intensity and complexity of the conflict. Violence, in the usual sense of any attack on persons or property, has taken diverse forms ranging from simple assaults to small-scale military actions. It has been undertaken by different people for different reasons. Above all, it has been prolific. Official statistics give the number of shooting incidents from 1969 to 1977 (inclusive) as 25 613; the number of civilians reported injured was 11 706. Lesser forms of violence, such as groups of youths stoning army patrols or other youths, are almost daily events and may not even be recorded. A more important problem, however, is that the academic researcher, who must rely on publicly available material, rarely has access to the information needed to identify the persons responsible and their motives. Moreover, in Northern Ireland there is often fundamental disagreement as to the "facts" of an incident, such as whether the dead person was armed.

This study, therefore, has been confined to two categories of violence, deaths and explosions. These were chosen because they are the incidents that arouse greatest public and political concern, they have the greatest impact on the community, and, not least, they are the best documented. Nevertheless, the information that was available for this chapter was limited to certain basic features of each incident.

The main source of data was two lists, covering the years 1969–1977, one each for deaths and explosions, supplied by the Royal Ulster Constabulary (R.U.C.) Information Office; these were supplemented by reference to newspaper reports. The information extracted from the deaths list covered the date and location of the incident (for a number of fatalities the location recorded was that where the body was found since the location of the killing was unknown); the age, sex and affiliation (Protestant, Roman Catholic or security forces) of the victim; the cause of death. The Protestant and Catholic categories include not only "pure" civilians but also members of paramilitary groups such as the Provisional I.R.A. (P.I.R.A.) or Ulster Defence Association (U.D.A.) as there was insufficient information to do otherwise. The security forces were classified as police (Royal Ulster Constabulary), Ulster Defence Regiment (U.D.R.)—a locally-recruited regiment of the British army, mainly part-timers—or regular British army. The newspaper reports yielded a superficial description of the circumstances. The explosions list gave data on the date and location of the incident and the target. For both types of incident the location was coded using the system of wards developed for "Northern Ireland: A Census Atlas" (Compton, 1978); under this system the 526 wards into which Northern Ireland was divided for the 1971 Population Census was reduced to 332 by aggregating urban wards and treating most towns as one unit.

CHARACTERISTICS OF THE VIOLENCE

Tables 12.1 and 12.2 summarise the temporal trends in the levels of violence. Although the general trends are similar, for deaths and explosions, and for Northern Ireland as a whole and the Belfast Urban Area, there are noticeable variations. The peak year for deaths in Belfast, as in Northern Ireland, was 1972 but the highest figure for explosions in the Belfast area was a year earlier. The proportion of Northern Ireland's fatalities which occurred in Belfast was consistently higher than that of the explosions, except in 1969 and 1977. Finally, after 1972 the annual variation in level was greater for explosions than deaths.

TABLE 12.1. Annual Number of Deaths.[a]

Year	N. Ireland (No.)	(%)	Belfast Urban Area (No.)	(%)	Belfast as a percentage of N. Ireland
1969	13	1	11	1	85
1970	25	1	17	2	68
1971	176	10	118	11	67
1972	467	26	294	28	63
1973	248	14	135	13	54
1974	219	12	116	11	53
1975	245	14	137	13	56
1976	293	16	159	15	54
1977	112	6	63	6	56
Total	1798	100	1050	100	58

[a] The date used is the date of the incident and not the date when death occurred.

TABLE 12.2. Annual Number of Explosions.

Year	N. Ireland (No.)	(%)	Belfast Urban Area (No.)	(%)	Belfast as a percentage of N. Ireland
1969	6	0	6	0	100
1970	170	3	103	5	61
1971	1034	18	527	23	51
1972	1424	25	469	21	33
1973	959	17	323	14	34
1974	664	12	227	10	34
1975	354	6	118	5	33
1976	633	11	286	13	45
1977	346	6	221	10	64
Total	5590	100	2280	100	41

TABLE 12.3. Characteristics of Victims.

| | N. Ireland | | Belfast Urban Area | | Belfast as a percentage |
	(No.)	(%)	(No.)	(%)	of N. Ireland
(a) Sex (Northern Ireland civilians only)					
Male	1169	89	768	88	66
Female	149	11	102	12	68
Total	1318	100	870	100	66
(b) Affiliation					
Catholic civilians	846	47	567	54	67
Protestant civilians	461	26	303	29	66
Police	106	6	35	3	33
Army	275	15	121	12	44
U.D.R.	81	5	11	1	14
Other	29	2	13	1	45
Total	1798	100	1050	100	58
(c) Age (Northern Ireland civilians only)					
Under 17	103	8	72	8	70
17–50	907	69	575	66	63
Over 50	157	12	104	12	66
Unknown	151	11	119	14	79
Total	1318	100	870	100	66

Table 12.3 indicates some of the personal characteristics of the people who have died as a result of the violence. The outside image of the violence in Northern Ireland is that it is indiscriminate; the figures in this table show that this is not the case. Females and young people are grossly under-represented amongst the "civilian" casualties by comparison with their numbers in the general population. The typical "civilian" victim has been a male of military age. This is not because most were actually members of paramilitary organisations. It has been estimated (McKeown, 1977) that only about 20% of Roman Catholic deaths and 10% of Protestant deaths fall into that category. The fact is that most "civilian" deaths appear to have been quite deliberate; even if the killers were not after a particular person they were at least clear on their affiliation. This is borne out by the figures in Table 12.4 which relate to the circumstances of the "civilian" deaths. The first five categories, which together account for 62% of these deaths, involve cases where the killers selected a person or group of people to kill. The largest category is of people killed while in a public house, club, or other social centre; because of the residential and social segregation in Northern Ireland most of such places will cater predominantly for one

ethnic group and thus anyone planning a murder can be reasonably sure of the affiliation of his victims by selecting an appropriate location. The typical case in the fifth category ("Found Body") involves a man seized while walking home at night through or near the "wrong" area and taken somewhere to be murdered, his body then being dumped elsewhere; the main reason for the murder was that the victim was from a different ethnic group.

TABLE 12.4. Circumstances of Deaths (N. Ireland Civilians Only).

Circumstances	N. Ireland (No.)	(%)	Belfast Urban Area (No.)	(%)	Belfast as a percentage of N. Ireland
Killed at home	136	10	85	10	63
Killed at work	90	7	69	8	77
Killed in pub, club, etc.	210	16	141	16	67
Attack in street[a]	183	14	124	14	68
Found Body[b]	203	15	153	18	75
Shot by security forces	144	11	84	10	58
Crossfire[c]	81	6	73	8	90
Own bomb	105	8	48	6	46
Other attacks[d]	33	3	19	2	58
Bystander[e]	86	7	39	4	45
Unclassified	47	4	35	4	74
Total	1318	100	870	100	66

[a]Persons killed while walking in the street or in a vehicle (including booby-traps).
[b]Persons whose body was dumped somewhere else after the murder.
[c]Persons killed in crossfire during gun battles.
[d]Persons killed while in another house, at church, in booby-trapped buildings.
[e]Persons killed by bombs in commercial premises, during robberies, by landmines, etc.

Some further points emerge from Tables 12.3 and 12.4. Although Roman Catholics make up only 37% of the general population they constitute 47% of all victims, 65% of the dead civilians; data not given in the tables indicate that they account for 88% of people shot by the security forces. Again, this discrepancy cannot fully be accounted for by the deaths of I.R.A. members because they constitute only a small proportion of the deaths; as McKeown (1977) points out, even the people shot by the security forces were mostly innocent civilians. (As in 1956–1962 over half the I.R.A. deaths have been the result of accidents with their own bombs; many of the others were killed by other Republicans.) When all residents of Northern Ireland are taken together (i.e. all civilians plus members of the R.U.C. and U.D.R.) it seems that about 58% of victims have been Roman Catholics, 42% Protestants (McKeown, 1977). The tables also show that the Belfast Urban Area accounts for a disproportionate number of certain types of fatality. The figures for the security forces, in particular the R.U.C. and U.D.R., are rather low while the levels of certain sectarian killings —notably persons killed at work or those seized and killed later ("Found Body")—are higher than the overall numbers. The most striking figure is that for persons killed in crossfire during two- (or even three-) sided gun battles; this is an inevitable consequence of urban guerilla warfare.

TABLE 12.5. Characteristics of Explosion Targets.

Target	N. Ireland (No.)	(%)	Belfast Urban Area (No.)	(%)	Belfast as a percentage of N. Ireland
Residential	323	6	224	10	69
Shops/Offices	1928	34	917	40	48
Industrial	468	8	230	10	49
Utilities	536	10	120	5	22
Government	433	8	86	4	20
Pubs/Clubs	685	12	346	15	51
Army/R.U.C.	749	13	189	8	25
Catholic premises[a]	116	2	51	2	44
Protestant premises[a]	78	1	27	1	35
Other	274	5	90	4	33
Total	5590	100	2280	100	41

[a]Catholic/Protestant premises: these are buildings owned by a sectarian organisation or which are generally used exclusively by one group, e.g. schools, church halls, Orange halls. Licensed premises, although frequently sectarian in use, have not been included here as it was not possible to assign each to one group or the other.

The next table (Table 12.5) summarises the circumstances of the bombing campaigns; although no proportions are available most of the explosions have been the work of the P.I.R.A., but Loyalist groups have also been involved. It is clear that these campaigns have been directed mainly at business targets. The targets that one expects to predominate in a guerilla war aimed (by the I.R.A.) at driving the British from Northern Ireland—government premises and the security forces—account for only about a fifth of the explosions; even if we include the other classic guerilla target, premises and installations of the public utilities (gas, electricity, public transport, roads, communications), the proportion only rises to about 30%. It is noticeable that this aspect of the bombing campaign has been carried out mainly outside the Belfast Urban Area. The two categories in which Belfast accounts for the highest proportion of explosions—attacks on residential areas or specific dwellings and attacks on public houses and drinking clubs—are those in which, because of residential segregation, there is the greatest chance of killing or injuring members of one or other ethnic group.

THE SPATIAL PATTERN

For this first stage of the spatial analysis no distinction is made between the different categories of fatalities or explosions. Their spatial distributions for the whole period under study are shown in Figs 12.1 and 12.2. Figure 12.1 shows the pattern of deaths.

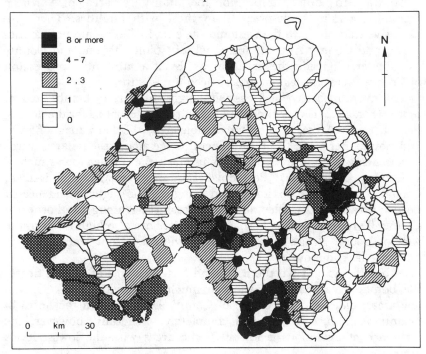

FIGURE 12.1. The Distribution of Deaths Due to Political Violence, Northern Ireland, 1969–1977.

Wards falling into one of the top two classes (i.e. four or more deaths since 1969) form five main areal groups: that is, clusters of at least six contiguous wards in one of the top two categories. The major one, in the sense of the number of deaths, is Belfast: just over half of all deaths occurred here. In the south of Northern Ireland there is another high area in south Armagh, stretching from Crossmaglen to Newry; this is the area that has been labelled "Bandit Country". To the north-west of this area is another group of wards with high values running west and east of Dungannon. Next we have the strip of wards along the Border in County Fermanagh. The final area is made up of the city of London-derry and its suburbs. In addition to these groupings there are a number of smaller concentrations of fatalities. These are mostly urban areas, notably Coleraine, Strabane, Portadown and Lurgan, Omagh and Armagh. The high value exhibited by the ward containing Claudy (just south-east of Londonderry) is the result of just one bomb attack on that village on 31 July 1972 which killed nine people.

Contrary to popular impression the fatality-free areas of Northern Ireland are more widespread than those with fatalities. There are extensive tracts in both the west and the east, including most of County Down and County Antrim, and much of County Tyrone and County Londonderry outside the urban areas. Even a substantial proportion of County Armagh has not experienced any deaths.

The overall pattern of areas with high numbers of bombs (ten or more) (Fig. 12.2) is very similar to that already described for the deaths. Belfast, south Armagh, the Dungannon area, the Fermanagh Border and Londonderry are again prominent. Once again, the isolated wards experiencing a high level of bombing mark the smaller towns such as Coleraine, Ballymena, Portadown-Lurgan, Armagh, Enniskillen, Omagh, Strabane, Cookstown and Bangor. The higher incidence in Border areas noted earlier now stretches further along the Border in County Tyrone as well as Fermanagh. There are also high levels to the west of Lough Neagh and adjacent to the road from Dungannon to Omagh via Pomeroy.

Although most of Northern Ireland has been free of violent death, the bombing campaigns have been much more widespread. Only a few areas, chiefly in the centre of County Down and in the north of County Antrim, have escaped completely. Generally, however, the incidence of explosions is lowest in the areas with the lowest levels of deaths.

This discussion of the spatial patterns of violence has been based on the absolute levels of deaths and explosions. The high violence areas have been identified as such on the basis of the actual numbers of in-cidents in these areas regardless of their total population. It is the usual practice in geography to convert such values to rates (the ratio of persons affected to the total persons at risk), to correct for areal dif-ferences in population size. Two earlier geographical studies of the violence, both confined to deaths (Schellenberg, 1977; Mitchell, 1979), converted their figures to rates for some analyses. Many commentators on the "troubles" have used rates to emphasise either the relatively high incidence of violent death in Northern Ireland in comparison with Great Britain or the low incidence by urban United States standards.

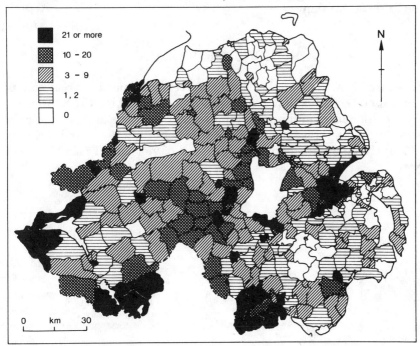

FIGURE 12.2. The Distribution of Bomb Explosions, Northern Ireland, 1969–1977.

This approach was rejected in the present study on two grounds. First, there are practical problems regarding the appropriate "population" to be used. For deaths, the total number of persons in a given area is irrelevant when a quarter of all victims are members of the security forces. One would require to calculate a separate rate for these deaths based on the average number of such personnel in the area at any time; this figure is unobtainable for any spatial unit smaller than Northern Ireland. Explosions present an even greater challenge since one would need information on all the potential targets of a given type in the area. (What is the "at risk" population for landmines—all culverts?) Even if such operational difficulties could be overcome, a more pertinent objection remains. Politicians, the mass media, and the general public do not think of violence in terms of rates. Violent events acquire social and political significance in terms of the actual numbers involved; the only rates that attract attention are the temporal. Since this study is concerned with violence as a social phenomenon it would seem more appropriate to adopt this definition of seriousness for its social meaning.

REGIONS OF VIOLENCE

It seems, then, that at the Northern Ireland scale five areas can be recognised which exhibit high levels of violence (Fig. 12.3). Allowing for the differences in the spatial units employed these are essentially the same areas as those identified by Schellenberg (1977) and Mitchell (1979). In approximate order of the level of violence (Table 12.6) they are:

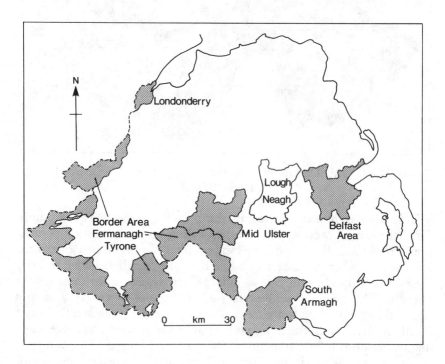

FIGURE 12.3. Areas with High Levels of Violence, Northern Ireland, 1969–1977.

TABLE 12.6 Incidents by Violence Area.

Area	Deaths		Explosions	
	(No.)	(%)	(No.)	(%)
Belfast	1068	59	2291	41
South Armagh	145	8	442	8
Londonderry	143	8	692	12
Border area in Fermanagh-Tyrone	76	4	520	9
Mid-Ulster	70	4	243	4
Remainder	296	16	1402	25
Total	1798	100	5590	100

(i) Belfast[1]—the main urban centre in Northern Ireland. The area of high violence includes much of the suburbs except those on the east of the city.

(ii) South Armagh—this area stretches from the town of Newry (actually in County Down) south-west to the Irish Border. It includes the village of Crossmaglen. This is a rural area of rolling hills, scrubland, small streams and winding roads.

(iii) Londonderry—Northern Ireland's second largest city, with a Roman Catholic majority. A city of particular symbolic value to Loyalists.

(iv) Border area in Fermanagh-Tyrone—the strip of country along the Border with the Irish Republic, running from the vicinity of Keady to Strabane. Most of this region lies in County Fermanagh. Like south Armagh it is predominantly rural and hilly.

(v) Mid-Ulster—another mainly rural area centred on the towns of Dungannon and Coalisland. This is a somewhat more prosperous, less hilly region than south Armagh and the Border.

At the risk of a certain degree of over-simplification, for the remainder of this chapter these five areas will be treated as three regions of violence: Belfast, Londonderry, and the Border (comprising the other three areas above). Although there are some variations within the Border region in the patterns of violence, the areas which constitute it are all adjacent to the international boundary between the Republic of Ireland and the United Kingdom, or within a few miles of it, and are predominantly rural in character.

The aim of this stage in the analysis is to examine and compare the characteristics of the violent incidents in the different regions. To do this, the deaths and explosions have each been re-classified into categories that seem to correspond broadly to the main forms of violence. Each explosion has been classified into one of three categories according to the type of target:

(i) Classical guerilla warfare—attacks on the security forces, on central and local government personnel and installations, and on the infrastructure of the state (public transport, utilities, communications, etc.).

(ii) Economic guerilla warfare—attacks on economic targets: commercial and office buildings, industrial premises.

(iii) Sectarian conflict—attacks on private houses, schools, public halls, clubs, any other building or location identified with one ethnic group.

This scheme is based entirely on the characteristics of the target itself and does not take any other factors into account, because in most cases there is no further information readily accessible. Thus, the classification of a particular incident may not reflect the perpetrators' motives. For example, many attacks on commercial or industrial premises have been claimed by the P.I.R.A. as attacks on the "British war machine"; on the other hand, the majority of premises are owned by Protestants and the motives may have been primarily sectarian. Without further information for all, or even most incidents, however, the present approach appears the least biased. Moreover, even if the motives are the same, the spatial distribution and the consequences will tend to vary with the type of target. Bombing a man's shop is a different act from bombing his home; it will affect more people, cost the state more in compensation, and probably occur in a different place.

The deaths, too, have been re-classified into three main categories according to the circumstances:

(i) Sectarian deaths—all civilians (including paramilitaries) killed at home, at work, in a place of leisure, in the street, or a "Found Body". The common feature of most of these deaths is that they appear to reflect a deliberate decision to kill a particular person, or, at least, persons of a particular ethnic group.

(ii) Security force deaths—all members of the security forces (regular army, R.U.C. and U.D.R.) killed on or off duty. The R.U.C./U.D.R. have been tabulated separately from the regular army.

(iii) Incidents—all civilians (including paramilitaries) who were shot by the security forces or killed by the premature explosion of their own bomb. As mentioned above, it seems that only a minority of persons shot by the army were engaged in paramilitary activities; nevertheless they have been included with the "own bomb" cases since both groups can be construed as incidents arising mainly from the conflict between the I.R.A. and the forces of the Crown.

TABLE 12.7. Categories of Explosions by Violence Region.[a]

Region		Classical		Economic		Sectarian		Total	
		(No.)	(%)	(No.)	(%)	(No.)	(%)	(No.)	(%)
Belfast	Number	406	23	1150	48	684	51	2240	41
	Percentage		18		51		31		100
Londonderry	Number	205	12	387	16	86	6	678	12
	Percentage		30		57		13		100
Border	Number	652	38	356	15	192	14	1200	22
	Percentage		54		30		16		100
Remainder	Number	472	27	503	21	377	28	1352	25
	Percentage		35		37		28		100
Total	Number	1735		2396		1339		5470	100
	Percentage		32		44		24		100

[a] The number of explosions recorded in this table is less than the total number recorded in Table 12.6. This is because some explosions could not be categorised according to the threefold scheme used here.

TABLE 12.8. Categories of Deaths by Violence Region.

Region		Sectarian (No.)	(%)	R.U.C./U.D.R. (No.)	(%)	Army (No.)	(%)	Incidents (No.)	(%)	Other (No.)	(%)	Total (No.)	(%)
Belfast	Number	600	71	46	25	123	45	132	53	167	68	1068	59
	Percentage		56		4		12		12		16		100
Londonderry	Number	29	3	18	10	50	18	36	14	10	4	143	8
	Percentage		20		13		35		25		7		100
Border	Number	92	11	54	29	78	28	43	17	24	10	291	16
	Percentage		32		19		27		15		8		100
Remainder	Number	123	15	67	36	25	9	38	15	43	18	296	16
	Percentage		42		23		8		13		15		100
Total	Number	844	100	185	100	276	100	249	100	244	100	1798	100
	Percentage		47		10		15		14		14		100

(iv) All other deaths—most cases in this category are of people who died in circumstances where there was apparently no intention to kill them. They include people caught in crossfire, in explosions of booby-traps or landmines probably intended for the security forces, or in bomb attacks on business premises.

These general categories, for both the explosions and the deaths, have been adopted in an attempt to reflect the main features of the violence in Northern Ireland since 1969. In the limited space available here it is not possible to examine in detail the processes behind that violence. For present purposes we will simply advance the argument that there have been three strands in the current conflict:

(i) The guerilla war waged between the I.R.A. and the security forces.

(ii) The "economic campaign" of the I.R.A. against commercial and industrial targets.

(iii) The sectarian conflict between Catholics and Protestants.

The variations within and between the three violence regions and the remainder of Northern Ireland for the categories of explosions and deaths are shown in Tables 12.7 and 12.8 respectively. Thus it can be seen that in Belfast the incidence of explosions directed against "classical" targets is less than expected (in relation to the overall incidence), while that of "economic" and "sectarian" targets is greater than expected; similarly there have been fewer security force deaths but more "sectarian" killings. In Londonderry, however, there has been a low level of "sectarian" incidents, both explosions and deaths, but a high proportion of security force deaths. The final region, the Border, exhibits a different pattern of violence from the two urban regions. In respect of the explosions the incidence of "classical" explosions is particularly high whereas that for "sectarian" targets is lower than expected; correspondingly, security force deaths are high, "sectarian" killings are low.

INTERPRETATION

This chapter has demonstrated that within Northern Ireland there have been significant spatial variations, of intensity and form, in the commission of acts of violence. Before attempting to account for these variations, however, we must tackle the problem of interpretation, that is, of assigning meanings to the events enumerated in the previous figures and tables. The various acts of violence are the manifestations of different underlying processes and it is the operations of these processes which presumably give rise to the spatial patterns of violence. Unfortunately, the lack of information on specific incidents makes it difficult to match events to processes and the task of inference is compounded by the complexity of groups and motives amongst the civilians. On the Republican side there are the Official Irish Republican Army (O.I.R.A.) and the Provisional Irish Republican Army (P.I.R.A.). There are also two major paramilitary groups amongst the Loyalists: the Ulster Defence Association (U.D.A.) and the Ulster Volunteer Force (U.V.F.).

The paramilitary groups mainly direct their actions outwards. Republicans attack Protestant, security force, and "establishment" targets; Loyalists attack Catholic targets (and, sometimes, the security forces). Republicans and Loyalists rarely attack their paramilitary opponents; their targets are almost always innocent civilians or their property. The activities of the security forces have been mainly directed against Republicans since the threat to the state has come from that direction but they have also taken firm and effective action against Loyalists. Within both the Republican and Loyalist groupings, however, the various organisations have also engaged in feuds with each other. These feuds are usually confined to Belfast where the two wings of the I.R.A. have fought, and the U.D.A. and U.V.F. have feuded. Other violence is the result of groups taking disciplinary action against their own members or civilians in their areas who have violated their rules.

Finally, a certain amount of the violence does not reflect the plans of these groups. Some reflects planning gone astray because of inadequate intelligence, bad luck, or incompetence; bombs have gone off prematurely, the wrong target has been attacked. Some of the violence in Northern Ireland has undoubtedly been undertaken from motives of individual gain alone. With the information currently available, however, the researcher cannot separate such incidents from the organised violence or, overall, accurately identify the persons or groups responsible for the different acts of violence and their motives.

While remaining aware of these difficulties, however, we intend to proceed on the assumption that the system of categorisation adopted in the tables above provides a reasonably adequate approximation to the main processes involved in the present disturbances. Thus the level of explosions directed at "classical" targets and of deaths of the security forces and of civilians killed in "incidents" indicates the intensity of the guerilla war, while explosions at "sectarian" targets and the deaths of civilians in "sectarian" circumstances provide measures of the level of sectarian violence. The final category, "economic" explosions, presents the greatest problems of interpretation. Some of these were undoubtedly sectarian in motive and there may be a spatial bias in this respect. In rural and small town situations, where ownership is likely to be individual rather than corporate, the majority of attacks on commercial premises may be sectarian.

Obviously there can be other interpretations, and hence categorisations, of the events discussed here. Some observers would argue that because of the identification of government within Northern Ireland with the Loyalist cause, attacks on local government buildings or officials, and particularly against the R.U.C. and U.D.R. (with their overwhelmingly Protestant membership), should be regarded as primarily sectarian. While it is no doubt true that the Loyalist community will react more vigorously to an attack on the R.U.C. or U.D.R. than to one on the army, it does not follow that the killings were sectarian in the sense used here, i.e. that the primary basis for victim selection was their ethnicity rather than some other attribute. It seems more likely, as McKeown (1977) has argued, that they were killed "because of the uniform they wore". Nevertheless, the R.U.C. and U.D.R. fatalities have been tabulated separately so that readers can draw their own conclusions.

Proceeding, then, on the assumptions and interpretations outlined above, the figures in Tables 12.7 and 12.8 suggest that for all three facets of the violence—the guerilla war, the economic campaign, and the sectarian conflict—most incidents have occurred in Belfast; this is in marked contrast to the I.R.A. guerilla campaign of 1956–1962 which avoided Belfast altogether in favour of the Border areas (Bowyer Bell, 1970). Moreover, most of the violence in Belfast has been of a "sectarian" nature. In Londonderry, however, there has been a relatively low level of "sectarian" violence. Most of the violence here has been related to the guerilla war and the economic campaign; deaths associated with guerilla warfare make up a higher proportion of the deaths in Londonderry than in any other region. The guerilla war also dominates the violent incidents in the Border region; the south Armagh area in particular has the highest incidence of security force deaths in Northern Ireland. Another feature of the violence in this Border region is that it is the only region in which Protestant victims of sectarian violence equal Catholics; elsewhere Roman Catholics outnumber Protestants.

EXPLANATION

The data presented here, and the interpretations made of them, pose many questions. In this chapter, however, we will only attempt to answer two: why has most of the violence occurred in Belfast, Londonderry and the Border region? Why have there been differences between these regions in the nature of that violence? At present, because of inadequacies in the data and the lack of other information, these questions cannot be properly answered here. Perhaps all we can say with any certainty is that the explanations will probably be complex. There are, nonetheless, indications as to the forms that the answers might take and to the factors that will need to be incorporated. Providing evidence for their action in particular areas, however, is rarely possible.

Since most of the violence is attributable to the P.I.R.A., whose support is drawn from the Roman Catholic community, and Catholics figure disproportionately amongst the casualties, the ethnic composition of an area might affect its level of violence. Schellenberg (1977), using a coarser system of only sixty-five areas, found in his study of violence that the number of deaths was highly positively correlated with proportion Roman Catholic. A comparison of Figs 12.1 and 12.2 with Fig. 4.2 (Chapter 4) shows that in fact the spatial correspondence between ethnicity and violence is not strong. Although Roman Catholics are in a majority in most of the Border region and in Londonderry, there are many other parts of Northern Ireland where they are equally predominant which exhibit low levels of violence. Conversely, however, areas with large Protestant majorities generally have the lowest levels of violence. In Belfast, the most violent region, Roman Catholics are in a minority overall but, because of residential segregation, are a majority in certain areas; these tend to be the areas with the most violence. Again, there has been relatively little violence in Protestant areas. It would appear, therefore, that a Catholic majority in an area (or within easy travelling distance) is a necessary condition for violence, particularly in the context of a guerilla war: as Mao Tse-Tung pointed out, the successful guerilla must be able to move amongst the people like a fish in water. It is not, however, a sufficient condition. Additional factors must be present to inhibit violence in some Catholic areas, or facilitate it in others.

One such element is the presence of historical precedents. Stewart (1977) has demonstrated that south Armagh has been an area of violent resistance to British authority for over a century. Many of the areas along the Border which today have high levels of violence, mainly directed against the Government, are the same areas which refused to recognise Northern Ireland in 1920–1921 (c.f. Chapter 5) and in which British soldiers had to force I.R.A. units from villages they had occupied. When the I.R.A. launched its 1956 campaign it expected to establish "liberated zones" in the south-west with the support of the local Roman Catholics (Bowyer Bell, 1970). In Belfast the violence of today, with its marked sectarian overtones, may simply reflect the continuation of a conflict originally engendered early in the nineteenth century by competition for jobs; the traditional hostility persists to be harnessed to changing slogans (Boyd, 1970; Budge and O'Leary, 1973). Even the main locations for sectarian clashes have remained remarkably constant since the riots of the last century (Boal and Murray, 1977). This historical factor is important because before people will resort to social violence there must be present an ideology of violence, a set of beliefs and values which sanction violence as legitimate, even praiseworthy, behaviour for certain purposes. A tradition of the use of violence, which is common to both ethnic groups in Northern Ireland, can provide a potent source for such an ideology. To be most effective this ideology must be shared by the majority of the community.

Public support is vital. Although a guerilla campaign may be possible without the active support of the majority of even one's own people it cannot survive their active hostility. Thus, unless their opponents commit acts which are even more objectionable, a group is constrained by what its potential supporters regard as acceptable. Burton (1978), in an analysis of the sources of the P.I.R.A.'s legitimacy in the Roman Catholic community, describes how it is seen as performing essentially a defensive role against the Loyalists or the security forces. When it exceeds this role and engages in offensive actions, particularly those leading to retaliation against Catholics, or activities which are not obviously related to a military role, it alienates many members of the community. As we have seen, very few of the victims of violence have been women or young children (Table 12.3) and most of these have been killed inadvertently; the majority of the civilian dead have been men of military age (although most have had no paramilitary connections). Even in a civil war there are some deaths which even one's own supporters will not condone.

A third necessary condition is the existence of social divisions; members of an integrated society do not make war on one another. Such a division clearly exists in Northern Ireland society. The double minority model (Chapter 1) implies that within Northern Ireland a group's position on the integration–division continuum will depend not only on their relative numbers in an area but also on the location of that area. Thus the Roman Catholics who will be most opposed to the Partition of Ireland will be those most aware of being in a majority in the island. Other things being equal we would expect that they would be those living in predominantly Catholic areas along the Border since their awareness will be reinforced by their frequent cross-Border contacts. Roman Catholics living in rural areas in the east, on the other hand, may be in a local majority in some areas but be less conscious of being members of an island majority because of their lack of direct links with the Irish Republic. A second source of a sense of division is spatial division; social segregation is reinforced by residential segregation (Boal, 1969). The degree of segregation, at least in urban areas, seems to vary spatially in a manner generally consistent with the observed pattern of violence.

To these three necessary conditions—a Roman Catholic majority, a tradition of violence, a high degree of social division—must be added a fourth factor, an environment which facilitates the expression of violence. Such an area will have two attributes: it will contain a relatively large number of potential targets, people or buildings, and the terrain, natural or built, will provide cover and the means of escape from pursuit. The Border region illustrates this last point. The rugged terrain aids concealment and the nearby territory of the Irish Republic offers a relatively secure base. In cities the high density of buildings, the large populations, and the existence of highly segregated areas combine to furnish the urban guerilla with a secure environment that also provides many opportunities for violence.

The importance of spatial variations in potential targets is demonstrated by the bombing campaigns (Tables 12.5 and 12.7). Only in Belfast and Londonderry were most explosions aimed at "economic" targets. These are Northern Ireland's only important cities and hence contain a greater quantity and quality (in the sense of value, importance, and publicity) of such targets. Conversely, "classical" targets— such as the security forces, government buildings, or public utilities— will tend to be more plentiful (this applies particularly to the last group) or easier to attack, or both, in mainly rural areas. To take one example, of the 433 explosions involving central or local government premises 131 (30%) were directed at customs posts along the Border. Moreover, although there are a large number of official buildings in Belfast and Londonderry they are often the most important of their type and hence the best protected. It seems likely, although we have no evidence, that the factor of scale is also a partial explanation for the high level of "sectarian" bombings in Belfast, the largest group within this category being attacks on public houses or clubs. Because in absolute terms residential segregation is on a greater scale in Belfast, premises of this kind which are exclusively Protestant or Roman Catholic are more common there than elsewhere.

To sum up then, it is argued that a high level of violence, particularly of violence arising from the conflict between the Government and the I.R.A., in an area depends on four factors: a majority of Roman Catholics in the population; a history of political violence in the area; a high degree of alienation, social and political, of the Catholic population from Protestant society; an environment which provides the guerilla with both targets and security. Moreover, all four must be present together before a high incidence of violence occurs. In fact, because the processes generating, and generated by, the first three factors tend to be mutually reinforcing these factors will occur together in any case. As far as high levels of sectarian violence are concerned one change needs to be made to this set of necessary conditions. Instead of a Catholic majority the area now requires a Protestant majority but not an overwhelming one; because of its size the Belfast Urban Area contains Roman Catholic and Protestant majority areas and thus exhibits high levels of both anti-Government and sectarian violence.

CONCLUSION

The deaths and the injuries, and the physical damage caused by the explosions, are not the only consequences of the years of violence. Some of the social, psychological, and economic effects have been discussed elsewhere (e.g. Lyons, 1971; Fraser, 1973; Darby and Williamson, 1978; Compton *et al.*, 1980). In the context of the present book, however, we are concerned with the possible effects of the violence on integration or division. In the spatial sense there is no doubt that in some parts of Northern Ireland, notably in Belfast and Londonderry, violence has led to increased residential segregation (Darby and Morris, 1974; Boal *et al.*, 1976). In the social and political spheres violence seems to have had both integrative and divisive effects. It seems unlikely that many people will change their beliefs or values in response to attacks on them or on other members of their own ethnic group. More probably such attacks will tend to strengthen a group's sense of solidarity. In that respect, therefore, violence probably serves only to harden attitudes and to reinforce the divisive trends in Northern Ireland. It seems more likely to bring about a reconstruction of ideologies amongst the same ethnic group as its perpetrators. Violence demonstrates the consequences of previously held beliefs in a way that makes people acutely aware of the conflict between those beliefs and other values equally deeply held. If one's political beliefs seem to lead inevitably to violence as a means of realising them then perhaps it is time to change the beliefs and adopt a new goal.

ACKNOWLEDGEMENTS

I should like to thank Mr W. McGookin, R.U.C. Press and Information Office, for supplying the raw data; Mr I. Alexander, Geography Department, Queen's University, Belfast, who drew the maps; and, above all, Miss J. Orr of the Geography Department who bore the brunt of the data coding.

NOTE

1. The Belfast "violence area", composed of the city and a number of contiguous wards, is not the same areal unit as the Belfast Urban Area, the latter being the area employed in Tables 12.1–12.5. The Belfast "violence area" excludes the eastern suburbs of the Belfast Urban Area but is more extensive to the north-west than the latter.

REFERENCES

Boal, F. W. (1969). Territoriality on the Shankill-Falls Divide. *Irish Geography* **6**, 30–50.
Boal, F. W. and Murray, R. C. (1977). A City in Conflict. *Geographical Magazine* **49**, 364–371.
Boal, F. W., Murray, R. C. and Poole, M. A. (1976). Belfast: The Urban Encapsulation of a National Conflict. *In* "Urban Ethnic Conflict: A Comparative Perspective" (S. E. Clarke and J. L. Obler, eds.), pp. 77–131. Comparative Urban Studies Monograph No. 3, Institute for Research in Social Science, University of North Carolina, Chapel Hill.
Bowyer Bell, J. (1970). "The Secret Army." Anthony Blond, London.
Boyd, A. (1970). "Holy War in Belfast." Anvil Press, Tralee.
Budge, I. and O'Leary, C. (1973). "Belfast—Approach to Crisis: A Study of Belfast Politics, 1613–1970." Macmillan, London.
Burton, F. (1978). "The Politics of Legitimacy." Routledge and Kegan Paul, London.
Cameron, Lord (1969). "Disturbances in Northern Ireland: Report of the Commission Appointed by the Governor of Northern Ireland" (Cmd. 532). Her Majesty's Stationery Office, Belfast.

Compton, P. A. (1978). "Northern Ireland: A Census Atlas." Gill and Macmillan, Dublin.

Compton, P. A., Murray, R. and Osborne, R. D. (1980). Conflict and its Impact on the Urban Environment of Northern Ireland. *Studies in Geography in Hungary* **15**, 83–98.

Darby, J. and Morris, G. (1974). "Intimidation in Housing." Northern Ireland Community Relations Commission, Belfast.

Darby, J. and Williamson, A., eds. (1978). "Violence and the Social Services in Northern Ireland." Heinemann, London.

Fraser, R. M. (1973). "Children in Conflict." Secker and Warburg, London.

Kirk, W. (1978). The Road from Mandalay: Towards a Geographical Philosophy. *Institute of British Geographers, Transactions* **3** (New Series), 381–394.

Lyons, H. A. (1971). Psychiatric Sequelae of the Belfast Riots. *British Journal of Psychiatry* **118**, 265.

McKeown, M. (1977). Considerations on the Statistics of Violence. *Fortnight* **151**, 4–5.

Mitchell, J. K. (1979). Social Violence in Northern Ireland. *Geographical Review* **69**, 179–201.

Scarman, Hon. Mr. Justice (1972). "Violence and Civil Disturbance in Northern Ireland in 1969: Report of the Tribunal of Inquiry" (Cmd. 566). Her Majesty's Stationery Office, Belfast.

Schellenberg, J. A. (1977). Area Variations of Violence in Northern Ireland. *Sociological Focus* **10**, 69–78.

Stewart, A. T. Q. (1977). "The Narrow Ground." Faber and Faber, London.

Sunday Times Insight Team (1972). "Ulster." Deutsch, London.

CHAPTER 13

OVERVIEW

Frederick W. Boal and J. Neville H. Douglas

THE INTERWEAVE

As our contributors show, the varied aspects of integration and division in Northern Ireland are reflected in the time-polished facets of everyday life. Time and the ever-present sense of history are crucial—they provide the cultural context referred to constantly and relied upon as the touchstone for contemporary behaviour.

The Plantation of Ulster holds a central place in this history; it provided the framework for the subsequent interweave of Protestant and Roman Catholic. Although incoming Planters caused displacement of population, the many Gaels who remained or were brought on to Plantation estates ensured that an intricately complicated interwoven pattern of settlement and cultural diversity would emerge. Northern Ireland's varied physical geography added to the intricacies of the weave. Poorer hill land and ill-drained lowland offered fewer attractions to the Planter and remained strong Gaelic areas. Since lowland and upland—good land and poorer land—are seldom far apart in Northern Ireland, the evolving mesh of Planter and Gael was reinforced and further complicated. As Philip Robinson shows in Chapter 2, this complicated pattern of settlement woven in the seventeenth century remained relatively unchanged into the twentieth.

The nineteenth century did witness the addition of one major strand to the pattern. This took place as industrialisation affected the towns of Northern Ireland. Previously the urban centres had been overwhelmingly Protestant, but large-scale population movement off the land gave them a new Catholic component. Rapid urban growth, particularly in Belfast, was generally paralleled by the emergence of distinct districts of Roman Catholic settlement. Again, the stability of these patterns is worthy of note for, as Mike Poole shows in Chapter

333

11, the urban residential segregation of the 1970s had its origin in the selective, community-based urbanisation of the nineteenth century.

The delimitation of the international boundary in 1921—the Border, as it is described in Ireland—was undertaken to separate two groups who, because of divergent national aspirations, could no longer live together. Yet, as a separator, the Border had only limited success. The close interweave of Catholic and Protestant settlement inevitably meant that the Border encapsulated within the new political unit of Northern Ireland two substantial communities whose ensuing relations have been conditioned, not simply by their contrasting aspirations, but also by the complex intermingling and settlement spacing of their members.

In this new political framework, with a new majority (the Protestants) and a new, yet significant, minority (the Roman Catholics), the concepts of territoriality and dominance–subordination behaviour can be used to aid understanding of emerging inter-group relations. Sommer (1969, p. 12) suggests that the processes involved in these concepts are used by communities to build security and limit aggression. An individual either refrains from going where he is likely to be involved in disputes or, based on his knowledge of who is above or below him, engages in ritualised dominance–subordination behaviour rather than in actual combat. With the failure of Partition to separate Protestant and Catholic effectively, it was perhaps inevitable that group relations became structured along these lines. Interestingly, the territoriality/dominance alternatives were posed as early as 1901 by the Irish Catholic journalist D. P. Moran. He wrote: ". . . the only thinkable solution of the Irish national problem is that one side gets on top and absorbs the other until we have one nation, or that each develops independently" (Hepburn, 1980, p. 64).

Within the territorial frame of Northern Ireland, avoidance of dominance at the local level became important and, to a degree, possible through territorial escape. By retreating into community territory in town or country, an individual could become a member of the locally dominant group, relatively secure and less directly subject to alien dominance pressure. As Bob Osborne points out in Chapter 6, avoidance of subordination took shape rapidly in relation to electoral behaviour within the new state. Each group recognised and established the electoral territory it could dominate and then avoided intervention beyond this territory where electoral defeat (subordination) would have been the certain outcome.

ETHNICITY AND NATIONALISM

While the concepts of territoriality and dominance–subordination are an aid to the student of group relations in Northern Ireland, the extent to which they have been applied by each group in everyday life is an even more striking indication of the degree of group divergence. Territorial security, dominance and avoidance of subordination become vitally important to groups when central values and longed-for aspirations are involved—such is the case in Northern Ireland. However, attempts to dominate, stubborn avoidance and territorial retreat all produce a reaction and in Northern Ireland the plural society (see Chapter 1), already in existence before Partition, found reason for further and more deep-seated division.

Precisely how plural the society is remains the fundamental question, as the degree of plurality can influence not just the effective functioning of the state but its very existence. Pluralism which does not involve a clash of separate national identities and aspirations can, with statesmanship, usually be solved within the existing state framework. However, when a plural society involves opposing national aspirations within the same state a permanent solution to social conflict can rarely be found. The contributions to this book demonstrate clearly the existence of a wide range and variety of plural elements present in Northern Ireland. How deep and how significant are these plural traits?

Reviewing the literature on the nature of ethnic groups, Donnan (1980) indicates that the members of each group should share certain cultural values and a common past, that the group should be self-reproductive, that it should have a network of internal contacts and that the members should self-identify and be identified by others as distinctive. Overall, Donnan concludes that Roman Catholics and Protestants in Northern Ireland do form two ethnic groups. Ronnie Buchanan, in Chapter 3, demonstrates that, historically, differences in material culture between Planter and Gael were not as great as some have suggested. Equally, however, he points out that differences of a non-material kind became, with time, particularly powerful differentiators.

Ethnic differentiation may go beyond questions of relations within an existing state to questions of political separation. Lieberson (1972, p. 200) suggests that nationalism is essentially an ethnic movement in which the distinctive characteristics of a "people" are emphasised and praised, and where the true and full expression of their unique national qualities requires recognition in a separate and sovereign political

territory, i.e. a state. In Ireland, ethnicity became the basis of nationalism, and the processes of ethnic elaboration became part of the processes of nation-building. For instance, the promotion of Gaelic games
and the regeneration of the Irish language as elements of the Celtic
revival were part of nation-building for the Irish Catholic nation. This,
however, also widened the perceived differences between Protestant
and Roman Catholic, contributed to the sense of ethnic difference
on the part of Protestants and in time fed into the process of nation-
building amongst Protestants in north-east Ireland.

The Irish nationalist movement, seeking separation from the United
Kingdom, developed because the people of Catholic Ireland did not
feel themselves to be British and wanted to set up an independent
state in which Gaelic and Catholic culture could be secured. In
addition, political independence required a degree of economic
independence, and such economic independence was not seen as
conflicting with the existing economic interests of much of Ireland.
The Protestants of north-east Ireland, on the other hand, did not
want to be Gaelic or Catholic but wanted to be British. Their economic
interests, related to the large-scale industrialisation of the Belfast
area during the nineteenth century, also pointed in the same direction.
Partition was the only possible democratic solution to the problem
(Boal, 1980), and is one that has emerged frequently with the wind-
down of the British Empire—for instance Palestine, the Indian sub-
continent, Cyprus and (unsuccessfully) Nigeria.

As is so frequently the case, however, those who most loudly demand
self-determination for themselves tend to be equally strong in denying
such a right to others. This was certainly the outcome in Ireland, where
Catholic nationalists attempted to deny the Protestants of the north-
east of the island the right of self-determination, whilst the Protestants,
in turn, showed little concern for the right of self-determination for
those Irish Catholics who were encapsulated within Northern Ireland.

Protestant nationalism, as a mechanism of group self-interest, causes
confusion to some observers. They fail to recognise it as a fallback
position. The Protestant community did not seek a national territory
separate from all others, but rather the maintenance of integration with
the United Kingdom system. As Heslinga (1962, p. 62) viewed the
question, the fulfilment of the "Ulster" nation was not sought by the
attainment of political independence but by the maintenance of the
constitutional link with the British Crown. The Protestant community
in north-east Ireland, at the beginning of the twentieth century, placed
this link, and not the provision of a local parliament in Belfast, as its
top priority. Whyte (1978, p. 263) has objected to the treatment of the

two "nations" in Ireland as equals. He claims that the "two nations theory" makes no allowance for the possibility that there may be degrees of nationhood where the "mainstream, predominantly Catholic Irish nation ranks high . . . On the same scale the Protestant or Unionist nation ranks much lower". In the conflict over nationalism in Ireland, this is precisely the situation one would expect to find. The Irish Catholic nation was seeking separation and, to achieve this, difference from the predominant "British" nation had to be emphasised and indeed promoted. The Ulster Protestant nation, on the other hand, while wishing to be distinguished from the Irish Catholic nation, had no interest in emphasising differences from the other groups (the English, the Scots and the Welsh) that comprised the United Kingdom. We can support Boserup (1972, p. 180) when he says that "Northern Irish nationalism is no new phenomenon, but it has not been clearly visible hereto because it took the form of Unionism as long as the union with Britain was the best safeguard for Northern Ireland's independence from the South".

Within Northern Ireland aspects of pluralism built upon ethnicity and formulated in terms of nationality endlessly emerge. To quote Anders Boserup again, "one could liken the society of Ulster to a crystal: whichever the strains acting upon it or within, it always breaks in much the same way" (1972, p. 161). The strength of this cleavage is highlighted by Bob Osborne in Chapter 6 when he demonstrates that even among the "middle ground" electors who give their first preference vote to the Alliance Party, which supports a power-sharing structure for Northern Ireland, second preferences break down along the Protestant–Roman Catholic divide—Protestants for political integration within the United Kingdom, Catholics for a politically united Ireland.

GROUP RELATIONS

Clearly, group relations in Northern Ireland exist in a most difficult milieu—a milieu characterised by territorial segregation in which dominance and avoidance of subordination behaviours are employed to preserve and, indeed, strengthen the central ethnic values and national aspirations of each group. In this context group relations creating discord can be expected to prevail, pushing the plural society towards the division end of the integration–division continuum (Chapter 1). Yet, as the preceding chapters show, group relations take many forms, varying in time and place. The diversity of these relations can now be considered.

Group relations can be characterised in a number of ways. The first way is where avoidance is the most marked feature; the second, where conflict of a non-violent kind is predominant; the third, where violent conflict is the central theme and the fourth, where group relations are characterised by integrative processes or, at least, by processes that constrain the deepening of division.

Avoidance

Upon the establishment of Northern Ireland as a distinct political unit in 1920, significant elements of the Roman Catholic minority "opted out" of the new state. This occurred in two ways—first, local councils with Irish nationalist majorities refused to recognise the authority of the new government (see Chapter 5), and secondly, at the level of the Northern Ireland Parliament, Irish nationalists either refused to stand for election or would not take their seats when elected. The actions by the local councils could be considered a virtual declaration of independence from Northern Ireland, while abstention not only signalled non-recognition but also an assessment which suggested that it was not worthwhile becoming involved since the Northern Ireland state was likely to collapse in a short time.

It was quite impossible for any state worthy of the name to tolerate the behaviour of the dissident local councils. They were thus taken over and run by Commissioners appointed by the government. Subsequent to the abolition of proportional representation in 1923, when local government electoral boundaries came up for review, the re-arrangements proposed by Unionists were accepted, these not unnaturally being to their advantage; the local nationalists made hardly any proposals since they were boycotting Northern Ireland institutions at the time.

Given the distribution of the Roman Catholic population, the geography of opt-out and boycott was particularly marked on the Border periphery of Northern Ireland. This periphery emerged as a zone where Unionist candidates at Stormont elections rarely intervened electorally (see Chapter 6). It also became a zone of considerable violence, this characteristic being dramatically manifested in the 1970s, as Russell Murray's data clearly show (Chapter 12). The opt-out periphery provided an enormous irritant to inter-group relations within Northern Ireland—it still does.

The process of avoidance can also be seen in the maintenance and, indeed, further development of residential segregation, particularly in the urban areas. Since this segregation is also, at least in part, a response to violence or the fear of violence, it will be discussed in a later section.

Although the boycott of elections and of local and regional government disappeared in the 1930s and abstention by elected representatives declined in use as a symbolic weapon, other methods of community avoidance evolved. Evidence of this is given by the variety of voluntary and self-help organisations which drew support from and worked within the Roman Catholic community. These organisations permitted that community to avoid giving, at least in some degree, recognition to the state and to avoid complete dependence upon a government which it did not trust. Organisations such as St. Vincent de Paul, concerned with charity and social work centred on the Church and with Church advocacy, could expect regular financial contributions from Church members for their work in the Catholic community. The development of a separate school system, although eventually funded mainly by the state, avoided handing over the young to the state system of education and instead focussed educational activity upon the Church. Other self-help organisations concerned, for example, with the co-operative provision of houses or with the development of industry, such as the Tyrone Crystal factory at Dungannon, helped to spread a range of activities within the Catholic community which emphasised group distinctiveness and encouraged avoidance of contact with and dependence upon the majority community and the government (Griffiths, 1978).

Conflicting Non-Violent Relationships

Protestants and Roman Catholics come into non-violent conflict through the operation of various processes in the demographic, economic and political spheres. Indeed the three spheres are not separate entities but impinge on each other, usually in ways which exacerbate conflict.

Demographic differentials between Roman Catholics and Protestants have contributed significantly to stressful group relations in Northern Ireland. As Paul Compton demonstrates in Chapter 4, higher Roman Catholic fertility and emigration rates have impinged on society in a number of ways. Higher fertility creates the potential for a more rapid increase in the numbers of Roman Catholics than of Protestants. This will have electoral significance in certain local government areas and, more importantly, in Northern Ireland as a whole. Thus Protestants feel threatened demographically while Roman Catholics may calculate on the "revenge of the cradle" as a future prospect. Both situations destabilise group relations.

The higher fertility rate of Roman Catholics is also significant in that it leads potentially to a growth in their relative and absolute demand for housing space, schools and jobs. In a condition of shortage as discussed below, this creates a zero-sum situation—if one group gets more the other gets less. It also leads to what Paul Compton calls accusations of preferential treatment, levelled by Protestants against Roman Catholics, and of discrimination, made by Roman Catholics.

The higher rate of Roman Catholic emigration has contributed significantly to the process whereby higher Catholic fertility has not led to a rapid increase in the Catholic proportion of the total population of Northern Ireland. This higher rate of emigration may be partly generated by the demographic characteristics of the Roman Catholic section of the population itself. Nonetheless, it has been a source of resentment for Catholics and forms another divisive factor in terms of group relations.

A question occurs at this point. Why has the Protestant population not responded reproductively to the challenge of higher Roman Catholic fertility? Possible answers include the fact that higher Catholic emigration has largely removed the Catholic fertility-based potential for population growth. It may also be true that Protestants have not been prepared to trade off possible gains in electoral security against the perceived advantages, in economic terms, of relatively small family size.

One final situation where demography impinges on group relations concerns the absolute size of the Roman Catholic and the Protestant sections of the population. At the scale of urban segregation, Mike Poole demonstrates in Chapter 11 that the most important variable correlating with high levels of segregation is that measuring absolute group size. Specifically, where the minority group in a town (the minority usually being the Roman Catholic) is large, the levels of Protestant–Roman Catholic segregation are high. This may derive from the joint operation of two factors—a large minority group providing for itself the base for a high degree of social self-sufficiency, and such a large minority being perceived as a significant threat to the local majority.

Group size is also important at the level of Northern Ireland as a whole. Roman Catholics are a large minority, creating a situation very close to that observed at the scale of individual towns, with the self-sufficiency/threat complex impinging critically on group relations. A smaller minority would have been less self-sufficient and would have been perceived as less of a threat. The Protestant minority in the Republic of Ireland is a case in point. At something less than 5% of the population they form no kind of threat to the majority and are so small that they suffer problems of self-sufficiency. Indeed, the group is on the verge of complete disappearance, due in particular to exogamous marriage with Roman Catholics, with the Irish Roman Catholic Church exerting strong pressures for the offspring of such marriages to be brought up as Catholics.

The economic environment is a further factor that has negative effects on inter-group relations. Tony Hoare (Chapter 8) refers to Northern Ireland as a problem region with a regional problem. The problem region exists as one where there has been a high level of unemployment. Competition for the jobs that are available operates in what has already been referred to as a zero-sum situation. Milton Esman (1972, pp. 237–238) writes:

> In an atmosphere of pervasive scarcity re-enforced by mutual distrust, the more fundamental motivations of both groups seem to be defensive ... In a culture of poverty they are least likely to look for ways to expand available values and solve problems by an equitable distribution of the increments.

Esman could be writing about Northern Ireland—he is, in fact, writing about Malaysia.

Since 1978, for which Paul Doherty supplies unemployment statistics (Chapter 9), the general economic environment has deteriorated further, with the overall unemployment rate in Northern Ireland having reached 19·0% by November 1981. This is influenced by general economic conditions outside Northern Ireland, but the conditions act with a peculiarly sharp brutality on the local economy. The contraction of regional employment leads us to agree with Don Parson (1980, p. 83) that: "Just as reserve labour 'is the last hired and the first fired' so reserve space [peripheral regions such as Northern Ireland] suffers a similar fate in regard to industrial investment". This introduces elements of further competition between the two ethnic groups in Northern Ireland and adds an additional dimension to the stress on inter-group relations. Paul Doherty goes so far as to suggest that there is a dual economy of core and periphery. The problem undoubtedly is a serious one in its own right. Like so many other things in Northern Ireland, however, it gains in seriousness when it impinges on the community divide. In many countries peripheral areas suffer more severely economically than core areas, but in Northern Ireland the added significance derives from the peripheral areas having higher proportions of Roman Catholics than the core. This has become another element in the whole structure of what Edwards (1970) has called "conspiracy consciousness", in which most resource allocation decisions are viewed as favouring one or other group and in which Catholic–Protestant differentials are frequently interpreted in terms of deliberate discrimination, no matter how complex the actual explanation for the differentials may be. This point is reinforced in Chapter 8, where Tony Hoare demonstrates that Roman Catholic–Protestant differentials in economic opportunity are derived from the interaction of a whole set of factors, only one of which falls under the heading of discriminatory behaviour.

Conflict in group relations, however, has been engendered and sustained most consistently by political behaviour. Each major political event since 1920 seems to have reinforced the cultural cleavages that separate the two communities. Conflict results from group competition, in this case for the most important of all scarce resources—political power and the control it confers. Partition, in essence, created a community of power holders and a community divorced from power— either from its wielding or from the influencing of its use. In addition, the reform of local government electoral areas by the 1923 Local Government (Northern Ireland) Act created strong suspicions that Unionist control at this level was being unfairly strengthened (Chapter 5). Indeed, members of the nationalist community interpreted the reform as a large-scale gerrymander and a unionist plot to deprive them of houses and jobs and to force many either to accept lower status or emigrate.

The suspicion at local political level was mirrored at regional level where, in the years of uninterrupted Unionist Party control from 1921 to 1972, only one opposition-sponsored Bill gained government approval and passed through Parliament. This Bill, which became the Wild Bird Act of 1931, clearly lay beyond the controversial use of power even in Northern Ireland. With its strong power base, the Unionist Government was not required to make concessions and group relations received few integrative stimuli. Divisive relations became so entrenched that reforming political behaviour since 1969, concerned with equal voting rights, equality in housing provision and the establishment of complaints procedures against all forms of discriminatory behaviour, has done little, as yet, to shift the balance towards the integrative end of the continuum.

In such a political environment the problems of demonstrating political activity to be objective and integrative are formidable. In Northern Ireland, conspiracy consciousness, creating suspicion and the search for ulterior motive, pervades both communities and finds

ample scope for activity when, as David Smith (1979, p. 50) observes—
"Every decision to build or invest, whether private or public, is in the
end a locational decision, for what is to be done must be done *somewhere.*
And where it is done . . . where the factory is set up, the motorway
constructed or the hospital built . . . has a bearing on the differentiation
of human life chances". As Bob Osborne and Dale Singleton show in
Chapter 7, every policy choice, however innocuous on the surface,
has communal implications which, when a conspiracy consciousness
predominates, can lead more readily to division than to integration.
It is all too easy to point to public policies and exaggerate the group
disadvantage which may result and then "explain" that disadvantage
strictly in terms of discriminatory behaviour by the group perceived
as being advantaged. Indeed the discrimination "explanation" has been
a useful tool, in the hands of some Irish nationalists, for cultivating
among the Northern Irish Roman Catholic community an antagonism
and militant opposition to the existence of Northern Ireland as a
political unit distinct within the island of Ireland.

In situations of strong competition over scarce economic and political
resources groups attempt to develop concerted organisational responses.
The concepts of territoriality and dominance–subordination behaviour,
already noted in this chapter, are two such responses. Frank Parkin
has drawn on the work of Max Weber to suggest another, although
allied, response. He suggests that a process of social closure is implemented whereby "social collectivities seek to maximise rewards by
restricting access to resources and opportunities to a limited circle of
eligibles . . . Its purpose is always the closure of social and economic
opportunities to outsiders" (1979, p. 144). He further suggests that
closure strategies include not only those of an exclusionary kind (which
relate to dominance behaviour) but also those adopted by the excluded
themselves (which relate to avoidance of dominance) as a direct
response to their status as outsiders, these latter strategies being called
usurpationary. Minority groups are frequently the target for exclusionary closure and may, in response, adopt usurpationary closure strategies.
Exclusionary closure may also be employed in the process of building
a base for usurpation. Both processes can readily be observed in Northern
Ireland, with the ethnic groups (Protestant and Roman Catholic)
being their focus. It might be argued that the greatest gain to the under-
privileged would derive from joint action by both the Protestant and
Roman Catholic sections of the working class. However, and with
direct reference to Northern Ireland, Parkin (1979, p. 95) has observed:

Workers who opt for closure against a minority group can hardly be declared guilty of irrationality in choosing to retain the proven benefits of exclusion in preference to the uncertain or doubtful payoff resulting from combined usurpation . . . It probably always requires considerably less expenditure of political energy to effect exclusionary closure against a visible and vulnerable minority group than to mount collective usurpationary action against a powerful dominant class.

It may also be noted that many of the gains in working-class conditions in Northern Ireland, certainly since the Second World War, occurred without the need for combined working-class action in Northern Ireland itself. The gains were achieved through working-class action on the United Kingdom mainland, the welfare consequences of which were transferred subsequently to Northern Ireland.

Conflicting-Violent Relationships

In Northern Ireland conflicting group relationships frequently boil over into violence. This results from the non-negotiable nature of some of the aspirations and demands of the two groups (the "Law of Contradiction", discussed in Chapter 1), most particularly over the issue of sovereignty in regard to the area now constituting Northern Ireland. Some members of the Roman Catholic community attempt to achieve, by violent means, the abolition of Northern Ireland as a separate political entity; some members of the Protestant community respond with their own counter-violence. Frustrations have also been built up historically over the inflexibility of the political system in regard to issues other than those of a directly constitutional nature.

Inter-group relations in the early years of the existence of Northern Ireland were particularly strained and provided a most unhelpful context for constructive political development. A. T. Q. Stewart writes (1977, p. 174): "the state called into existence by the 1920 Act forged its essential identity in bitter suffering and adversity, for the I.R.A. launched in the north a campaign of murder and outrage with the object of making it impossible for the new government to function". Violence has also emerged within Northern Ireland where exclusionary actions have greatly reduced the ability of those excluded to influence the political system through the democratic process.

Violence occurs in situations where inter-ethnic conflict escalates in a process designated "polarisation" by Leo Kuper—the process of increasing aggregation into hostile groups; the escalation of conflict by reciprocal violence, with terrorism and atrocity (1977, p. 248). This process may be a particular manifestation of group closure. To quote Kuper:

> Aggregation may proceed not only by the action of each of the parties, as they consolidate their own support, but as a reaction to the measures taken by the antagonist . . . In polarising societies . . . repressive violence often takes the form of the imposition of collective responsibility . . . Subordinate groups too act on the principle of collective responsibility, when their terrorists engage in indiscriminate violence, in the sense that the target is any member of the dominant section. (1977, p. 261)

In such a situation attacks on people are viewed as attacks on the whole person and not just a person in one role (policeman, soldier, worker). We would emphasise the fusion of identities that makes almost all murders in Northern Ireland political *and* sectarian, whether in intent or in interpretation, or in both.

The recourse to violence in group relations may be due to the perception of those involved that violence is the only effective tool for the achievement of particular objectives. The Welsh Nationalist leader, Gwynfor Evans, has made an appropriate comment on this—"if there were less Irishmen ready to live than to shoot and die for Ireland it was because of the uncritical Irish acceptance of the convention that violence is alone heroic and effective" (Birch, 1977, p. 77).

Violence is not only outwardly directed—it may also be inwardly directed. Where there is conflict the development of effective closure by an ethnic group may be an important objective in that such closure will result in the strengthening of the group's organisation and identity. Closure strategies result in groups becoming not only intolerant of outsiders, but also intolerant of anything more than limited internal departures from the norms of group identity (Coser, 1956, p. 103). In Northern Ireland, group conformity can be enforced by the threat of violence against the supposed deviant or by the taking of violent action—"tarring and feathering", "kneecapping" or even "execution".

Recurrent violence leads to residential segregation as people seek the security of living in an area occupied predominantly (in many cases, overwhelmingly) by fellow ethnic group members. Evidence in Chapters 10 and 11 demonstrates the longevity of residential segregation in many Northern Ireland towns, reflective of long-continued intergroup mistrust. This segregation is not just a response to the threat of violence, it is also evidence of the operation of group relations in their "avoidance" form as discussed earlier.

Without any doubt, outbursts of physical violence move group relations in Northern Ireland along the integration–division continuum in a markedly divisive direction.

Constrained Conflict Relationships

Books and articles have appeared with titles such as "Prejudice and Tolerance in Ulster" (Harris, 1972) or "Opposition and Integration in Ulster" (Leyton, 1974). Indeed, our own book continues this theme with its title "Integration and Division". The implication is that, while there are many divisive factors at work in Northern Ireland, there must also be factors that provide some "glue" to prevent complete social division or, at the least, to prevent even more severe violence than has occurred already. Leyton raises this issue bluntly when he states that "the true enigma is not why so many died: rather it is why so *few* have been killed . . . The matter . . . entails the analysis of the social mechanisms which limited a casualty rate which might otherwise have been catastrophic" (1974, p. 185). He then proceeds to an analysis of the integrative and divisive factors delineating the "structural cement". For the area studied, he mentions as integrative between Roman Catholic and Protestant a notion of shared values, a sense of regional identity, a common ideology regarding the workings of the political system and the shared interest of certain institutions on both sides of the ethnic divide in the *status quo*, particularly in regard to the roles of churches and schools.

Religion provides not only the labels for the conflicting ethnic groups in Northern Ireland, it is also deeply entwined in the conflict (see below). The question arises, however, as to whether "Christian" values put a brake on extreme forms of divisive activities. A number of churchmen have claimed this to be so and it is also mentioned by Leyton (1974). In a different geographical context, Kuper (1977, p. 230) suggests that "there must also have been some influence of the Christian ethic on inter-personal relations between Tutsi and Hutu" in a situation of otherwise severe group conflict in Rwanda, although he does not think that it was a significant restraining influence.

Lijphart (1977) discusses the significance of "cross-cutting cleavages" as influences restraining the development of societal division along one fundamental divide. It may be that the cross-cut of ethnic division and social class division in Northern Ireland functions in this way—that is, at times, both Roman Catholic and Protestant members of the middle class may recognise a commonality of interests and objectives that override the ethnic divide; similarly with the working class. The argument here is that if on some issues the ethnic divide is paramount while on others the class divide is predominant then "divide switching" weakens the overall significance of both.

The internal fragmentation of both ethnic groups along a number of lines of cleavage, only one of which is class based, may well exert a braking influence on the process of polarisation. These other lines of cleavage may reflect differences in strength of religious commitment or differing positions on a political spectrum that has two types of extremism forming its end points. Little attempt has been made by researchers to explore the nature and significance of such segmentation.

In his analysis of Malay–Chinese relations in Malaysia, Esman (1972, pp. 238–239) states:

the communities *co-exist* in a condition of precarious *mutual deterrence* or unstable equilibrium. Since each community is in a position both to defend itself and to inflict unacceptable damage on the other, there are strong incentives, particularly among leadership elements, to pursue policies of peaceful, if competitive coexistence and mutual, if competitive accommodation. Neither community, notwithstanding the fantasies of their more chauvinistic members, is strong enough to expel or destroy the other without risking heavy punishment to itself, nor do the patterns of settlement make geographic partition a possibility. Thus Malaysia seems fated to a process of competitive communal coexistence.

Later Esman claims that, although distinctive, Malaysia is in no way unique (1972, p. 241). The relevance of the above quotation to the situation in Northern Ireland strongly reinforces this claim.

A further source of "glue", and indeed a critical one, may be the existence in Northern Ireland of significant levels of British army presence. Since Northern Ireland is part of the United Kingdom, it is entirely appropriate that contingents of the army of that state be stationed in part of it. Certain elements may demand "Troops Out" but it may well be the presence of these very same troops which permits these elements the luxury of making such a demand. Several writers without roots in Ireland have pointed to the significance of the British presence. Leo Kuper (1977, p. 265) has suggested that "The history of Protestant–Catholic conflict in Belfast in the nineteenth and twentieth centuries is a reminder that even where the reciprocity of violence has become established as tradition, it need not result in an extreme escalation of the level of violence, *though no doubt the British presence may be the crucial restraining factor*" (our emphasis). David Miller (1978, p. 151) notes:

... it is one of the salutary ironies of the Anglo-Irish nexus that despite their disdain for both Irish communities Englishmen cannot bring themselves to regard the Irish as foreigners in quite the same sense as Cypriots or Pakistanis. Westminster has implicitly used the modest power deriving from its military presence to impose upon the problem the constraint that its solution must not entail a "bloodbath" or massive forced population transfers.

Thus there is a British umbrella under which the two communities in Northern Ireland shelter. The consequences of the removal of this umbrella elsewhere in the world (India, Palestine, Cyprus, etc.) are only too evident. Miller's statement also indirectly suggests that both Roman Catholic and Protestant, though highly aware of their differences in the Northern Ireland context, are also part of a wider political and cultural "western" world that provides a common set of cultural and material values, aspirations and actualities.

Pushing the consideration of societal conflict to the ultimate of genocide, Kuper (1977, p. 277) claims that in most societies there are restraints on such an outcome—"the unwillingness of the parties to engage in so fearful a crime, the capacity of potential victims to defend themselves, and pressures from the outside world". Yet there may be great danger in taking societal "glue" too much for granted—"things may get bad for a little while, but they will not go right over the brink". Leyton (1974, p. 186) feared that forces outside Northern Ireland might crush "the fragile integrative structures". Certainly it should never be assumed that ethnic conflict escalation will not spin right out of control. It is necessary to understand what the societal "glue" is, how to preserve and indeed develop its holding qualities, and how to tend it with care.

The refusal of the ethnic groups in Northern Ireland to become completely polarised is a sign of the strength of the glue. Unfortunately it also means that pseudo-normality has permitted the current outburst of violent conflict to drag on for more than a decade, albeit most of the time in a relatively low key.

Telling

The different forms of group relations discussed above involve reduced levels of contact between members of the two ethnic groups. Contact does still occur, however, creating situations where it is necessary to distinguish the group membership of individuals. At a conference on ethnic segregation in the spring of 1980, one of the authors was asked by a black American geographer how Protestants and Roman

Catholics in Northern Ireland told each other apart. The American was well aware of the clear visual clues employed in race relations in the United States, but was unclear as to what identification process was used in Northern Ireland. This "problem" has been touched on by a number of non-Northern Irish academic investigators in the course of their studies of communities in different parts of Northern Ireland. For instance, Leyton observed (1974, p. 190) that "the culture provides an elaborate code through which an individual's side can be determined ... Once this affiliation is known, the dichotomous world view permits a rapid and accurate assessment of the associated values and symbols". The elaborate code is necessary in a divided society where the group affiliation of any individual is not necessarily immediately obvious and where the degree of ethnic segregation of residence, employment, shopping, etc. is not sufficient to prevent the meeting of members of the two ethnic groups. As Barth (1969, p. 15) says, "if a group maintains its identity when members interact with others, this entails criteria for determining membership and ways of signalling membership and exclusion". The process whereby these criteria are employed has been called "telling" by Burton in his study of a Belfast working-class community (1978, p. 48). It was observed by Harris, in her work on a predominantly rural area, that "many Ulster people seem to have developed an extreme sensitivity to signs other than explicit badges that denote the affiliations of those they meet" (1972, p. 148). Telling criteria include surnames and first names, schools attended, addresses, subtleties of physical appearance, pronunciations, use of certain phrases and swear words, games played, sporting equipment carried, newspapers read and kind of bread bought (at least when bread is delivered to the housewife's door). None of these telling indicators guarantees 100% accuracy. Cairns (1980) suggests that each indicator has a particular probability of correctness. The important point is that a battery of such indicators is available to the knowledgeable "teller". Most significantly, the telling assessment having been made, its conclusion will profoundly influence subsequent behaviour.

Religion

Group relations have been discussed in terms of relations between Protestants and Roman Catholics. However, we have indicated that these religious labels are, in fact, ethnic. On the other hand this is not to suggest that religion *sensu stricto* is not involved. Many churchmen in Ireland deny that the conflict is about "religion". They are right insofar as doctrinal difference does not bring bombers and gunmen on to

the streets. They are utterly wrong if they claim that religion does not
impinge centrally on the conflict. Ronnie Buchanan, in Chapter 3,
confronts the issue when he writes:

> Deeply rooted divisions in matters of faith and doctrine ensured that
> denominational integrity was preserved intact, but even more important
> in maintaining divisions between the groups was the all-pervasive
> influence of religion in social life, in values, attitudes and relationships.

Other differences, some of which may have been relatively minor in
themselves, have become hitched on to this underlying religious division.
Fulton (1977, p. 200) views the same question from a slightly different
angle, noting that the opposing theological viewpoints become rooted
in "living and opposing communities"—the two religious cognitive
systems having "greater power in Ireland because they came to legitimate the ethnic, cultural and political divide".

Religion also enters into the conflict through what Spencer (1977)
calls the process of sacralisation. This process defines phenomena as
sacred—phenomena such as goals, values, norms, persons, animals,
places, objects, symbols, time and behaviour. From the geographical
perspective, the sacralisation of territory becomes particularly important: "this sacred territory is contaminated when a member of the
other community moves in" (Spencer, 1974, p. 86). The sacred territorial goal of incorporating Northern Ireland in an all-Ireland nation
state is widely recognised as a major factor in the Northern Ireland
conflict. O'Brien (1980, p. 59) refers to the Irish nationalist axiom of
sacral insularity, vividly proclaimed in the statement by Connolly
(1916), quoted in Chapter 5, that "the frontiers of Ireland, the inefface-
able marks of the separate existence of Ireland, are as old as Europe
itself, the handiwork of the Almighty, not of politicians" (MacAonghusa
and Ó Réagain, 1967, p. 193). Fifty-eight years later a former cabinet
minister in the government of the Irish Republic reminds us that sacral
insularity is still around—"Ireland is one island, one nation, one
country because God made it one" (*Irish Times*, 14 January 1974).
Sacral insularity denudes the concept of nationalism of all human
choice.

Religion is also used as a weapon in national struggle through the
process of sacralisation—for instance by adoption of the term "Easter
Rising" or by the elevation of the blood sacrifice to a sacred plane. No
one has put this with greater clarity than the Irish nationalist, Patrick
Pearse, in 1913:

I do not know if the Messiah has yet come, and I am not sure that there will be any visible and personal Messiah in this redemption: the people itself will perhaps be its own Messiah, the people labouring, scourged, crowned with thorns, agonizing and dying, to rise again immortal and impassible ... Bloodshed is a cleansing and a sanctifying thing ... (Hepburn, 1980, pp. 79–80)

Against such arguments who can deny that religion fundamentally affects the ethnic-national conflict?

Finally, as has been pointed out in Chapter 3, the religious factor is of the greatest importance socially in that a high degree of religiously endogamous marriage goes a long way towards ensuring that kin networks do not cross the religious-ethnic divide (Harris, 1972, p. 143).

EXTERNAL RELATIONS

The preceding chapters have concentrated on questions of integration and division within Northern Ireland. However, these issues exist in a wider context, which in turn impinges very significantly on the internal situation. The fact that Northern Ireland is a part of the "United Kingdom of Great Britain and Northern Ireland" indicates one element of this wider context. The territorial claim to Northern Ireland, enshrined in Article 2 of the constitution of the Republic of Ireland, provides another. O'Brien (1980) suggests the concept of a triangle composed of Great Britain, Northern Ireland and the Republic of Ireland. He notes, however, that the triangle is liable, at its apex in Northern Ireland, to turn into a rectangle. Pakenham (1981), in a review of Robert Kee's book, "Ireland: A History" (1980), suggests that there is an historical puzzle consisting of a set of ill-fitting Chinese boxes:

The outside box is the British Isles, where, as we all know, English Protestants have predominated since the Reformation. Trapped inside is Ireland, a box full of Catholics, the majority of the island since the time of St. Patrick. Trapped inside that is Ulster, a box of northern Protestants, the majority of the northeast since they were settled there in the seventeenth century. And at the heart of the puzzle are the northern Catholics, outnumbered two to one in Northern Ireland, yet part of the island's overall Catholic majority.

From either of these two perspectives, the Protestant and Roman Catholic groups in Northern Ireland are not only uncomfortably articulated with each other but also with the Republic of Ireland and with Great Britain.

Both ethnic-national groups within Northern Ireland reach out for external support (Boal, 1980, p. 41). In addition, they each work to reduce the external support of the other. These objectives involve attempts to redraw the frame of the conflict: Irish Catholic nationalists attempt to alleviate their numerical minority position within Northern Ireland by seeking support from the Irish Republic, while Northern Ireland Protestants seek to bolster their position by reinforcing links with Great Britain (Kuper, 1977, p. 257).

The "double minority" relationship between Protestants and Roman Catholics in Northern Ireland, discussed in Chapter 1, means that the attitudes and behaviour of the two groups cannot be fully understood in terms of Northern Ireland majority–minority relationships alone. Irish Catholic nationalism presents itself as an "inclusive nationalism" whereby Irish Catholics are prepared conditionally to accept Protestants within the "Irish nation", a relatively easy thing for them to do in that they would then form a very substantial majority. Conversely, Northern Ireland Protestant nationalism tends to be exclusive, in that if such nationalism included those Irish Catholics who currently reside in Northern Ireland, logic would indicate a possible political fusion of Protestant and Roman Catholic in the whole island of Ireland, which would, in turn, place Protestants in a minority. Perhaps the most balanced comment on the inclusive/exclusive argument has been made by F. S. L. Lyons:

> ... the work of the historians, the geographers, the archaeologists, the folklorists, the language specialists and others who began to discover both what was common to the whole island and what was not. In doing so they demonstrated the co-existence of cultural unity and cultural diversity, thus challenging both the exclusiveness of Ulster nationalism and the inclusiveness of Irish nationalism. (1979, p. 24)

Ronnie Buchanan's discussion in Chapter 3 of our book reinforces this position.

The external relations dimension of problems of integration and division within Northern Ireland is also influenced by the large scale "diasporas" of Roman Catholics from both the area that is now Northern Ireland and the area of the present-day Irish Republic and of Protestants from Northern Ireland. These population movements have been predominantly to England and the United States, but very significant numbers have also moved to Canada, Scotland, Australia and New Zealand.

Although no studies have been carried out, it would appear that Protestants from Northern Ireland have been more readily assimilated in the countries to which they have emigrated than have Irish Roman Catholics. The result of this differential assimilation has been that Irish Catholics have existed as self-conscious ethnic groupings overseas. This has been particularly important in the United States, with the consequence, as O'Brien points out, that interaction between Ireland and America has hinged on the interaction of Catholics—Irish Catholics at home in Ireland and descendants of Irish Catholics in the United States (O'Brien, 1980, p. 66).

The fact that Irish Catholic immigrants in the United States have retained their group identity to a significant degree has meant that, as a group, they have been in a position to exert leverage within the political system of their host country (Boal, 1977). From time to time this leverage has been applied in such a way as to influence American governmental and party political attitudes towards the ethnic conflict in Northern Ireland. The attitudes so influenced have usually contributed to the deepening of division within Northern Ireland.

SOLUTIONS

It has been said (Rose, 1976, p. 139) that there are no solutions to the Northern Ireland problem. This is wrong: it is not that there are no solutions but that the solutions are either unpleasant or extremely difficult to achieve, or both. Complex interaction between problem and solution leads to further difficulty. Generally problems help define their own solutions. However, in the Northern Ireland case, desired solutions tend to define the problem. Thus, those who desire a politically united island of Ireland will define the problem as being one deriving from the political partition; those who wish to maintain the partition will define the problem as being one deriving from the unwillingness of Irish Republicans to accept the partition.

In Chapter 1, we have defined the problem as one of pluralism and mutual insecurity. Earlier in this chapter we have suggested that dominance and territoriality are two alternative behavioural strategies for the reduction of conflict, and we now return to these, seeking pointers to possible solutions to the Northern Ireland problem.

Dominance means that one group (the Protestants or the Roman Catholics) gains control in Northern Ireland. If this comes about, one side will have lost or, as Richard Rose puts it (1976, p. 166), "We will only know that the 'Troubles' have once again ended because of the palpable, even brutal, evidence that someone has lost". Louis Cullen (1980, p. 100) seems to suggest that dominance is a likely outcome because

> harmony is attainable in Irish circumstances only when one side is dominant; if it [i.e. harmony] has increased on balance it has done so to a large extent because outside the north, the Protestant community, even more mobile than the Catholic, has suffered even more from emigration. In the north, by contrast, a conspicuously immobile Catholic population, less mobile in part for cultural and economic reasons than its southern Protestant counterpart, has threatened the fragile inter-community balance.

The dominance solution might suit the winner, and may motivate either or both groups if they think that they can become dominant. Basically it is a nasty solution that contains the seeds of further conflict.

An alternative is territoriality, which was the solution attempted in 1920 with the partition of the island. It probably would have worked if the two political units produced by Partition (i.e. Northern Ireland and what was then the Irish Free State) had been ethnically homogeneous. This was almost true of the Free State, but, as we have indicated earlier, it was not true of Northern Ireland, due to the complex geographical interweave of Roman Catholic and Protestant and to the large absolute and relative size of the minority. A territorial solution today would probably mean a redrawing of the international boundary that separates the Northern Ireland component of the United Kingdom from the Irish Republic. It would probably also mean large-scale population movement because, as has been demonstrated in Chapters 4 and 5, boundary change alone would leave very significant minorities on both sides of the new boundary line. If a relocated Border and population exchange could be agreed, then the territorial solution might not be a nasty one; however, such an agreed outcome is unlikely. Instead, repartition would seem to be possible only after all-out war, and, to quote Conor Cruise O'Brien (1972, p. 301):

> Ireland would be left, once more, with two States, but of even more virulent shades of green and orange than before. The Orange State would be smaller than before—probably about four counties—but would be homogeneously Protestant, without the tiniest Catholic crack or crevice for a new I.R.A. to take root in. The Green State, with its massive ingestion of embittered and displaced Ulster Catholics, would be an uncongenial environment for Protestants, most of whom would probably leave.

Thus, the territorial solution is also unpalatable, but in the long term perhaps less so than a solution based on dominance.

Is there another solution concerned not with separation or victory and defeat but with co-operation and co-existence? There is such a possibility, though in practice perhaps less easy to achieve. This we call the mutuality solution. The only published work that suggests a similar approach is a little-noted pamphlet by T. J. Pickvance, "Peace with Equity", published in 1975.

A clue to the nature of the mutuality solution is contained in Paul Compton's discussion (Chapter 4) of the demographic characteristics of Northern Ireland:

> A summary glance at the basic demographic characteristics of the constituent parts of the British Isles would seem to suggest that there exists a distinctive Northern Ireland demography, the area forming a sort of demographic half-way house between Great Britain on the one hand and the Irish Republic on the other ... Such distinctiveness, however, is not a product of a unique Northern Ireland demography common to both Protestants and Roman Catholics but, on the contrary, is a function of the fact that the British and Irish realms overlap in Northern Ireland ...

The mutuality solution recognises the British–Irish overlap and attempts to build from this recognition an individual solution to a problem with some unique attributes. Pickvance talks of the "Ulster-British" and the "Ulster-Irish" as being the two basic groups (to be correlated, although not entirely, with Protestants and Roman Catholics). The solution involves the development of a Northern Ireland with a considerable degree of autonomy, but constructed within a framework of agreement between Great Britain and the Irish Republic. These two countries would act as joint guarantors to the two communities in Northern Ireland. Northern Ireland would be governed on a power-sharing basis between Ulster-British and Ulster-Irish. No changes in the overall constitutional structures could be made without majority electoral support from *both* communities, voting separately. Thus the mutuality solution would create a situation of considerable stability, where one group would not have to fear the possibility that the other was using the power-sharing structures as mere stepping stones to some preferred (inevitably territorial or dominance) objective, as seems inherent, for instance, in the "condominium" proposals made some years ago by the Social Democratic and Labour Party (S.D.L.P., 1973). There would be no threat and no gains from shifts in the ethnic demography of Northern Ireland since both Ulster-Irish and Ulster-British would have a veto on undesired change. Conservative, liberal or socialist power-sharing groupings could be constructed, depending on the outcomes of the electoral process, and any such grouping would be acceptable, provided that it cross-cut the ethnic divide to a significant extent.

The mutuality solution requires that the absolute sovereignty presently exercised by the United Kingdom be withdrawn, and that the claim to absolute sovereignty made by the Irish Republic be similarly removed. Absolute sovereignty requires that Northern Ireland be either British *or* Irish *or* independent. The withdrawal of such absolutism would not mean complete independence for Northern Ireland, but a considerable degree of autonomy within the supportive framework of Great Britain and the Republic of Ireland. Complete independence would be undesirable because of inter-ethnic mistrust and also because the British–Irish overlap nature of Northern Ireland requires recognition through some linkage with both Great Britain and the Irish Republic.

The mutuality solution is difficult and would be a delicate creation, at least at first. The presence of constraints to the conflict in Northern Ireland, referred to earlier as the "glue", provides, however, a base from which to build. This building should be carried out without undue haste—indeed the mutuality solution should be approached not so much as a single event in time but as an extended process.

Most importantly, however, it should be recognised that the mutuality solution contains within it the possibility for the creation of an environment favourable to many positive developments, where neither group would feel that it had wholly won or lost, though it would need to be acknowledged that while the Ulster-Irish were being asked to yield on an aspiration (a united Ireland), the Ulster-British were being asked to yield on an existing reality (a United Kingdom).

One final point: for mutuality to thrive, the economic environment of Northern Ireland would have to be greatly improved. This is where many of those in Great Britain, the Republic of Ireland, the United States and the European Economic Community who express a concern that a solution to the Northern Ireland problem be found could bring material resources to bear in a very significant way. Indeed, once progress towards a mutuality solution was under way, the improved environment within Northern Ireland would itself be conducive to economic (as well as political and social) development.

CONCLUSION

The theme of cultural integration and division followed in this volume has permitted a two-stage approach to the problems of Northern Ireland's plural society. At the first stage, integration and division considered as cultural attributes encourage the portrayal of the varied and complex human characteristics of each community within the plural society of Northern Ireland; the cultural components of pluralism are clarified. At the second stage, integration and division considered as cultural processes build in the dynamic element which shows how, as a consequence of culture group behaviour, a plural society evolves and maintains itself over time. Beckett (1958, p. 192) states that "the real partition of Ireland is not on the map but in the minds of men". Study of cultural processes shows that Partition is both on the map *and* in the mind, as a consequence of long-established integrative and divisive behaviour. It also makes clear that Irish unity, the Partition of Ireland and the cultural integration and division that exists at different scales within the island have not been pre-ordained by divine intervention nor conditioned by some natural geopolitical order. Instead, these political and cultural realities result from human behaviour and its integrative and divisive consequences.

In pluralism, since division and conflict result from man's own actions so must the achievement of co-operation and integration. This must be the objective of all communities who set co-existence before conflict and peace before war.

Postscript 10 April 1981

At a by-election held on 9 April 1981 for the Fermanagh-South Tyrone seat in the Westminster Parliament, the vote was 30 492 for Bobby Sands (a member of the Provisional I.R.A. convicted on arms charges and, at the time of the by-election, on hunger strike in the Maze Prison), 29 046 for Harry West of the Official Unionist Party. It had been predicted that a sufficient number of Irish Catholic nationalists would have abstained from voting for a member of an organisation dedicated to a violent "solution" to the Northern Ireland problem to have prevented Sands' election. That prediction proved incorrect. In Fermanagh-South Tyrone, at least, there appears to be no middle ground upon which the beginnings of a mutuality solution can be built. The territoriality (repartition) or dominance solutions have thus been given a marked boost.

REFERENCES

Barth, F. (1969). Introduction. *In* "Ethnic Groups and Boundaries" (F. Barth, ed.), pp. 9–38. Universitets Forlaget, Oslo.

Beckett, J. C. (1958). "A Short History of Ireland." Hutchinson, London.

Birch, A. H. (1977). "Political Integration and Disintegration in the British Isles." George Allen and Unwin, London.

Boal, F. W. (1977). Who are the Irish Americans? *Fortnight* **155**, 4–5.

Boal, F. W. (1980). Two Nations in Ireland. *Antipode* **13**, 38–44.

Boserup, A. (1972). Contradictions and Struggles in Northern Ireland. *Socialist Register* **9**, 157–192.

Burton, F. (1978). "The Politics of Legitimacy." Routledge and Kegan Paul, London.

Cairns, E. (1980). The Development of Ethnic Discrimination in Children in Northern Ireland. *In* "A Society under Stress: Children and Young People in Northern Ireland" (J. and J. Harbison, eds.), pp. 115–127. Open Books, Shepton Mallet.

Coser, L. (1956). "The Functions of Social Conflict." Free Press, New York.

Cullen, L. M. (1980). The Cultural Basis of Modern Irish Nationalism. *In* "The Roots of Nationalism: Studies in Northern Europe" (R. Mitchison, ed.), pp. 91–106.

Donnan, H. (1980). "The Ethnic Group and its Possible Relevance in Northern Ireland." Unpublished Paper Presented to the Ethnic Relations Group, Institute of Irish Studies, Queen's University, Belfast.

Edwards, O. D. (1970). "The Sins of Our Fathers: Roots of Conflict in Northern Ireland." Gill and Macmillan, Dublin.

Esman, M. J. (1972). Malaysia: Communal Coexistence and Mutual Deterrence. *In* "Racial Tensions and National Identity" (E. Q. Campbell, ed.), pp. 227–243. Vanderbilt University Press, Nashville, Tennessee.

Fulton, J. (1977). Is the Irish Conflict Religious? A Sociology for the Irish Churches. *Social Studies: Irish Journal of Sociology* **5**, 190–201.

Griffiths, H. (1978). Community Reaction and Voluntary Involvement. *In* "Violence and the Social Services in Northern Ireland" (J. Darby and A. Williamson, eds.), pp. 165–200. Heinemann, London.

Harris, R. L. (1972). "Prejudice and Tolerance in Ulster: A Study of Neighbours and 'Strangers' in a Border Community." Manchester University Press, Manchester.

Hepburn, A. C. (1980). "The Conflict of Nationality in Modern Ireland." Edward Arnold, London.

Heslinga, M. W. (1962). "The Irish Border as a Cultural Divide." Van Gorcum, Assen.

Kee, R. (1980). "Ireland: A History." Weidenfeld and Nicolson, London.

Kuper, L. (1977). "The Pity of It All: Polarisation of Racial and Ethnic Relations." Duckworth, London.

Leyton, E. (1974). Opposition and Integration in Ulster. *Man* **9** (New Series), 185–198.

Lieberson, S. (1972). Stratification and Ethnic Groups. *In* "Readings in Race and Ethnic Relations" (A. H. Richmond, ed.), pp. 199–209. Pergamon Press, Oxford.

Lijphart, A. (1977). "Democracy in Plural Societies." Yale University Press, New Haven, Connecticut.

Lyons, F. S. L. (1979). "The Burden of Our History" (W. B. Rankin Memorial Lecture). Queen's University, Belfast.

MacAonghusa, P. and Ó Réagain, L., eds. (1967). "The Best of Connolly." Mercier Press, Cork.

Miller, D. W. (1978). "Queen's Rebels: Ulster Loyalism in Historical Perspective." Gill and Macmillan, Dublin.

O'Brien, C. C. (1972). "States of Ireland." Hutchinson, London.

O'Brien, C. C. (1980). "Neighbours." Faber and Faber, London.

Pakenham, T. (1981). In the Irish Fog. *Sunday Times*, 18 January 1981.

Parkin, F. (1979). "Marxism and Class Theory: A Bourgeois Critique." Tavistock Publications, London.

Parson, D. (1980). Spatial Underdevelopment: The Strategy of Accumulation in Northern Ireland. *Antipode* **13**, 73–87.

Pickvance, T. J. (1975). "Peace with Equity." The Author, Birmingham.

Rose, R. (1976). "Northern Ireland: A Time of Choice." Macmillan, London.

Smith, D. M. (1979). "Where the Grass is Greener: Living in an Unequal World." Penguin, Harmondsworth.

Social Democratic and Labour Party (1973). "Towards a New Ireland: Proposals." Social Democratic and Labour Party, Belfast.

Sommer, R. (1969). "Personal Space: The Behavioral Basis of Design." Prentice-Hall, Englewood Cliffs, New Jersey.

Spencer, A. E. C. W. (1974). Urbanisation and the Problem of Ireland. *Aquarius*, 82–90.

Spencer, A. E. C. W. (1977). The Religious and the Sacred in the Northern Ireland Conflict. *In* "Sociological Association of Ireland: Proceedings of Third Annual Conference, Dublin, 1976" (A. E. C. W. Spencer, ed.), pp. 34–45. Department of Social Studies, Queen's University, Belfast.

Stewart, A. T. Q. (1977). "The Narrow Ground." Faber and Faber, London.

Whyte, J. (1978). Interpretations of the Northern Ireland Problem: An Appraisal. *Economic and Social Review* **9**, 257–282.

Subject Index